The *Modernized* INTERNATIONAL JEWISH COOK BOOK

By Florence Kreisler Greenbaum

1400 Favorite Recipes of
AMERICA, AUSTRIA, GERMANY, RUSSIA,
FRANCE, POLAND, HUNGARY, ROMANIA,
ENGLAND, SERBIA, IRELAND, TURKEY,
SPAIN, and MEXICO.

Originally published in 1919

Modernized in 2016 for 21st century cooks & kitchens
by New York History Review

The Modernized International Jewish Cook Book
By Florence Kreisler Greenbaum

Originally published as *The International Jewish Cook Book* in 1919. This new edition has been modified/modernized for 21st century kitchens by New York History Review.

Copyright © 2016 New York History Review.
Some rights reserved.
For more information www.NewYorkHistoryReview.com

ISBN: 978-0-9965353-8-0

Printed in the United States of America.

For Zelda

PUBLISHERS' NOTE

This is a new and improved modernized version of an old favorite *The International Jewish Cook Book.* Our editors took great care to make sure these recipes can be made in today's kitchens by today's cooks. Gone are requirements making your own aspic, and skinning your own geese. We have made changes to some recipes by re-wording them for modern accuracy, safety, and ease of acquiring ingredients. In this modern edition, our editors have assumed that modern cooks have access to refrigerators, gas or electric stoves, and are not cooking over coal or wood stoves. We also assume that cooks have access to supermarkets, groceries, and farmers' markets for their meats and produce.

The author Mrs. Florence K. Greenbaum wasan expert Jewish cook. She graduated from Hunter College of New York City after studying diet and food chemistry. She was instructor in Cooking and Domestic Science in the Young Women's Hebrew Association of New York, and was also instructor and lecturer for the Association of Jewish Home Makers and the Central Jewish Institute.

REMARKS

The Jewish housewife enjoys the enviable reputation of being a good cook; in fact she is quite famous for her savory and varied dishes. Her skill is due not so much to a different method of cooking as to her ingenuity in combining food materials. The very cuts of meat she has been always accustomed to use, are those which modern cooks are now advising all to use. The use of vegetables with just enough meat to flavor, as for instance in the Shabbos Shalet, is now being highly recommended.

While it is not given to each and every woman to be a good cook, she can easily acquire some knowledge of the principles of cooking, namely:

1. That heat from coal, charcoal, wood, gas or electricity is used as a medium for toasting, broiling or roasting.
2. That heat from water is used as a medium for boiling, simmering, stewing or steaming.
3. That heat from fat is used as a medium for deep fat frying.
4. That heat from heated surfaces is used in pan-broiling, sauté, baking, braising or pot-roasting.

The length of time required to cook different articles varies with the size and weight of same -and here is where the judgment of the housewife counts. She must understand how to keep the fire at the proper temperature, and how to manage the stove or stove.

In planning meals try to avoid monotony; do not have the same foods for the same days each week. Try new and unknown dishes by way of variety. Pay attention to garnishing, thereby making the dishes attractive to the eye as well as to the palate.

The recipes in this book are planned for a family of five, but in some instances desserts, puddings and vegetables may be used for two meals. Cakes are good for several days.

Do not consider the use of eggs, milk and cream an extravagance where required for certain desserts or sauces for vegetables, as their use adds to the actual food value of the dish.

As a rule the typical Jewish dish contains a large proportion of fat which when combined with cereal or vegetable, fruits, nuts, sugar or honey, forms a dish supplying all the nourishment required for a well-balanced meal. Many of these dishes, when combined with meat, require but a small proportion of same.

Wherever fat is called for, it is intended that melted fat or dripping be used. In many of the dishes where fat is required for frying, any of the good vegetable oils or butter substitutes may be used equally well. These substitutes may also be used in place of butter or fat when same is required as an ingredient for the dish itself. In such cases less fat must be used, and more salt added. It is well to follow the directions given on the containers of such substitutes.

It is understood that all meats be made kosher.

Before preparing any dish, gather all materials, and see that all the ingredients are at hand.

RULES FOR KASHERING

In the religious and dietary laws of the Jewish people, the term "kasher" is applied to the preparation of meat and poultry, and means "to render fit" or "proper" for eating.

1. To render meat "fit" for food, the animal must be killed and cut up according to the Jewish method of slaughter, and must be purchased from a Jewish butcher.
2. The meat should be put into a pan, especially reserved for this purpose, entirely covered with cold water, and left to soak for half an hour. Before removing the meat from the water every particle of blood must be washed off. It should then be put upon the salting board (a smooth wooden board), placed in a slanting position, or upon a board with numerous perforations, in order to allow the blood to freely flow down. The meat should then be profusely sprinkled on all sides with salt, and allowed to remain in salt for one hour. It is then removed, held over a sink or pan, and well rinsed with cold water three times, so that all the salt is washed off. Meat left for three days or more unsoaked and unsalted, may be used only for broiling over coals; it may not be cooked in any other way. The ends of the hoofs and the claws of poultry must be cut off before the feet are kashered.

Bones with no meat or fat adhering to them must be soaked separately, and during the salting should not be placed near the meat.

3. The liver must be prepared apart from the meat. It must be cut open in both directions, washed in cold water, and broiled over the fire, and salted while it is broiling. It should be seared on all sides. Water must then be poured over it, to wash the blood away. It may then be used in any manner, as the heat has drawn out the blood. Small steaks and chops may be kashered in the same way.

4. The heart must be cut open, lengthwise, and the tip removed before being soaked, so that the blood may flow out. The lungs likewise must be cut open before being soaked. Milt must have veins removed.

5. The head and feet may be kashered with the hair or skin adhering to them. The head should, however, be cut open, the brain taken out, and kashered separately.

6. To kasher suet or fat for clarifying, remove skin, and proceed as with meat.

7. Joints from hind-quarters must not be used, until they have been "porged," which means that all veins of blood, forbidden fat, and prohibited sinew have been removed. In New York City no hind-quarter meat is used by Orthodox Jews.

8. All poultry must be drawn, and the inside removed before putting in water.

Cut the head off and cut the skin along the neck; find the vein which lies between the tendons, and trace it as far back as possible; at the back of the neck it divides into two branches, and these must be removed.

Cut off the tips of the wings and the claws of the feet. Proceed as with meat, first cutting open the heart and the liver. Eggs found inside of poultry, with or without shells, must be soaked and when salted be placed in such a position that the blood from the meat does not flow upon them. Such eggs may not be eaten with milk foods.

In conducting a kosher kitchen care must be taken not to mix meat and milk, or meat and butter at the same meal.

The utensils used in the cooking and serving of meat dishes may not be used for milk dishes. The should never be mixed.

Only soaps and scouring powders which contain no animal fat are permitted to be used in washing utensils. Kosher soap, made according to directions for making hard soap, may be used in washing meat dishes and utensils.

To follow the spirit as well as the letter of the dietary laws, scrupulous cleanliness should always be observed in the storing, handling and serving of food.

It is very necessary to keep the hands clean, the flours and cereals clean, the ice-box clean, and the pots and pans clean.

CONTENTS

TABLE OF WEIGHTS AND MEASURES

All measurements should be made level.

2 gills = 1 cup
2 cups = 1 pint
2 pints = 1 quart
4 quarts = 1 gallon
16 ounces = 1 pound
8 quarts = 1 peck
4 pecks = 1 bushel
60 drops = 1 teaspoon
3 teaspoons = 1 tablespoon
4 tablespoons = 1/4 cup
4 tablespoons = 1 wineglass
2 tablespoons of butter, sugar, salt = 1 ounce
4 tablespoons of flour = 1 ounce
16 tablespoons = 1 cup
4 cups of flour = 1 pound
2 cups of solid butter = 1 pound
2 cups of granulated sugar = 1 pound

PUBLISHERS' NOTE	6
REMARKS	7
RULES FOR KASHERING	8
TABLE OF WEIGHTS & MEASURES	11
APPETIZERS	15
SANDWICHES	22
SOUPS	27
GARNISHES & DUMPLINGS FOR SOUPS	43
FISH	47
SAUCES FOR FISH AND VEGETABLES	64
SAUCES FOR MEATS	68
FRYING	71
ENTREES	73
MEATS	85
POULTRY	98
STUFFINGS FOR MEAT & POULTRY	107
VEGETABLES	109
POTATOES	136
VEGAN DISHES	146
SALADS & SALAD DRESSINGS	150
FRESH FRUITS & COMPOTE	167
PASTA MEHLSPEISE (FLOUR FOODS)	175
CEREALS	192
EGGS	197
CHEESE	206
BREAD	211
COFFEE CAKES (KUCHEN)	219

MUFFINS & BISCUITS 231
PANCAKES, FRITTERS, ETC 238
CAKES 245
ICINGS & FILLINGS FOR CAKES 265
PIES & PASTRY 269
COOKIES 284
DESSERTS 295
PUDDING SAUCES 311
FROZEN DESSERTS 314
CANDIES & SWEETS 321
BEVERAGES 324
JELLIES & PRESERVES 334
PICKLED VEGETABLES 340
PASSOVER DISHES 342
INDEX 363

APPETIZERS

CANAPÉS

For serving at the beginning of dinner and giving a zest to the appetite, canapés are extremely useful. They may be either hot or cold and made of anything that can be utilized for a sandwich filling. The foundation bread should be two days old and may be toasted or fried crouton fashion. The nicest way is to butter it lightly, then set it in a hot oven to brown delicately, or fry in hot fat.

The bread should be cut oblong, diamond shaped, in rounds, or with a cutter that has a fluted edge. While the toast is quite hot, spread with the prepared mixture and serve on a small plate with sprigs of watercress or points of lemon as a garnish.

Another way is to cut the bread into delicate fingers, pile it log-cabin fashion, and garnish the center with a stuffed olive. For cheese canapés sprinkle the toast thickly with grated cheese, well seasoned with salt and pepper. Set in a hot oven until the cheese melts and serve immediately.

SARDINE CANAPÉS
Toast lightly diamond-shaped slices of stale bread and spread with a sardine mixture made as follows: Skin and bone six sardines, put them in a bowl and run to a paste with a silver spoon. Add two tablespoons of lemon juice, a few drops of Worcestershire sauce, a dash of pepper, two teaspoons of chopped parsley and four tablespoons of creamed butter. Garnish with a border of whites of hard boiled eggs, finely chopped, and on top scatter shredded olives.

WHITE CAVIAR
Take roe of any fish, remove skin, salt; set aside over night. Next day beat roe apart, pour boiling water over it and stir; when roe is white,

pour off the water and let drain; then put in pan with two tablespoons of oil and salt, pepper, a little vinegar, and mix well. Let stand a few days before using. This caviar may be substituted in all recipes for the Russian caviar or domestic caviar may be procured in some shops.

CAVIAR CANAPÉS
Cut the bread about ¼ inch thick and two inches square (or round), and after it is toasted spread over each slice a teaspoon of ice cold caviar. Mix one teaspoon of chopped onion and one teaspoon chopped parsley; spread the mixture over the caviar and serve with quarters of lemon.

ANCHOVY CANAPÉS
Cut the bread as for caviar canapés and spread with anchovy paste. Chop separately the yolks and whites of hard boiled eggs and cover the canapés, dividing them into quarters, with anchovies split in two lengthwise, and using yolks and whites in alternate quarters.

ANCHOVY CANAPÉS WITH TOMATOES
For each person take a thin slice toast covered with anchovy paste. Upon this place whole egg which has been boiled four minutes, so that it can be pealed whole and the yolk is still soft. Around the toast put tomato sauce.

CHOPPED ONION AND CHICKEN FAT
Chop one yellow onion very fine, add four tablespoons of chicken fat (melted), salt to taste. Serve on slices of rye bread. If desired, a hard-boiled egg chopped very fine may be mixed with the onions.

BRAIN (APPETIZER)
Cook brains, let cool and add salt; beat up with chopped onions, juice of one and a half lemons and olive oil. Serve on lettuce leaves.

BLACK OLIVES
Pit black olives, cut them very thin, and prepare as brain appetizer; beat well with fork.

CHICKEN LIVER PASTE, No. 1
Wash thoroughly several fowls' livers and then let them simmer until tender

in a little strong soup stock, adding some sliced mushroom, minced onion, and a little pepper and salt. When thoroughly done mince the whole finely, or pound it in a mortar. Now put it back in the sauce pan and mix well with the yolks of sufficient eggs to make the whole fairly moist. Warm over the heat, stirring frequently until the mixture is quite thick, taking care that it does not burn. It should be served upon rounds of toast on a hot dish garnished with parsley.

IMITATION PATÉ DE FOIS GRAS

Take as many livers and gizzards of any kind of fowl as you may have on hand; add to these three tablespoons of chicken or goose fat, a finely chopped onion, one tablespoon of pungent sauce, and salt and white pepper to taste. Boil the livers until quite done and drain; when cold, rub to a smooth paste. Take some of the fat and chopped onion and simmer together slowly for ten minutes. Strain through a thin muslin bag, pressing the bag tightly, turn into a bowl and mix with the seasoning; work all together for a long time, then grease a bowl or cups and press this mixture into them; when soft cut up the gizzards into bits and lay between the mixture. You may season this highly, or to suit taste.

CHICKEN LIVER PASTE, No. 2

Take ¼ pound chicken livers that have been boiled soft; drain and rub through grater, add one-quarter cup of fresh mushrooms that have been fried for three minutes in two tablespoons of chicken fat, chop these, mix smooth with the liver, moistening with the fat used in frying the mushrooms, season with salt, pepper, paprika and a little onion and lemon juice. Spread on rye bread slices. Garnish plate with a red radish or sprigs of parsley.

CHOPPED HERRING

Soak herring a few hours, when washed and cleaned, bone and chop. To one herring - take one onion, one sour apple, a slice of white bread which has been soaked in vinegar, chop all these; add one teaspoon oil, a little cinnamon and pepper. Put on platter in shape of a herring with head at top and tail at bottom of dish, and sprinkle the chopped white of a hard-boiled egg over fish and then the chopped yolk.

CHEESE BALLS

Take mashed cream cheese - add butter, cream and a little paprika. You can chop either green peppers, almonds or olives in this mixture, or the juice of an onion. Roll into small balls and serve on lettuce leaves. This is also very good for sandwiches.

EGG APPETIZER

Boil eggs hard. Cut slice off the end, so that the egg will stand firm. Dip egg in French dressing, then with a pastry bag arrange sardellen (herring) butter on the top of egg. Have ready small squares of toasted bread, spread with a thin layer of sardellen butter, on which to stand the eggs. Caviar, mixed with some finely chopped onion, pepper and lemon juice, may be used instead of the sardellen butter, but mayonnaise must be used over the caviar.

DEVILED EGGS WITH HOT SAUCE

Take six hard-boiled eggs, cut lengthwise, remove yolk and add to same: one dessertspoon of melted butter, cayenne pepper, salt and chopped parsley. Mash this mixture very fine and refill the whites of the eggs and turn over on platter.

Sauce:
One tablespoon of butter, one tablespoon of flour, a pinch of cayenne pepper, salt and one pint of milk. Stir this mixture continually until it thickens; beat the yolk of one egg and pour the hot gravy over the same. Dress with chopped parsley and eat very hot. Sherry wine can be added if desired.

STUFFED YELLOW TOMATOES

Take small yellow tomatoes, scrape out the center and fill with caviar. Serve on lettuce or watercress.

A DELICIOUS APPETIZER

Take as many slices of delicately browned toast as people to serve, several large, firm tomatoes sliced, one green pepper, and store cheese. Place a slice of tomato on each slice of toast and season with salt and pepper and a dot of butter. Place several long, curly strips of pepper around the tomato, and cover with a thin slice of the cheese. Place in the oven until the cheese is melted. Serve piping hot.

CELERY RELISH

Boil about six pieces of celery root. When soft, peel and mash. Season with salt, pepper, a little onion powder, a teaspoon of home-made mustard and plenty of mayonnaise. Shape into pyramids, put mayonnaise on the top of the pyramid, and on top of that either a little well-seasoned caviar or some sardellen (herring) butter shaped in a pastry bag. Serve on a slice of beets and a lettuce leaf.

SARDELLEN

Take ¼ pound salted sardellen (herring) and soak in water over night. Bone the next morning, put in cloth and press until dry; chop very fine, almost to a paste; take ½ pound sweet butter, stir to a cream and add the sardellen. Serve on toasted cracker or bread. Sprinkle with the grated yellow and grated white of egg.

STUFFED EGGS

Hard boil eggs, drop into cold water, remove shells, cut each in half lengthwise. Turn out yolks into a bowl. Carefully place whites together in pairs, mash yolks with back of a spoon. For every six yolks put into bowl one tablespoon melted butter, ½ teaspoon prepared mustard, one teaspoon salt, dash of cayenne pepper. Rub these together thoroughly with yolks. Make little balls of this paste the size of the yolks. Fit one ball into each pair whites.

NUT AND CHEESE RELISH

Mix one package cream cheese with one cup of chopped nut meats, one teaspoon of chopped parsley, two tablespoons of whipped cream, salt and red pepper. Roll into balls and serve cold, garnished with parsley and chopped nuts.

GRAPEFRUIT COCKTAIL

Cut the grapefruit into halves, crosswise, and scoop out the pulp, rejecting the white inner skin as well as the seeds. Clean the shells; cut the edges with a sharp knife into scallops and throw them into cold water. Set the pulp on the ice. At serving time put a teaspoon of cracked ice in the bottom of each shell; fill with the pulp, mixed thoroughly with powdered sugar and a little sherry, if desired; and place a maraschino cherry or bit of bright-colored jelly in the center of each. Lay on paper doilies or surround with bits of asparagus fern.

AMBROSIA

Fill glass with alternate layers of sliced orange and coconut; cover with powdered sugar and place a maraschino cherry on the top of each.

PEACH COCKTAIL

Fill the glasses with sliced peaches; cover with orange or lemon juice; sweeten to taste; add a little shaved ice and serve. Apricot and cherry cocktails may be made in the same way.

RASPBERRY COCKTAIL

Mash 2 cups ripe, red currants; strain them through cheesecloth; pour the juice over a pint of red raspberries and set on the ice to chill. At serving time sweeten to taste and pour into the glasses, putting one teaspoon of powdered sugar on the top of each.

PINEAPPLE AND BANANA COCKTAIL

Take equal parts of banana and fresh or canned pineapple; cut into small cubes and cover with lemon or pineapple juice. Serve in glasses or orange shells placed on autumn leaves or sprays of green fern.

STRAWBERRY COCKTAIL

Slice five or six large strawberries into each glass and squeeze over them the juice of an orange. At serving time add one heaping teaspoon of powdered sugar and one tablespoon of shaved ice.

MUSK MELONS

Cut melon in half, seed and put on ice one hour before serving. When ready to serve, fill with crushed ice and sprinkle with powdered sugar. Allow one-half melon for each person. Very refreshing for summer luncheons or dinners. For dinner serve before soup.

FILLED LEMONS

Select good-sized lemons; cut off tip to stand the lemon upright; cut top for cover. Scoop out all the lemon pulp, and put in a bowl; put shells in a bowl of cold water. For six lemons take one box of boneless sardines, six anchovies, and two green peppers, cut very fine. Wet with lemon-juice until moist; fill in shells after wiping dry; insert a pimento on top; put on cover of lemon; serve on doily with horseradish and watercress.

RED PEPPER CANAPÉS

Mix together two chopped hard-boiled eggs, one tablespoon of chopped red peppers, a ¼ of a teaspoon of salt, a tiny pinch of mustard and two tablespoons of grated American cheese with sufficient melted butter to form a paste; spread over the rounds of fried bread and place in a very hot oven for about three minutes. Serve on a folded napkin, garnished with watercress.

SALTED PEANUTS

Shell and skin freshly roasted peanuts and proceed as in salting almonds.

SALTED ALMONDS

Pour boiling water on the almonds; cool and remove the skins; dry thoroughly and brown in a hot oven, using a half tablespoon of butter or olive oil, to each cup of nuts, which must be shaken frequently. When brown, sprinkle well with salt and spread on paper to dry and cool. A still easier way to prepare the nuts is to cook them over the fire, using a larger quantity of olive oil. As the oil can be saved and used again, this method is not necessarily extravagant.

SANDWICHES

Bread should be twenty-four hours old and cut in thin, even slices. If fancy forms are desired, shape before spreading with butter. Cream butter and spread evenly.

ANCHOVY SANDWICHES
Pound the anchovies to a paste and mix with an equal quantity of olives stoned and finely chopped.

CELERY SANDWICHES
Two cups of chopped celery, two tablespoons of chopped walnuts, two tablespoons of chopped olives, a ¼ cup of mayonnaise dressing. Spread between slices of thin buttered bread.

FISH SANDWICHES
Spread one piece of bread with any kind of cold fish that has been shredded and mixed with tartar sauce. Then put a lettuce leaf on that and then a slice of hard-boiled egg that has been dipped in tartar sauce. Cover with a slice of buttered bread.

NUT AND RAISIN SANDWICHES
Take equal quantities of nuts and raisins; moisten with cream or grape juice and spread on thin slices of bread.

BROWN BREAD SANDWICHES
Season one cup of cottage cheese with salt, cayenne, and add one pimento cut in shreds. Cut white and brown bread in finger lengths about one inch wide. Spread with cheese mixture and place a brown and white slice together.

CHEESE AND NUT SANDWICHES
Cut thin rounds from rye bread. Spread with the following mixture: take one cream cheese, rub to a cream, season to taste with salt and paprika,

add one stalk of chopped celery, and one-fourth cup of chopped nut meats. Spread on buttered bread and place a slice of stuffed olive on top, in the center of each piece of bread.

LETTUCE SANDWICHES
Put fresh lettuce leaves, washed and dried, between thin layers of bread. Spread with Mayonnaise or Boiled Dressing.

OLIVE SANDWICHES
Take either ripe or green olives; remove the seeds; mince and mix thoroughly with Mayonnaise dressing. Spread between slices of whole-wheat or graham bread.

SARDINE SANDWICHES
Remove the skin and bones from the sardines. Rub to a paste, adding an equal quantity of chopped hard-boiled eggs, seasoned with salt, cayenne, lemon juice or vinegar. Moisten with melted butter and spread between slices of bread.

DATE AND FIG SANDWICHES
Wash equal quantities of dates and figs; stone the dates; add blanched almonds in quantity about one-fourth of the entire bulk; then run the whole mixture through a food chopper. Moisten with orange juice and press tightly into baking powder tins. When ready to use, dip the box in hot water; turn out the mixture; slice and place between thin slices of buttered bread.

FIG SANDWICHES
Remove the stems and chop the figs fine. Put in a double boiler with a little water and cook until a paste is formed. Add a few drops of lemon juice; set aside; when cool spread on thin slices of buttered bread.

EGG SANDWICHES
Hard boil the eggs, place them immediately into cold water. When cold, remove the shells carefully, cut the eggs in half lengthwise and butter slightly. Lay one or two sardellen on one half of the egg and press the one half gently on the other half which has the sardellen. The egg must appear

whole. Now tie lengthwise and across with the narrowest, various colored ribbons you can find.

CHESTNUT SANDWICHES
One slice each of white and brown bread, cut thin and buttered, and spread with chestnuts that have been boiled tender, peeled and rubbed through a sieve, then mashed with hard-boiled eggs to a paste and moistened with Mayonnaise.

SALMON AND BROWN BREAD SANDWICHES
Flake one cup salmon and rub it to a paste. Add mustard, salt, and cayenne. Spread on the bread, cover with a layer of thin slices of cucumber, then another piece of bread, press lightly and arrange with sprigs of parsley on the platter.

WHITE AND BROWN BREAD SANDWICHES
If a novel sandwich is wanted, butter alternate slices of brown and white bread and pile them one above the other in a loaf. Cut the new loaf across the slices, butter them and pile them so that when this second loaf is cut, the slices will be in white and brown blocks. Press the slices very closely together before cutting at all.

TOASTED CHEESE SANDWICHES
The filling for the toasted cheese sandwiches calls for a cup of soft, mild cheese, finely cut, and stirred over the fire with a tablespoon of butter until the cheese is melted. Enough milk to moisten, perhaps not more than one-eighth of a cup, is then added, with salt, mustard, and paprika to taste, and the whole is stirred until creamy and smooth. Slices of bread are very thinly buttered, the cheese mixture spread on generously, each slice covered with another slice, and set away until the filling cools and hardens, when the sandwiches are toasted on both sides and served hot.

POACHED EGG SANDWICHES
slice as many pieces of bread, from a round loaf, as you have persons to serve. Toast these slices and let cool. Across each slice place three strips of pimentoes, on top of that place a cold poached egg, put a teaspoon of mayonnaise on the top of the egg and sprigs of watercress encircling the toast.

MUSTARD SARDINE PASTE FOR SANDWICHES

Take one box of mustard sardines; bone and mash; add to the mixture one tablespoon of tomato catsup, one teaspoon of Worcestershire sauce, juice of one lemon, a pinch of cayenne pepper, as much white pepper as will cover the end of a knife, two tablespoons of vinegar, and one tablespoon of olive oil. Mix thoroughly until it becomes a paste. Then spread on thinly cut bread for sandwiches.

CAVIAR AND SALMON SANDWICHES

Take a piece of rye bread, cut round (with a biscuit cutter), spread with mustard; put some caviar in center of the bread, strips of smoked salmon around the caviar and strips of pickle around the salmon.

RIBBON SANDWICHES

Cut two slices of white bread and two of brown. Butter three and spread with a thick paste made of hard-boiled egg very finely chopped and mixed with mayonnaise dressing. Build the slices up one above the other, alternating brown and white, and placing the unbuttered slice on top. Before serving, slice down as you would a layer cake.

EGG AND OLIVE SANDWICHES

Chop four eggs which have been boiled fifteen minutes, add two tablespoons of chopped olives, season and moisten with olive oil and vinegar. Spread between thin slices of buttered bread.

RUSSIAN SANDWICHES

Spread bread with thin slices of Neufchatel cheese, cover with finely chopped olives moistened with mayonnaise dressing.

SURPRISE SANDWICHES

Take orange marmalade, pecan nuts and cream cheese in equal quantities and after mixing thoroughly spread on thin slices of buttered bread.

CHICKEN SANDWICHES

Mince some cold roast or boiled chicken in a chopping bowl, then mix the gravy with it, adding a few hard-boiled eggs, which have been minced to a powder. Mix all into a soft paste. Then cut thin slices of bread, spread the chicken between the slices (if desired you may add a little mustard); press the pieces gently together.

CHICKEN SANDWICHES WITH MAYONNAISE
Grind up chicken in meat chopper. To each cup of chicken add one tablespoon of mayonnaise, and one tablespoon of chicken soup. Mix into soft pasate, and put in finger-rolls.

DEVILED TONGUE SANDWICHES
Grind up tongue in meat chopper; to a cup of ground tongue add one teaspoon of mustard, one tablespoon of soup, and one teaspoon of mayonnaise. Mix into soft paste; spread on white bread cut very thin.

MINCED GOOSE SANDWICHES
Take either boiled or roast goose (which has been highly seasoned) and mince in a chopping bowl, add one or two pickles, according to quantity, or a teaspoon of catsup. Spread thin slices of bread or nice fresh rolls, with a thin coating of goose oil, slightly salted, then spread the minced goose and cover with a layer of bread which has been previously spread.

VEAL SANDWICHES
May be prepared as above, or slice the veal in thin slices and spread with mustard.

BOILED, SMOKED, OR PICKLED TONGUE SANDWICHES
Remove the crust from the bread (unless it is very soft), place the slices of tongue (cut very thin) and lettuce leaves between the slices.

SOUPS

Soups are wholesome and palatable and should form part of the meal whenever possible. It is a good plan to have some sort of vegetable or meat stock always at hand, as this renders the making of the soup both easy and economical. With milk at hand, cream soups are easily made.

SOUP STOCK

In making soup, bring the cold water in the soup pot with the meat and bones to a boil slowly, and let it simmer for hours, never boiling and never ceasing to simmer. If clear soup is not desired soup may be allowed to boil. Bones, both fresh and those partly cooked, meats of all kinds, vegetables of various sorts, all may be added to the stock pot, to give flavor and nutriment to the soup.

One quart of cold water is used to each pound of meat for soup; to four quarts of water, one each of vegetables of medium size and a bouquet.

Make the soup in a closely covered kettle used for no other purpose. Remove scum when it first appears; after soup has simmered for four or five hours add vegetables and a bouquet.

Parsley wrapped around peppercorn, bayleaf, six cloves and other herbs, excepting sage, and tied, makes what is called a bouquet and may be easily removed from the soup.

Root celery, parsley, onions, carrots, asparagus and potatoes are the best vegetables to add to the soup stock. Never use celery leaves for beef soup. You may use celery leaves in potato soup, but sparingly, with chopped parsley leaves.

Vegetables, spices and salt should always be added the last hour of cooking. Strain into an earthen bowl and let cool uncovered, by so doing stock is less apt to ferment.

A cake of fat forms on the stock when cold, which excludes air and should not be removed until stock is used. To remove fat run a knife around edge of bowl and carefully remove the same. A small quantity will remain, which should be removed by passing a cloth, wrung out of hot water, around edge and over top of stock. This fat should be clarified and used for drippings. If time cannot be allowed for stock to cool before using, take off as much fat as possible with a spoon, and remove the remainder by passing tissue or any absorbent paper over the surface. Bouillon should always be thickened with yolks of eggs, beat up with a spoon of cold water. Ordinary beef soup or tomato soup may be thickened with flour. To do this properly heat a scant spoon of soup drippings, stir in briskly a spoon of flour, and add gradually a large quantity of soup to prevent it becoming lumpy.

WHITE STOCK
Veal, turkey, chicken and fish are used.

BROWN STOCK
Follow directions given for bouillon, adding a slice of beef and browning some of the meat in the marrow from the bone.

BEET SOUP - RUSSIAN (FLEISCHIG) [with meat]
Cut one large beet and ½ pound of onions in thick pieces and put in kettle with one pound of fat brisket of beef; cover with water and let cook slowly two hours; add ¾ of a cup of sugar and a little lemon juice to make it sweet and sour and let cook another hour; season and serve hot.

BORSHT
Take some red beetroots, wash thoroughly and peel, and then boil in a moderate quantity of water from two to three hours over a slow fire, by which time a strong red liquor should have been obtained. Strain off the liquor, adding lemon juice, sugar, and salt to taste, and when it has cooled a little, stir in sufficient yolks of eggs to slightly thicken it. May be used either cold or hot. In the latter case a little home-made beef stock may be added to the beet soup. If after straining off the soup the remaining beetroot is not too much boiled away, it may be chopped fine with a little onion, vinegar and dripping, flavored with pepper and salt, and used as a vegetable.

SCHALET OR TSCHOLNT (SHABBAS SOUP)
Wash one pint of white haricot beans and one pint of coarse barley and put them into a covered pot or pan with some pieces of fat meat and some pieces of marrow bone, or the backs of two fat geese which have been skinned and well spiced with ginger and garlic. Season with pepper and salt and add sufficient water to cover. Cover the pot up tightly. Cook until tender. This takes the place of soup for the Sabbath dinner.

BOUILLON

Put on 1 three-pound chicken to boil in six quarts cold water. Take 1½ or 2 pounds of beef and the same quantity thick part of veal, put in a baking-pan, set in the stove and brown quickly with just enough water to keep from burning. When brown, cut the meat in pieces, add this with all the juice it has drawn, to the chicken soup. Set on the back of the stove, and cook slowly all day. Set in a cold place, or on ice over night, and next morning after it is congealed, skim off every particle of fat.

Melt and season to taste when ready to serve. Excellent for the sick. When used for the table, cut up carrots and French peas already cooked can be added while heating. If cooked on gas stove, cook over the simmering flame the same number of hours.

CONSOMMÉ

Take three pounds of beef, cut in dice and cover with three quarts of cold water. Simmer slowly for four hours. The last hour add ½ cup each of carrots, celery, onion, and season with one-half teaspoon of peppercorns and one tablespoon of salt. Strain, cool, remove fat and clear (allowing one egg shell broken fine and the slightly beaten white of one egg to each quart of stock). Add to the stock, stir constantly until it has reached the boiling point. Boil two minutes and serve.

CHICKEN SOUP, No. 1

Take one large chicken, cook with four quarts of water for two or three hours. Skim carefully, when it begins to boil add parsley root, an onion, some asparagus, cut into bits. Season with salt, strain and beat up the yolk of an egg with one tablespoon of cold water, add to soup just before serving. This soup should not be too thin. Rice, barley, noodles or dumplings may be added. Make use of the chicken either for salad or stew.

CHICKEN SOUP, No. 2

Take a cold, cooked chicken and break into small pieces. Add ½ cup of chopped celery and one onion chopped fine. Cover with cold water; simmer slowly for two hours. Strain, add salt and pepper to taste.

CHICKEN BROTH

Cut the chicken into small pieces and place it in a deep oven-safe dish; add one quart of water; cover it and set over a kettle of boiling water, letting it steam until the meat of the chicken has become very tender. Strain off the broth and let it stand over night. In the morning remove the fat and return the liquid to the original earthen dish.

JULIENNE SOUP

Have soup stock ready. Boil in water until tender one cup green peas, three carrots cut up in small pieces, and some cabbage chopped fine. brown two tablespoons of flour in a skillet in hot fat, then stir in the vegetables. Fry some livers and gizzards of fowls, if handy, and add, then stir in the strained soup stock.

RICE BROTH

May be made either of beef or mutton, adding all kinds of vegetables. Boil ½ cup of rice separately in a farina kettle. Strain the beef or mutton broth. Add the rice and boil one-half hour longer, with potatoes, cut into dice shape; use about two potatoes; then add the beaten yolk of an egg. Strained stock of chicken broth added to this soup makes it very palatable and nutritious for the sick.

MOCK TURTLE SOUP

Take one calf's head, wash well; put on to boil with 4½ quarts of water; add two red peppers, onions, celery, carrots, cloves, salt to taste, and a little cabbage; boil six hours; also, have ready some meat stock; the next day put fat in a skillet with two large tablespoons of flour; let it brown; then take the calf's head and cut all the meat from it in pieces; add the calf's tongue, cut in dice. slice hard-boiled eggs, one glass of sherry, and one lemon sliced; put all in the stock; allow it to come just to a boil.

MUTTON BROTH

Cut three pounds of neck of lamb or lean shoulder into small pieces; cover closely and boil with three quarts of water, slowly, for two hours; add two tablespoons well-washed rice to the boiling soup. Cook an hour longer, slowly; watch carefully and stir from time to time. Strain and thicken it with a little flour; salt and pepper to taste.

MULLIGATAWNY SOUP
Add to three quarts of liquor, in which fowls have been boiled, the following vegetables: three onions, two carrots, and one head of celery cut in small dice. Keep the kettle over a high heat until soup reaches the boiling point; then place where it will simmer for twenty-five minutes. Add one tablespoon of curry powder, one tablespoon of flour mixed together; add to the hot soup and cook five minutes. Pass through a sieve. Serve with small pieces of chicken or veal cut in it.

FARINA SOUP
When the soup stock has been strained and every particle of fat removed, return it to the kettle to boil. When it boils hard stir in carefully quarter of a cup of farina, do this slowly to prevent the farina from forming lumps. Stir into the soup bowl the yolk of one egg, add a teaspoon of cold water. Pour the soup into the bowl gradually and stir constantly until all has been poured into the bowl. Serve at once.

NOODLE SOUP
For six persons, select a piece of meat off the neck, about 2½ pounds; add three quarts of water, an onion, one celery root, two carrots, a large potato, some parsley, three tomatoes and the giblets of poultry. Cook in a closely covered kettle, letting the soup simmer for four or five hours. Remove every bit of scum that rises. Strain; add salt and remove every particle of fat; put in noodles; boil about five minutes and serve at once. If allowed to stand it will become thick.

MUSHROOM AND BARLEY SOUP
Take one quart of hot bouillon, add a ¼ pound barley which has been boiled in water; and one ounce of dried mushrooms which have been thoroughly washed and cut in pieces, an onion, carrot, bay leaf, parsley and dill. Boil all these and when the vegetables are nearly tender, remove from soup, add the meat from the bouillon, cut up in small pieces, let soup come to a boil and serve.

OXTAIL SOUP
Wash two large oxtails and cut into pieces. Cut one onion fine and fry in one tablespoon of drippings. When brown, add oxtails to brown, then put

into soup kettle with four quarts cold water. Add one tablespoon of salt, one tablespoon of mixed herbs, four cloves, four peppercorns. Simmer for three or four hours. Skim off fat, strain. Vegetables cut into fancy shapes and boiled twenty minutes may be added.

GREEN PEA SOUP
Make your soup stock as usual, adding a pint of washed pea pods to the soup. Heat a tablespoon of drippings, put in the peas, with a little chopped parsley, cover closely and let simmer; keep adding soup stock when dry. When the peas are tender put into the strained soup. Season with one teaspoon of salt and two teaspoons of sugar, add drop dumplings to this soup before serving.

PIGEON SOUP
Make a beef soup, and an hour before wanted add a pigeon. Boil slowly, with all kinds of vegetables. Strain, add the beaten yolk of an egg, salt to taste.

TURKEY SOUP
Cut up any bones or meat of cold turkey, and cook like soup made of leftover chicken and chicken bones.

OKRA GUMBO SOUP (SOUTHERN)
Take one quart of ripe tomatoes, stew with one quart of okra, cut into small rings. Put this on to boil with about two quarts of water and a piece of soup meat (no bone), chop up an onion, a carrot and a sprig of parsley, add this to the soup. Fricassee one chicken with some rice, dish up with the soup, putting a piece of chicken and one tablespoon of rice into each soup plate before adding the soup. Let the soup simmer four or five hours; season with salt and pepper. A little corn and lima beans may be added; they should be cooked with the soup for several hours. Cut the soup meat into small cubes and leave in the soup to serve.

TCHORBA - TURKISH SOUP
Take one pound of meat, cover with water and boil until meat is tender. Boil rice in another pan until it is creamy, when ready to serve, add one beaten egg and juice of ½ lemon. Broken rice is best for this dish.

BARLEY SOUP
Take one cup of barley, two onions cut fine, ½ cup of carrots diced, one teaspoon of salt, pepper to taste; add two quarts of water and simmer two or three hours. When water has evaporated add soup; if you are making fresh soup, keep adding the "top soup," strained, to the barley and let boil until tender, one-half cup of celery root boiled with the barley improves the flavor.

DRIED PEA SOUP
Soak one cup of picked and cleaned dried split peas in cold water over night, drain, put on with two quarts cold water, a smoked beef-cheek or any other smoked meat; let boil slowly but steadily four hours or more; add one-half cup of celery, diced, one small onion cut fine, one teaspoon of salt, ⅛ teaspoon of pepper, cook until the meat and peas are tender. Remove meat when tender. Skim fat off the top of the soup. Heat one tablespoon of the fat in a frying pan, add one tablespoon of flour and gradually the rest of the soup. Season to taste and serve with the smoked meat, adding croutons.

LENTIL SOUP (LINZEN), No. 1
Soak two cups of lentils over night in cold water. Drain and add to a sliced onion which has been browned in two tablespoons of drippings; when these have been fried for five minutes, add three stalks of celery cut in small pieces or some celery seed, pepper and salt to taste, and two quarts of warm water, boil all these slowly, stirring occasionally until the lentils are quite soft. Pass all through a sieve, return to saucepan, heat again and serve.

LENTIL SOUP, No. 2
Made same as Dried Pea Soup. One cup of strained tomatoes may be added or small slices of sausage.

SOUR SOUP FOR PURIM
Take one pound of soup meat and two soup bones, put on to boil in boiling water. Cut two leeks in slices like noodles, some cooked tomatoes which have been cooled and strained, some cauliflower, two tablespoons of sugar, a pinch sour salt, pepper and salt, and let cook steadily. When the soup is done thicken it with two egg yolks that have been beaten up with a little salt and some cold water. Do not cook after adding yolks of eggs.

TOMATO SOUP

Take a large soup bone or two pounds of soup meat, the latter preferred, one or two onions, a few potatoes, a few carrots, a turnip, soup greens and a can of tomatoes or a quart of fresh ones, cook two hours, and in season add two ears of sweet corn grated. Season with salt and pepper. Thicken with a tablespoon of flour, dissolved in cold water. A nice addition to this soup is a handful of noodles cut into round disks with a thimble.

VEAL SOUP

Boil a piece of veal, off the neck, and one or two veal bones in two quarts of water, add a sprig of parsley, one onion, cut up into small pieces. Strain and thicken with the yolks of two eggs slightly beaten with a tablespoon of cold water. Season with salt and pepper to taste.

VEGETABLE SOUP

Take a small soup bone, cover with cold water. Cut ½ cup each of celery, carrots, and onion. Brown in fat, cooking five to ten minutes; add one tablespoon of chopped parsley and ½ cup of potatoes. Add to soup bone and cook one hour. Season with salt and pepper. Remove bone and serve.

HOW TO MAKE CREAM SOUPS

Cream soups are all made by blending two tablespoons of butter with two tablespoons of flour and then adding slowly one cup of cold milk or half cream and milk. One cup for a thin soup or purée, to one quart of liquid. More according to the thickness of soup desired. Any cooked vegetable or fish may be added to the cream sauce. Less milk is used when the water in which the vegetables are cooked is added.

Purées are made from vegetables or fish, forced through a strainer and retained in soup, milk and seasonings. Generally thicker than cream soup. Use a double boiler in making cream sauces and the cream sauce foundation for soups.

To warm over a thick soup it is best to put it in a double boiler. It must not be covered. If one does not have a double boiler set soup boiler in a pan of hot water over fire. Cream soups and purées are so nutritious that with bread and butter, they furnish a satisfactory meal.

CREAM OF ALMOND SOUP
Blanch, and grind or pound one-half pound almonds, let simmer slowly in one pint of milk for five minutes. Melt one tablespoon of butter, blend with one of flour. Do not allow to bubble. Add one cup of milk and thicken slightly. Then add the almond mixture and simmer again until creamy. Remove from fire and add one cup of cream. Season with salt and pepper to taste. Cream may be whipped or left plain.

CREAM OF CELERY SOUP
Break three stalks of celery in one-inch pieces and pound in a mortar. Cook in double boiler with one slice of onion and three cups of milk for twenty minutes. Remove onion, heat two tablespoons of butter, add two tablespoons of flour, ¼ teaspoon of pepper, one teaspoon of salt ; first ⅔ cup, and gradually the rest of the celery broth, add one cup of cream; cook until smooth and serve at once.

CREAM OF ASPARAGUS SOUP
Proceed as with cream of celery soup, substituting one-half bundle of fresh asparagus or an equal amount of canned for the stalk of celery. Or, the tips

of a bundle of asparagus may be cut off for table use and the remainder used for soup. In either case the asparagus will be better if mashed through a colander, thus removing the woody portions.

CREAM OF CAULIFLOWER SOUP
Take a solid head of cauliflower, scald it to take away the strong taste; separate the flowers and proceed as with cream of celery soup.

CREAM OF CORN SOUP
Take a six ears of corn. Run a sharp knife down through the center of each row of kernels, and with the back of a knife press out the pulp, leaving the husk on the cob. Break the cobs and put them on to boil in sufficient cold water to cover them. Boil thirty minutes and strain the liquor. Return the liquor to the stove, and when boiling add the corn pulp and bay leaf. Cook fifteen minutes; add the cream sauce and serve.

CREAM OF HERRING SOUP (RUSSIAN)
Place two cups of milk, two cups of water, one small onion, salt and pepper to taste in a saucepan, and boil for ten minutes, add two herrings which have been previously soaked and cut in small pieces; cook until herring is tender.

MILK, OR CREAM SOUP
Heat a quart of milk or cream, add a tablespoon of sweet butter and thicken with a spoon of flour or cornstarch, wet with cold milk. Pour, boiling, over pieces of toasted bread cut into dices; crackers may also be used.

FISH CHOWDER
Skin and bone 1½ pounds of codfish or haddock. Cut six large tomatoes, six large potatoes, two large onions in small pieces, add salt, pepper, three pints of water and cook one hour. Add ½ pint of cream, ¼ cup of butter, and paprika. Cook five minutes and serve.

MOCK FISH CHOWDER
Omit fish and use same ingredients, sprinkle with chopped parsley and serve.

GLOBE ARTICHOKE OR TURNIP SOUP
Heat two tablespoons of butter, add 1½ pounds of sliced turnips or arti-

chokes and stir them in the butter, add one tablespoon of flour, a little salt, three cups of hot milk, three cups of hot water, stirring them in slowly. When the vegetables are done, rub them through a sieve, put them back in the saucepan, add a little sugar and more seasoning, if required, and heat thoroughly. A little cream or butter may be put into the tureen, and the soup stirred into it.

SPINACH SOUP

Wash, pick over and cook two quarts of spinach for twenty minutes; drain, chop and rub through a sieve and return to the water in which it was cooked, add ½ cup of chopped onions, cook until thoroughly done, thicken with a white sauce made by melting two tablespoons of butter to which is added two tablespoons of flour; stir until smooth, add two cups of milk; season with ½ teaspoon each of salt and pepper and add the spinach mixture.

CREAM OF LETTUCE SOUP

Proceed as with spinach, substituting lettuce for spinach.

CREAM OF TOMATO SOUP

Cook one quart tomatoes (fresh or canned) with one pint water until done, and strain through a sieve. Meanwhile melt two tablespoons of butter, add two tablespoons of flour, add gradually 1½ cups of milk (or half cream and half milk), one teaspoon of salt, one teaspoon of sugar, ¼ teaspoon of pepper; add a little chopped parsley and celery, and let this boil for fifteen minutes. Just before ready to serve add ¼ teaspoon of baking soda to the hot strained tomatoes, pour gradually into the cream sauce stirring constantly and serve at once.

CREAM OF LENTIL SOUP

Soak one cup of lentils over night. Drain and boil slowly for one hour in water containing one-half teaspoon of baking soda, drain and boil again very gently in fresh water; when the lentils are tender drain off most of the liquid and return to the fire. Add two tablespoons of butter, or butter substitute, two teaspoons of salt, and ½ teaspoon of sugar. Bring three cups of milk to a boil in the double-boiler. Just before serving mash the lentils through a strainer directly into the milk. Serve in cups and pass croutons with the soup.

ONION SOUP

Slice two or three large onions; fry them in a tablespoon of butter until they are soft and red, then add three tablespoons of flour and stir until it is a little cooked. To this add slowly a pint of boiling water, stirring all the time, so it will be smooth. Boil and mash three good-sized potatoes. Add to them slowly a quart of scalded milk, stirring well so it will be smooth. Add the potato and milk mixture to the onion mixture. Season with salt and pepper. Let it get very hot, and pass it through a strainer into the tureen. Sprinkle over the top a little parsley chopped very fine, and a few croutons.

CREAM WINE SOUP

Put one cup of white wine and ½ cup of cold water on to boil, add a few pieces of stick cinnamon and seven lumps of cut loaf sugar; while boiling scald a cup of sweet cream in double boiler. Have ready the well-beaten yolks of two eggs, pour over this the hot cream, stirring all the time, then pour in the boiling wine, being careful to stir well or it will curdle. Can be eaten hot or cold.

VEGETABLE SOUP (MILCHIG) [has dairy ingredients]

Brown ½ cup of chopped onion in one tablespoon of butter, add one and a half quarts of boiling water, two cups of shredded cabbage, ½ cup of chopped carrot, one leak, one tablespoon of chopped peppers, one tablespoon of chopped celery. Boil rapidly for ten minutes, then gently for one hour. Add one medium-sized potato diced and a tomato, 1½ teaspoons of salt, and ¼ teaspoon of pepper, a pinch of paprika and thyme. Cook one hour longer. Have the cover partially off the kettle during the entire time. Ten minutes before serving thicken with two tablespoons of flour mixed with ¼ cup of cold milk.

BRAUNE MEHLSUPPE (BROWN FLOUR SOUP), No. 1

Heat a spoon of butter in a sauce pan, add a spoon of flour, stir briskly, but do not let it get black; pour boiling water over it, add salt and caraway seeds.

BROWN FLOUR SOUP, No. 2

Heat two tablespoons of fresh butter in a sauce pan, add four tablespoons of flour to it and brown to light golden brown, then add one quart water, stirring constantly. Season with salt and pepper and a little nutmeg. Add one pint of milk, let boil up once or twice and serve at once.

BEER SOUP

To one pint of beer add one cup of water, let come to a boil, season with salt and cinnamon if desired. Beat two egg yolks well with a little sugar and flour mixed, add one cup of milk, stir until smooth, stir all together in the hot beer mixture, let come almost to the boiling point, fold in the beaten whites of the two eggs and serve at once with croutons. If desired for a meat meal equal parts of water and beer may be used instead of milk.

SOUR MILK SOUP

Let the milk stand until it jellies, but does not separate. Put it into a sauce pan and let simmer one minute. Then thicken with two generous tablespoons of flour; blend to a smooth paste with butter. Strain through a fine sieve and serve in cups or soup plates and sprinkle the top with maple sugar.

POTATO SOUP

Boil and mash three or four potatoes, one tablespoon of butter, ½ tablespoon of flour, and one teaspoon of chopped onion, letting the onion cook in the butter a few minutes before adding the flour. When this is cooked add to it 2 cups milk, making a thin, white sauce. Add this to the mashed potato and pass the whole through a strainer. Return it to the heat for a few minutes to heat and blend it. Season it with salt and pepper. Sprinkle on the soup chopped parsley and a few croutons.

For Fleischig Soup - This soup may be made with fat instead of butter, and the water in which the potatoes have been boiled may be used instead of the milk; any left-over meat gravy will give the soup a rich flavor.

GREEN PEA PURÉE

Cook one quart of green peas until very tender. Then mash through colander. To this amount heat one quart of milk in double boiler. Add butter, salt and pepper to taste, and last the mashed green peas.

LEEK SOUP

Put a small piece of butter in saucepan and then six or eight leeks cut in small pieces. Keep turning for about five minutes so they will get brown; add water for amount desired; season with salt and pepper and put in piece of stale bread. Strain through the strainer. Put in croutons and serve with grated cheese.

RED WINE SOUP

Put on to boil one cup of good red wine and ½ cup of water, sweeten to taste, add three whole cloves and three small pieces of cinnamon bark, let boil ten minutes, and pour while boiling over the well-beaten yolk of one egg. Eat hot or cold. This quantity serves one person.

SPLIT PEA SOUP (MILCHIG)

Soak peas in lukewarm water over night. Use one quart of peas to one gallon of water. Boil about two hours with the following vegetables: a few potatoes, a large celery root, a little parsley and a little onion, a small carrot cut up in cubes and a small clove of garlic. When boiled down to half the quantity, press all through colander. If soup is too thin, take a tablespoon of flour blended with a little cold water in a saucepan and add to the peas already strained. Serve with croutons.

TOMATO SOUP WITH RICE

Brown slightly one minced onion in one tablespoon of butter, add one can of tomatoes or a quart of medium sized tomatoes cut in small pieces, season with salt, pepper, one tablespoon of sugar and a pinch of paprika. Simmer a half hour, strain and thicken with one tablespoon of flour moistened with cold water, add the strained tomatoes and one cup of boiled rice; let come to a boil and serve.

MILK AND CHEESE SOUP

Thicken three cups of milk with ½ tablespoon of flour and cook thoroughly in a double boiler, stirring very often. When ready to serve add one cup of grated cheese and season with salt and paprika.

BLACK BEAN SOUP

Soak one pint of beans over night, drain, add cold water and rinse thoroughly. Fry two tablespoons of chopped onion in two tablespoons of butter, put in with the beans, add two stalks of celery or a piece of celery root and two quarts of water. Cook slowly until the beans are soft, three or four hours, add more boiling water as it boils away; rub through a strainer, add ⅛ teaspoon of pepper, ¼ teaspoon of mustard, a few grains of cayenne. Heat one tablespoon of butter in saucepan with two tablespoons of flour, then ⅔ cup and then the rest of the soup gradually; cut a lemon (removing seeds) and two hard-boiled eggs in slices and serve in the soup.

BARLEY AND VEGETABLE SOUP

Take ½ cup of coarse barley and two quarts of water. Let boil for one hour and skim. Then add two onions, a bunch of carrots, parsley, two turnips, one green pepper and six tomatoes (all chopped fine). Add a few green peas, lima beans, two ears of corn cut from cob; pepper and salt to taste. Cook for one hour or more until done. Then add a small piece of butter, quarter teaspoon of sage and thyme, if you like, and if soup is too thick add more water.

BEER SOUP (PARVE)

Mix the beer with ⅓ water, boil with sugar and the grated crust of stale rye bread, add stick cinnamon and a little lemon juice. Pour over small pieces of zwieback. Some boil a handful of dried currants. When done add both currants and juice.

BEET SOUP (RUSSIAN)

Cut two small beets in strips, cover with water and let cook until tender, add a dash lemon juice, and a little sugar to make sweet and sour, a little salt, and ¾ cup of sour cream. Serve cold. Sweet cream may be used and while hot gradually poured over the well-beaten yolks of two eggs, keeping the soup over the stove and stirring all the time until thick and smooth. Remove from stove and serve cold.

CHERRY SOUP

This soup is a summer soup and is to be eaten cold. Cook two tablespoons of cornstarch in one cup of boiling water until tender, add more as water boils down. Put one quart of large red or black cherries, one cup of claret, one tablespoon of broken cinnamon, ¼ cup sugar, and ½ lemon sliced fine, up to boil and let boil fifteen minutes; add the cornstarch, let boil up and pour very gradually over the well-beaten yolks of two eggs. Serve cold. Raspberry, strawberry, currant, gooseberry, apple, plum or rhubarb soups are prepared the same way, each cooked until tender and sweetened to taste. The juice of lemon may be used instead of the wine.

FRUIT SOUP

Take two pounds of plums, cherries, or red currants and raspberries, which carefully pick and wash, and boil to a pulp with a pint of water. Let it slightly cool and then stir in the beaten yolk of an egg and a little sugar. Strain the soup, which should be served cold.

COLD SOUR SOUP
Take a pound of sour grass (sorrel), remove leaves, wash well, cut and squeeze well. Peel three potatoes, mince a bunch of young onions, salt and set on to boil, when boiling add the sour grass and let boil well, add two tablespoons of sugar, and a bit of sour salt, let simmer a bit, afterward add two well-beaten eggs. Do not boil this soup after adding the eggs. This soup is to be eaten cold. It can be kept for some time in jars.

GARNISHES AND DUMPLINGS FOR SOUPS

NOODLES
Beat one large egg slightly with ¼ teaspoon of salt, add enough flour to make a stiff dough; work it well for fifteen or twenty minutes, adding flour when necessary. When the dough is smooth place on slightly floured board and roll out very thin and set aside on a clean towel for an hour or more to dry. Fold in a tight roll and cut crosswise in fine threads. Toss them up lightly with fingers to separate well, and spread them on the board to dry. When thoroughly dry, put in a jar covered with cheese cloth for future use. Drop by handfuls in boiling soup, ten minutes before serving. Noodles for vegetables or for puddings are made in the same way, but to each egg, one-half egg-shell full of cold water may be added. The strips are cut one-half inch wide.

PLÄTCHEN
Take noodle dough, roll out thin in same manner as noodles, when dry cut in three-inch strips, place the strips on top of one another, then cut into ½ inch strips, crosswise, cut again to form one-half inch squares. Dry same as noodles. Drop by handfuls in boiling soup.

KREPLECH OR BUTTERFLIES
Roll noodle dough into pieces 2½ inches square. Place on each one tablespoon of force-meat, then fold squares into three corned pockets, pressing edges well together. Drop in boiling soup or salted water and boil fifteen minutes.

FORCE-MEAT FOR KREPLECH
Chop one pound of beef, soup meat, cold veal, or take lamb chopped very fine, season with one teaspoon of salt, ⅛ teaspoon of pepper, ginger or nutmeg, ½ teaspoon of onion juice, mix with one egg. This force-meat may also be made into balls ½ inch in diameter, roll the balls in flour and cook them in the boiling soup, or fry them in fat.

BAKING POWDER DUMPLINGS
Sift one cup of flour, ¼ teaspoon of salt, one teaspoon of baking powder, stir in scant ½ cup of milk or water and mix to a smooth batter. Drop one teaspoonful at a time in the boiling soup; cover pot, let boil five minutes and serve at once.

CROUTONS
Cut stale bread into cubes, place in pan and brown in the oven; or butter the bread, cut into cubes and then brown the same way. Fry small cubes of stale bread in deep hot fat until brown or fry them in a little butter or fat in a hot sauce pan until brown.

PFARVEL OR GRATED EGG FOR SOUP
Into the yolk of one egg stir enough flour until it is too stiff to work. Grate on coarse grater, and spread on board to dry. After soup is strained, put in and boil ten minutes before serving.

SPÄTZEN or SPÄTZLE
Beat one egg well, add ½ teaspoon of salt, ¾ cup of flour, and ⅓ cup of water, stirring to a stiff, smooth batter. Drop by teaspoons into boiling soup ten minutes before serving.

EGG CUSTARD
Beat slightly the yolks of two eggs, add two tablespoons of milk, and a few grains of salt. Pour into small buttered cup, place in pan of hot water and bake until firm; cool, remove from cup and cut in fancy shapes with French vegetable cutters.

GRATED IRISH POTATO
Peel, wash and grate one large Irish potato, or two medium-sized ones. Put it in a sieve and let hot water run over it until it is perfectly white. Have the white of one egg beaten to a very stiff froth, then stir in the potatoes and twenty minutes before serving add it to the boiling soup. Beat the yolk of one egg up in the soup tureen, and pour the hot soup over it, stirring carefully at first.

FARINA DUMPLINGS
Put in a double boiler one kitchen spoon of fresh butter, stir in one cup of milk. When it begins to boil stir in enough farina to thicken. Take off the stove and when cold add the yolks of two eggs and the stiffly beaten whites, and a little salt and nutmeg, and ½ cup grated almonds, if desired. Let cool, then make into little balls, and ten minutes before soup is to be served, drop in boiler and let boil up once or twice.

BOILED FLOUR BALLS WITH ALMONDS
Two yolks of eggs beaten very light, add a pinch of salt, pepper and finely-chopped parsley. Add six blanched almonds grated, enough sifted flour to make stiff batter, then add the stiffly beaten whites of eggs and ½ teaspoon baking powder. Drop by teaspoons in soup ten minutes before serving.

EINLAUF (EGG DROP)
Beat one egg, add ⅛ teaspoon of salt, three tablespoons of flour, and ¼ cup water, stir until smooth. Pour slowly from a considerable height from the end of a spoon into the boiling soup. Cook two or three minutes and serve hot; add one teaspoon of chopped parsley to the soup.

EGG DUMPLINGS FOR SOUPS
Rub the yolks of two hard-boiled eggs to a smooth paste, add a little salt and grated nutmeg and ½ teaspoon melted butter. Add the chopped whites of two eggs and a raw egg yolk to be able to mold the dough into little marbles, put in boiling soup one minute.

SCHWEM KLÖßE
Take three tablespoons of flour; stir with one egg, and ½ cup milk; pour this in a pan in which some butter was melted; stir until it loosens from the pan. When it is cold, add two more eggs and some salt, and shortly before needed form in little dumplings and put in boiling hot soup for five minutes.

DUMPLINGS FOR CREAM SOUPS
Scald some flour with milk or water, mix in a small piece of butter and salt, and boil until thick. When cool beat in yolk of an egg, if too stiff add the beaten white.

DROP DUMPLINGS
Break into a cup the whites of three eggs; fill the cup with milk, put it with a tablespoon of fresh butter and one cup of sifted flour in a sauce pan and stir as it boils until it leaves the sauce pan clean. Set aside until cool and stir in the yolks of three eggs. Season with salt, pepper and nutmeg, mix thoroughly and drop by teaspoons in the boiling soup ten minutes before ready to be served.

LEBERKLÖSE (LIVER DUMPLINGS)
Brown a small onion minced in one tablespoon of chicken fat, add a small liver chopped fine, chopped parsley, two tablespoons of flour. Season with nutmeg, red and white pepper, and add two eggs. Drop with teaspoon in the boiling soup, let cook ten minutes. Serve.

FRITTER BEANS
Beat one egg until light, add ¾ teaspoon salt, ½ cup flour, and two tablespoons of water. Put through colander into deep hot fat and fry until brown. Drain and pour hot broth over them.

SPONGE DUMPLINGS
Separate three eggs, beat the yolks, and add one cup of soup stock, ¼ teaspoon salt, then add the beaten whites. Pour into a greased cup and place in pan of hot water and steam until firm; cool, remove from cup and cut into small dumplings with a teaspoon; pour the boiling soup over and just before serving add chopped parsley.

FISH

Fish that is not fresh is a very dangerous food and great care should be taken in selecting only fish fit to eat. If the fish is hard in body and the eyes are clear and bright, the gills a bright red and slimy, the flesh so firm that when pressed the marks of the fingers do not remain, the scales not dry or easy to loosen, then the fish is fresh.

In the refrigerator fish will taint butter and other foods if placed in the same compartment, so that in most cases it is better to lay it on a plate on a pan of ice, or wrap it in parchment or waxed paper and put it in the ice box.

Pickerel weighing more than five pounds should not be bought. If belly is thick it is likely that there is another fish inside. This smaller fish or any found in any other fish may not be used as food. Salt fish should be soaked in fresh water, skin side up, to draw out the salt.

Each fish is at its best in its season, for instance:--

Bluefish, Butterfish, Sea, Striped Bass, Porgies, Sea-trout or Weakfish are best from April to September.

Fluke and Flounders are good all year round, but the fluke is better than the flounder in summer. Carp may be had all year, but care must be taken that it has not been in polluted water.

Cod, Haddock, Halibut, Mackerel, Red Snapper, Salmon, Whitefish are good all year.

In the different states of the United States there are laws governing the fishing for trout, so the season for that fish differs in the various states.

Black Bass, Perch, Pickerel and Pike are in season from June 1st to December 1st.

Shad, April to June.

Smelts, November 10th to April.

TO CLEAN FISH

The fish may be cleaned at the market, but needs to be looked over carefully before cooking. To remove the scales hold the fish by the tail and scrape firmly toward the head with a small sharp knife, held with the blade slanting toward the tail. Scrape slowly so that the scales will not fly, and rinse the knife frequently in cold water. If the fish is to be served whole, leave the head and tail on and trim the fins; otherwise remove them.

TO OPEN FISH

To open small fish cut under the gills and squeeze out the contents by pressing upward from the middle with the thumb and finger. To open large fish split them from the gills half way down the body toward the tail; remove the entrails and scrape clean, opening far enough to remove all the blood from the backbone, and wiping the inside thoroughly with a cloth wrung out of cold, salted water.

TO SKIN FISH

To skin a fish remove the fins along the back and cut off a narrow strip of the skin the entire length of the back. Then slip the knife under the skin that lies over the bony part of the gills and work slowly toward the tail. Do the same with the other side.

TO BONE FISH

To bone a fish clean it first and remove the head. Then, beginning at the tail, run a sharp knife under the flesh close to the bone, scraping the flesh away clean from the bone. Work up one side toward the head; then repeat the same process on the other side of the bone. Lift the bone carefully and pull out any small bones that may be left in the flesh.

BOILED FISH

To cook fish properly is very important, as no food, perhaps, is so insipid as fish if carelessly cooked. It must be well done and properly salted. A good rule to cook fish by is the following: Allow ten minutes to the first pound and five minutes for each additional pound; for example: boil a fish weighing five pounds thirty minutes. By pulling out a fin you may ascertain whether your fish is done; if it comes out easily and the meat is an opaque white, your fish has boiled long enough. Always set your fish on to boil in hot water, hot from the teakettle, adding salt and a dash of vinegar to keep the meat firm; an onion, a head of celery and parsley roots are always an acceptable flavor to any kind of boiled fish, no matter what kind of sauce you intend to serve with the fish. If you wish to serve the fish whole, tie it in a napkin and lay it on an old plate at the bottom of the kettle; if you have a "regular "fish kettle" this is not necessary. In boiling fish avoid using too much water. To thicken sauces, where flour is used, take a level teaspoon of flour to a cup of sauce, or the yolk of an egg to a cup of sauce.

BAKED FISH

Wash and dry the fish, rubbing inside and outside with salt; stuff with a bread stuffing and sew. Sprinkle with salt and pepper and place in a hot oven without water. As soon as it begins to brown add hot water and butter and baste every ten minutes. Bake until done, allowing an hour or more for a large fish, twenty or thirty minutes for a small one. Remove to a hot platter; draw out the strings; garnish with slices of lemon well covered with chopped parsley and serve with Hollandaise sauce.

BROILED FISH

For broiling, large fish should be split down the back and head and tail removed; salmon and halibut should be cut into one-inch slices, and smelts and other small fish left whole. Wipe the fish as dry as possible; sprinkle with salt and pepper and if the fish is dry and white brush the flesh side well with olive oil or butter. Put in a well-greased broiler, placing the thickest parts of the fish toward the middle or back of the broiler. Hold over a hot fire until the flesh side is nicely browned; then cook the skin side just long enough to make the skin crisp. Small fish require from ten to fifteen minutes, large fish from fifteen to twenty-five. To remove from the broiler loosen one side first, then the other, and lift carefully with a cake turner. Place on a platter; spread with butter and stand in the oven for a few minutes. Garnish with lemon and serve with Maître d'hôtel butter.

JEWISH METHOD OF FRYING FISH

Scale the fish with the utmost thoroughness, remove the entrails, wash very thoroughly, and salt both inside and out. Then cut the fish into convenient slices, place them on a strainer and leave them there for an hour. Meanwhile, place some flour in one plate and some beaten eggs in another, and heat a large frying pan half full of oil or butter. Now wipe your fish slices thoroughly with a clean cloth, dip them first in flour and then in beaten eggs and finally fry until browned. In frying fish very hot oil is required. If a crumb of bread will brown in twenty seconds the oil is hot enough. Put fish in a frying basket, then into the hot oil and cook five minutes. Drain on brown paper and arrange on platter. Do not stick knife or fork into fish while it is frying. When the oil has cooled, strain it, pour it into a jar, cover it and it will be ready for use another time. It can be used again for fish only.

ANOTHER METHOD OF FRYING FISH

Thoroughly mix six ounces of flour with an ounce of olive oil, the yolk of an egg, and a pinch of salt. Stir in one gill of tepid water and allow the whole to stand for half an hour in a cool place. Next, beat the white of an egg stiff and stir into the batter. Dip each fish into the mixture, then roll in breadcrumbs and cook in boiling oil. Butter must not be used. In frying fish do not allow the fish to remain in the sauce pan after it has been nicely browned, for this absorbs the fat and destroys the delicate flavor. Be sure that the fish is done. This rule applies to fish that is sauted.

SAUTÉED FISH

Clean fish, sprinkle with salt and pepper, dip in flour or cornmeal and cook in sauce pan with just enough hot butter to prevent it sticking to the pan. Shake the pan occasionally. Brown well on under side, then turn and brown on the other side.

LEMON FISH

Boil three tablespoons of vinegar, one sliced onion, six whole peppers, salt, one piece of stick cinnamon, and a little water, then add sliced fish. When fish has boiled twenty minutes remove and arrange on platter. Strain the gravy and add the well-beaten yolks of two eggs, juice of two lemons, sugar to taste and twelve grated almonds. Let all come to a boil, then pour over the fish, sprinkle finely chopped parsley on top and garnish with sliced lemons. Bluefish, mackerel, shad, salmon and porgies may be cooked with this sauce.

SWEET SOUR FISH

First cut up and salt the fish. Shad, trout or carp can be used. Put on fish kettle with 1½ cups of water, and one cup of vinegar, add one onion cut in round slices, one dozen raisins, one lemon cut in round slices, two bay leaves, six cloves. When this mixture begins to boil, lay in your fish and cook thoroughly. When done remove fish to platter. Put liquor back on stove, add three tablespoons of granulated sugar (which has been melted and browned in a pie plate without water), then add two tablespoons of flour which has been rubbed smooth with a little water. Let boil well and pour over fish. If not sweet enough add more sugar. Serve cold.

SWEET AND SOUR FISH

Place the fish in strong salt water for one hour before cooking. Take three parts of water and one of vinegar, put in saucepan with some sliced onions and some raisins, and let boil until tender. Add brown sugar to taste, a piece of rye bread from which the crust has been removed, and some molasses. Boil the sauce, then place the fish in and let all cook twenty minutes. When done, arrange on platter with sliced lemon and chopped parsley.

SWEET SOUR FISH WITH WINE

Put on to boil in fish kettle, one glass water, ½ glass vinegar, two tablespoons of brown sugar, six whole cloves, ½ teaspoon of ground cinnamon, one onion cut in round slices. Boil thoroughly, then strain and add to it one lemon cut in round slices, one goblet of red wine, one dozen raisins, one tablespoon of pounded almonds; put on stove again, and when it comes to a boil, add fish that has been cut up and salted. Cook until done, remove fish to a platter, and to the liquor add a small piece Lebkuchen or ginger cake, and stir in the well-beaten yolks of four eggs; stir carefully or it will curdle. If not sweet enough add more sugar. Pour over fish. Shad or trout is the best fish to use.

FISH STOCK

Put in a saucepan a tablespoon of butter or butter substitute, add a tablespoon each of chopped onion, carrot and turnip. Fry them without browning, then add fish-bones, head, and trimmings, a stalk of celery, sprigs of parsley and of thyme, a bay-leaf, a tomato or a slice of lemon. Cover with water and let them simmer for an hour or more. Season with salt and pepper and strain.

PIKE WITH EGG SAUCE

Clean the fish thoroughly, and wash it in hot water, wipe dry and salt inside and out. If you heat the salt it will penetrate through the meat of the fish in less time. Take a kettle, lay in it a piece of butter about the size of an egg; cut up an onion, some celery root, parsley root and a few slices of lemon, lay the fish in, either whole or cut up in slices; boil in enough water to just cover the fish, and add more salt if required, add a dozen whole peppers, black or white; season with ground white pepper. Let the fish boil quickly. In the meantime beat up the yolks of two eggs, and pound a dozen almonds to a paste, add to the beaten yolks, together with a tablespoon of cold water. When done remove the fish to a large platter; but to ascertain whether the fish has cooked long enough, take hold of the fins, if they come out readily your fish has cooked enough. Strain the sauce through a sieve, taking out the slices of lemon and with them garnish the top of the fish; add the strained sauce to the beaten eggs, stirring constantly as you do so; then return the sauce to the kettle, and stir until it boils, remove quickly and pour it over the fish. When it is cold garnish with curly parsley.

GEFILLTE FISCH

Prepare trout, pickerel, or pike in the following manner: After the fish has been scaled and thoroughly cleaned, remove all the meat that adheres to the skin, being careful not to injure the skin; take out all the meat from head to tail, cut open along the backbone, removing it also; but do not disfigure the head and tail; chop the meat in a chopping bowl, then heat about a ¼ pound of butter in a sauce pan, add two tablespoons chopped parsley, and some soaked white bread; remove from the fire and add an onion grated, salt, pepper, pounded almonds, the yolks of two eggs, also a very little nutmeg grated. Mix all thoroughly and fill the skin until it looks natural. Boil in salt water, containing a piece of butter, celery root, parsley and an onion; when done remove from the stove and lay on a platter. The fish should be cooked for 1¼ hours, or until done. Thicken the sauce with yolks of two eggs, adding a few slices of lemon. This fish may be baked but must be rolled in flour and dotted with bits of butter.

RUSSIAN FISH CAKES

Take three pounds of fish (weakfish or carp, pickerel or haddock or whitefish, any fat fish with a fish poor in it). Remove skin and bones from the fish and chop flesh very fine, add a good-sized onion, minced or grated, make a depression in the center of the chopped fish and add ¾ cup water, ½ cup soft breadcrumbs, salt and pepper to taste, ¼ cup sugar, two egg whites and two tablespoons of melted butter. Chop until very smooth and form into cakes containing a generous tablespoonful each. Put the bones and skins into a sauce pan with an onion sliced and a tablespoon of butter and add the fish cakes. Cover with water and simmer for 1¼ hours. Then remove the cakes and strain off the gravy into the two egg yolks which have been slightly beaten together with one teaspoon of sugar; stir over the heat until thickened, but do not boil it. Pour over fish cakes and serve either hot or cold. The butter and sugar may be omitted if so desired.

GEFILLTTE FISCH WITH EGG SAUCE
Cut a five-pound haddock into four-inch slices. Cut a big hole into each slice, preserving the backbone and skin. Put this meat, cut from the fish, into a wooden tray, add to it four large onions and a sprig of parsley. Chop until very fine, then add two eggs, a dash of pepper and cinnamon, a pinch of salt, and a tablespoon of sugar. To this add enough cracker dust to stiffen it. Put this filling into the holes cut in the fish.

Take a saucepan, put in one sliced onion, a sprig of parsley, a small sliced carrot, a dash of pepper, and a pinch of salt. Put the fish into the saucepan, cover with cold water, and let it boil slowly for one hour. At the end of the hour take out the fish, and put on a platter. Preserve the water or gravy in which the fish was boiled for the sauce.

Egg sauce for fish: Beat the yokes of two eggs thoroughly. Into the beaten yolks slowly pour the gravy in which the fish was boiled, stirring constantly. Stand this on the back of the stove to boil for five minutes, stirring constantly so as to prevent burning.

FILLED FISH - TURKISH STYLE No. 1.
Bone some fat fish, boil in salt and water; when done take a little of the fish soup, one egg, beat until light, add gradually the juice of ½ lemon.

FRITADA No. 2.
Steam the fish and bone. Take four good-sized tomatoes, cut them up, add chopped parsley, scallions or leeks cut in small pieces, a little celery, salt and pepper to taste and four eggs well-beaten; mix all these ingredients very well with the boned fish, form in omelet shape. Place in oven in pan greased with olive oil and bake until well browned.

HECHT (PICKEREL)
This fish is best prepared "scharf" [highly seasoned]. Clean your fish thoroughly and salt the day previous; wrap it in a clean towel and lay it

on ice until wanted. Line a kettle with celery and parsley roots; cut up an onion, add a lump of fresh butter, and pack the fish in the kettle, head first, either whole or cut up; sprinkle a little salt and white pepper over all and add about a dozen peppercorns; put on enough water to just cover, and add a whole lemon cut in slices. Do not let the fish boil quickly. Add about a dozen pounded almonds. By this time the fish will be ready to turn, then beat up the yolks of two eggs in a bowl, to be added to the sauce after the fish is boiled. Try the fish with a fork and if the meat loosens readily it is done. Take up each peace carefully, if it has been cut up, and arrange on a large platter, head first and so on, make the fish appear whole, and garnish with the slices of lemon and sprigs of parsley; then mince up some parsley and garnish top of the fish, around the lemon slices. Thicken the gravy by adding the beaten yolks, add a tablespoon of cold water to the yolks before adding to the boiling sauce; stir, remove from the fire at once and pour over the fish. If you prefer the sauce strained, then strain before adding the yolks of the eggs and almonds. Haddock, sea-bass, pike, perch, weakfish and porgies may be cooked "scharf" [highly seasoned].

FRESH COD OR STRIPED BASS
Cut into pieces ready to serve, after which salt them for an hour. Into the fish kettle put a quantity of water, large onion sliced, carrot also sliced, turnip, celery root, and boil fifteen minutes. Add the fish and two tablespoons of butter, tiny piece of cinnamon, pepper to taste. Boil fifteen minutes longer, then add teaspoon of flour mixed with cold water. Boil up well and add salt or pepper if needed. Remove fish and arrange on platter. Beat yolks of two eggs with a tablespoon of cold water; after straining out vegetables, add the hot gravy in which fish was boiled. Return to fire and stir till thick enough. Garnish with chopped parsley.

AHILADO SAUCE (TURKISH)
Mix some tomato sauce, olive oil, parsley, salt and pepper. Boil sauce first, and add boiled sea-bass or flounders.

BOILED TROUT
Cut up a celery root, one onion, and a sprig of parsley, tie the fish in a napkin and lay it on this bed of roots; pour in enough water to cover and add

a dash of vinegar - the vinegar keeps the fish firm - then boil over a quick fire and add more salt to the water in which the fish has been boiled. Lay your fish on a hot platter and prepare the following sauce: set a cup of sweet cream in a kettle, heat it, add a tablespoon of fresh butter, salt and pepper, and thicken with a tablespoon of flour which has been wet with a little cold milk, stir this paste into the cream and boil about one minute, stirring constantly; pour over the fish. Boil two eggs, and while they are boiling, blanch about a dozen or more almonds and stick them into the fish, points up; cover the eggs with cold water, peel them, separate the whites from the yolks, chop each separately; garnish the fish, first with a row of chopped yolks, then whites, until all is used; lay chopped parsley all around the platter. Fresh cod and striped bass may be cooked in this way.

FISH PIQUANT
Cook any large fish in salt water - salmon is particularly nice prepared in this style - add one cup of vinegar, onions, celery root and parsley. When the fish is cooked enough, remove it from the fire, kettle and all - letting the fish remain in its sauce until the following sauce is prepared: Take the yolks of two eggs, ½ teaspoon of dry mustard, salt, pepper, a tablespoon of butter, a tablespoon of vinegar, ½ glass water and some fish gravy. Boil in double boiler until thick. Take some parsley, green onions, capers, shallots and one large vinegar pickle and some tarragon, chop all up very fine; chop up the hard-boiled whites separately and then add the sauce; mix all this together thoroughly, then taste to see if seasoned to suit.

SALMON CUTLETS
Take the remains of some boiled salmon or a small can of salmon, three tablespoons of mashed potatoes, one of breadcrumbs, one of chopped parsley, a little flour, mace, an egg, pepper and salt. Mix the ingredients well together, bind with the egg, let stand an hour, then form into little flat cutlets, roll in breadcrumbs and fry in hot oil, drain on paper and send to table garnished with parsley.

PAPRIKA CARP
Slice and salt three pounds of carp. Steam four sliced onions with one cup of water, to which has been added one teaspoon of paprika, add the sliced carp and cook very slowly until the fish is done.

RED SNAPPER WITH TOMATO SAUCE

Scale thoroughly, salt and pepper inside and out, and lay upon ice, wrapped in a clean cloth overnight. When ready to cook cut up the celery or parsley root, or both, two large onions, a carrot or two, and let this come to a boil in about one quart of water, then lay in the fish, whole or in pieces, let the water almost cover the fish; add a lump of fresh butter and three or four tomatoes (out of season you may use canned tomatoes, say three or four large spoonfuls); let the fish boil half an hour, turning it occasionally. Try it by taking hold of the fins, if they come out readily, the fish is done. Take it up carefully, lay on a large platter and strain the sauce; let it boil, thicken it with the well-beaten yolks of two eggs, adding the sauce gradually to the eggs and stirring constantly. Garnish the fish with chopped parsley, letting a quantity mix with the sauce. Red snapper is also very good fried.

BONED SMELTS, SAUTÉED

Take a dozen raw smelts; split them from the back lengthwise, leaving the head and tail intact; take out the large center bone without opening the stomach and season with salt. Put four ounces of butter into a saucepan, and when quite hot place the smelts in it, so that the side which was cut open is underneath. When they have attained a nice color, turn them over and finish cooking. When ready, arrange them on a very hot dish, pour the butter in which they were cooked over them, squeeze a little lemon on them, then add over all some finely chopped green parsley. Serve.

FISH WITH HORSERADISH SAUCE

Clean three pounds of fresh salmon, bone, salt and let stand several hours. Place in fish kettle with boiling salt water (one teaspoon of salt to one quart of water), and let boil ½ hour or until well cooked. Lift out carefully, place on hot platter and pour over ¼ cup melted butter, and sprinkle well with one tablespoon of parsley. Serve in a separate bowl the following sauce; a large spoonful with each portion of fish: Peel ¼ pound horseradish root, grate, and mix well with one pint of cream beaten stiff. The fish must be hot and the sauce cold.

FISH WITH SAUERKRAUT

Fry an onion in butter (or vegetable oil), add sauerkraut and cook. Boil the fish in salt water, then bone and shred. Fry two minced onions in butter or oil, put them into the kettle with the fish, add two egg yolks, butter or oil, a little pepper and a tablespoon of breadcrumbs; steam for half hour and serve with the kraut.

FILLET OF SOLE Á LA MOUQUIN
Thoroughly wash and pick over a pound of spinach, put it over the fire with no more water than clings to the leaves and cook for ten minutes; at the end of that time drain the spinach and chop it fine. Have ready thin fillets of flounder, halibut, or whitefish. Cover them with acidulated warm water - a slice of lemon in the water is all that is wanted, and add a slice of onion, a sprig of parsley and a bit of bay leaf. Simmer for ten minutes and drain. Put the minced spinach into the bottom of the buttered baking dish, arrange the fillets on it, cover with a cream sauce to which a tablespoon of grated cheese has been added, and brown in the oven.

FILLET OF SOLE Á LA CREOLE
Fillet some large flounders, and have a fishman send you all the bones; put the bones on to boil; wash, dry, and season the fillets; roll them (putting in some bits of butter), and fasten each one with a wooden toothpick. Strain the water from the bones; thicken with a little brown flour and onion; add to this one-half can of tomatoes, a little cayenne pepper, salt, and chopped green peppers. Let this sauce simmer for a couple of hours (this need not be strained); put the fillets in a casserole, and pour some of this sauce over them, and put in the oven for about fifteen minutes. Then pour over the rest of the tomato sauce, sprinkle a little chopped parsley and serve. One can add a few mushrooms to the sauce. The mushrooms must be fried in butter before being added to the sauce.

BAKED BLACK BASS
After having carefully cleaned, salt well and lay it in the baking-pan with a small cup of water, and strew flakes of butter on top, also salt, pepper and a little chopped parsley. Bake about one hour, basting often until brown.

Serve on a heated platter; garnish with parsley and lemon and make a sauce by adding a glass of sherry, a little catsup and thicken with a teaspoon of flour, adding this to fish gravy. Serve potatoes with fish, boiled in the usual way, making a sauce of two tablespoons of butter. Add a bunch of parsley chopped very fine, salt and pepper to taste, a small cup of sweet cream thickened with a tablespoon of flour. Pour over potatoes.

BAKED FLOUNDERS

Clean, wipe dry, add salt and pepper and lay them in a pan; put flakes of butter on top, an onion cut up, some minced celery and a few breadcrumbs. A cup of hot water put into the pan will prevent burning. Baste often; bake until brown.

BAKED BASS Á LA WELLINGTON

Remove the scales and clean. Do not remove the head, tail, or fins. Put into a double boiler one tablespoon of butter, two cups of stale breadcrumbs, one tablespoon of chopped onion, one teaspoon of chopped parsley, two teaspoons of chopped capers, ¼ cup sherry. Heat all the above ingredients, season with paprika and salt, and stuff the bass with the mixture. Sew up the fish, put into a hot oven, bake and baste with sherry wine and butter. A fish weighing four or five pounds is required for the above recipe.

BAKED FISH - TURKISH

Take perch and stuff with steamed onion to which has been added one well-beaten egg, two tomatoes cut up in small pieces, some breadcrumbs, chopped parsley or celery, salt and pepper to taste. Bake until the fish is nicely browned.

SAUCE AGRISTOGA

Fry any fish in oil, and serve the following: Beat very well two whole eggs, add two tablespoons of flour diluted with cold water, add gradually the juice of one lemon.

ZUEMIMO SAUCE

Heat one teaspoon of oil, add one tablespoon of flour, add slowly ½ cup of vinegar diluted with water; season with salt and sugar. If no other fish can be procured, salt herring may be used.

SHAD ROE
Parboil the roe in salted water ten minutes. Drain; season with salt, pepper and melted butter; form into balls, roll in beaten egg and cracker crumbs and fry in hot oil or any butter substitute. The roe can be baked and served with tomato sauce.

BAKED SHAD
Clean and split a three-pound shad. Place in a buttered dripping pan. Sprinkle with salt and pepper, brush with melted butter and bake in a hot oven thirty minutes.

SCALLOPED FISH ROE
Boil three large roes in water with a little vinegar for ten minutes. Plunge into cold water; wipe the roe dry. Mash the yolks of three hard-boiled eggs into a cup of melted butter, teaspoon of anchovy paste, tablespoon of chopped parsley, juice of half a lemon, salt and pepper to taste. Add a cup of breadcrumbs and then mix in lightly the roe that has been broken into pieces. Put all in baking dish, cover with breadcrumbs and flakes of butter, and brown in oven.

BAKED MACKEREL
Split fish, clean, and remove head and tail. Put in buttered pan, sprinkle with salt and pepper and dot over with butter (allowing one tablespoon to a medium-sized fish), pour over ⅔ cup of milk. Bake twenty-five minutes in a hot oven.

STUFFED HERRING
Make a dressing of two tablespoons of breadcrumbs, one tablespoon of chopped parsley, two tablespoons of butter, juice of ½ lemon, and pepper and salt to taste. Add enough hot water to make soft. Fill the herrings, roll up, tie in shape. Cover with greased paper and bake ten to fifteen minutes.

FISH WITH GARLIC
Clean, salt fish one half hour, wash and dry with a clean cloth; cut garlic very thin, rub over fish; place in oven to bake; bake until odor of garlic has disappeared, then let fish cool.

BAKED CHOPPED HERRING

Soak herring one hour in water and then one and a half in sweet milk, skin, bone and chop; cut up a medium-sized onion, fry in butter until golden brown, add a cup of cream, two egg yolks and ¼ cup white breadcrumbs, then put in a little more cream. Butter pan, sprinkle with crumbs or cracker dust, then put in herring, pepper slightly. Bake in 350° oven for forty-five minutes.

MARINIRTE (PICKLED) HERRING

Take a New Holland herring, remove the heads and scales, wash well, open them and lay the herring in milk or water over night. Next day lay the herring in a stone jar with alternate layers of onions cut up, also lemon cut in slices, a few cloves, whole peppers and a few bay leaves, some capers and whole mustard seed. Stir in a spoon of brown sugar and vinegar and pour it over the herring.

SALT HERRING

Soak salt herring over night in cold water, so that the salt may be drawn out. Drain and serve with boiled potatoes, or bone and place in kettle of cold water, let come to a boil and let simmer a few minutes until tender, drain and pour melted butter over them and serve hot with boiled or fried potatoes.

BROILED SALT MACKEREL

Freshen the fish by soaking it over night in cold water, with the skin uppermost. Drain and wipe dry, remove the head and tail, place it upon a butter broiler, and slowly broil to a light brown. Place upon a hot dish, add pepper, bits of butter, a sprinkling of parsley and a little lemon juice.

BOILED SALT MACKEREL

Soak mackerel over night in cold water, with the skin side up, that the salt may be drawn out, change the water often, and less time is required. Drain. Place mackerel in shallow kettle, pour water over to cover and boil ten to fifteen minutes or until flesh separates from the bone. Remove to platter and pour hot, melted butter over and serve with hot potatoes. They may also be boiled and served with a White Sauce.

MARINIRTE FISH
Take pickerel, pike or any fish that is not fat, cut into two-inch slices, wash well, salt and set aside in a cool place for a few hours. When ready to cook, wash slightly so as not to remove all salt from fish. Take heads and set up to boil with a whole onion for twenty-five minutes, then add the other pieces and two cups of vinegar, one cup of water, four bay leaves and twelve allspice, a little pepper and ginger. Cook for thirty-five minutes longer. Taste fish, add a little water or a little more vinegar to taste. Then remove fish carefully so as not to break the pieces and let cool. Strain the sauce, return fish to same, adding a few bay leaves and allspice. Set in a cool place until sauce forms a jelly around the fish. Can be kept covered and in a cool place for some time.

SOUSED HERRING
Split and half three herrings, roll and tie them up. Place them in a pie plate, pour over them a cup of vinegar, add whole peppers, salt, cloves to taste and two bay leaves. Bake in a slow oven until soft (about twenty minutes).

SALMON LOAF
Blend together one can of salmon, one cup of grated breadcrumbs, two beaten eggs, one cup of milk, one teaspoon of lemon juice, ½ teaspoon paprika, ½ teaspoon of salt, one tablespoon of chopped parsley and one tablespoon of onion juice. Place in a greased baking dish. Sprinkle top with thin layer of breadcrumbs. Bake in hot oven for thirty minutes or until the crumbs that cover the dish are browned. Serve with a white sauce.

CREAM SALMON
Remove salmon from the can, place it in a colander and wash under running water or scald with boiling water. Break into small pieces, stir into one cup of hot cream sauce; bring all to a boil and serve in patty cups or on toasted bread or crackers.

PICKLE FOR SALMON
Take equal parts of vinegar, white wine and water. Boil these with a little mace, a clove or two, a bit of ginger root, one or two whole peppers and some grated horseradish. Take out the last named ingredient when sufficiently boiled, and pour the pickle over the salmon, previously boiled in strong salt and water.

KEDGEREE

Cut up in small pieces about a pound of any kind of cooked fish except herring. Boil two eggs hard and chop up. Take one cup of rice and boil in the following manner: After washing it well and putting it on in boiling water, with a little salt, let it boil for ten minutes, drain it almost dry and let it steam with the lid closely shut for ten minutes longer without stirring. Take a clean pot and put in the fish, eggs, rice, a tablespoon of butter, and pepper and salt to taste. Stir over the fire until quite hot. Press into a mold and turn it out at once and serve.

SWISS CREAMED FISH

Mix smoothly in one cup of cold water a teaspoon of flour. Stir it into one cup of boiling milk and when thick and smooth add the meat of any cold fish, picked free from skin and bones. Season with salt, pepper and a tablespoon of butter. If the cream is desired to be extra rich one well-beaten egg may be added one minute before removing from the fire. Serve hot. A pinch of cayenne or a ¼ of a teaspoon of paprika is relished by many.

COD FISH BALLS

Put the fish to soak over night in lukewarm water. Change again in the morning and wash off all the salt. Cut into pieces and boil about fifteen minutes, pour off this water and put on to boil again with boiling water. Boil twenty minutes this time, drain off every bit of water, put on a platter to cool and pick to pieces as fine as possible, removing every bit of skin and bone. When this is done, add an equal quantity of mashed potatoes, a tablespoon of butter, a very little salt and pepper, beat up one egg and a little milk, if necessary, mix with a fork. Flour your hands well and form into biscuit-shaped balls. Fry in hot oil.

FINNAN HADDIE

Parboil ten minutes and then broil like fresh fish. To bake, place the fish in a pan, add one cup of milk and one cup of water; cover. Cook ten minutes in 400° oven. Remove cover, drain, spread with butter and season with pepper.

FINNAN HADDIE AND MACARONI

Break up and cook until tender about a package of macaroni. Pick up the finnan haddie until you have about three-quarters as much as you have macaroni. Mix in a greased baking dish and pour over a drawn butter sauce, made with cornstarch or with any good milk or cream dressing, then cover with bread or cracker crumbs or leave plain to brown in oven. Bake at 350° from twenty to thirty minutes.

SCALLOPED FISH, No. 1
Line a buttered baking dish with cold flaked fish. Sprinkle with salt and pepper; add a layer of cold cooked rice, dot with butter; repeat and cover with cracker or breadcrumbs. Bakeat 350° for fifteen to twenty minutes.

SCALLOPED FISH, No. 2
Butter a dish, place in a layer of cold cooked fish, sprinkle with breadcrumbs, parsley, salt, butter and pepper; repeat. Cover with white sauce, using one tablespoon of flour to two tablespoons of butter and one cup of milk. Sprinkle top with buttered breadcrumbs and bake.

SAUCES FOR FISH AND VEGETABLES

These sauces are made by combining butter and flour and thinning with water or other liquid. A sauce should never be thickened by adding a mixture of flour and water, as in that case the flour is seldom well cooked; or by adding flour alone, as this way is certain to cause lumps. The flour should be allowed to cook before the liquid is added. All sauces containing butter and milk should be cooked in a double boiler. If so desired, any neutral oil--that is, vegetable or nut oil--may be substituted for the butter called for in the recipe. Care in preparation of a sauce is of as much importance as is the preparation of the dish the sauce garnishes.

DRAWN BUTTER SAUCE
Melt two tablespoons of butter and stir in two tablespoons of flour. Add carefully one cup of boiling water, then season with ½ teaspoon of salt and a dash of pepper and paprika. Many sauces are made with drawn butter as a foundation. For caper sauce add three tablespoons of capers. For egg sauce add one egg, hard-boiled and chopped fine.

BEARNAISE SAUCE
There are several ways of making Bearnaise sauce. This is one very simple rule: Bring to the boil two tablespoons each of vinegar and water. Simmer in it for ten minutes a slice of onion. Take out the onion and add the yolks of three eggs beaten very light. Take from the fire, add salt and pepper to season, and four tablespoons of butter beaten to a cream, and added slowly.

QUICK BEARNAISE SAUCE
Beat the yolks of four eggs with four tablespoons of oil and four of water. Add a cup of boiling water and cook slowly until thick and smooth. Take from the fire, and add minced onion, capers, olives, pickles, and parsley and a little tarragon vinegar.

CUCUMBER SAUCE
Pare two large cucumbers; remove seeds, if large; chop fine and squeeze dry. Season with salt, vinegar, paprika and add ½ cup of cream.

HOLLANDAISE SAUCE
Mix one tablespoon of butter and one of flour in a saucepan and add gradually one cup of boiling water. Stir until it just reaches the boiling point; take from the heat, and add the yolks of two eggs. Into another saucepan put a slice of onion, a bay leaf, and a clove of garlic; add four tablespoons of vinegar, and stand this over the fire until the vinegar is reduced by half. Turn this into the sauce, stir for a moment; strain through a fine sieve; add half a teaspoon of salt and serve. This sauce may be varied by adding lemon juice instead of vinegar, or by using the water in which the fish was boiled. It is one of the daintiest of all sauces.

MUSTARD SAUCE
Mix two tablespoons of vinegar and one of mustard, one teaspoon of oil or butter melted, pepper and salt to taste. Add this to two hard-boiled eggs chopped fine, with a small onion and about the same quantity of parsley as eggs; and mix all well together.

Maître d'hôtel BUTTER
Work into ½ cup of butter, all the lemon juice it will take, and add a teaspoon of minced parsley.

PICKLE SAUCE
Cream two tablespoons of butter, add one teaspoon of salt and one tablespoon of chopped pickle. A speck of red pepper may be added.

SARDELLEN, OR HERRING SAUCE
Brown a spoon of flour in heated fat, add a quantity of hot fish stock and a few sardellen chopped fine, which you have previously washed in cold water, also a finely-chopped onion. Let this boil a few minutes, add a little vinegar and sugar; strain this sauce through a wire sieve and add a few capers and a wineglass of white wine and let it boil up once again and thicken with the yolk of one egg.

SAUCE VINAIGRETTE
Rub the mixing bowl with a clove of garlic, add ½ teaspoon salt, dash of white pepper, and a teaspoon of cold water or a bit of ice, then four tablespoons of oil. Mix until the salt is dissolved, remove the ice and add ten

drops of Tabasco sauce, two tablespoons tarragon vinegar, one tablespoon grated onion, one tablespoon chopped parsley and one chopped gherkin.

ANCHOVY SAUCE

Mix six tablespoons of melted butter and 1½ teaspoons anchovy paste, place in double boiler and allow to boil for about six minutes. Flavor with lemon juice.

SAUCE PIQUANTE

To one pint of drawn butter add one tablespoon each of vinegar and lemon juice and two tablespoons each of chopped capers, pickles, and olives, one-half teaspoon onion juice, a few grains cayenne pepper.

SAUCE TARTARE (TARTAR SAUCE)

Add to a half pint of well-made mayonnaise dressing two olives, one gherkin and one small onion, chopped fine. Chop sufficient parsley to make a tablespoonful, crush it in a bowl and add it first to the mayonnaise. Stir in at least a tablespoon of drained capers and serve with fried or broiled fish.

WHITE SAUCE FOR VEGETABLES

Place two tablespoons of butter in a saucepan; stir until melted: add two tablespoons of flour mixed with ¼ of a teaspoon of salt, and a few grains of pepper. Stir until smooth. Add one cup of milk gradually and continue to stir until well mixed and thick. Chopped parsley may be added. Used for creamed vegetables - potatoes, celery, onion, peas, etc.

CREAM MUSTARD SAUCE

Make white sauce as directed above. Mix one tablespoon of mustard with a teaspoon of cold water and stir into the sauce about two minutes before serving. The quantity of mustard may be increased or diminished, as one may desire the flavor strong or mild.

CURRY SAUCE

Use one teaspoon of curry in the flour while making white sauce.

SPANISH SAUCE
Cook one onion and green pepper chopped fine in hot butter; add four tablespoons of flour, stir until smooth. Add two cups of strained tomatoes. Season with salt and pepper.

TOMATO SAUCE
Brown one tablespoon butter with one minced onion, then add one tablespoon of flour. When brown stir in two cups of tomatoes which have previously been cooked and strained, add also one teaspoon of sugar, a pinch of salt, pepper, and red pepper, also one tablespoon of vinegar and one tablespoon of tomato catsup.

SAUCES FOR MEATS

APPLE SAUCE
Pare and quarter tart apples. Put them in a saucepan with just enough water to keep them from burning; bring to a boil quickly and cook until the pieces are soft. Then press through a colander and add four tablespoons of sugar (or less) to each pint of apples. If desired, cinnamon or grated nutmeg may be sprinkled over the top after the apple sauce is in the serving dish, or a little stick cinnamon or lemon peel may be cooked with the apples. Serve with goose.

BROWN SAUCE
Fry one tablespoon chopped onion in one tablespoon fat. Add one tablespoon of flour, one cup of soup stock, one teaspoon lemon juice, salt and pepper to taste. Strain before serving. The following sauces can be made by using brown sauce as a foundation:
Mushroom Sauce. Add ½ cup mushrooms.
Olive Sauce. Add twelve olives, chopped fine.
Wine Sauce. Add ½ cup wine and one tablespoon currant jelly. Thicken with flour.

CRANBERRY SAUCE
To one pint of cranberries take 1¼ cups of water. Put the cranberries on with the water and cook until soft; strain through a cloth; weigh and add three-fourths of a pound of sugar to every pint of juice. Cook ten minutes; pour into molds and set aside to cool. Serve with poultry, game or mutton.

STEWED CRANBERRIES
Boil together 1½ cups of sugar, and one cup of water for seven minutes, then add three cups of cranberries, well washed and picked, and cook until the berries burst. Serve the same as cranberry sauce.

SAUCE BORDELAISE
Nice for broiled steaks. Take one medium-sized onion chopped very fine

and browned in fat; add a cup of strong beef gravy and a cup of claret or white wine; add pepper, salt and a trifle of finely-chopped parsley; allow this to simmer and thicken with a little browned flour.

CARAWAY, OR KIMMEL SAUCE

Heat a tablespoon drippings in a sauce pan; add a little flour; stir smooth with a cup of soup stock, added at once, and half a teaspoon of caraway seeds.

ONION SAUCE

Stew some finely-chopped onions in fat; you may add half a clove of garlic, cut extremely fine; brown a very little flour in this, season with salt and pepper and add enough soup stock to thin it.

LEMON SAUCE

Boil some soup stock with a few slices of lemon, a little sugar and grated nutmeg; add chopped parsley; thicken with a teaspoon of flour or yolk of egg. Mostly used for stewed poultry.

MINT SAUCE

Chop some mint fine; boil ½ cup of vinegar with one tablespoon of sugar; throw in the mint and boil up once; pour in a sauceboat and cool off a little before serving.

RAISIN SAUCE

Brown some fat in a sauce pan, stir in a tablespoon of flour; stir until it becomes a smooth paste; then add hot soup, stirring constantly; add a handful of raisins, some pounded almonds, a few slices of lemon, also a tablespoon of vinegar; brown sugar to taste: flavor with a few cloves and cinnamon, and if you choose to do so, grate in part of a stick of horseradish and the crust of a rye loaf.

HORSERADISH SAUCE, No. 1

Grate a good-sized stick of horseradish; take some soup stock and a tablespoon of fat, salt and pepper to taste, a little grated stale bread, a few pounded almonds. Let all boil up and then add the meat.

HORSERADISH SAUCE, No. 2

Heat one tablespoon of fat in a frying pan, when hot cut up ¼ of an onion in it, and fry light brown, then brown one tablespoon cracker meal or flour and add two tablespoons of grated horseradish; let this brown a bit, then add some soup stock, one tablespoon of brown sugar, two cloves, two bay leaves, salt, pepper and two tablespoons of vinegar. Let cook a few minutes then add one more tablespoon of horseradish and if necessary a little more sugar or vinegar. Lay the meat in this sauce and cover on back of stove until ready to serve. If gas stove is used, place over the simmering flame.

KNOBLAUCH SAUCE (GARLIC SAUCE)

Heat a tablespoon of drippings, either of meat or goose in a frying pan; cut up one or two cloves of garlic very fine and let it brown slightly in the heated fat; add a tablespoon of flour, a cup of soup stock or warm water, salt, pepper to taste.

Maître d'hôtel SAUCE

Take a heaping tablespoon of drippings or goose fat, heat it in a sauce pan, stir two teaspoons of flour into this, then add gradually and carefully a small cup of hot soup or water, the former is preferable; add some chopped parsley, also the juice of a lemon; salt and pepper; stir up well. May be used either with roast or boiled meats.

FRYING

PREPARED BREADCRUMBS FOR FRYING

All scraps of bread should be saved for crumbs, the crusts being separated from the white part, then dried, rolled, and sifted, and put away until needed in a covered glass jar. The brown crumbs are good for the first coating, the white ones for the outside, as they give better color. Cracker crumbs give a smooth surface, but for most things breadcrumbs are preferable. For meats a little salt and pepper, and for sweet articles, a little sugar, should be mixed with the crumbs. Crumbs left on the board should be dried, sifted, and kept to be used again.

FRYING

Frying is cooking in very hot fat or oil, and the secret of success is to have the fat hot enough to harden the outer surface of the article to be fried immediately and deep enough to cover these articles of food. As the fat or oil can be saved and used many times, the use of a large quantity is not extravagant. To fry easily one must have, in addition to the deep, straight-sided frying pan, a frying-basket, made from galvanized wire, with a side handle. The bale handles are apt to become heated, and in looking for something to lift them, the foods are over-fried. The frying pan must be at least six inches deep with a flat bottom; iron, granite ware or copper may be used, the first two are preferable. There must be sufficient fat to wholly cover the articles fried, but the pan must not be too full, or there is danger of overflow when heavy articles are put in. After each frying, drain the fat or oil, put it into a receptacle kept for the purpose, and use it over and over again as long as it lasts. As the quantity begins to lessen, add sufficient fresh fat or oil to keep up the amount. Always put the fat or oil in the frying pan before you stand it over the fire. Wait until it is properly heated before putting in the articles to be fried. Fry a few articles at a time. Too many will cool the fat or oil below the point of proper frying and they will absorb grease and be unpalatable. Put articles to be fried in the wire frying-basket and lower into the boiling hot fat or oil. Test the fat by lowering a piece of stale bread into it, if the bread browns in thirty seconds the fat is sufficiently hot. Fry croquettes a light brown; drain over the fat, life the frying-basket from the hot fat to a round plate, remove the articles from the basket quickly to brown paper, drain a moment and serve. When frying fish or any food that is to be used at a milk meal, use oil. Olive oil is the best, but is very expensive for general use. Any other good vegetable oil or nut oil will do as substitute. When the food is intended for a meat meal; fat may be prepared according to the following directions and used in the same manner as oil.

TO RENDER GOOSE, DUCK OR BEEF FAT

Cut the fat into small pieces. Put in a deep, iron kettle and cover with cold water. Place on the stove uncovered; when the water has nearly all evaporated, set the kettle back and let the fat try out slowly. When the fat is still and scraps are shriveled and crisp at the bottom of the kettle, strain the fat through a cloth into a stone crock, cover and set it away in a cool place. The water may be omitted and the scraps slowly tried out on back of stove or in moderate oven. When fat is tried out, pour in crock. Several slices of raw potato put with the fat will aid in the clarifying. All kinds of fats are good for drippings except mutton fat, turkey fat and fat from smoked meats which has too strong a flavor to be used for frying, but save it with other fat that may be unsuitable for frying, and when six pounds are collected make it into hard soap.

ENTREES

CROQUETTES

Combine ingredients as directed in the recipe, roll the mixture lightly between the hands into a ball. Have a plentiful supply of breadcrumbs spread evenly on a board; roll the ball lightly on the crumbs into the shape of a cylinder, and flatten each end by dropping it lightly on the board; put it in the egg (to each egg add one tablespoon of water, and beat together), and with a spoon moisten the croquette completely with the egg; lift it out on a knife-blade, and again roll lightly in the crumbs. Have every part entirely covered, so there will be no opening through which the grease may be absorbed. Where a light yellow color is wanted, use fresh white crumbs grated from the loaf (or rubbed through a purée sieve) for the outside, and do not use the yolk of the egg. Coarse fresh crumbs are used for fish croquettes, which are usually made in the form of chops, or half heart shape. A small hole is pricked in the pointed end after frying, and a sprig of parsley inserted. Have all the croquettes of perfectly uniform size and shape, and lay them aside on a dish, not touching one another, for an hour or more before frying. This will make the crust more firm. The white of an egg alone may be used for egging them, but not the yolk alone. Whip the egg with the water, just enough to break it, as air bubbles in the egg will break in frying, and let the grease penetrate. Serve the croquettes on a platter, spread them on a napkin and garnish with sprigs of parsley.

CHICKEN CROQUETTES, No. 1

Cook ½ tablespoon of flour in one tablespoon chicken-fat, add ½ cup soup stock gradually, and ½ teaspoon each of onion juice, lemon juice, salt, and ¼ teaspoon pepper, 1½ cups of veal or chicken, chopped very fine, one pair of brains which have been boiled, mix these well, remove from the fire and add one well-beaten egg. Turn this mixture out on a flat dish and place in ice box to cool. Then roll into small cones, dip in beaten egg, roll again in powdered bread or cracker crumbs and drop them into boiling fat, fry until a delicate brown.

CHICKEN CROQUETTES, No. 2
Chop the chicken very fine, using the white meat alone, or the dark meat alone, or both together. Season with salt, pepper, onion juice, and lemon juice. Chopped mushrooms, sweetbreads, calf's brains, tongue, or truffles are used with chicken, and a combination of two or more of them much improves the quality of the croquettes.

CROQUETTES OF CALF'S BRAINS
Lay the brains in salt water an hour, or until they look perfectly white, then take out one at a time, pat with your hands to loosen the outer skin and pull it off. Beat or rub them to a smooth paste with a wooden spoon, season with salt and pepper and a very little mace; add a beaten egg and about ½ cup breadcrumbs. Heat fat in a sauce pan and fry large spoonfuls of this mixture in it.

MEAT CROQUETTES
Veal, mutton, lamb, beef and turkey croquettes may be prepared in the same way as chicken croquettes.

MEAT AND BOILED HOMINY CROQUETTES
Equal proportions.

SWEETBREAD CROQUETTES
Cut the boiled sweetbreads into small dice with a silver knife. Mix with mushrooms, using half the quantity of mushrooms that you have of sweetbreads. Use two eggs in the sauce.

VEAL CROQUETTES
Veal is often mixed with chicken, or is used alone as a substitute for chicken. Season in same manner and make the same combinations.

CAULIFLOWER CROQUETTES
Finely chop cold cooked cauliflower, mix in one small, finely chopped onion, one small bunch of parsley finely chopped, ½ cup breadcrumbs and one well-beaten egg. Carefully mix and mold into croquette forms, dip in cracker dust and fry in deep, smoking fat until a light brown.

EGGPLANT CROQUETTES (ROMANIAN)
Peel the eggplant, place in hot water and boil until tender, drain, add two eggs, salt, pepper, two tablespoons of matzoth or white flour or breadcrumbs, beat together; fry in butter or oil by tablespoonfuls.

CROQUETTES OF FISH
Take any kind of boiled fish, separate it from the bones carefully, chop with a little parsley, salt and pepper to taste. Beat up one egg with one teaspoon of milk and flour. Roll the fish into balls and turn them in the beaten egg and cracker crumbs or bread. Fry a light brown. Serve with any sauce or a mayonnaise.

POTATO CROQUETTES
Work into two cups of mashed potatoes, a tablespoon of melted butter, until smooth and soft; add one egg well beaten and beat all together with a wooden spoon. Season with salt and nutmeg. Roll each in beaten egg then in breadcrumbs, fry in hot oil or butter substitute. If desired chicken fat may be substituted for the butter and the croquettes fried in deep fat or oil.

SWEET POTATO CROQUETTES
Press through a ricer sufficient hot baked sweet potatoes to measure one pint. Place over the fire. Add one teaspoon of butter or drippings, the beaten yolks of two eggs, pepper and salt to taste, and beat well with a fork until the mixture leaves the sides of the pan. Cool slightly, form into cones, roll in fine breadcrumbs; dip in beaten eggs, roll again in crumbs and fry in hot oil or fat.

PEANUT AND RICE CROQUETTES
To one cup of freshly cooked rice allow one cup of peanut butter, four tablespoons of minced celery, one teaspoon of grated onion, one tablespoon of canned tomatoes, and salt and pepper to taste. Mix well, add the white of one egg, reserving the yolk for coating the croquettes. Shape into croquettes and let stand in a cold place for an hour, then coat with the egg yolk mixed with one tablespoon of water and roll in stale bread crumb dust until well covered. Fry in any hot oil or butter substitute.

RICE CROQUETTES, No. 1

Separate the white and yolk of one egg and reserve about half the yolk for coating the croquette. Beat the rest with the white. Mix with two cups of boiled or steamed rice, and ½ teaspoon salt, form into oblong croquettes or small balls. Mix the reserved part of the egg yolk with a tablespoon of cold water. Dip croquettes in this and then roll in fine breadcrumbs. Repeat until well coated, then fry brown in deep oil.

RICE CROQUETTES, No. 2

Put on with cold water one cup of rice, and let boil until tender. Drain, and mix with the rice, one tablespoon of butter, yolks of three eggs, and pinch of salt. About one tablespoon of flour may be added to hold the croquettes together. Beat the whites of the three eggs to a stiff froth, reserving some of the beaten white for egging croquettes, mix this in last, shape into croquettes and fry in hot oil or butter substitute. Place on platter and serve with a lump of jelly on each croquette.

CALF'S BRAINS (SOUR)

Lay the brains in ice water and then skin. They will skin easily by taking them up in your hands and patting them, this will help to loosen all the skin and clotted blood that adheres to them. Lay in cold salted water for an hour at least, then put on to boil in half vinegar and half water (a crust of rye bread improves the flavor of the sauce). Add one onion, cut up fine, ten whole peppers, one bay leaf, one or two cloves and a little salt, boil altogether about fifteen minutes. Serve on a platter and decorate with parsley. Eat cold.

CALF'S BRAINS FRIED

Clean as described in calf's brains cooked sour; wipe dry, roll in rolled cracker flour, season with salt and pepper, and fry as you would cutlets.

BRAINS (SWEET AND SOUR)

Clean as described above. Lay in ice-cold salted water for an hour. Cut up an onion, a few slices of celery root, a few whole peppercorns, a little salt and a crust of rye bread. Lay the brains upon this bed of herbs and barely cover with vinegar and water. Boil about fifteen minutes, then lift out the brains with a perforated skimmer, and lay upon a platter to cool. Take a Lebkuchen, some brown sugar, a tablespoon of molasses, ½ teaspoon cinnamon, a few seedless raisins and a few pounded almonds. Moisten this with vinegar and add the boiling sauce. Boil the sauce ten minutes longer and pour scalding over the brains. Eat cold and decorate with slices of lemon.

DEVILED BRAINS
Put one tablespoon of fat in skillet, and when hot add two tablespoons of flour, rub until smooth, and brown lightly, then add ½ can of tomatoes, season with salt, pepper, finely chopped parsley, and a dash of cayenne pepper, and the brains that have previously been cleaned, scalded with boiling water, and cut in small pieces. Cook a few minutes, and then fill the shells with the mixture. Over each shell sprinkle breadcrumbs, and a little chicken-fat. Put shells in pan and brown nicely. Serve with green peas.

BRAINS WITH EGG SAUCE
Wash brains well, skin, boil fifteen minutes in salt water; slice in stew-pan some onions, salt, pepper, ginger and a cup of stock. Put in the brains with a little marjoram; let it cook gently for 30 minutes. Mix yolks of two eggs, juice of a lemon, a teaspoon of flour, a little chopped parsley; when it is rubbed smooth, stir it into saucepan; stir well to prevent curdling.

JELLIED CHICKEN
Boil a chicken in as little water as possible until the meat falls from the bones, chop rather fine and season with pepper and salt. Put into a mold a layer of the chopped meat and then a layer of hard-boiled eggs, cut in slices. Fill the mold with alternate layers of meat and eggs until nearly full. Boil down the liquor left in the kettle until half the quantity. While warm, add one-quarter of a cup aspic, pour into the mold over the meat. Set in a cool place overnight to jelly.

PRESSED CHICKEN
Boil one or more chickens just as you would for fricassee, using as little water as possible. When tender remove all the meat from the bone and take off all the skin. Chop as fine as possible in a chopping bowl (it ought to be chopped as fine as powder). Add all the liquor the chicken was boiled in,

which ought to be very little and well seasoned. Press it into the shape of a brick between two platters, and put a heavy weight over it so as to press hard. Set away to cool in ice chest and garnish nicely with parsley and slices of lemon before sending to the table. It should be placed whole upon the table, and sliced as served. Serve pickles and olives with it. Veal may be pressed in the same way, some use half veal and half chicken, which is equally nice.

HOMEMADE CHICKEN TAMALES
Boil until tender one large chicken. Have two quarts of stock left when chicken is done. Remove chicken and cut into medium-sized pieces. Into the stock, pour gradually one cup of corn meal or farina, stirring until it thickens. If not the proper consistency, add a little more meal. Season with one tablespoon of chili sauce, three tablespoons of tomato catsup, salt, one teaspoon of Spanish pepper sauce. Simmer gently thirty minutes, then add chicken. Serve in ramekins.

CHICKEN FRICASSEE, WITH NOODLES
Prepare a rich chicken fricassee (recipe for which you will find among poultry recipes; see index), but have a little more gravy than usual. Boil some noodles or macaroni in salted water, drain, let cold water run through them, shake them well and boil up once with chicken. Serve together on a large platter.

SWEETBREAD GLACÉ SAUCE JARDINAIRE WITH SPAGHETTI
Put on some poultry drippings to heat in a saucepan, cut up an onion, shredded very fine and then put in the sweetbreads, which have been picked over carefully and lain in salt water an hour before boiling. Salt and pepper the sweetbreads before putting in the kettle, slice two tomatoes on top and cover up tight and set on the back of stove to simmer slowly. Turn once in a while and add a little soup stock. Boil ½ cup of string beans, ½ a can of canned peas, ½ cup currants, cut up extremely fine, with a tablespoon of drippings, a little salt and ground ginger. When the vegetables are tender, add to the simmering sweetbreads. Thicken the sauce with a teaspoon of flour. Have the sauce boiled down quite thick. Boil the spaghetti in salted water until tender. Serve with the sweetbreads.

CHICKEN Á LA SWEETBREAD
Take the breast of chicken that has been fricasseed, cut up into small pieces, and add mushrooms. Make brown sauce. Serve in Pâte à Choux shells.

SWEETBREADS
Wash the sweetbreads very carefully and remove all bits of skin and fatty matter. Cover with cold water, salt and boil for fifteen minutes. Then remove from the boiling water and cover with cold water. Sprinkle with salt and pepper, roll in beaten egg and breadcrumbs, and fry a nice brown in hot fat.

SWEETBREAD SAUTÉ WITH MUSHROOMS
Clean sweetbread, boil until tender, and cut in small pieces. Take one tablespoon of fat, blend in one tablespoon of flour; add half the liquor of a can of mushrooms and enough soup stock to make the necessary amount of gravy; add a little catsup, mushroom catsup, and a few drops of Kitchen Bouquet, a clove of garlic, and a small onion; salt and pepper to taste. Cook this about an hour, and then remove garlic and onion. Add sweetbreads, mushrooms, and two hard-boiled eggs chopped very fine.

VEAL SWEETBREADS (FRIED)
Wash and lay your sweetbreads in slightly salted cold water for an hour. Pull off carefully all the outer skin, wipe dry and sprinkle with salt and pepper. Heat some goose fat in a sauce pan, lay in the sweetbreads and fry slowly on the back of the stove, turning frequently until they are a nice brown.

CALF'S FEET, PRUNES AND CHESTNUTS
Two calf's feet, sawed into joints, seasoned with pepper and salt a day before using. Place in an iron pot, one-half pound Italian chestnuts that have been scalded and skinned, then the calf's feet, 2 ounces raisins, one pound of fine prunes, one small onion, one small head of celery root, two olives cut in small pieces, ⅛ teaspoon paprika, one cup of soup stock. Stew slowly for five hours, and add one hour before serving, while boiling, a wine glass claret and a wine glass sherry. Do not stir.

CALF'S FEET, SCHARF [HIGHLY SEASONED]

Take calf's feet, saw into joints; put on to boil within cold water and boil slowly until the gristle loosens from the bones. Season with salt, pepper, and a clove or two of garlic. Serve hot or cold to taste.

CALF'S FOOT JELLY, No. 1

After carefully washing one calf's foot, split and put it on with one quart water. Boil from four to five hours. Strain and let stand overnight. Put on stove next day and when it begins to boil add the stiff-beaten whites of two eggs; boil until clear, then strain through cheesecloth. Add sherry and sugar to taste. Let it become firm before serving.

SULZE VON KALBSFUESSEN (CALF'S FOOT JELLY), No. 2

Take one calf's head and four calf's feet, and clean carefully. Let them lay in cold water for half an hour. Set on to boil with four quarts of water. Add two or three small onions, a few cloves, salt, one teaspoon of whole peppers, two or three bay leaves, juice of a large lemon (extract the seeds), one cup of white wine and a little white wine vinegar (just enough to give a tart taste). Let this boil slowly for five or six hours (it must boil until it is reduced one-half). Then strain through a fine sieve and let it stand ten or twelve hours. Remove the meat from the bones and when cold cut into fine pieces. Add also the boiled brains (which must be taken up carefully to avoid falling to pieces). Skim off every particle of fat from the jelly and melt slowly. Add one teaspoon of sugar and the whipped whites of three eggs, and boil very fast for about fifteen minutes, skimming well. Taste, and if not tart enough, add a dash of vinegar. Strain through a flannel bag, do not squeeze or shake until the jelly ceases to run freely. Remove the bowl and put another under, into which you may press out what remains in the bag (this will not be as clear, but tastes quite as good). Wet your mold, put in the jelly and set in a cool place. In order to have a variety, wet another mold and put in the bits of meat, cut up, and the brains and, lastly, the jelly; set this on ice. It must be thick, so that you can cut it into slices to serve.

ASPIC (SULZ)

Set on to boil two calf's feet, chopped up, one pound of beef and one calf's head with one quart water and one cup of white wine. Add one celery root, three small onions, a bunch of parsley, twelve whole peppercorns, half a dozen cloves, two bay leaves and a teaspoon of fine salt. Boil steadily for eight hours and then pour through a fine hair sieve. When cold remove every particle of fat and set on to boil again, skimming until clear. Then break two eggs, shells and all, into a deep bowl, beat them up with one cup of vinegar, pour some of the soup stock into this and set all back on the stove to boil up once, stirring all the while. Then remove from the fire and pour through a jelly-bag as you would jelly. Pour into jelly glasses or one large mold. Set on ice.

GANSLEBER IN SULZ (GOOSE LIVER ASPIC)
Fry a large goose liver in goose fat. Season with salt, pepper, a few whole cloves and a very little onion. Cut it up in slices and mix with the sulz and the whites of hard-boiled eggs.

GANSLEBER PURÉE IN SULZ
After the liver is fried, rub it through a sieve or colander and mix with sulz.

GOOSE LIVER
If very large cut in half, dry well on a clean cloth, after having lain in salted water for an hour. Season with fine salt and pepper, fry in very hot goose fat and add a few cloves. While frying cut up a little onion very fine and add. Then cover closely and smother in this way until you wish to serve. Dredge the liver with flour before frying and turn occasionally. Serve with a slice of lemon on each piece of liver.

GOOSE LIVER WITH GLACÉED CHESTNUTS
Prepare as above and garnish with chestnuts that have been prepared thus: Scald until perfectly white, heat some goose fat, add nuts, a little sugar and glaze a light brown.

GOOSE LIVER WITH MUSHROOM SAUCE
Take a large white goose liver, lay in salt water for an hour (this rule applies to all kinds of liver), wipe dry, salt, pepper and dredge with flour. Fry in hot goose fat. Cut up a piece of onion, add a few cloves, a few slices of celery, cut

very fine, whole peppers, one bay leaf, and some mushrooms. Cover closely and stew a few minutes. Add lemon juice to sauce.

SPANISH LIVER

Boil in salt water ½ pound calf's liver. Drain and cut into small cubes. Chop one onion, one tablespoon parsley, some mint; add two cloves, a little cinnamon, a little Tabasco sauce, one tablespoon olive oil, and one cup of soup stock. Add one cup of breadcrumbs that have been soaked in hot water and then drained. Mix all with the liver and bring to a boil. Serve with Spanish rice.

CALF'S LIVER SMOTHERED IN ONIONS

Heat some goose fat in a sauté pan with a close-fitting lid. Cut up an onion in it and when the onion is of a light yellow color, place in the liver that you have previously sprinkled with fine salt and dredged with flour. Add a bay leaf, five cloves and two peppercorns. Cover up tight and stew the liver, turning it occasionally and when required adding a little hot water.

CHICKEN LIVERS

Slice three or four livers from chicken or other fowl and dredge well with flour. Fry one minced onion in one tablespoon of fat until light brown. Put in the liver and shake the pan over the fire to sear all sides. Add ½ teaspoon salt, ⅛ teaspoon paprika, and ½ cup strong soup stock. Allow it to boil up once. Add one tablespoon claret or sherry and serve immediately on toast.

KISCHKES - RUSSIAN STYLE

Buy beef casings of butcher. Make a filling of fat, flour (using ⅓ cup fat to one cup flour) and chopped onions. Season well with salt and pepper, cut them in short lengths, fasten one end, stuff and then fasten the open end. If they are not already cleaned the surface exposed after filling the casing is scraped until cleaned after having been plunged into boiling water. Slice two large onions in a roasting-pan, and roast the kischkes slowly until well done and well browned. Baste frequently with liquid in the pan.

KISCHKES

Prepare as above. If the large casings are used they need not be cut in shorter lengths. Boil for three hours in plenty of water and when done, put in frying pan with one tablespoon of fat, cover and let brown nicely. Serve hot.

TRIPE Á LA CREOLE
Boil tripe with onion, parsley, celery, and seasoning; cut in small pieces, then boil up in the following sauce: Take one tablespoon of fat, brown it with two tablespoons of flour; then add one can of boiled and strained tomatoes, one can of mushrooms, salt and pepper to taste. Serve in ramekins.

TRIPE, FAMILY STYLE
Scald and scrape two pounds tripe and cut into inch squares. Take big kitchen spoon of drippings and put in four large onions quartered and three small cloves of garlic cut up very fine. Let steam, but not brown. When onions begin to cook, put in tripe and steam half an hour. Then cover tripe with water and let cook slowly three hours. Boil a few potatoes and cut in dice shapes and add to it. Half an hour before serving, add the following, after taking off as much fat from the tripe as possible: Three tablespoons of flour thinned with little water; add catsup, paprika, ginger, and one teaspoon of salt. It should all be quite thick, like paste, when cooked.

BOILED TONGUE, (SWEET AND SOUR)
Lay the fresh tongue in cold water for a couple of hours and then put it on to boil in enough water to barely cover it, adding salt. Boil until tender. To ascertain when tender run a fork through the thickest part. A good rule is to boil it, closely covered, from three to four hours steadily. Pare off the thick skin which covers the tongue, cut into even slices, sprinkle a little fine salt over each piece and then prepare the following sauce: Put one tablespoon of drippings in a kettle or sauce pan (goose fat is very good). Cut up an onion in it, add a tablespoon of flour and stir, adding gradually about a pint of the liquor in which the tongue was boiled. Cut up a lemon in slices, remove the seeds, and add two dozen raisins, a few pounded almonds, a stick of cinnamon and a few cloves. Sweeten with four tablespoons of brown sugar in which you have put one-half teaspoon of ground cinnamon, one tablespoon of molasses and two tablespoons of vinegar. Let this boil, lay in the slices of tongue and boil up for a few minutes.

FILLED TONGUE

Take a pickled tongue, cut it open; chop or grind some corned beef; add one egg; brown a little onion, and add some soaked bread; fill tongue with it, and sew it up and boil until done.

SMOKED TONGUE

Put on to boil in a large kettle, fill with cold water, enough to completely cover the tongue; keep adding hot water as it boils down so as to keep it covered with water until done. Keep covered with a lid while boiling and put a heavy weight on the top of the lid so as not to let the steam escape. It should boil very slowly and steadily for four hours. When tongue is cooked set it to cool in the liquor in which it was boiled. If the tongue is very dry, soak overnight before boiling. In serving slice very thin and garnish with parsley.

SMOTHERED TONGUE

Scald tongue, and then skin. Season well with salt and pepper and slice an onion over it. Let it stand overnight. Put some drippings in a covered iron pot, and then the tongue, with whatever juice the seasoning drew. Cover closely and let it cook slowly until tender - about three hours.

PICKLED BEEF TONGUE

Select a large, fresh beef tongue. Soak in cold water for thirty minutes. Mix one teacup of salt, one teaspoon of pepper, three small cloves of garlic cut fine. Drain water off tongue. With a pointed knife prick tongue; rub in seasoning. Put tongue in crock; add the balance of salt, etc.; cover with plate and weight. Allow to stand from four to five days. Without washing off the seasoning, boil in fresh water until tender.

MEATS

The majority of the cuts of meat which are kosher are those which require long, slow cooking. These cuts of meat are the most nutritious ones and by long, slow cooking can be made as acceptable as the more expensive cuts of meat; they are best boiled or braised.

In order to shut in the juices the meat should at first be subjected to a high degree of heat for a short time. A crust or case will then be formed on the outside, after which the heat should be lowered and the cooking proceed slowly. This rule holds good for baking, where the oven must be very hot for the first few minutes only; for boiling, where the water must be boiling and covered for a time, and then placed where it will simmer only; for broiling, where the meat must be placed under the broiler flame of the gas stove at first, then held farther away. Do not pierce the meat with a fork while cooking, as it makes an outlet for the juices. If necessary, to turn it, use two spoons.

PAN ROAST BEEF
Take a piece of cross-rib or shoulder, about 2½ to 3 pounds, put in a small frying pan with very little fat; have the pan very hot, let the meat brown on all sides, turning it continually until all sides are done, which will require thirty minutes altogether. Lift the meat out of pan to a hot platter, brown some onions, serve these with the meat.

AN EASY POT ROAST
Take four pounds of brisket, season with salt, pepper and ginger, add three tablespoons of tomatoes and an onion cut up. Cover with water in an iron pot and a close-fitting cover, put in oven and bake from three to four hours.

POT ROAST, BRAISED BEEF
Heat some fat or goose fat in a deep iron pot, cut half an onion very fine and when it is slightly browned put in the meat. Cover up closely and let the meat brown on all sides. Salt to taste, add a scant ½ teaspoon of paprika, ½ cup of hot water and simmer an hour longer, keeping covered closely all the time. Add ½ sweet green pepper (seeds removed), one small carrot cut in slices, two tablespoons of tomatoes and two onions sliced. Two and a

half pounds of brisket shoulder or any other meat suitable for pot roasting will require three hours slow cooking. Shoulder of lamb may also be cooked in this style. When the meat is tender, remove to a warm platter, strain the gravy, rubbing the thick part through the sieve and after removing any fat serve in a sauce boat. If any meat is left over it can be sliced and warmed over in the gravy, but the gravy must be warmed first and the meat cook for a short time only as it is already done enough and too much cooking will render it tasteless.

BRISKET OF BEEF (BRUSTDECKEL)
If the brisket has been used for soup, take it out of the soup when it is tender and prepare it with a horseradish sauce, garlic sauce or onion sauce. (See Meat Sauces.)

BRISKET OF BEEF WITH SAUERKRAUT
Take about three pounds of fat, young beef (you may make soup stock of it first), then take out the bones, salt it well and lay it in the bottom of a kettle, put a quart of sauerkraut on top of it and let it boil slowly until tender. Add vinegar if necessary, thicken with a grated raw potato and add a little brown sugar. Some like a few caraway seeds added.

SAUERBRATEN
Take a piece of cross-rib or middle cut of chuck about three pounds, and put it in a large bowl and pour enough boiling vinegar over it to cover; you may take ⅓ water. Add to the vinegar when boiling four bay leaves, some whole peppercorns, cloves and whole mace. Pour this over the meat and turn it daily. Keep in refrigerator. Three days is the longest time allowed for the meat to remain in this pickle. When ready to boil, heat one tablespoon drippings in a stew pan. Cut up one or two onions in it; stew until tender and then put in the beef, salting it on both sides before stewing. Stew closely covered and if not acid enough add some of the brine in which it was pickled. Stew about three hours and thicken the gravy with flour.

ROLLED BEEF – POT ROASTED
Take 1½ pound of tenderloin, sprinkle it with parsley and onion; season with pepper and salt; roll and tie it. Place it in a pan with soup stock (or

water if you have no stock), carrot and bay leaf and pot roast in oven at 400° for 1½ hours. Serve with tomato or brown sauce.

MOCK DUCK

Take the tenderloin, lay it flat on a board after removing the fat. Make a stuffing as for poultry. Spread this mixture on the meat evenly; then roll and tie it with white twine; turn in the ends to make it even and shapely. Cut into dice an onion, turnip, and carrot, and place them in a baking pan; lay the rolled meat on the bed of vegetables; pour in enough stock or water to cover the pan one inch deep; add a bouquet made of parsley, one bay leaf and three cloves; cover with another pan, and let cook slowly for four hours, basting frequently. If can be done in a pot just as well, and should be covered as tight as possible; when cooked, strain off the vegetables; thicken the gravy with one tablespoon of flour browned in fat and serve it with the meat. Long, slow cooking is required to make the meat tender. If cooked too fast it will not be good.

ROAST BEEF, No. 1

Take prime rib roast. Cut up a small onion, a celery root and part of a carrot into rather small pieces and add to these two or three sprigs of parsley and one bay leaf. Sprinkle these over the bottom of the dripping-pan and place your roast on this bed. The 400° oven should be very hot when the roast is first put in, but when the roast is browned sufficiently to retain its juices, moderate the heat and roast more slowly until the meat is done. Do not season until the roast is browned, and then add salt and pepper. Enough juice and fat will drop from the roast to give the necessary broth for basting. Baste frequently and turn occasionally, being very careful, however, not to stick a fork into the roast.

ROAST BEEF, No. 2

Season meat with salt and paprika. Dredge with flour. Place on rack in dripping pan with two or three tablespoons fat, in 400° oven, to brown quickly. Reduce heat and baste every ten minutes with the fat that has fried out. When meat is about half done, turn it over, dredge with flour, finish browning. If necessary, add a small quantity of water. Allow fifteen to twenty minutes for each pound of meat. Three pounds is the smallest roast practicable.

ROAST BEEF (RUSSIAN)

Place a piece of cross-rib or shoulder weighing three pounds in roasting pan, slice some onions over it, season with salt and pepper, add some water and let it cook well at 400°. Then peel a few potatoes and put them under the meat. When the meat becomes brown, turn it and cook until it browns on the other side.

WIENER BRATEN - VIENNA ROAST

Take a shoulder, have the bone taken out and then pound the meat well with a mallet. Lay it in vinegar for twenty-four hours. Heat some fat or goose oil in a deep pan or kettle that has a cover that fits air tight and lay the meat in the hot fat and sprinkle the upper side with salt, pepper and ginger. Put an onion in with the meat; stick six whole cloves in the onion, and add one bay leaf. Now turn the meat over and sprinkle the other side with salt, pepper and ginger. Cut up one or two tomatoes and pour some soup stock over all, and a dash of white wine. Cover closely and stew very slowly for three or four hours, turning the meat now and then; in doing so do not pierce with the fork, as this will allow the juice to escape. Do not add any water. Make enough potato pancakes to serve one or two to each person with "Wiener Braten."

FRIED STEAK WITH ONIONS

Season the steak with salt and pepper, and dredge with flour. If tough, chop on both sides with a sharp knife. Lay in a pan of hot fat, when brown on one side, turn and brown on the other. While the steak is frying, heat some fat in another fryer and drop in four of five white onions that have been cut up. Fry crisp but not black. Remove the steak to a hot platter, stir one tablespoon of flour in the fryer until smooth, add ½ cup of boiling water. Lay the crisp onions over the steak, then over all pour the brown gravy.

FRIED BEEFSTEAK

Take third cut of chuck or the tenderloin. Have the sauce pan very hot, use just enough fat to grease the sauce pan. Lay in the steak, turning very often to keep in the juice, season with salt and pepper. Serve on a hot platter.

BRUNSWICK STEW

Cook one pound of brisket of beef and three pounds of young chicken with one pint of soup stock or water, one pint of lima beans, four ears of cut corn (cut from cob), three potatoes diced, two tomatoes quartered; one small onion, one teaspoon of paprika and one teaspoon of salt. Let all these simmer until tender, and before serving remove the meat and any visible chicken bones. This stew may be made of breast of veal omitting the chicken and brisket.

SHORT RIBS AND YELLOW TURNIPS

Get the small ribs and put on with plenty of water, an onion, pepper and salt. After boiling about one and one-half hours add a large yellow turnip cut in small pieces; thirty minutes before serving add six potatoes cut in small pieces. Water must be added as necessary. A little sugar will improve flavor, and as it simmers the turnip will soften and give the whole dish the appearance of a stew.

MEAT OLIVES

Have a flank steak cut in three-inch squares. Spread each piece with the following dressing: one cup of breadcrumbs, two tablespoons of minced parsley, one chopped onion, a dash of red pepper and one teaspoon of salt. Moisten with one-fourth cup of melted fat. Roll up and tie in shape. Cover with water and simmer until meat is tender. Take the olives from the sauce and brown in the oven. Thicken the sauce with ¼ cup flour moistened with water to form a thin paste.

SPANISH SHORT RIB OF BEEF

Get the small ribs of beef and put on with water enough to cover, seasoning with salt, pepper, an onion and a tiny clove of garlic. Let it cook about two hours, then add a can of tomatoes and season highly either with red peppers or paprika. Cook at least three hours.

BRAISED OXTAILS

Two oxtails, jointed and washed; six onions sliced and browned in pot with oxtails. When nicely browned add water enough to cover and stew slowly one hour; then add two carrots, if small; one green pepper, sprig of parsley, ½ cup of tomatoes and six small potatoes, and cook until tender. Thicken with browned flour. Cook separately eight lengths of macaroni; place cooked macaroni on dish and pour ragout over it and serve hot. To brown flour take one-half cup of flour, put in pan over moderate heat and stir until nicely browned.

HUNGARIAN GOULASH

Have two pounds of beef cut into one-inch squares. Dredge in flour and fry until brown. Cover with water and simmer for two hours; the last half hour add one tablespoon of salt, and ⅛ of a teaspoon of pepper. Make a sauce by cooking one cup of tomatoes and one stalk of celery cut in small pieces, a bay leaf and two whole cloves, for twenty minutes; rub through a sieve, add to stock in which meat was cooked. Thicken with four tablespoons of flour moistened with two tablespoons of water. Serve meat with cooked diced potatoes, carrots, and green and red peppers cut in strips.

RUSSIAN GOULASH

To one pound beef, free from fat and cut up as pan stew, add one chopped green pepper, one large onion, two blades of garlic (cut fine), pepper and salt, with just enough water to cover. Let this simmer until meat is very tender. Add a little water as needed. Put in medium sized can of tomatoes an hour or so before using and have ready two cups of cooked spaghetti or macaroni and put this into the meat until thoroughly heated. This must not be too wet; let water cook away just before adding the tomatoes.

MEAT LOAF

To two pounds of chopped beef take three egg yolks, three tablespoons of parsley, three tablespoons of melted chicken-fat, four heaping tablespoons of soft breadcrumbs, ½ teaspoon Kitchen Bouquet, two teaspoons of lemon juice, grated peel of one lemon, one teaspoon of salt, ½ teaspoon onion juice and one teaspoon of pepper. Mix and bake twenty minutes in a 400° oven with ¼ cup of melted chicken fat, and ½ cup boiling water. Baste often.

HAMBURGER STEAK

Take one pound of ground beef, season with salt and pepper, grate in part of an onion or fry with onions. Make into round cakes a little less than ½ inch thick. Heat pan blue hot, grease lightly; add cakes, count to sixty, then turn them and cook on the other side until brown. When well browned they are done if liked rare. Cook ten minutes if liked well done.

BITKI (RUSSIAN HAMBURGER STEAK)

Take two cups of ground beef, and two cups of breadcrumbs that have been soaked in a little water, leaving them quite moist, mix thoroughly with the beef, season with pepper and salt and shape into individual cakes. Fry as directed for Hamburger Steak.

GROUND MEAT WITH RAISINS (ROMANIAN)

Take a pound of ground meat, add grated onion, an egg, matzoth flour, white pepper, mix and form into small balls, put in pot with ½ cup of water, fat, sugar, a ¼ cup large black raisins, a few slices of lemon and let stew 30 minutes, then thicken gravy with tablespoon of flour browned in a tablespoon of fat and serve.

CARNATZLICH (ROMANIAN)

One pound of ground beef, add an egg, a little paprika, black pepper, salt and four cloves of garlic (which have been scraped, and let stand in a little salt for ten minutes, and then mashed so it looks like dough). Form this meat mixture into short sausage-like rolls; boil thirty minutes and serve at once. Serve this dish with Slaietta. (See Vegetables.)

BAKED HASH

Mix together one cup of ground meat, one cup of cold mashed potatoes, ½ an onion, minced, one well-beaten egg and ½ cup soup stock. Season rather highly with salt, if unsalted meat is used, paprika and celery salt, turn into greased baking dish and bake for twenty minutes in a well heated oven. The same mixture may be fried, but will not taste as good.

SOUP MEAT

The meat must be cooked until very tender then lift it out of the soup and lay upon a platter and season while hot. Heat a tablespoon of fat or drippings of roast beef in a sauce pan, cut up a few slices of onion in it, also half a clove of garlic, add a tablespoon of flour, stirring all the time; then add soup stock or rich gravy, and the soup meat, which has been seasoned with salt, pepper and ginger. You must sprinkle the spices on both sides of the meat, and add ½ teaspoon of caraway seed to the sauce, and if too thick add more soup stock and a little boiling water. Cover closely and let it simmer about fifteen minutes.

LEFTOVER MEAT

There are many ways to utilize leftover meat. Indeed, not one particle of meat should ever be wasted. Cold roasts of beef, lamb, mutton or any cold joint roasted or boiled may be made into soups, stews, minces or used for sandwiches, or just served cold with vegetables or salads.

SPAGHETTI AND MEAT

Break spaghetti in small pieces and boil until tender. Put leftover meat through grinder and mix with the spaghetti, salt, pepper, and a little onion juice. Grease a baking dish and put in the meat and spaghetti, sprinkle on top with breadcrumbs and bake in a moderate oven.

MEAT PIE

Cut any leftover beef, lamb or veal in small pieces, removing all excess of fat; parboil one green pepper (seeds removed) cut in strips, two cups of potatoes, ½ cup of diced carrots, and one onion chopped fine. Add to the meat. Thicken with ¼ cup flour moistened in cold water. Put in a baking dish. The crust is made as follows: One cup of flour, one heaping teaspoon of drippings, pinch of salt, ¼ teaspoon of baking powder, one teaspoon of sugar and cold water to mix, about ⅓ cup. Roll out to fit baking dish, cut holes for steam to escape, after covering the contents of the dish. Bake in a quick hot oven for thirty minutes.

BOILED CORNED BEEF

Put corned beef into cold water; using enough to cover it well; let it come slowly to the boiling point; then place where it will simmer only; allow thirty minutes or more to each pound. It is improved by adding a few soup vegetables the last hour of cooking. If the piece can be used a second time, trim it to good shape; place it again in the water in which it was boiled; let it get heated through; then set aside to cool in the water, and under pressure, a plate or deep dish holding a flat-iron being set on top of the meat. The water need not rise above the meat sufficiently to wet the iron. When cooled under pressure the meat is more firm and cuts better into slices. Cabbage is usually served with hot corned beef, but should not be boiled with it.

ENCHILADAS

Make a dough of cornmeal and wheat flour and water. Roll it out in thin, round cakes; cook quickly in a pan that has not been greased, then roll in a cloth to keep soft and warm. Grind one cup of sausage, add ½ grated onion, one tablespoon of Worcestershire sauce, and fill the warm cakes with this mixture. Roll them when filled, and pour over them a sauce made of two tablespoons of drippings into which two tablespoons of flour have been smoothed. Add one cup of soup stock, one cup of strained tomatoes, two tablespoons of vinegar, one tablespoon of Spanish pepper sauce.

VIENNA SAUSAGE

Wash and put on in boiling water. Boil ten minutes, fill a deep dish with hot water, put sausages in, cover, and serve in hot water. To be eaten with grated horseradish or French mustard.

SMOKED BEEF

Soak overnight in cold water; next morning place it in cold water, and simmer until quite tender, reckoning 30 minutes to the pound.

ROAST VEAL

The shoulder and breast of veal are best for roasting. Always buy veal that is fat and white. Prepare for the oven in the following manner: Wash and then dry; rub it well with salt, a very little ground ginger, and dredge it well with flour. Lay in roasting pan and put slices of onion on top with a few tablespoons of goose fat or drippings. Cover tightly and roast at 350°, allowing twenty minutes to the pound and baste frequently. Veal must be well done. When cold it slices up as nicely as turkey.

ROASTED BREAST OF VEAL

Roast as directed above. Have the butcher cut a pocket to receive the stuffing. Prepare bread stuffing and sew up the pocket. Sprinkle a little caraway seed on top of the roast. A tablespoon of lemon juice adds to the flavor. Baste often.

STEWED VEAL

Prepare as above, but do not have the meat cut in small pieces. If desired ½ teaspoon of caraway seed may be used instead of the parsley. Mashed potatoes and green peas or stewed tomatoes are usually served with veal. Any of the flour or potato dumplings are excellent served with stewed or fricasseed veal.

FRICASSEED VEAL WITH CAULIFLOWER

Use the breast or shoulder for this purpose, the former being preferable, and cut it up into pieces, not too small. Sprinkle each piece slightly with fine salt and ginger. Heat a tablespoon of oil or poultry drippings in a stew-pan, and lay the veal in it. Cut up an onion and one or two tomatoes (a tablespoon of canned tomatoes will do), and add to this a little water, and stew two hours, closely covered. When done mix a teaspoon of flour and a little water and add to the veal. Chop up a few sprigs of parsley, add it and boil up once and serve. Place the cauliflower around the platter in which you serve the veal. Boil the cauliflower in salt and water, closely covered.

STUFFED SHOULDER OF VEAL

Have the blade removed, and fill the space with a stuffing made of breadcrumbs, thyme, lemon juice, salt, pepper to taste and one egg, also chopped mushrooms if desired. Sew up the opening, press and tie it into good shape and roast. The stuffing may be made of minced meat, cut from the veal, and highly seasoned.

VEAL LOAF

Take two pounds of chopped veal, four tablespoons of breadcrumbs, two beaten eggs, season with salt, pepper, ginger, nutmeg and a little water. Add a tablespoon of chicken fat; grease the pan, mix ingredients thoroughly, form into a loaf, spread or lay piece of chicken fat on top. Bake in oblong tin until done, basting frequently.

SHOULDER OR NECK OF VEAL - HUNGARIAN

Brown four onions light brown in a tablespoon of fat, add one teaspoon mixed paprika, and the meat cut in pieces; leave the pan uncovered for a few moments, cover; add one sweet green pepper, cut up, and let cook; add a little water whenever the gravy boils down; when the meat is tender serve with dumplings.

IRISH STEW
Cut 1½ pounds of lamb into small pieces. Dredge each piece of meat in flour. Brown in the frying pan. Put in kettle, cover with water and cook slowly one hour or until tender. Add one quart of potatoes cut in small dice, ½ a cup of carrots and three onions, after cooking thirty minutes. Season with salt, pepper, and thicken with two tablespoons of flour moistened in enough cold water to form a smooth paste. Serve with dumplings. (See Dumpling.)

LAMB AND MACARONI
Dilute one can of concentrated tomato sauce with one quart of water; mince two medium-sized onions very fine and fry slowly in olive oil or drippings until they are a golden brown, and add to tomatoes. Fry 1½ pounds of lean neck of lamb in a little drippings until the meat is nicely browned all over and add to the tomatoes, season with one clove of garlic, two bay leaves, two teaspoons of sugar, pepper and salt, and let it simmer for about 1½ hours, or until the meat is tender and the sauce has become the consistency of thick cream. Have ready some boiled macaroni, put in with the meat and stir well. Serve hot. Short ribs of beef may be cooked in the same manner.

LAMB STEW - TOCANE
Brown slices of leeks or young onions in one tablespoon of drippings, add neck or breast of lamb, cut in small pieces; season with white pepper, salt and parsley; cook until tender, just before serving season with dill.

CURRIED MUTTON
Have three pounds of mutton cut in one-inch squares. Wipe, put in kettle and cover with cold water. Cook for five minutes, drain and again cover with boiling water. Add one cup of chopped onion, one teaspoon of peppercorns, and ½ of a red pepper, cut in small strips. Place on back of stove and allow it to simmer until tender. Strain liquor and thicken with flour. Add two tablespoons of drippings, one tablespoon of minced parsley, one teaspoon of curry powder, and ½ teaspoon of salt. Serve with molded rice.

GEWETSH (SERBIAN)
Brown one large onion in a tablespoon of oil, add one teaspoon of paprika and two pounds of neck or shoulder of lamb, cook one hour; have ready one

pound of rice that has been boiled for twenty minutes. Take a twelve inch baking dish, grease, place a layer of sliced tomatoes on bottom of pan, then half the rice, half the meat, two sliced green peppers, sprinkle a little salt and pour part of gravy over this; place another layer of tomatoes, rice, meat, with two sliced peppers and tomatoes on top, salt, and pour remainder of gravy, put lumps of fat here and there; bake in hot oven for forty-five minutes. Use plenty of gravy and fat for this dish or else it will be too dry. Six large tomatoes are required.

ROAST MUTTON WITH POTATOES
Take a shoulder of mutton - wash the meat well and dry with a clean towel. Rub well with salt, ginger and a speck of pepper, and dredge well with flour. Lay it in a covered roasting pan. Put a few pieces of whole mace and a few slices of onion on top; pour a cup of water into the pan. Cover it up tight and set in a 400° oven to roast, basting frequently. Allow twenty minutes to the pound for roasting mutton; it should be well done. Add more water if necessary (always add hot water so as not to stop the process of boiling), skim the gravy well and serve with currant or cranberry jelly. Pare potatoes of uniform size and wash and salt them about three-quarters of an hour before dinner. Lay the potatoes in pan around the roast and sprinkle them with salt and return to the oven to roast . Let them brown nicely.

BREAST OF MUTTON STEWED WITH CARROTS
Salt the mutton on both sides, adding a little ground ginger; put on to boil in cold water, cover up tightly and stew slowly. In the mean time pare and cut up the carrots, add these and cover up again. Pare and cut up about half a dozen potatoes into dice shape and add them forty-five minutes before dinner. Cover up again, and when done, make a sauce as follows: Skim off about two tablespoons of fat from the mutton stew, put this in a sauce pan and heat. Brown a tablespoon of flour in the fat, add a heaping tablespoon of brown sugar, some cinnamon and pour the gravy of the stew into the sauce pan, letting it boil up once, and then pour all over the carrots and stew until ready to serve. White turnips may be used instead of carrots.

MUTTON OR LAMB CHOPS
Trim off some of the fat and heat in the sauce pan. Season the chops with salt and pepper, or salt and ginger. Have the sauce pan very hot with very

little fat in it. To be nice and tender they must be sautéed quickly to a nice brown. Or the chops may be broiled, eight or ten minutes is all the time required; serve at once.

SHOULDER OF MUTTON STUFFED
Have the butcher carefully remove the blade from the shoulder and fill the space with a bread stuffing; (see stuffing). Sew up the opening, roast in the oven with a very little water in the pan, and baste frequently. Serve with the gravy from the pan after the grease has been carefully removed.

POULTRY

TO TRUSS A CHICKEN
Press the thighs and wings close against the body; fasten securely with skewers and tie with string. Draw the skin of the neck to the back and fasten it.

ROAST CHICKEN
Stuff and truss a chicken, season with pepper and salt and dredge with flour. Put in a roasting pan with two or three tablespoons of chicken fat if the chicken is not especially fat. When heated add hot water and baste frequently. 400° oven for about an hour and a half. When done, remove the chicken, pour off the grease and make a brown sauce in the pan.

CHICKEN CASSEROLE
Bake chicken in covered casserole at 350° until nearly tender, then add three potatoes cut in dice; boil small pieces of carrots, green peas, and small white onions - each to be boiled separately. Just before serving, thicken gravy with a teaspoon of flour mixed with a half cup of soup stock or water. Season to taste and place vegetables around the dish.

BOILED CHICKEN, BAKED
Make chicken soup with an old hen. Remove chicken from soup just as soon as tender. Place in roasting pan with three tablespoons of chicken-fat, one onion sliced, one clove of garlic, ½ teaspoon each of salt and paprika. Sprinkle with soft breadcrumbs. Baste frequently and when sufficiently browned, cut in pieces for serving. Place on platter with the strained gravy pour over the chicken and serve.

BROILED SPRING CHICKEN
Take young spring chickens of 1 to 1½ pounds in weight, and split down the back, break the joints and remove the breast bone. Sprinkle with salt and pepper and rub well with chicken fat. Place in broiler and broil twenty minutes over a clear fire, or under the broiler, being careful to turn that all

parts may be equally browned. The flesh side must be exposed to the broiler the greater part of the time as the skin side will brown quickly. Remove to hot platter. Or chicken may be placed in dripping-pan, skin side down, seasoned with salt and pepper and spread with chicken-fat, and bake fifteen minutes in a 400° oven and then broiled to finish. Serve with giblet sauce.

FRIED SPRING CHICKEN
Cut it up as for fricassee and see that every piece is wiped dry. Have ready heated in a sauce pan some goose fat or other poultry drippings. Season each piece of chicken with salt and ground ginger, or pepper. Roll each piece of chicken in sifted cracker or breadcrumbs (which you have previously seasoned with salt). Fry in the sauce pan, turning often, and browning evenly. You may cut up some parsley and add while frying. If the chicken is quite large, it is better to steam it before frying.

GIBLETS
Heart, liver and gizzard constitute the giblets, and to these the neck is usually added. Wash them; put them in cold water and cook until tender. This will take several hours. Serve with the chicken; or mash the liver, mince the heart and gizzard and add them to the brown sauce. Save the stock in which they are cooked for making the sauce.

CHICKEN FRICASSEE
Take a chicken, cut off the wings, legs and neck. Separate the breast from the chicken, leaving it whole. Cut the back into two pieces. Prepare a mixture of salt, ginger and a little pepper in a saucer and dust each piece of chicken with this mixture. When you are ready to cook the chicken, take all the particles of fat you have removed from it and lay in the bottom of the kettle, also a small onion, cut up, some parsley root and celery. Lay the chicken upon this, breast first, then the leg and so on. Cover up tight and let it stew slowly over low heat), adding hot water when necessary. Just before serving chop up some parsley, fine, and rub a teaspoon of flour in a little cold water, and add. Let it boil up once. Shake the kettle back and forth to prevent becoming lumpy. The parsley root and celery may be omitted if so desired. Duck can be prepared in this manner.

CHICKEN WITH RICE
Joint a chicken; season with salt and ground ginger and boil with water enough to cover. Allow ½ pound of rice to one chicken. Boil this after chicken is tender. Serve together on a large platter.

CHICKEN (TURKISH)
Brown a chicken, cover with water and season, cook until tender. When chicken is tender; slash the skin of chestnuts, put them in oven and roast, then skin them, put in chicken and let come to a boil and serve with the chicken.

AMASTICH
Cook one pound of rice in a quart of stock for thirty minutes, stirring frequently. Then add a chicken stuffed and trussed as for roasting; cover closely and cook thoroughly. After removing the chicken, pass the liquor through a strainer, add the juice of a lemon and the beaten yolk of an egg, and pour over the bird.

CHICKEN WITH SPAGHETTI EN CASSEROLE
Prepare and truss a young chicken, as if for roasting. Put it in a casserole, and pour over it two tablespoons of olive oil, a cup of white wine, a cup of bouillon, salt and cayenne to taste, one spoon of dried mushrooms soaked in one cup of water and chopped fine, and ½ can of mushrooms. Cover tightly and put in a 325° oven for about an hour, turning the chicken occasionally; add a dozen olives and a tablespoon of chicken-fat, smoothed with one tablespoon of flour, and bring to a boil. Remove the chicken and add about a pint of boiled spaghetti to the sauce. Place the chicken on a platter, surround with the spaghetti, and serve.

STUFFED CHICKEN (TURKISH)
Steam chicken and when it is almost tender stuff it with the following: Take 4 ounces of almonds, chopped; season with parsley, pepper and salt to taste, add one tablespoon of breadcrumbs and bind this with one well-beaten egg. Put chicken in roasting pan and roast at 400° until done.

SMOTHERED CHICKEN

Two tender chickens cut in half, split down the back; place the pieces in a colander to drain well, after having been well salted; season with pepper; grease well the bottom of a baking pan; add one stalk finely chopped celery, onion; lay the chicken on breast, side up; sprinkle lightly with flour, fat; two cups of hot water. Have the oven 400° when putting chickens in. As soon as browned evenly, cover with a pan, fitting closely. Reduce the heat of the oven; allow to cook slowly an hour or so longer, until tender. Place on a hot platter; set in oven until sauce is made, as follows: put the pan on top of stove in which chickens were smothered; add level tablespoon of flour, thinned in cold water; add minced parsley; let this all cook two or three minutes, then add large cup of strong stock, to the chickens. Broil one can of mushrooms, and pour these over chicken when ready to serve.

CHICKEN CURRY

Cut chickens in pieces for serving; dredge in flour and sauté in hot fat. Cut one onion in thin pieces, add one tablespoon of curry powder, ¾ tablespoon of salt and one tablespoon of wine vinegar. Add to chicken, cover with boiling water; simmer until chicken is tender. Thicken sauce and serve with steamed rice.

CHICKEN PAPRIKA WITH RICE

Cut a three and one-half pound fat chicken in pieces to serve, salt it and let stand several hours. Heat ¼ cup of fat in an iron kettle, add one medium-sized onion, minced; fry golden brown and set aside. Fry the chicken in the fat and when nicely browned, add paprika to taste and boiling water to cover, and let simmer one hour. Soak one cup of rice in cold water, drain, add the fried onion and one teaspoon of salt and gradually three cups of chicken broth, more if necessary. When nearly done add the chicken and finish cooking in a 325° oven, 30 minutes.

CHILI CON CARNE

Cut two broilers in pieces for serving. Season with salt, pepper, and dredge in flour; brown in hot fat. Parboil six large red peppers until soft, rub through a wire sieve. Chop two small onions fine, three cloves of garlic and one-fourth cup of capers. Combine, add to chicken, cover with water and cook until chicken is tender. Thicken the sauce with fat and flour melted together.

PILAF (RUSSIAN)
Follow recipe below but substitute cooked lamb for the chicken, and add chicken livers fried and cut in small pieces.

PILAF (TURKISH)
Soak one cup of rice in cold water for one hour. Pour off the water, and put the rice with two cups of soup stock, and ¼ a white onion on to boil. Stew until the rice absorbs all the stock. Stew ½ can of tomatoes thoroughly and season with olive oil or chicken-fat, salt and pepper. Mix it with the rice. Sauté in chicken-fat to a light color, a jointed chicken slightly parboiled, or slices of cold cooked chicken or turkey. Make a depression in the rice and tomato, put in the chicken and two tablespoons of olive oil or chicken-fat, and stew all together for twenty minutes. Serve on a platter in a smooth mound, the red rice surrounding the fowl.

SPANISH PIE
Take one pint of cold chicken, duck or any poultry. Cut it into flakes and place it in a pudding dish that has been lined with a thin crust. On the layer of meat place a layer of sweet red peppers (seeds removed), cut in slices; next, a layer of thinly sliced sausage, and so on until the dish is full. Over this, pour a glass of claret into which have been rubbed two tablespoons of flour. Cover with a thin crust of pastry, and bake.

CHICKEN Á LA ITALIENNE
Cut the remains of cold chicken (or turkey) into pieces about an inch long and marinate them in a bowl containing one tablespoon of olive oil, one teaspoon of tarragon vinegar or lemon juice, a few drops of onion juice, salt and pepper. At the end of thirty minutes sprinkle with finely chopped parsley, dip them in fritter batter, and fry in boiling fat. Drain on a brown paper, and serve with or without tomato or brown sauce. In some parts of Italy this dish is made of several kinds of cold meats, poultry, brains, etc. (the greater the variety the better), served on the same platter, and in Spain all kinds of cold vegetables are fried in batter and served together.

ROAST GOOSE
All goose meat tastes better if it is well rubbed with salt, ginger and a little garlic a day previous to using. Stuff goose with bread dressing, or chestnut

dressing, a dressing of apples is also very good. Sew up the goose, then line a roasting pan with a few slices of onion and celery and place the goose upon these, cover closely, roast at 325° three hours or more, according to weight. If the goose browns too quickly, lower the heat of the oven. Baste every fifteen minutes.

GESCHUNDENE GANS

Take a very fat goose for this purpose. Cut off neck, wings and feet. Lay the goose on a table, back up, take a sharp knife, make a cut from the neck down to the tail. Begin again at the top near the neck, take off the skin, holding it in your left hand, your knife in your right hand, after all the skin is removed, place it in cold water; separate the breast from back and cut off joints. Have ready in a plate a mixture of salt, ginger and a little garlic or onion, cut up fine. Rub the joints and small pieces with this, and make a small incision in each leg and four in the breast. Put in each incision a small piece of garlic or onion, and rub also with a prepared mixture of salt and ginger. Put in refrigerator overnight or until you wish to use.

GÄNSEKLEIN

Rub wings, neck, gizzard, heart and back of goose with salt, ginger, pepper and garlic and set on the fire in a stew-pan with cold water. Cover tightly and stew slowly but steadily for four hours. When done skim off all the fat. Now put a sauce pan over the fire, put into it about two or three tablespoons of the fat that you have just skimmed off and then add the fat to the meat again. Cut up fine a very small piece of garlic and add a heaping teaspoon of flour (brown). Add the hot gravy and pour all over the goose. Cover up tightly and set on low burner until you wish to serve. You may cook the whole goose in this way after it is cut up.

GOOSE CRACKLINGS (GRIEBEN)

Cut the thick fat of a fat goose in pieces as big as the palm of your hand, roll together and run a toothpick through each one to fasten. Put a large pot on a hot stove burner, lay in the cracklings, sprinkle a tiny bit of salt over them and pour in a cup or two of cold water; cover closely and let cook not too fast, until water is cooked out. Then add the soft or "linda" fat, keep top off and let all brown nicely. About one to two hours is required to cook them. If you do not wish the scraps of "Greben" brittle, take them out of the fat before they are browned. Place strainer over your fat crock, to catch the clear fat and let greben drain. If greben are too greasy place in baking pan in oven a few minutes to try out a little more. Serve at lunch with rye bread.

ROAST GOOSE BREASTS
The best way to roast a goose breast is to remove the skin from the neck and sew it over the breast and fasten it with a few stitches under the breast, making an incision with a pointed knife in the breast and joints of the goose, so as to be able to insert a little garlic (or onion) in each incision, also a little salt and ginger. Keep closely covered all the time, so as not to get too brown. They cut up nicely cold for sandwiches.

STEWED GOOSE, PIQUANTE
Cut up, after being skinned, and stew, seasoning with salt, pepper, a few cloves and a very little lemon peel. When done heat a little goose fat in a frying pan, brown half a tablespoon of flour, add a little vinegar and the juice of half a lemon.

MINCED GOOSE (HUNGARIAN)
Take the entire breast of a goose, chop up fine in a chopping bowl; grate in part of an onion, and season with salt, pepper and a tiny piece of garlic. Add some grated stale bread and work in a few eggs. Press this chopped meat back on to the breast bone and roast, basting very often with goose fat.

DUCK
Wash duck thoroughly and rub well with salt, ginger and a little pepper, inside and out. Now prepare this dressing: Take the liver, gizzard and heart and chop to a powder in chopping bowl. Grate in a little nutmeg, add a piece of celery root and half an onion. Put all this into your chopping bowl. Soak some stale bread, squeeze out all the water and fry in a sauce pan of hot fat. Toss this soaked bread into the bowl; add one egg, salt, pepper and a speck of ginger and mix all thoroughly. Fill the duck with this and sew it up. Lay in the roasting pan with slices of onions, celery and

specks of fat. Put some on top of fowl; roast at 325° for two hours, covered up tight and baste often. Stick a fork into the skin from time to time so that the fat will trickle out.

ROAST DUCK
Draw the duck; stuff, truss and roast the same as chicken. Serve with giblet sauce and currant jelly. If small, the duck should be cooked in an hour.

DUCK Á LA MODE IN JELLY
One duckling of about five pounds, one calf's foot, eight to ten small onions, as many young carrots, one bunch of parsley. Cook the foot slowly in one quart of water, one teaspoon of salt and a small bay leaf. Put aside when the liquor has been reduced to half. In the meanwhile fry the duck and when well browned wipe off the grease, put in another pan, add the calf's foot with its broth, one glass of dry white wine, a tablespoon of brandy, the carrots, parsley and the onions - the latter slightly browned in drippings - pepper and salt to taste and cook slowly under a covered lid for one hour. Cool off for about an hour, take off the grease, bone and skin the duckling and cut the meat into small pieces; arrange nicely with the vegetables in individual earthenware dishes, cover with the stock and put on the ice to harden.

SQUABS, OR NEST PIGEONS
Clean and season them well inside and out, with salt mixed with a little ginger and pepper, and then stuff them with well-seasoned bread dressing. Pack them closely in a deep stew pan and cover with flakes of goose fat, minced parsley and a little chopped onion. Cover with a lid that fits close and stew gently, adding water when necessary. Do not let them get too brown. They should be a light yellow.

BROILED SQUABS
Squabs are a great delicacy, being peculiarly savory and nourishing. Clean the squabs; lay them in salt water for about ten minutes and then rub dry with a clean towel. Split them down the back and broil in oven. Season with salt and pepper; lay them on a heated platter, grease them liberally with goose fat and cover with a deep platter. Toast a piece of bread for each pigeon, removing the crust. Dip the toast in boiling water for an instant. In serving lay a squab upon a piece of toasted bread.

PIGEON PIE

Prepare as many pigeons as you wish to bake in your pie. Salt and pepper, then melt some fat in a stew-pan, and cut up an onion in it. When hot, place in the pigeons and stew until tender. In the mean time line a deep pie plate with a rich paste. Cut up the pigeons, lay them in, with hard-boiled eggs chopped up and minced parsley. Season with salt and pepper. Put flakes of chicken fat rolled in flour here and there, pour over the gravy the pigeons were stewed in, cover with a crust. Bake at 325° until done.

SQUAB EN CASSEROLE

Take fowl and brown in a skillet the desired color, then add to this enough water (or soup stock preferred), put it in casserole and add vegetables; add first those that require longest cooking. Use mushrooms, carrots, small potatoes and peas. If you like flavor of sherry wine, add small wine glass; if not, it is just as good. Season well and cook in hot oven not too long, as you want fowl and vegetables to be whole. You may add soup stock if it is too dry after being in oven.

ROAST TURKEY

Wash and clean the turkey the same as chicken. Fill with plain bread stuffing or chestnut stuffing. Tie down the legs and rub entire surface with salt and let stand overnight. Next morning place in large drippings or roasting-pan on rack and spread breast, legs and wings with one-third cup of fat creamed and mixed with ¼ cup of flour. Dredge bottom of pan with flour. Place in a 400° oven and when the flour on the turkey begins to brown, reduce the heat and add two cups of boiling water or the stock in which the giblets are cooking, and baste with ¼ cup of fat and ¾ cup of boiling water. When this is all used, baste with the fat in the pan. Baste every fifteen minutes until tender; do not prick with a fork, press with the fingers; if the breast meat and leg are soft to the touch the turkey is done. If the oven is too hot, cover the pan; turn the turkey often, that it may brown nicely. Remove strings and skewers and serve on hot platter. Serve with giblet sauce and cranberry sauce. If the turkey is very large it will require three hours or more, a small one will require only an hour and a half.

STUFFED TURKEY NECK (TURKISH)

Take neck of turkey, stuff with following: One-quarter pound of almonds or walnuts chopped fine and seasoned with chopped parsley, pepper and salt, put two hard-boiled eggs in the center of this dressing; stuff neck, sew up the ends and when roasted slice across so as to have a portion of the hard-boiled egg on each slice; place on platter and surround with sprigs of parsley.

STUFFINGS FOR MEAT AND POULTRY

TO STUFF POULTRY

Use enough stuffing to fill the bird but do not pack it tightly or the stuffing will be soggy. Close the small openings with a skewer; sew the larger one with linen thread and a long needle. Remove skewers and strings before serving.

CRUMB DRESSING

Take one tablespoon of chicken fat, mix in two cups of breadcrumbs, pinch of salt and pepper, a few drops of onion juice, one tablespoon of chopped parsley, and lastly one well-beaten egg. Mix all on stove in skillet, remove from heat and stuff fowl.

BREAD DRESSING FOR FOWL

In a fryer on the stove heat two tablespoons of drippings or fat, drop in ½ onion cut fine, brown lightly and add ¼ loaf of stale baker's bread (which has previously been soaked in cold water and then thoroughly squeezed out). Cook until it leaves the sides of the fryer, stirring occasionally. If too dry add a little soup stock. Remove from the stove, put in a bowl, season with salt, pepper, ginger, and finely chopped parsley, add a small lump of fat, break in one whole egg, mix well and fill the fowl with it.

MEAT DRESSING FOR POULTRY
In some ground beef, mix in some ground veal. Season with salt, pepper, nutmeg or thyme. Grate in a piece of celery root and a piece of garlic about the size of a bean, add a small onion, a minced tomato, a ¼ loaf of stale bread, also grated, and mix up the whole with one egg. If you prefer, you may soak the bread, press out every drop of water and dry in a heated sauce pan with fat.

POTATO STUFFING
Add two cups of hot, mashed Irish or sweet potatoes to bread stuffing. Mix well and stuff in goose, stuffed veal or lamb breast.

CHESTNUT STUFFING
Shell and blanch two cups of chestnuts. Cook in boiling salted water until tender. Drain and force through a colander or a potato ricer. Add ¼ cup of melted chicken fat, ¼ teaspoon of pepper, ¾ teaspoon of salt, one cup of grated breadcrumbs, and enough soup stock to moisten.

RAISIN STUFFING
Take three cups of stale breadcrumbs; add ½ cup of melted chicken fat, one cup of seeded raisins cut in small pieces, one teaspoon of salt, and ¼ teaspoon of white pepper. Mix thoroughly.

VEGETABLES

All vegetables should be thoroughly cleansed just before being put on to cook. Green vegetables, such as cabbage, cauliflower and Brussels sprouts, should be soaked heads down in salted cold water, to which a few spoons of vinegar may be added. To secure the best results all vegetables except beans, that is the dried beans, should be put in boiling water and the water must be made to boil again as soon as possible after the vegetables have been added and must be kept boiling until the cooking is finished. In cooking vegetables, conserve their juices. The average housewife pours down the sink drainpipe the juices from all the vegetables which she cooks; she little realizes that she thus drains away the health of her family. Cook vegetables with just sufficient water to prevent them from burning, and serve their juices with them; else save the vegetable "waters" and, by the addition of milk and butter, convert them into soups for the family use. Such soups, derived from one or several vegetables, alone or mixed together, make palatable and healthful additions to the family bill-of-fare.

ASPARAGUS

Cut off the woody part, scrape the lower part of the stalks. Wash well and tie in bunches. Put into a deep stew pan, with the cut end resting on the bottom of the stew-pan. Pour in boiling water to come up to the tender heads, but not to cover them. Add one teaspoon of salt for each quart of water. Place where the water will boil. Cook until tender, having the cover partially off the stew pan. This will be from fifteen to thirty minutes, depending upon the freshness and tenderness of the vegetable. Have some slices of well-toasted bread on a platter. Butter them slightly. Arrange the cooked asparagus on the toast, season with butter and a little salt and serve at once. Save the water in which the asparagus was boiled to use in making vegetable soup.

ARTICHOKES (FRENCH OR GLOBE)

French artichokes have a large scaly head, like the cone of a pine tree. The flower buds are used before they open. The edible portion consists of the thickened portion at the base of the scales and the receptacle to which the leaf-like scales are attached. When the artichoke is very young and tender the edible parts may be eaten raw as a salad. When it becomes hard, as it does very quickly, it must be cooked. When boiled it may be eaten as a salad or with a sauce. The scales are pulled with the fingers from the cooked head, the base of each leaf dipped in a sauce and then eaten. The bottoms (receptacles), which many consider the most delicate part of the artichoke, may be cut up and served as a salad, or they may be stewed and served with a sauce. To prepare the artichoke remove all the hard outer leaves. Cut off the stem close to the leaves. Cut off the top of the bud. Drop the artichokes into boiling water and cook until tender, which will take from thirty to fifty minutes, then take up and remove the choke. Serve a dish of French salad dressing with the artichokes, which may be eaten either hot or cold. Melted butter also makes a delicious sauce for the artichokes if they are eaten hot.

JERUSALEM ARTICHOKE

This vegetable is in season in the fall and spring, and may be cooked like kohl-rabi and served in a white cream or sauce. The artichoke may also be cooked in milk. When this is done, cut the washed and peeled artichoke into cubes, put in a pan, and cover with milk (a generous pint to a quart of cubes). Add one small onion and cook twenty minutes. Beat together one tablespoon of butter and one level tablespoon of flour, and stir this into the boiling milk. Then season with one teaspoon of salt and ¼ teaspoon of pepper, and continue the cooking thirty minutes longer. The cooking should be done in a double boiler. The artichoke also makes a very good soup.

FRENCH ARTICHOKES WITH TOMATO SAUCE

Pick off from the solid green globes the outer tough petals. Scoop out with a sharp-pointed knife the fuzzy centers, leaving the soft base, which is the luscious morsel. Cut each artichoke in halves, wash, drain and fry brown on each side in olive oil. Make tomato sauce and cook thirty minutes in that mixture. Then serve.

BEET GREENS

Beets are usually thickly sowed, and as the young plants begin to grow they must be thinned out. These plants make delicious greens, and even the tops of the ordinary market beets are good if properly prepared. Wash thoroughly in several waters, and put on stove in a large kettle of boiling water. Add one teaspoon of salt for every two quarts of greens; boil rapidly about thirty minutes or until tender; drain off the water; chop well and season with butter and salt.

*Original recipe's boiling time may be too long for modern tastes. Cook until the tenderness of the vegetable meets your approval.

BOILED BEETS

Carefully wash any earth off the beets, but every care is needed to avoid breaking the skin, roots or crown; if this is done much of their color will be lost, and they will be a dull pink. Lay them in plenty of boiling water, with a little vinegar; boil them steadily, keeping them well covered with water for about 1½ hours for small beets, and two to three hours for large ones. If they are to be served hot, cut off the roots and crown and rub off the skin directly, but if to be served cold, leave them until they have become cold and then cut into thin slices and sprinkle with salt and pepper and pour some vinegar over them. If to be eaten hot, cut them into thin slices, arrange them on a hot vegetable dish and pour over white sauce or melted butter, or hand these separately.

*Original recipe's boiling time may be too long for modern tastes. Cook until the tenderness of the vegetable meets your approval.

BAKED BEETS

Boil large beetroot about two hours, being careful not to pierce it. When cold mash very smooth, add a little drippings, pepper, salt and stock. Place in a greased pan and bake one hour.

SOUR BUTTERED BEETS

Wash as many beets as required and cook in boiling water until tender. Drain and turn into cold water for peeling. Remove the skins, slice and sprinkle with as much salt as desired. Melt ½ cup of butter in a large frying-pan and add two tablespoons of strained lemon juice. Stir the butter and lemon juice until blended, keeping the fire low. Now turn the beets into this sauce, cover the pan and shake and toss until the sauce has been well distributed. Serve hot at once.

CELERIAC
This vegetable is also known as "knot celery" and "turnip-rooted celery." The roots, which are about the size of a white turnip, and not the stalks are eaten. They are more often used as a vegetable than as a salad. Pare the celeriac, cut in thin, narrow slices, and put into cold water. Drain from this water and drop into boiling water and boil thirty minutes. Drain and rinse with cold water. The celeriac is now ready to be prepared and served the same as celery.

PURÉE OF CELERIAC
Boil as directed above and press through a sieve. To one quart take two tablespoons of butter blended with two tablespoons flour and cooked until smooth and frothy, add the strained celeriac and cook five minutes, stirring frequently. Add one teaspoon of salt, and a ½ cup of cream, cook five minutes longer and serve hot on toast or fried bread.

CAULIFLOWER
Trim off the outside leaves and cut the stalk even with the flower. Let it stand upside down in cold salted water for twenty minutes. Put it into a generous quantity of rapidly boiling salted water and cook it uncovered about twenty minutes or until tender, but not so soft as to fall to pieces. Remove any scum from the water before lifting out the cauliflower. If not perfectly white, rub a little white sauce over it. Serve with a white, a Béchamel, or a Hollandaise sauce; or it may be served as a garnish to chicken, sweetbreads, etc., the little bunches being broken off and mixed with the sauce.

*Original recipe's boiling time may be too long for modern tastes. Cook until the tenderness of the vegetable meets your approval.

SPANISH CAULIFLOWER
Finely chop one medium-sized onion and a small bunch of parsley. Melt one tablespoon butter in a pan and fry the onion until it is brown. Season with celery salt. Blend in one tablespoon flour, add one cup boiling water

and let simmer for thirty minutes. Carefully clean the cauliflower and boil for thirty minutes. Drain the onion sauce, add three tablespoons tomato catsup, drain the cauliflower, turn into a baking pan, pour over the sauce, place in a moderate oven for five minutes and serve hot.
*Original recipe's boiling time may be too long for modern tastes. Cook until the tenderness of the vegetable meets your approval.

CAULIFLOWER WITH BROWN CRUMBS
Drain and place the hot cauliflower in serving dish, and pour over it two tablespoons fine breadcrumbs browned in one tablespoon of hot butter or fat. Serve hot. Asparagus may be served in this style.

CAULIFLOWER OR ASPARAGUS (HUNGARIAN)
Cook in salt water until tender. Spread with breadcrumbs and butter. Pour some sour cream over the vegetable and bake until the crumbs are a golden brown.

SCALLOPED CAULIFLOWER
Boil and drain off the water, grease a baking dish, line with a layer of cauliflower, add a layer of toasted breadcrumbs, another of cauliflower and so on alternately, letting the top layer be of breadcrumbs. Over all pour one cup of boiling milk, dot the top with butter and bake in a moderate oven for twenty minutes.

CAULIFLOWER (ROMANIAN)
Brown a minced onion, add cauliflower cut in pieces with a small quantity of water; stew, add salt, white pepper, a little sour salt and red tomatoes; when half done add ¼ cup of rice. Cook until rice is done. The onion may be browned either in butter, fat or olive oil, as desired.

CREAMED CELERY
Remove the leaves from the stalks of celery; scrape off all rusted or dark spots; cut into small pieces and drop in cold water. Having boiling water ready; put the celery into it, adding ½ teaspoon of salt for every quart of water. Boil until tender, leaving the cover partly off; drain and rinse in cold water. Make a cream sauce; drop the celery into it; heat thoroughly and serve.

BOILED LETTUCE

Wash four or five heads of lettuce, carefully removing thick, bitter stalks and retaining all sound leaves. Cook in plenty of boiling salted water for ten or fifteen minutes, then blanch in cold water for a minute or two. Drain, chop lightly, and heat in stew pan with some butter, and salt and pepper to taste. If preferred, the chopped lettuce may be heated with a pint of white sauce seasoned with salt, pepper, and grated nutmeg. After simmering for a few minutes in the sauce, draw to a cooler part of the stove and stir in the well-beaten yolks of two eggs.

GREEN LIMA BEANS

Cover the shelled beans with boiling water; bring to a boil quickly; then let them simmer slowly until tender. Drain and add salt, pepper and butter or hot cream or cream sauce.

CARROTS

Scrape the carrots lightly; cut them into large dice or slices and drop them into salted boiling water, allowing one teaspoon of salt to one quart of water. Boil until tender; drain and serve with butter and pepper or with cream sauce.

LEMON CARROTS

Dice carrots, and simmer in salted water until tender. Drain, return to the fire, and for one pint of carrots add one teaspoon of minced parsley, a grating of loaf sugar, ½ teaspoon of paprika, one tablespoon of butter, and the juice of ½ lemon. Heat through, shaking the dish now and then, so that each piece of the vegetable will be well coated with the mixture or dressing.

SIMMERED CARROTS

Wash, scrape and slice one quart of carrots. Put them in a sauce pan with one tablespoon of butter or drippings, three tablespoons of sugar and one teaspoon salt. Cover closely and let simmer on a slow fire until tender.

FLEMISH CARROTS

Scrape, slice and cook one quart of carrots in one quart of boiling water to which has been added one teaspoon of salt, until tender; drain. Heat two tablespoons fat, add one small onion, brown lightly, add the carrots, season with one teaspoon of sugar, ¼ teaspoon salt, ⅛ teaspoon white pepper and shake well over the fire for ten minutes, add 1½ cups of soup stock, cover and simmer for thirty minutes, then add one teaspoon chopped parsley and serve hot.

CARROTS WITH BRISKET OF BEEF

Salt and pepper two pounds of fat brisket of beef and let stand several hours. Wash and scrape two bunches of carrots and cut in small cubes. Place in kettle with meat, cover with boiling water and cook several hours or until the meat and carrots are tender, and the water is half boiled away. Heat two tablespoons of fat in a sauce pan, let brown slightly, add two tablespoons of flour and gradually one cup of carrot and meat liquid. Place in kettle with meat and carrots and boil until carrots become browned.

COMPOTE OF CARROTS (RUSSIAN)

Make a syrup of one cup of sugar and one cup of water by boiling ten minutes. To this syrup add two cups of carrots diced, which have previously been browned in two tablespoons hot fat or butter. Cook all together until carrots are tender. Brown in oven and serve.

CORN ON THE COB

Free the corn from husks and silk; have a kettle of water boiling hard; drop the corn into it and cook ten minutes (or longer if the corn is not young). If a very large number of ears are put into the water they will so reduce the temperature that a longer time will be needed. In no case, however, should the corn be left too long in the water, as overcooking spoils the delicate flavor.

*Original recipe's boiling time may be too long for modern tastes. Cook until the tenderness of the vegetable meets your approval.

CORN OFF THE COB

Corn is frequently cut from the cob after it is cooked and served in milk or butter; but by this method much of the flavor and juice of the corn itself is wasted. It is better to cut the corn from the cob before cooking. With a sharp knife cut off the grains, not cutting closely enough to remove any of the woody portion of the skins. Then with a knife press out all the pulp and milk remaining in the cob; add this to the corn; season well with salt, pepper and butter; add a little more milk if the corn is dry; cook, preferably in the oven, for about ten minutes, stirring occasionally. If the oven is not hot, cook over the fire.

SUCCOTASH

Mix equal parts of corn, cut from the ear, and any kind of beans; boil them separately; then stir them lightly together, and season with butter, salt, and pepper and add a little cream if convenient.

DANDELIONS

Wash one peck of dandelions; remove roots. Cook one hour in two quarts of boiling salted water. Drain, chop fine; season with salt, pepper and butter. Serve with vinegar.
*Original recipe's boiling time may be too long for modern tastes. Cook until the tenderness of the vegetable meets your approval.

STUFFED CUCUMBERS

Cut four cucumbers in half lengthwise; remove the seeds with a spoon, lay the cucumbers in vinegar overnight; then wipe dry and fill with a mixture made from one cup pecans or Brazil nuts chopped, six tablespoons of mashed potatoes, one well-beaten egg, one teaspoon of salt, two tablespoons of chopped parsley, ¼ teaspoon white pepper, dash of nutmeg, and two tablespoons of melted butter. Bake at 350° in a buttered dish until tender. Serve hot with one cup of white sauce, dash of powdered cloves, one well-beaten egg, salt and pepper to taste.

FRIED CUCUMBERS

Daintily prepared fried cucumbers are immeasurably superior to fried egg plant and are especially nice with boiled chicken. Peel and slice the cucumbers lengthwise in about the same thickness observed with eggplant.

Lay these slices in salt and water for about an hour, then dip in beaten egg and cracker dust, and fry in boiling fat, taking care to carefully drain in a colander before serving.

COLD SLAW

Take a firm, white head of cabbage; cut it in halves; take out the heart and cut as fine as possible on slaw-cutter. Cut up one onion at the same time and a sour apple. Now sprinkle with salt and white pepper and a liberal quantity of white sugar. Mix this lightly with two forks. Heat one tablespoon of oil or butter, and mix it thoroughly in with the cabbage. Heat some white vinegar in a sauce pan; let it come to a boil and pour over the slaw, boiling. Keep covered for a short time. Serve cold.

BOILED SAUERKRAUT

Take a 2 to 3 pound brisket of beef. Set it on to boil in two quarts of water, a little salt and the usual soup greens. When the meat is tender take it out, salt it well and put on to boil again in a pot, having previously removed all the bones. Add about a cup of the soup stock and as much sauerkraut as you desire. Boil about one hour; tie one tablespoon of caraway seed in a bag and boil in with the kraut. Thicken with two raw potatoes, grated, and add one tablespoon of brown sugar just before serving. If not sour enough add a dash of vinegar. This gives you meat, vegetables and soup. Mashed potatoes, Kartoffelklöße or any kind of flour dumpling is a nice accompaniment. Sauerkraut is just as good warmed over as fresh, which may be done two or three times in succession without injury to its flavor.

TO BOIL CABBAGE

Cut a small head of cabbage into four parts, cutting down through the stock. Soak for half an hour in a pan of cold water to which has been added one tablespoon of salt; this is to draw out any insects that may be hidden in the leaves. Take from the water and cut into slices. Have a large stew pan half full of boiling water; put in the cabbage, pushing it under the water with a spoon. Add one tablespoon of salt and cook from twenty to thirty minutes. Turn into a colander and drain for about two minutes. Put in a chopping bowl and mince. Season with butter, pepper, and more salt if it requires it. Allow one tablespoon of butter to a generous pint of the cooked vegetable. Cabbage cooked in this manner will be of delicate flavor and may be generally eaten without distress. Have the kitchen windows open at the top while the cabbage is boiling, and there will be little if any odor of cabbage in the house.

FRIED CABBAGE

Cut one medium head of cabbage fine, soak ten minutes in salt water. Drain, heat three tablespoons of fat (from top of soup stock preferred), add cabbage, one sour apple peeled and cut up, caraway seed to taste, salt, paprika, and ½ onion minced. Cover very closely and cook slowly for one hour.

CREAMED NEW CABBAGE

To one pint of boiled and minced new cabbage add one cup of hot milk, one tablespoon of butter, one teaspoon of flour, ½ teaspoon each of salt and pepper, one teaspoon finely minced parsley, and a generous dash of sweet paprika. The butter and flour should be creamed together before stirring in. Let simmer for about ten minutes, stirring occasionally to keep from burning. Serve hot on toasted bread.

HOT SLAW

Cut the cabbage into thin shreds as for cold slaw. (Use a plane if convenient). Boil it until tender in salted fast-boiling water. Drain it thoroughly, and pour over it a hot sauce made of one tablespoon of butter, one-half teaspoon of salt, dash of pepper and of cayenne, and ½ cup of vinegar, according to its strength. Cover the saucepan and let it stand on the side of the stove for five minutes, so that the cabbage and sauce will become well incorporated.

CARROTS BOILED WITH CABBAGE

Pare the carrots and cut them into finger lengths, in thin strips. Put a breast of lamb or mutton on to boil, having previously salted it well. When boiling, add the carrots and cover closely. Prepare the cabbage as usual and lay in with the mutton and carrots; boil two hours at least; when all has boiled tender, skim off some of the fat and put it into a sauce pan. Add to this one tablespoon of flour, one tablespoon of brown sugar and ½ teaspoon cinnamon. Keep adding gravy from the mutton until well mixed, and pour all over the mutton and vegetables. Serve together on a platter.

STEWED CABBAGE
Clean and drain cabbage, cut in small pieces and boil until tender. Drain and rinse in cold water; chop fine, heat one tablespoon of drippings in sauce pan, ¼ of an onion cut fine, and one tablespoon of flour; brown all together, add one cup of soup stock, add cabbage and cook ten minutes longer. Salt and pepper to taste.

FILLED CABBAGE
Take a large, solid head of cabbage; take off the large top leaves, and scoop out the center of the cabbage so as to leave the outside leaves intact for refilling. Chop your cabbage fine as for slaw; take a quarter of a loaf of stale bread, soak it in water and squeeze very dry. Heat two tablespoons of drippings in a sauce pan, add a large onion chopped fine, do not let the onion get too brown; then add the bread, one pound of chopped beef well minced and the chopped cabbage and let it get well heated; take off stove and add two eggs, pepper, salt, nutmeg, a little parsley and a little sage, season very highly. Use a little more cabbage than bread in the filling. Put this all back in the cabbage, and cover this with the large leaves, put into small bread-pan and bake at 325° for two hours, put just enough water in to keep the pan from burning; don't baste. It doesn't harm if the leaves scorch.

KAL DOLMAR
Boil cabbage whole for ten minutes. Let it cool and boil the rice. Mix chopped meat, rice, and salt and pepper. Separate the cabbage leaves; put about three tablespoons of the meat and rice in the leaves, roll up and tie together with string. Then fry in fat until brown. Boil for thirty minutes in a little water. Make brown gravy and pour over.

SAVOY CABBAGE WITH RICE
Boil cabbage whole for five minutes; drain, separate the leaves after it has cooled. Mix one cup of boiled rice with three dozen raisins, pinch of salt, one teaspoon of cinnamon and two tablespoons of drippings. Put

two tablespoons of this mixture in three or four leaves, roll them and tie together with string. Place in pan and let cook for an hour until done. This dish is just as good warmed up a second time. There must be sufficient fat and gravy to prevent the cabbage rolls from sticking to the bottom of the pan which must be kept closely covered.

BELGIAN RED CABBAGE

Put two or three sticks of cinnamon, salt and pepper, ½ teaspoon cloves, one onion sliced thin, one bay leaf, two cups of water, three tablespoons of drippings in sauce pan, then add five or six greening apples, peeled and cut in quarters. Lastly, put in one medium-sized red cabbage, cut in halves and then sliced very thin. Cook three hours and then add two tablespoons each of sugar and vinegar; cook one minute more.

RED CABBAGE

Cut fine on slaw cutter, put cabbage in a colander, pour boiling water over it and let it stand over another pan for ten minutes; salt, mix well, and cut up a sour apple in the cabbage. Heat one tablespoon goose or soup drippings, brown in this an onion cut fine, add the cabbage and stew slowly, keep covered. Add a little hot water after it has boiled about five minutes. When tender add a few cloves, vinegar, brown sugar and cinnamon to taste, and serve. White cabbage may be cooked in this way.

RED CABBAGE WITH CHESTNUTS AND PRUNES

Clean cabbage and cut off outside leaves, cut on cabbage-cutter and blanch as above. Take one tablespoon of butter, put in kettle and let brown, add cabbage, let simmer about ten minutes more. Add about one cup of water, ¼ cup vinegar, and one tablespoon of sugar, salt and pepper to taste. Add ¼ cup raisins and blanched chestnuts and cook until tender, adding to cabbage just before serving. Take one tablespoon of flour smooth with cold water, add to cabbage, let cook a few minutes and serve.

VEGETABLE HASH

Hash may be made with one or many vegetables and with or without the addition of meat and fish. Potato is the most useful vegetable for hash, because it combines well with meat or other vegetables. The vegetables must be chopped fine, well seasoned with salt and pepper, and parsley, onion, chives or green pepper if desired, and moistened with stock, milk or water, using a ¼ cup to a pint of hash. Melt ½ tablespoon butter or savory drippings in a pan; put in the hash, spreading it evenly and dropping small pieces of butter or drippings over the top. Cover the pan; let the hash cook over moderate heat for half an hour; fold over like an omelet and serve. If properly cooked there will be a rich brown crust formed on the outside of the hash.

Original recipe's cooking time may be too long for modern tastes. Cook until it meets your approval.

BAKED EGGPLANT

Parboil eggplant until tender, but not soft, in boiling salted water. Cut in half crosswise with a sharp knife. Scrape out the inside and do not break the skin. Heat one tablespoon of butter, add a minced onion, brown, then scraped eggplant, breadcrumbs, salt and pepper to taste and an egg yolk. Mix well together, refill shells, place in dripping pan in 350° oven - baste with butter or sprinkle cracker crumbs on top with bits of butter - baste often and brown nicely.

BROILED OR FRIED EGGPLANT

For preparing eggplant, either to fry or boil, use small eggplant as they are of more delicate flavor than the large ones. Do not cook too rapidly.

BROILED EGGPLANT

Slice the eggplant and drain it as for frying; spread the slices on a dish; season with salt and pepper; baste with olive oil; sprinkle with dried breadcrumbs and broil.

EGGPLANT FRIED IN OIL (TURKISH)

Arrange in oiled pan in layers: one layer of sliced eggplant, one layer of chopped meat seasoned with egg, chopped parsley, salt and pepper; as many layers as desired, add a little olive oil, cover with water. Bake at 350° for thirty minutes.

EGGPLANT (ROMANIAN)

Brown onion, peel eggplant raw, cut in quarters, put in when onions are brown with a little water and stew; add salt, white pepper, sour salt, red tomatoes; when half done add ¼ cup of rice, cook until rice is tender.

FRIED EGGPLANT

Pare eggplant, cut in very thin slices. Sprinkle with salt, pile slices on a plate. Cover with a weight to draw out juice; let stand one hour. Dredge with flour and fry slowly in a little butter until crisp and brown, or dip in egg and cracker and fry in deep fat.

GREEN PEAS

Shell the peas and cover them with water; bring to a boil; then push aside until the water will just bubble gently. Keep the lid partly off. When the peas are tender add salt and butter; cook ten minutes longer and serve. If the peas are not the sweet variety, add one teaspoon of sugar.

Original recipe's boiling time may be too long for modern tastes. Cook until the tenderness of the vegetable meets your approval.

SUGAR PEAS

Sugar peas may be cooked in the pods like string beans. Gather the pods while the seeds are still very small; string like beans and cut into pieces. Cover with boiling water and boil gently for thirty minutes or until tender. Pour off most of the water, saving it for soup; season the rest with salt and butter and serve.

Original recipe's boiling time may be too long for modern tastes. Cook until the tenderness of the vegetable meets your approval.

CARROTS AND PEAS

Wash, scrape and cut one pint of carrots in small cubes, cook until tender, drain and reserve one-half cup of carrot water. Mix carrots well with one pint cooked green peas. Sprinkle with two tablespoons of flour, salt, pepper and sugar to taste, add two tablespoons of fat or butter, one-half cup of milk or soup stock and carrot water, boil a little longer and serve.

GREEN PEAS AND EGG BARLEY (PFARVEL)
Make the pfarvel. Heat ¼ cup of butter or other fat, add the pfarvel and when golden brown, add one quart of boiling water, ½ cup sugar, ½ teaspoon of salt, and one can or ½ peck of green peas strained. Set in moderate oven and bake thirty minutes or until every kernel stands out separately. Serve hot.

GREEN PEAS AND RICE
Shell ½ peck of green peas and wash them well; if canned peas are used pour off liquid and rinse with cold water. Heat ¼ cup butter or other fat in a sauce pan, add one cup of rice and let simmer, stirring constantly until rice is a golden brown; add one quart of boiling water, then the drained peas and ½ teaspoon of salt, and ½ cup granulated sugar. Place in pudding dish, set in the 325° oven and bake until rice is tender. (Serve hot.)

GREEN PEPPERS
Sweet green peppers, within the last ten years have gained a place in cookery in this country. Their flavor is depended on for soups. They are used in stews. They are used for salad, and they are used much as a separate vegetable in dozens of different ways.

STUFFED PEPPERS
Select six tender, sweet peppers. Soak in water breadcrumbs sufficient to make one pint when the water is pressed out; mix with ¼ teaspoon basil, herbs and two teaspoons of salt, add two tablespoons of butter. Cut off the stem end of each pepper; carefully remove the interior and fill the peppers with the prepared dressing. Place in a shallow baking pan and pour around them white sauce thinned with two cups of water. Bake at 325° about one hour, basting frequently with the sauce.

PEPPERS STUFFED WITH MEAT
Cut a slice from the blossom end of each pepper, remove seeds and parboil ten minutes. Chop one onion fine and cook in fat until straw color; add ¼ cup cold cooked chicken or veal, and ¼ cup mushrooms; cook two minutes, add ½ cup of water and two tablespoons of breadcrumbs. Cool,

sprinkle peppers with salt and a pinch of red pepper. Fill with stuffing, cover with crumbs and bake at 400° ten minutes.

STUFFED PEPPERS (ARDAY-INFLUS)
Take sweet green peppers, cut off blossom end; prepare the following: To one pound of chopped meat take one egg, grate in one onion, a little salt, mix all together. Place this mixture in the peppers, but do not fill too full. Set the entire top of peppers in place. Melt one tablespoon of fat in a sauce pan, add sliced tomatoes, then the stuffed peppers and ½ cup water; let steam about thirty minutes. Make sweet sour with a little lemon juice, and sugar to taste. Thicken gravy with ½ tablespoon flour, browned with ½ tablespoon oil.

GREEN PEPPERS STUFFED WITH VEGETABLES
Brown large white onions, add ½ cup uncooked rice, a little salt, fill peppers, stew with tomatoes. Or fill peppers with red cabbage which has been steamed with onions and fat, and add moistened rice.

PEPPERS STUFFED WITH NUTS
Another good way to stuff peppers is to parboil them and then stuff them with a forcemeat made of chopped nuts and breadcrumbs moistened with salt and pepper. Bake at 350°, basting occasionally with melted butter for twenty minutes.

STEWED PEPPERS
Cut the peppers in half and remove the seeds and pith. Then cut them in neat, small pieces and throw into boiling salted water. Boil for half an hour. Drain them and then add salt to taste, one tablespoon of butter and four tablespoons of cream - to four peppers. Heat thoroughly and serve.
*Original recipe's boiling time may be too long for modern tastes. Cook until the tenderness of the vegetable meets your approval.

BROILED GREEN PEPPERS
Broil on all sides; place the broiled peppers in a dish of cold water so that the skin can be easily removed. When the peppers are all peeled put in a bowl or crock, add French dressing, and cover closely. These peppers will keep all winter.

RADISHES
There are many varieties of radishes, round and long, black, white, and red. The small red radish may be obtained all year. They are served uncooked, merely for a relish. The large varieties are peeled, sliced and salted for the table. To serve the small ones for table, remove tip end of root, remove the leaves and have only a small piece of stem on radish. They may be made to look like a tulip by cutting into six equal parts from the root end, down three-quarters of the length of the radish.

BROILED MUSHROOMS
Wash the mushrooms; remove the stems and peel the caps. Place them in a broiler for five minutes, with the cap side down during the first half of broiling. Serve on circular pieces of buttered toast, sprinkling with salt and pepper and putting a small piece of butter on each cap.

CREAMED MUSHROOMS
First wash them thoroughly in cold water, peel them and remove the stems, then cut them in halves or quarters, according to their size. Melt one tablespoon of butter in a saucepan over the fire then add the mushrooms and let them simmer slowly in the butter for five minutes; season them well with salt and black pepper, freshly ground. After seasoning, add a ½ cream and while it is heating sift one tablespoon of flour in a bowl, add one cup milk. Stir these briskly until flour is all dissolved, then pour it gradually in the saucepan with the mushrooms and cream, stirring the whole constantly to keep it from lumping. Let it just bubble a moment, then add another tablespoon of butter and pour the creamed mushrooms over hot buttered toast on a hot platter and serve. Cooked like this mushrooms have more nutritive value than beef.

SCALLOPED MUSHROOMS
Sauté mushrooms and prepare two cups of white sauce for one pound of mushrooms, add one teaspoon of onion juice. Into a well-greased baking dish place one-quarter of the mushrooms, then one-quarter of the sauce, and one-quarter of the breadcrumbs, continue in this way until all the sauce is used, pour one cup of cream over this and sprinkle the remaining crumbs over the top. Bake fifteen minutes at 350°, or until the crumbs are browned.

SAUTÉED MUSHROOMS

Wash, peel caps and stems of one pound of mushrooms, drain dry between towels. Place in sauce pan with two tablespoons of butter and ¼ teaspoon of salt. Cover and cook twenty minutes, tossing them. Serve on hot slices of toast.

*Original recipe's cooking time may be too long for modern tastes. Cook until it meets your approval.

BOILED OKRA

Wash and cut off the ends of young pods, cover with boiling salted water and cook about twenty minutes, until tender. Drain, add cream (a scant cup to a quart of okra), a tablespoon of butter, and salt and pepper to taste. Another way of stewing is to cook it with tomatoes. To a pint of okra pods, washed and sliced, allow a dozen ripe tomatoes, peeled and sliced, and one medium-sized onion. Stew slowly for an hour, adding one tablespoon of butter, a scant teaspoon of salt and pepper to season. No water will be required, the tomato juice sufficing. In the West Indies lemon juice and cayenne are also added to stewed okra.

BOILED ONIONS

Peel the onions and cut off the roots; drop each into cold water as soon as it is peeled. When all are ready, drain and put in a saucepan well covered with boiling water, adding a teaspoon of salt for every quart of water. Boil rapidly for ten minutes with the cover partly off; drain and return to the fire with fresh water. Simmer until tender; add pepper and butter and serve, or omit the butter and pepper and pour a cream sauce over the onions.

SPANISH ONION RAREBIT

Boil two large onions until very soft, drain, chop, and return to the sauce pan with a small piece of butter. Add milk, salt, pepper, a dash of Tabasco sauce, one teaspoon of prepared mustard, ½ cup of grated cheese. Stir until of the consistency of custard.

SCALLOPED ONIONS

Cut boiled onions into quarters; put them in a baking dish and mix well with cream sauce; cover with breadcrumbs and bits of butter and place in the oven until the crumbs are browned.

STEWED SQUASH

Peel squash, cut in quarters, put on to boil in cold water, and cook until tender. Drain, mash fine and smooth, add ½ cup of milk or cream, one tablespoon of butter, pinch of salt and pepper, and put back on stove to keep hot. Beat well with a spoon to make light and smooth.

PARSNIPS

First scrape parsnips, then boil in weak salt water until tender; drain, and put in white sauce. Oyster plant [salsify] may be prepared same way.

SPINACH

Spinach with large leaves is best. It is richest in mineral matter and is less liable to conceal insects that are difficult to dislodge. Buy the crisp, green spinach that has no withered leaves or stalks. That is the freshest and healthiest. Cut off the roots and pick it over carefully, cutting off all the withered leaves and stems, put the leaves in cold salt water to soak for half an hour. That refreshens them, and makes any minute insects crawl out and come to the surface. Shake the leaves about and turn them over several times, drop them in a large pan of water; rinse well; lift them out separately and drop back into a second pan of water. Continue washing in fresh water until there is not a grain of sand to be found in the bottom of the pan. In cooking be careful not to put too much water in the pot. That is the trouble with most spinach. It is drowned in water; a cup is plenty for one quart of spinach. Let the water come to a boil. Then lift the spinach out of the pan with the cold water dripping from it and put it into the pot, into the boiling water. Put the lid on the pot. Turn the heat to low and let it cook slowly for fifteen minutes, stirring every now and then to keep it from sticking to the bottom of the pot. Just before taking up the spinach put some salt in it; then drain off the water and put a big tablespoon of butter, and ¼ teaspoon pepper in it. Take it out of the pot and place it in a long, flat dish. slice some hard-boiled eggs and place the slices all around the spinach for a kind of border.

SPINACH WITH CREAM SAUCE
Cook as directed, drain through colander, and grind through machine, make a rich cream sauce. Stir spinach in this sauce, add pepper, salt, nutmeg to taste, and garnish with slices of hard-boiled egg.

SPINACH - FLEISCHIG
Boil a quart of spinach about fifteen minutes, drain thoroughly through a colander and chop extremely fine. Heat one tablespoon of drippings in a saucepan, rub one tablespoon of flour in it, add salt, pepper and ginger to taste. Add one cup of soup stock to the whole or some beef gravy. Put the spinach in the sauce, let boil for five minutes. Garnish with hard-boiled eggs or use only the hard-boiled whites for decoration, rub the yolks to a powder and mix through the spinach.

SAVOY CABBAGE
Cut off the faded outside leaves and hard part of the stalk, and wash the vegetable well. Cook in boiling salted water. Drain, chop very fine and proceed as with spinach in the foregoing recipe.

BRUSSELS SPROUTS
Remove any wilted leaves from the outside of the sprouts, and let them stand in cold salted water from fifteen to twenty minutes. Put the sprouts into salted, rapidly boiling water and cook, uncovered, fifteen or twenty minutes or until tender, but not until they lose their shape. Drain them thoroughly in a colander; then place them in a saucepan with butter, pepper and salt, and toss them until seasoned; or mix them lightly with just enough white sauce to coat them.
*Original recipe's boiling time may be too long for modern tastes. Cook until the tenderness of the vegetable meets your approval.

OYSTER PLANT - SALSIFY
Wash, scrape and put at once in cold water with a little vinegar to keep from discoloring. Cut ½-inch slices and cook in boiling, salted water until soft. Drain and serve in white sauce. Or boil in salted, boiling water until tender and cut in four pieces lengthwise, dredge with flour and sprinkle with a little salt and fry in hot butter or fat until nicely browned.

SCALLOPED SALSIFY

Boil and slice the salsify as in preceding recipe. Butter a baking dish; fill it by adding alternate layers of salsify and small bits of cheese. Season with salt, pepper and butter. Pour over it a sufficient quantity of milk or cream to moisten thoroughly. Bake at 350° for thirty minutes. Breadcrumbs may be added if desired.

PLUMS, SWEET POTATOES AND MEAT

Wash one pound of prunes or plums and put on to boil with one pound of brisket of beef or any fat meat; when the meat is tender add five medium-sized sweet potatoes which have been pared and cut in small pieces. Place the meat on top, add ½ cup sugar, and a splash of lemon juice. Cover and bake at 400° until nicely browned. If gravy should cook away add some warm water.

TSIMESS

Take equal portions of parboiled spinach and sorrel, season to taste with ground nutmeg, pepper and salt, and add sufficient drippings to make all moist enough. Place in a covered oven-safe dish in a 350° oven. This is prepared on Friday and left in the oven to keep hot until needed for Shabbas dinner. All green vegetables may be prepared in the same way.

TURNIPS

Do not spoil turnips by overcooking. The flat white summer turnip when sliced will cook in thirty minutes. The winter turnip requires from forty-five to sixty minutes.

BOILED TURNIPS

Have the turnips peeled and sliced. Drop the slices into a pan with boiling water enough to cover generously. Cook until tender, then drain well. They are now ready to mash or chop. If they are to be served mashed, put them back in the pan; mash with a wooden vegetable masher, as metal is apt to impart an unpleasant taste. Season with salt, butter, and a little pepper. Serve at once.

HASHED TURNIPS

Chop the drained turnips into rather large pieces. Return to the pan, and for 1½ pints of turnips add one teaspoon of salt, ¼ teaspoon of pepper, one tablespoon of butter, and four tablespoons of water. Cook over a very hot burner until the turnips have absorbed all the seasonings. Serve at once. Or the salt, pepper, butter, and one tablespoon of flour may be added to the hashed turnips; then the pan may be placed over the hot fire and shaken frequently to toss up the turnips. When the turnips have been cooking five minutes in this manner add one cup of meat stock or of milk and cook ten minutes. When meat or soup stock is used substitute drippings for the butter in the above recipe.

KOHL-RABI WITH BREAST OF LAMB

Strip off the young leaves and boil in salt water. Then peel the heads thickly, cut into round, thin slices, and lay in cold water for an hour. Put on to boil a breast of mutton or lamb, which has been previously well salted, and spice with a little ground ginger. When the mutton has boiled thirty minutes add the sliced kohl-rabi, and boil covered. In the meantime, drain all the water from the leaves, which you have boiled separately, and chop them, but not too fine, and add them to the mutton. When done thicken with flour, season with pepper and more salt if needed.

KOHL-RABI

Kohl-rabi is fine flavored and delicate, if cooked when very young and tender. It should be used when it has a diameter of not more than two or three inches. Wash, peel and cut the kohl-rabi root in dice and cook in salt water until tender. Cook the greens or tops in another pan of boiling water until tender, drain and chop very fine in a wooden bowl. Heat butter or fat, add flour, then the chopped greens, and one cup of liquor the kohl-rabi root was cooked in or one cup of soup stock. Add the kohl-rabi, cook altogether, and serve. Use same quantities as for turnips.

KALE

Remove all the old or tough leaves; wash the kale thoroughly and drain. Put it into boiling water to which has been added salt in the proportion of ½ tablespoon to two quarts of water. Boil rapidly, uncovered, until the

vegetable is tender; pour off the water; chop the kale very fine; return it to the kettle with one tablespoon of drippings and two of meat stock or water to every pint of the minced vegetable. Add more salt if necessary; cook for ten minutes and serve at once. The entire time for cooking varies from thirty to fifty minutes. The leaves are sweeter and more tender after having been touched by the frost. The same is true of Savoy cabbage.
Original recipe's boiling time may be too long for modern tastes. Cook until the tenderness of the vegetable meets your approval.

SWISS CHARD
This vegetable is a variety of beet in which the leaf stalk and mid rib have been developed instead of the root. It is cultivated like spinach, and the green, tender leaves are prepared exactly like this vegetable. The midribs of the full-grown leaves may be cooked like celery.

STEWED TOMATOES
Pour boiling water over the tomatoes; remove the skins; cut into small pieces and place in a saucepan over the fire. Boil gently for twenty or thirty minutes and season, allowing for each quart of tomatoes one generous teaspoon each of salt and sugar and one tablespoon of butter. If in addition to this seasoning a slice of onion has been cooked with the tomatoes from the beginning, the flavor will be greatly improved.

CANNED TOMATOES, STEWED
Salt, pepper; add a lump of butter the size of an egg and add one tablespoon of sugar. Thicken with one teaspoon of flour wet with one tablespoon of cold water, stir into the tomatoes and boil up once.

FRIED TOMATOES
Cut large, sound tomatoes in halves and flour the insides thickly. Season with a little salt and pepper. Allow a pan with butter to get very hot before putting in the tomatoes. When brown on one side, turn, and when done serve with hot cream or thicken some milk and pour over the tomatoes hot.

FRIED GREEN TOMATOES
Cut into thin slices large green tomatoes, sprinkle with salt and dip into cornmeal, fry slowly in a little butter until well browned; keep the frying pan covered while they are cooking, so they will be perfectly tender. These are very delicately flavored, and much easier to fry than ripe tomatoes. They make an excellent breakfast dish.

TOMATO PURÉE
Scald the tomatoes, take off the skins carefully and stew with one teaspoon each of butter and sugar; salt and pepper to taste. This is enough seasoning for a quart of tomatoes. When the tomatoes are very soft strain through a coarse sieve and if necessary thicken with one teaspoon of flour.

SCALLOPED TOMATOES
Drain off part of the juice from one quart of tomatoes and season with pepper, salt, and onion juice. Cover the bottom of a baking dish with rolled crackers, dot over with dabs of butter, pepper, and salt, then another layer of tomatoes, then of crumbs, and so on until a layer of crumbs covers the top. If fresh tomatoes are used bake at 350° one hour, if canned, thirty minutes. If the crumbs begin to brown too quickly cover the dish with a tin plate.

STUFFED TOMATOES
Select tomatoes of uniform size, cut a slice from the stem end and scoop out a portion of the pulp. Have in readiness a dressing made from grated breadcrumbs, parsley, a slice of minced onion, a high seasoning of salt and paprika and sufficient melted butter to moisten. Fill this into the tomatoes and heap it up in the centers. Place a bit of butter on top of each and bake in a 425° oven until the vegetables are tender and the tops are delicately browned.

TOMATOES WITH RICE
Take six large tomatoes, pour boiling water over them and skin them. Scrape all the inside out with a spoon, put in sauce pan together with two onions, a tablespoon of butter, 2 cups water; let this boil for a little while; strain, place on low heat, pour into this 1 cup of rice, let it cook tender;

add salt, pepper, a tablespoon of butter and a little grated cheese. Fill the tomatoes with this mixture, dip them in egg and breadcrumbs, then fry until nice and brown.

TOMATO CUSTARDS
Simmer for fifteen minutes in a covered sauce pan, four cups chopped tomatoes, four eggs, one sliced onion, one bay leaf, and sprig of parsley. Strain and if there be not two cups of liquid, add water. Beat four eggs and add to liquid. Pour into greased baking cups and stand them in a pan of water and bake until firm - about fifteen minutes. Turn out and serve with cream sauce containing green peas.

BAKED TOMATO AND EGG PLANT
Take a deep oven-safe dish, pour into it a cup of cream; cut several slices of eggplant very thin, salt well, and line the dish with them; slice two large tomatoes, place a layer of these on the eggplant, next a layer of spaghetti (cooked); sprinkle with grated cheese, pieces of butter, salt, and pepper; cover this with layer of tomatoes; salt well and sprinkle with chopped green pepper, and a top layer of eggplant, which also salt and pepper well. Bake for an hour and a half in 325° oven.

CREOLE TOMATOES
Take one small onion and half a green pepper, chop them fine and cook until tender in a tablespoon of butter. Cut six tomatoes in half, sprinkle with a little sugar, season on both sides with salt, pepper and a little flour, and put them into the pan with skin-side down to cook partially, then turn them once; they must cook over a slow fire. Then sprinkle one tablespoon of chopped parsley over them, pour in one cup of thick cream and when this has become thoroughly hot, and has been combined with the other ingredients, the tomatoes are ready to serve. They have not been disturbed since the first turning, and have retained their shape. Half a tomato is placed on a slice of toast, with sufficient gravy to moisten. At the season of the year, when tomatoes are hard and firm, they may be peeled before cooking. Later they will likely fall to pieces unless the skin is left on. This is one method of cooking tomatoes in which they lose the sharp acid taste, disagreeable to so many persons.

STRING BEANS WITH TOMATOES

Cut off both ends of the beans, string them carefully and break into pieces about an inch in length and boil in salt water. When tender drain off this brine and add fresh water (boiling from the kettle). Add a piece of butter, three or four large potatoes cut into squares, also four large tomatoes, cut up, and season with salt and pepper. Melt one tablespoon of butter in a sauce pan, stir into it one tablespoon of flour, thin with milk, and add this to the beans.

STRING BEANS WITH LAMB

Take a small breast of lamb, two large onions, one-quarter peck of beans (string and cut in long thin pieces); skin six large tomatoes, and add two cups of water. Cook until the beans are tender, then add one tablespoon of flour to thicken.

STRING OR WAX-BEANS, SWEET AND SOUR

Put the beans into sufficient boiling water to just cover them; cook for one hour and a half to two hours, depending upon the tenderness of the beans. Meanwhile, prepare for each quart of beans five sour apples; peel, core and cut in pieces. When the beans are done, add the apples, the thin peel of one lemon, the juice of one and one-half lemons, a small teaspoon of salt, and two tablespoons of cider vinegar. Let the apples cook on top of the beans until they are thoroughly done, then mix well with a good quarter cup of granulated sugar. This dish will be better by being served the next day warmed up

SWEET SOUR BEANS

If you use canned string beans, heat some fat in a sauce pan and put in one tablespoon of flour; brown slightly; add one tablespoon of brown sugar, a pinch of salt, some cinnamon and vinegar to taste; then add the beans and let them simmer on the back of stove, but do not let them burn. The juice of pickled peaches or pears is delicious in preparing sweet and sour beans.

STRING OR GREEN SNAP BEANS

Cut off the tops and bottoms carefully; break the beans in pieces about an inch long and lay them in cold water, with a little salt, for ten or fifteen minutes. Heat one tablespoon of drippings in a pan, in which you have cut up part of an onion and some parsley; cover this and cook about ten minutes. In the meantime, drain the beans, put into the pan with salt and pepper (meat gravy or soup stock will improve them). You may pare about six potatoes, cut into dice shape, and add to the beans. If you prefer, you may add cream or milk instead of soup stock and use butter.

POTATOES

Potatoes are valuable articles of food and care should be taken in cooking them. The most economical method is to cook them in their "jackets" as there is not nearly as much waste of potato or of the salts that are valuable as food.

POTATOES BOILED IN THEIR JACKETS
Potatoes should be well brushed and put on to boil in a pot of boiling water; they should continue boiling at the same degree of heat until they are done, when a fork will easily pierce them. This may take from twenty-five to thirty minutes. Drain, draw the pot to low heat, place a clean cloth folded over the top of the saucepan and press the lid down over it. This dries the potatoes and makes them a good color. Hold the potatoes in a cloth and peel them, then reheat for one minute and serve. New potatoes, if well brushed or scraped do not require peeling.

POTATOES FOR TWENTY PEOPLE
To serve twenty people one-half peck of potatoes is required.

BOILED POTATOES
Peel six or eight potatoes, and put them on in boiling water to which has been added one teaspoon of salt. Boil as above.

BAKED POTATOES, No. 1
Select fine, smooth potatoes and boil them about twenty minutes. Drain off the water, remove the skins and pack in a buttered dish. Lay a small piece of butter on each potato, sprinkle with salt and pepper, and sprinkle fine breadcrumbs over all, with a few tablespoons of cream. Bake in a 425° oven until a nice light brown. Serve in the same dish. Garnish with parsley.

BAKED POTATOES, No. 2
Wash large potatoes and bake in a 425° oven until soft, which will take about forty-five minutes. This is the most wholesome way of cooking potatoes.

POTATO BALLS WITH PARSLEY
Pare very thin, medium potatoes as near a size as possible. Have ready a pot of boiling water, salted, drop in the potatoes and keep them at a quick boil until tender. Serve with a batter made by beating to a cream two tablespoons of butter, ½ tablespoon of lemon juice, and one tablespoon of finely minced parsley; add salt and a dash of cayenne pepper; spread over the hot potatoes, and it will melt into a delicious dressing. This is especially nice to serve with fish.

NEW POTATOES
Brush and scrape off all the skin of six potatoes and boil for thirty minutes in salted boiling water, drain, salt and dry for a few minutes, and then pour melted butter over them and sprinkle with chopped parsley.

MASHED POTATOES
Pare as many potatoes as required. Boil in salt water, drain thoroughly when done and mash them in the pot with a potato masher, working in a large tablespoon of butter and enough milk to make them resemble dough, do not allow any lumps to form in your dish. Garnish with parsley.

SCALLOPED POTATOES, No. 1
Grease a pan with butter. Choose the potatoes that are so big or misshapen you wouldn't want to use them for boiling or baking. Cut them in thin slices. Spread them in the pan in a layer an inch thick. Sprinkle with pepper and salt to taste. Dot with butter here and there, perhaps a half teaspoon for each layer. Four or six bits of butter should be sprinkled over each layer. Repeat the layers of the raw potatoes until the pan is full. Cover them with milk. Place in a 325° oven and bake for one hour.

SCALLOPED POTATOES, No. 2
Cut two cups of cold boiled potatoes into cubes; mix well with two cups of cream sauce, adding more seasoning if necessary; pour into a baking dish; cover with one cup of breadcrumbs and dot with small pieces of butter and bake at 400° for about half an hour.

CREAMED POTATOES
Make a cream sauce, a little thinner than usual by adding a little extra milk. Cut two cups of boiled potatoes into small cubes and mix them thoroughly with the same. Cook in a double-boiler until the potatoes are thoroughly hot, add a little chopped parsley if desired, and serve.

POTATOES *AU GRATIN*
Slice two cups of cold boiled potatoes and add them to two cups of hot cream sauce. Bring all to a boil; remove and add three tablespoons of grated cheese, salt and pepper to taste. Pour all into a baking dish, sprinkle buttered breadcrumbs over the top and set a 400° oven to brown.

GERMAN FRIED POTATOES
Cut up some raw potatoes quite thin, salt and pepper and drop in boiling fat. Cover up at first to soften them. Turn frequently to prevent burning and then remove the cover to brown slightly.

SARATOGA CHIPS
Proceed as above; but do not cover and do not take as many potatoes at one time.

HASHED BROWN POTATOES, LYONNAISE
Finely hash up six cold boiled potatoes and keep on a plate. Heat one tablespoon of butter in a fryingpan, add a finely chopped onion, and lightly brown for three minutes, then add the potatoes. Season with ½ teaspoon of salt, and ½ teaspoon of white pepper, evenly sprinkled over, then nicely brown them for ten minutes, occasionally tossing them meanwhile. Give them a nice omelet form, brown for a few minutes more, sprinkle a little freshly chopped parsley over and serve. These potatoes may be prepared with fat in place of butter.

CURRIED POTATOES
Melt two tablespoons of fat in a frying pan; add one onion chopped fine and cook until straw color. Add two cups of boiled potatoes, cut in dice, ½ cup of stock, and one tablespoon of curry powder. Cook until the stock has been absorbed; then add ½ teaspoon salt, a dash of red pepper, and one teaspoon of lemon juice.

POTATO CAKES

Take cold mashed potatoes, or cold baked or boiled potatoes, that have been mashed and seasoned; roll into balls, dusting the hands well with flour first. Flatten into cakes and sauté in butter, or place on a buttered baking sheet with a small piece of butter on top of each and bake in a 400° oven until golden brown.

POTATOES AND CORN

Butter well a deep baking dish, holding a quart or more. In the bottom place a layer of pre-cooked cold potatoes, sliced thin, then a layer of corn, using half of the contents of a can. On this sprinkle a little grated onion and season with salt, pepper and bits of butter. Add another layer of potatoes, then the rest of the corn, seasoning as before, and cover the whole with a layer of cracker crumbs. Dot well with butter, pour on milk until it comes to the top, and bake 350°.

FRENCH FRIED POTATOES

Pare the potatoes and place them into cold water until needed. Dry them with a towel; cut into small pieces lengthwise of the potato; drop them into hot fat and remove when lightly browned. It is better to fry only a few at a time, letting those done stand in a colander in the oven to keep hot. When all are done, sprinkle with salt and serve at once. For variety, and for use in garnishing, cut the potatoes into balls, using the vegetable cutter which comes for this purpose.

POTATOES WITH CARAWAY SEEDS

Boil medium-sized potatoes in their jackets until tender, peel while hot. Put two tablespoons of butter or fat in sauce pan, when hot add potatoes, brown well all over. Drain, sprinkle with salt and one teaspoon of caraway seeds and serve hot.

POTATOES AND PEARS

Heat two tablespoons of fat, add chopped onion and two tablespoons of flour; when flour is brown, add 1½ cups of water, stir and cook until smooth, add salt, brown sugar and a little cinnamon to taste. Quarter four medium-sized cooking pears, but do not peel, cook them in the brown sauce, then add six medium, raw potatoes, pared, and cook until tender.

POTATO RIBBON

Pare and lay in cold water (ice water is best) for half an hour. Select the largest potatoes, then cut round and round in one continuous curl-like strip (there is also an instrument for this purpose, which costs but a trifle); handle with care and fry a few at a time for fear of entanglement, in deep fat.

STEWED POTATOES WITH ONIONS

Take small potatoes, pare and wash them very clean, use one onion to about ten potatoes, add goose fat (in fact any kind of drippings from roast meat will answer) and put them in a pot or sauce pan. When hot cut up an onion very fine and add to the boiling fat. Then add the potatoes. Salt and pepper to taste. Pour some water over all, cover up tight and let them simmer for about forty-five minutes.

STEWED POTATOES, SOUR

Put a tablespoon of drippings in a kettle, and when it is hot cut up an onion fine and fry in the hot fat, cover closely. Put in potatoes, which have been previously pared, washed, quartered and well-salted. Cover them tight and stew slowly until soft, stirring them occasionally. Then heat in a sauce pan a little drippings. Brown in this a spoon of flour and add some soup stock, vinegar and chopped parsley. Pour this over the potatoes, boil up once and serve.

STEWED POTATOES

Pare and quarter, and put on to boil. When almost done drain off the water, add one cup of milk, one tablespoon of butter, a little chopped parsley and cook a while longer. Thicken with a little flour (wet with cold water or milk) stir, and take from the stove.

STUFFED POTATOES

Take as many potatoes as are needed; when done, cut off one end and take out inside; mash this and mix with it one tablespoon of butter, a sprig of parsley, pepper, salt, and enough milk to make quite soft. Put back in the potato skins and brown in 400° oven and serve very hot. If so desired the open end of each may be dipped in beaten egg before being put in oven.

BOHEMIAN POTATO PUFF

Pare, wash and boil potatoes until soft enough to mash well. Drain off nearly all the water, leaving just a little; add one teaspoon of salt, and return to the stove. It is better to boil the potatoes in salt water and add more salt if necessary after mashing. Sift ½ cup of flour into the potatoes after returning to the stove and keep covered closely for about five minutes. Then remove from the stove and mash them as hard as you can, so as not to have any lumps. They must be of the consistency of dough and smooth as velvet. Now put about two tablespoons of drippings or goose fat in a sauce pan, chop up some onions very fine, and heat them until they become a light brown, take a tablespoon and dip it in the hot fat and then cut a spoonful of the potato dough with the same spoon and put it in the sauce pan, and so on until you have used all. Be careful to dip your spoon in the hot fat every time you cut a puff. Let them brown slightly.

POTATOES (HUNGARIAN)

Wash, pare and cut potatoes in ½ inch pieces, there should be three cups; parboil three minutes, and drain. Add ⅓ cup butter, and cook on medium-low heat until potatoes are soft. Melt two tablespoons of butter, add a few drops of onion juice, two tablespoons of flour, and pour on gradually one cup of hot milk, season with salt and paprika, then add one well-beaten egg yolk. Pour sauce over potatoes and sprinkle with finely chopped parsley.

POTATO PUFF

Take two cups of cold mashed potatoes, and stir into them one tablespoon of melted butter, beating to a white cream before adding anything else. Then put with this two eggs beaten extremely light, one cup of cream, and salt to taste. Beat all well and pour into a deep oven-safe dish, and bake in a 400° oven until it is nice and brown. If properly mixed, it will come out of the oven light, puffy, and delectable.

POTATO SURPRISE

Take large potatoes, parboil without peeling, cut a small piece of one end of the potato and scoop out the inside. Mince two ounces cooked mutton, season with pepper and salt, mix with the potato pulp and a little gravy. Return end of potato to its place and bake in a 400° oven for about twenty minutes with a little fat on top of each potato.

BOILED SWEET POTATOES
Put on in boiling water, without any salt, and boil until a fork will easily pierce the largest. Drain off the water and dry.

FRIED SWEET POTATOES
Boil, peel and cut lengthwise into slices a quarter of an inch thick. Fry in sweet drippings or butter (cold boiled potatoes may also be fried in this way).

FRENCH FRIED SWEET POTATOES
Wash and cut small uncooked sweet potatoes into quarters; dry them and lower them into boiling hot fat. Brown thoroughly; remove with a skimmer; drain and dry on paper; sprinkle with salt and serve.

ROAST SWEET POTATOES
These are commonly called baked sweet potatoes. Select those of uniform size; wash, and roast in the 375° oven until done, which you can easily tell by pressing the potatoes. If done they will leave an impression when touched. It usually requires half an hour. Serve in their jackets.

SWEET POTATOES AND APPLES
Wash and pare long sweet potatoes. Cook in boiling salted water until almost soft; drain and cut slices crosswise, two inches high. Core, pare and cut apples in ½ inch rounds. Into a sauce pan, place the potatoes upright, with a slice of apple on top of each. Pour over ½ cup of maple syrup, ¼ cup of water and two tablespoons of butter. Baste frequently until apples are soft. Then pour one teaspoon of rum over each section, place a candied cherry in the center of each apple and bake ten minutes. Remove to platter and if desired, pour more rum over and around. Light the liquor and bring to the table burning.

CANDIED SWEET POTATOES
Boil sweet potatoes, peel and cut into long slices; place in an oven-safe dish; place lumps of butter or chicken fat if desired on each side, and sprinkle with sugar. A little water or juice of half a lemon may be added. Bake at 400° until the sugar and fat have candied and the potatoes are brown.

SWEET SOUR BEANS AND LINZEN
Soak overnight and drain the beans, boil in salted water until tender; drain and prepare by adding salt and pepper to taste, thicken with one tablespoon of drippings in which has been browned one tablespoon of flour and some soup stock. If the beans are to be made sweet sour add two tablespoons of vinegar and two tablespoons of brown sugar; boil for a few minutes and serve.

BAKED BEANS WITH BRISKET OF BEEF
Wash, pick over and soak overnight in cold water, two cups of navy beans. In the morning, drain and cover with fresh water, heat slowly and let cook just below the boiling point until the skins burst. When done, drain beans and put in a oven-safe baking dish with 1½ pounds of brisket of beef. Mix ½ tablespoon of mustard, one teaspoon of salt, one tablespoon of molasses, two tablespoons of sugar, ½ cup boiling water, and pour over beans, and add enough more boiling water to cover them. Cover dish and bake at 300° slowly six hours.

HARICOT BEANS AND BEEF
Wash two cups of haricot beans and leave them covered with two pints of water overnight. Next day brown one coarsely chopped onion in a little fat and put it with the beans and their water into a casserole. In a 325° oven, cook closely covered for one hour, then put in a pound of beef in fairly large pieces. An hour later, add one carrot cut into dice, half as many dice of turnip, and salt and pepper to taste. Continue the slow cooking until these vegetables are tender, and a few minutes before serving thicken the stew with pea meal or flour previously baked to a fawn color. Flavor with vinegar.

BEANS AND BARLEY
Soak ½ cup of navy beans in cold water overnight. Drain and cook in one quart boiling water with one teaspoon of salt, until tender but not broken, add ½ cup barley and let cook slowly until barley is tender, about thirty minutes. Add fat soup stock as the water evaporates. Season to taste and bake in 350° oven about thirty minutes or until dry, but not browned.

DRIED LIMA BEANS, BAKED

Wash one pound of dried lima beans, let soak overnight. Drain, add fresh water, bring quickly to the boiling point, then let simmer until tender. Add salt and paprika. Heat two tablespoons of poultry or beef fat in a sauce pan, add two tablespoons of flour, when brown add one cup of bean liquid, and the beans. Let simmer and bake at 325° in casserole for thirty minutes. Reserve the bean broth and add more if necessary.

FARSOLE

Soak dry lima beans overnight. To a pound of beans take two large onions. When the beans are soft add the onions browned in fat, salt, pepper, a tablespoon of sugar, a quarter cup of rice, and let all simmer until the rice is done.

FARSOLE DULCE

Soak dried lima beans in cold water overnight. Drain, put on with very little water, add one tablespoon of fat, peel of lemon or orange. When beans are half done, add a tablespoon of sugar which has been browned in a pan, stew slowly until the beans are tender.

SLAITTA (ROMANIAN)

Soak one pound medium-sized white beans overnight. Put on to boil in cold water, when soft, mash, adding a little warm water while mashing. Add salt and mashed garlic to beans and one or two teaspoons of sugar. To a pound of beans take a pound of onions. Brown the onions in oil and add water so they do not become too brown or greasy. When beans are tender serve on platter with browned onions poured over them. May be served either hot or cold. This dish is served with Carnatzlich. (See Meats.)

BAKED LENTILS (LINZEN)

Pick and wash ½ pound of lentils and soak them in cold water overnight. In the morning put them in a large saucepan with about a quart of water. As soon as the water begins to boil, the lentils will rise to the top. Remove them with a skimmer, put them in a baking dish with one small onion and three or four ounces of smoked fat meat in the center, and pour over them 2 cups of boiling water, in which ½ teaspoon of salt, and ¼ teaspoon pepper have been mixed. Bake in a 300° oven four or five hours. The lentils must be kept moist and it may be necessary to add a little water from time to time.

VEGAN DISHES

The following recipes can readily be substituted for meat at a meal.

LENTIL SAUSAGES
For each person soak one tablespoon of lentils overnight. Then drain and leave them spread on a dish for a day. When ready to use, chop them finely and cook gently in a pot with a littel water for about one hour, adding from time to time just as much water as they will absorb. When fully cooked, stir in about twice their bulk in breadcrumbs (preferably whole wheat), a slight flavoring of very finely chopped onion, powdered mixed herbs and nutmeg, salt and pepper to taste, and drippings to make the whole fairly moist. When cool, shape into sausages (or cutlets or round cakes), coat them with egg and breadcrumbs or seasoned flour, and brown them in a little fat in a frying pan or in a fairly hot oven. A sauce could be served with them. They are no less good when fried overnight and reheated in the gravy.

MOCK CHILE CON CARNE
Pick over and wash two cups of kidney beans, soak in one quart of water. Next morning bring to a boil in fresh water, drain, cover beans with boiling water and cook until tender. Half an hour before beans are to be served, put one tablespoon of butter in a sauce pan, chop and add four green peppers, one small red pepper, one onion, one pint of tomatoes, one teaspoon of salt, cook fifteen minutes, add to beans with three tablespoons of uncooked rice, simmer until thick.

SPANISH BEANS
Soak two cups of beans overnight. Drain and boil until the skin cracks, and let one cup of water remain on the beans. Chop fine one onion and two cloves of garlic and fry a light brown in one tablespoon of olive oil; then add ½ can of tomatoes, one teaspoon chili powder dissolved in a little cold water, salt to taste, and six olives chopped.

PEA PURÉE
Pick over and wash two cups of dried peas. Soak them overnight or for

several hours in cold water. Put them on to boil in three pints of fresh, cold water and let them simmer until dissolved. Keep well scraped from the sides of the kettle. When soft, rub through a strainer, add a little boiling water or soup stock, add 1½ teaspoons salt, ½ teaspoon sugar, and a speck of white pepper, and beat the mixture well. In a sauce pan, add a little olive oil, add a large onion cut in dice, and cook until a light yellow, and continue cooking until brown. Serve the purée like mashed potatoes. Pour the onion and oil over it before serving. Serve hot.

KIDNEY BEANS WITH BROWN SAUCE

Pick over and wash two cups of kidney beans, let soak overnight in cold water. Drain and cook in fresh salted water until tender. Drain; shake in sauce pan with one teaspoon butter three minutes. Add one cup of brown sauce and simmer five minutes.

BOILED CHESTNUTS

Boil the chestnuts a few minutes; drain and remove the shells and skins. Boil again until tender, adding sufficient salt to make them palatable. Drain again; shake over the burner until dry; cover with cream sauce and serve at once. If allowed to stand the chestnuts become heavy and unappetizing.

CHESTNUT PURÉE

Put one pound of chestnuts, which have been shelled and skinned, on to boil in two cups of milk and cook until tender, then mash smooth. If necessary add more milk while boiling. Strain and season with salt and pepper and one teaspoon of fresh butter. Serve hot.

PAN-ROASTED CHESTNUTS

Lay each chestnut on the flat side, and with a hammer hit each hard enough to break the shell; put them in a sauté pan and shake constantly over a hot burner for a few minutes to pan-roast them. Serve at once.

CHESTNUTS WITH CELERY (TURKISH)

Clean and cut table celery and some celery root. Take roasted chestnuts, season with two tablespoons of olive oil; put on to boil with the celery and one tablespoon of lemon juice; boil all until celery is tender, season with salt and pepper and serve hot.

CHESTNUTS AND PRUNES

Peel 2 cups chestnuts and skin, then boil until tender. Boil 2 cups of prunes until tender. Mix chestnuts and prunes together, leaving whatever of sauce there is on the prunes. Season with sugar, cinnamon, and lemon juice, and cook all together.

CHESTNUTS AND RAISINS

Remove the outer shells from one quart of chestnuts. Then pour boiling water over them and remove the skins; put in cold water for thirty minutes, then drain and put on in a boiler with cold water and boil until tender. Do not add any salt as it toughens them. In another boiler put one cup of raisins which have been stemmed and cleaned, cover with cold water, add two bay leaves and some stick cinnamon; boil until tender, then pour them into the boiler containing the chestnuts. Add a pinch of salt, and one teaspoon of butter and continue until chestnuts are done, then add two tablespoons of white wine, two tablespoons of sugar, ½ teaspoon of vinegar, and thicken with one tablespoon of flour dissolved in water. More sugar or vinegar may be added to suit taste. Boil a few minutes, then serve.

BOSTON ROAST

Mash one pound of cooked kidney beans and put them through a food chopper, add ½ pound of grated cheese (or vegan cheese), salt, and red pepper to taste and sufficient breadcrumbs to make the mixture stiff enough to form into a ball. Bake in a 350° oven, basting occasionally with butter and water. Serve with tomato sauce.

NUT LOAF

Mix two cups of soft breadcrumbs and one cup of chopped walnut meats with six tablespoons of butter or any butter substitute, ½ cup of hot water, 1½ teaspoons of salt, ¼ teaspoon of pepper, one tablespoon of chopped onion, a sprig of parsley chopped, and bind with one egg; shape into a loaf. Place in a greased baking dish and bake in a 350° oven one hour. As the liquor boils out of the loaf it may be used for basting. A brown sauce may be made in the dish in which the loaf is cooked.

NUT ROAST

Soak ½ cup of lentils overnight; in the morning drain, cover with fresh water and bring to a boil. Drain again, put in fresh water and cook until tender. Drain once more, throw away the water, and press the lentils through a colander. To them add ½ cup shelled roasted peanuts - either ground or chopped, ½ cup of toasted breadcrumbs, ½ teaspoon of salt, and ¼ of a teaspoon of pepper, and milk sufficient to make the mixture the consistency of mush. Put into a greased baking dish; bake in a 350° oven for an hour; turn out on a heated platter; garnish with parsley or watercress and serve.

VEGETABLE "MEAT" PIE

Soak ½ cup of dry lima beans overnight; in the morning let them boil rapidly for thirty minutes. Drain. Blanch ¼ cup of almonds, and chop them with ¼ cup of peanuts. Boil four potatoes, and when done cut two of them into small cubes. Mash the remaining two and use them for a dough, adding four tablespoons of hot milk, a little salt and ¼ cup of flour. Put a layer of beans in the bottom of the baking dish, a sprinkling of nuts, a little hard-boiled egg, then the potato blocks, and ½ tablespoon each of chopped parsley and chopped onion, ½ teaspoon of salt and ¼ of a teaspoon of pepper and so on until the material is all used. Roll out the potato dough the size of the baking dish; put it over the dish, brush with milk and bake thirty minutes in a 350° oven.

SALADS AND SALAD DRESSINGS

Salads are divided into two groups, dinner salads and the more substantial ones served at supper and luncheon in the place of meats. They are exceedingly wholesome. Nearly all the meats, vegetables, and fruits may be served as salads. The essential thing is to have the salad fresh and cold; and if green, to have the leaves crisp and dry. Lettuce, Romaine, endive and chicory or escarole make the best dinner salads, although one may use mixed cooked vegetables or well-prepared uncooked cabbage. Leftover green vegetables, string beans, peas, carrots, turnips, cauliflower, cooked spinach, leeks and beets may all take their place in the dinner salad. Use them mixed, alone, or as a garnish for lettuce. Lettuce and all green, raw salad vegetables should be washed and soaked in cold water as soon as they come from the market. After they have stood fifteen to twenty minutes in cold or ice water, free them from moisture by swinging them in a wire basket, or dry, without bruising, each leaf carefully with a napkin. Put them in a cheesecloth bag and on the ice, ready for service. In this way they will remain dry and cold, and will keep nicely for a week. The dressing is added only at the moment of serving, as the salad wilts if allowed to stand after the dressing is added. Meat of any kind used for salads should be cut into dice, but not smaller than one-half inch, or it will seem like hash. It should be marinated before being mixed with the other parts of the salad. Meat mixtures are usually piled in cone-shape on a dish, the mayonnaise then spread over it, and garnished with lettuce, capers, hard-boiled eggs, gherkins, etc.

To Marinate
Take one part oil and three parts vinegar, with pepper and salt to taste; stir them into the meat, and let it stand a couple of hours; drain off any of the marinade which has not been absorbed before combining the meat with the other parts of the salad. Use only enough marinade to season the meat or fish. If too much vinegar is added to mayonnaise it robs it of its consistency and flavor. All salads must be mixed at the last minute, at serving time.Mayonnaise dressing may be made hours before and the meat, lettuce and celery prepared, but each must be kept in a separate dish until mixing time.

SALAD DRESSINGS

MAYONNAISE DRESSING
Beat the yolk of one egg in a cold dish with a silver or wooden fork. If the weather is very warm, place the bowl in a larger vessel filled with chopped ice. When the egg is beaten add ½ teaspoon of salt, dash of red pepper, ½ teaspoon of dry mustard, and olive oil, drop by drop, being careful to beat well without reversing the motion for fear of curdling. When the dressing thickens, begin adding the vinegar or lemon juice, drop by drop. Then add more olive oil, then more acid, continuing until one cup of olive oil and two teaspoons of vinegar or lemon juice are all used. Be sure to have all the ingredients and dishes as cold as possible. If the mixture should curdle, begin immediately with a fresh egg in a fresh dish and when it is well beaten add carefully the curdled mixture, drop by drop. To serve twenty people one pint of mayonnaise is required.

MAYONNAISE WITH WHIPPED CREAM
When you are in want of a large quantity of dressing, mayonnaise or French, add one pint of whipped cream to your prepared dressing, stirring thoroughly, just before ready to serve.

COLORED MAYONNAISE
To color mayonnaise, chop parsley leaves very fine; pound them in a small quantity of lemon juice; strain and add the juice to the dressing.

WHITE MAYONNAISE
To make white mayonnaise, follow the ordinary directions, using lemon juice instead of vinegar, omitting the mustard and adding, when finished, ½ cup of whipped cream or half an egg white beaten very stiff.

RUSSIAN DRESSING
Make 2 cups of mayonnaise dressing and add to it the following: Two hard-boiled eggs chopped fine, two to four tablespoons of tomato catsup, one tablespoon of finely chopped parsley, one teaspoon of finely chopped or grated white onion or shallot, after these ingredients are mixed, fold them into one cup of mayonnaise and serve. Enough for ten people.

BOILED DRESSING WITH OLIVE OIL (PARVE)
Beat three whole eggs until very light, add two tablespoons of olive oil, stirring constantly, add a good pinch of salt, pepper, mustard and cayenne pepper. Heat ½ cup of vinegar with one teaspoon of sugar in it, stir while hot into the eggs and put it back on the stove in a double boiler or over hot water in another saucepan and stir until thick. Serve cold.

MUSTARD DRESSING
Take yolk of one hard-boiled egg and rub smooth in a bowl. Add two teaspoons of prepared mustard, salt, pepper, and little sugar. Add a little oil, and then a little vinegar. Garnish top with the white, cut in pieces.

SOUR CREAM DRESSING
Mix one cup of sour cream and three eggs, well beaten. Dissolve two tablespoons of sugar and one tablespoon of mustard in ½ cup vinegar; salt, pepper and paprika to taste, and then stir this slowly into the cream and eggs. Put in double boiler, cook until thick, then add butter the size of an egg and cook about five minutes longer.

BOILED DRESSING
Mix one teaspoon of salt, one tablespoon of mustard, one tablespoon of sugar, one tablespoon of flour and a few grains of cayenne. Beat three eggs until lemon-colored, and add the dry ingredients with ½ cup vinegar and two tablespoons of melted butter. Cook over boiling water until thick; strain, add ½ cup of cream or milk. Beat until smooth, and cool.

FRENCH DRESSING
Mix ½ teaspoon of salt, ¼ teaspoon of pepper, one teaspoon of sugar, a dash of paprika, two tablespoons of vinegar and four tablespoons of olive oil. Stir until well blended and use at once.

DRESSING FOR LETTUCE
Rub the yolks of two hard-boiled eggs to a paste, adding one teaspoon of salad oil or melted butter, being careful to add only a few drops at a time. Add ½ teaspoon salt, ½ teaspoon of prepared mustard, very little pepper, two tablespoons of white sugar. Stir very hard, then pour in gradually ½ cup of vinegar.

SALADS

GREEN SALADS
Imported or domestic endive, chicory, escarole and Romaine or lettuce must be washed, made crisp in cold water, and dried in a bag on the ice. Serve them with French dressing. Imported endive may, however, be served with mayonnaise, if desired.

LETTUCE
The French style of making lettuce salad is as follows: After dressing the salad, mix it in one tablespoon of oil, then take only two tablespoons of white wine vinegar, mixed with a very little pepper and salt, and just turn the lettuce over and over in this mixture.

CHIFFONADE SALAD
Lettuce, dandelion, chicory, a little chopped beet, chopped celery, a bit of tomato are mixed and covered with French dressing. The dressing is usually flavored both with onion and garlic.

ASPARAGUS SALAD
Boil the asparagus in salted water, being very careful not to break the caps; drain, and pour over it when cold a mayonnaise dressing, with some chopped parsley. Serve each person with three or four stems on a plate, with a little mayonnaise dressing. Do not use a fork; take the stems in the fingers and dip in the dressing.

BEET SALAD
Boil beets, when tender, skin quickly while hot and slice them into a bowl. Sprinkle salt, pepper, a tablespoon of brown sugar, some caraway seeds, one medium-sized onion in slices, and pour over all ½ cup of vinegar which has been boiled; with a fork mix the hot vinegar through the other ingredients.

BEET AND CAULIFLOWER SALAD

Take some thin slices of cooked beets, some cold cooked potatoes, some cold cooked cauliflower, and a little chopped parsley. Pour over the following dressing and add salt and pepper to taste. Put one level teaspoon of mustard, one teaspoon anchovy sauce, one tablespoon of milk or cream, and one dessertspoon of vinegar. Mix the mustard with the anchovy, then add the milk, and lastly the vinegar. Tomatoes are equally good served in the same way.

STRING BEAN SALAD

String and remove the ends from one quart of beans. Cut into short lengths. Cover with boiling water, add one level tablespoon of salt and cook until tender, but not soft. Drain and save one cup of the liquor. Cream one tablespoon of flour with two tablespoons of butter. Pour the liquid over the flour and butter, stirring constantly to avoid "lumping." Cook this sauce for five minutes, remove from stove and stir in two tablespoons of strained lemon juice. Pour this over the beans and serve.

BOHEMIAN SALAD

Cover the bottom of the salad bowl with crisp Romaine or lettuce; arrange over the top alternate slices of hard-boiled eggs and boiled beets. Sprinkle with finely chopped onion, cover with French dressing, toss and serve.

BOILED CELERY ROOT SALAD

Pare and wash the celery roots (they should be the size of large potatoes), put on to boil in a little salted water, and when tender remove from the water and set away until cool. Cut in slices about an $1/8$ inch thick; sprinkle each slice with fine salt, sugar and white pepper; pour enough white wine vinegar over the salad to cover. A few large raisins boiled will add to the appearance of this salad. Serve cold in a salad bowl, lined with fresh lettuce leaves.

CELERY ROOT BASKETS

Buy large celery roots, parboil them and cut in shape of baskets and scallop the edge; boil beets until soft and cut them in small balls (like potato-balls). Set celery root baskets in French dressing for several hours to flavor, and the beet-balls in boiling sugar and vinegar. Fill the baskets with pickled beet-balls; roll lettuce and cut it into shreds and put it around the celery root basket. The green lettuce, white basket and red balls form a pretty color scheme, and are delicious as a salad.

CHESTNUT SALAD
Equal parts of boiled chestnuts and shredded celery are combined. Bananas, apples, celery and chestnuts. Dress with mayonnaise and serve on lettuce leaves.

COLD SLAW OR CABBAGE SALAD
Select a small, compact cabbage; strip off the outside leaves and cut the head in quarters. With a sharp knife slice very thin; soak in cold water until crisp; drain and dry between clean towels. Mix with hot dressing and serve when cold.

DRESSING FOR COLD SLAW
Beat the yolks of two eggs until light, add one tablespoon of sugar, one teaspoon of pepper, ½ teaspoon each of salt and dry mustard, pour one cup of vinegar over, stir well and pour over the slaw. This dressing may be cooked over boiling water if so desired. Care must be taken in adding the vinegar gradually, and add sliced onions to the salad.

CUCUMBER SALAD
Pare thickly, from end to end, and lay in ice water one hour; wipe them, slice thin, and slice an onion equally thin. Strew salt over them, shake up a few times, cover and let remain in this brine for another hour. Then squeeze or press out every drop of water that has been extracted from the cucumbers. Put into a salad bowl, sprinkle with white pepper and scatter bits of parsley over them; add enough vinegar to cover. You may slice up an equal quantity of white or red radishes and mix with this salad.

CAULIFLOWER SALAD
Wash the cauliflower carefully, tie in a cloth and cook in boiling salt water until thoroughly tender. When done, remove the cloth, pour two tablespoons of lemon juice over the cauliflower and set it on the ice to cool. When ready to serve, separate the flowerets, lay them on lettuce leaves, cover with French dressing and sprinkle one tablespoon of chopped parsley over the top.

SALAD OF EGGPLANT (TURKISH)
Use small eggplants. Place on end of toasting fork under broiler until the peel is black; remove the skin. The eggplant will then be tender; chop with wooden spoon, add lemon juice, parsley chopped fine, and olive oil.

EGGPLANT SALAD (ROMANIAN)
Broil eggplant; when cool, skin, lay on platter, cut with wooden spoon, add a red onion cut fine, or garlic cut very fine, salt and a little vinegar.

TOMATO SALAD (FRENCH DRESSING)
Take six firm red tomatoes, wash and wipe them neatly, slice them in thin slices with a very sharp knife. Line a salad bowl with lettuce leaves, lay the sliced tomatoes in, sprinkle with salt and pepper, serve with French dressing.

MAYONNAISE OF TOMATOES (WHOLE)
Select tomatoes that are of uniform size, round, smooth and spotless, scald and take off outer skin, set away on ice until ready to serve. Serve on individual dishes, putting each on a lettuce leaf and pour a tablespoon of mayonnaise dressing over each tomato.

STUFFED TOMATOES
Select round, very firm and even sized tomatoes, cut off the top (reserve to use as a cover), scrape out the inside, being very careful to not break the tomato. Fill each tomato with some finely prepared "cold slaw," cover with the top of the tomato, lay them on lettuce leaves and pour a mayonnaise dressing over each. You may lay them en masse on a decorated platter, heaping them in the shape of a mound, or serve individually.

STUFFED TOMATOES, CHEESE SALAD
Wash and skin six small tomatoes. Cut a piece from the stem end of each and when cold remove a portion of the pulp from the center. Then sprinkle with salt and invert on the ice to chill. Mash to a paste one small block of cream cheese, add two tablespoons of chopped pimento, one tablespoon of prepared mustard. Blend well, moisten with a French dressing and fill into the tomato shells. Arrange on a bed of crisp lettuce leaves and pour over each tomato a tablespoon of thick boiled dressing.

LIMA BEAN SALAD
Take two cups cooked or canned lima beans, two stalks of chopped celery, twelve chopped olives, one teaspoon of onion juice, one teaspoon of salt, and a dash of red pepper. Mix thoroughly and serve on lettuce leaves with French dressing and garnish with green and red peppers cut in squares.

PEPPER AND CHEESE SALAD
Fill green peppers with a mixture of cream cheese and chopped olives. Set on the ice and then slice the peppers and serve a slice (shaped like a four-leaf clover) on a leaf of lettuce. Small brown bread sandwiches go well with this.

GREEN PEPPERS FOR SALAD
Put whole, green sweet pepper in boiling water and cook until tender. Place on platter and drain. Make a dressing of vinegar, salt, sugar and oil. Serve.

PEPPER SALAD
Cut the peppers lengthwise in half, and fill with a mixture of flaked, cold cooked fish and minced celery, mixed with mayonnaise.

POTATO SALAD, No. 1
Boil ten potatoes (small, round ones preferred) in their skins. When done, peel them while still hot and slice in thin, round slices. Spread over the potatoes one onion, sliced fine, and sprinkle generously with salt and pepper, add one tablespoon mustard seed, ½ tablespoon celery seed, and ½ tablespoon sugar. Beat one egg until light, pour two tablespoons of goose or chicken fat (or olive oil), melted, over the eggs, stir well, add ½ cup of vinegar, pour over the seasoned potatoes; then add ¼ cup of hot water and if necessary, add a little more vinegar, salt or pepper. One or two chopped hard-boiled eggs added improves the salad. Line a salad bowl with lettuce leaves, pour in the salad and decorate the top with grated hard-boiled eggs. Melted butter may be used if for a milk meal or heated olive oil for a parve salad in place of the melted fat.

POTATO SALAD, No. 2
Boil one quart of small potatoes. Do not peel them, just wash and scrub the potatoes thoroughly in cold water. Put them in a kettle with enough cold water, slightly salted, just to cover them; stand them over a medium-high with

the kettle covered until the water begins to boil; then turn down the heat, lift the cover of the kettle slightly and let the potatoes cook slowly until done. Drain off the water and stand the potatoes where they will get cold. But do not put them in a refrigerator. When quite cold, peel the potatoes and slice them very thin in a salad bowl. To every two layers of potato slices sprinkle over a very light layer of white onions sliced very thin. When the salad bowl is well filled pour over the salad a French dressing made of equal parts of oil and vinegar; let the vinegar be part tarragon; use a palatable amount of salt and pepper. When ready to serve, cover the surface of the salad with a stiff mayonnaise in which a suggestion of cream has been mixed. Garnish with quarters of hard-boiled eggs, boiled beets cut in fancy slices and a fringe of parsley around the edge of the bowl.

POTATO SALAD, No 3

Put into a bowl two tablespoons of olive oil, one tablespoon of sugar, one teaspoon of salt, some pepper and one tablespoon of vinegar and mix all together. Cut into this in slices six hot potatoes. Then cut into small pieces two small onions, a little garlic, some parsley, six stuffed olives, three hearts of celery (or the end of it), six radishes, three slices of red beets and two hard-boiled eggs. Add this to the gravy in the bowl, mix well, and season to taste. Put all into a glass dish and pour over this a prepared mayonnaise dressing. Decorate with parsley, olives (whole), some lettuce and put in the center some celery leaves.

ZUCCHINI SQUASH SALAD (TURKISH)

Grate off the skin of a zucchini, cut the squash in slices, ¼ of an inch thick, and fry in olive oil; prepare a sauce with a little vinegar, ½ teaspoon of prepared mustard, two tablespoons of olive oil, beat these ingredients very well; add two shallots or leeks, cut in small pieces, pour sauce over the squash and serve.

WALDORF SALAD

Mix an equal quantity of sliced celery and apples, add a ¼ pound of pecans or English walnuts, chopped fine. Put over a tablespoon of lemon juice and sufficient mayonnaise dressing to thoroughly cover. To be absolutely correct, this salad should be served without lettuce; it can, however, be dished on lettuce leaves.

WATER-LILY SALAD

Boil twenty minutes, one egg for each lily; remove shell and while still warm cut with silver knife in strips from small end nearly to base; very carefully lay back the petals on a heart of bleached lettuce; remove yolks and rub them with spoon of butter, vinegar, a little mustard, salt and paprika; form cone-shaped balls, and put on petals, sprinkling bits of parsley over balls. Two or three stuffed olives carry out the effect of buds; serve on cut-glass dishes to give water effect.

MARSHMALLOW SALAD

Cut up ¼ pound of marshmallows into small squares, also contents of one-half can of pineapple. Let the marshmallows be mixed with the pineapples quite a while before salad is put together; add to this ¼ pound of shelled pecans. Make a drip mayonnaise of one yolk of egg into which ½ cup of oil is stirred drop by drop; cut this with lemon juice, but do not use any sugar; to two tablespoons of mayonnaise, add four tablespoons of whipped cream. Serve on fresh, green lettuce leaves.

COTTAGE CHEESE SALAD

Mix thoroughly one pound of cheese, 1½ tablespoons of cream, one tablespoon of chopped parsley and salt to taste. First fill a rectangular tin mold with cold water to chill and wet the surface; line the bottom with waxed paper, then pack in three layers, putting two or three parallel strips of pimento between layers. Cover with waxed paper and set in a cool place until ready to serve; then run a knife around the sides and invert the mold. Cut in slices and serve on lettuce leaves with French dressing and wafers. Minced olives may be used instead of the parsley, and chopped nuts also may be added.

CREAM CHEESE SALAD

Moisten a cream cheese with cream and beat to a froth. Arrange in a mound shape on a dish and turn preserved gooseberries over it. Serve with biscuits.

CREAM CHEESE SALAD WITH PINEAPPLES
Serve one slice of Hawaiian pineapple on lettuce leaves. On the pineapple slice place a spoon of cream cheese and some chopped walnuts and top off with a dash of mayonnaise dressing.

FRUIT SALAD
Slice one pineapple, three oranges, and three bananas. Pour over it a French mayonnaise, put on lettuce leaves and serve at once. For those who do not care for the mayonnaise, make a syrup of one cup of sugar, and ½ cup of water, boil until thick, add juice of lemon, let slightly cool, then pour over fruit. Let stand on ice one to two hours. Another nice dressing is one cup of claret, ½ cup sugar, and piece of lemon. Always use lemon juice in preference to vinegar in fruit salads. All fruits that go well together may be mixed. This is served just before desert.

FRUIT AND NUT SALAD
Slice two bananas, two oranges and mix them with ½ cup of English walnuts and the juice of ½ lemon with French dressing. Serve on lettuce leaves.

GRAPEFRUIT SALAD
Cut the grapefruit in halves and remove the pulp, being careful to get none of the tough white skin. Mix with bananas and oranges and stir in white mayonnaise dressing. Remove all skin from the inside of the grapefruit and fill with the mixture, heaping it high and ornamenting with maraschino cherries. Lay each half in a bed of lettuce leaves and serve.

BANANA DAINTY
Cut the bananas in half crosswise and arrange them on a plate, radiating from the center. Sprinkle with grated nuts or nutmeg and heap white mayonnaise in the center. Garnish with maraschino cherries.

HUNGARIAN FRUIT SALAD
Mix together equal parts of banana, orange, pineapple, grapefruit and ½ cup of chopped nuts. Marinate with French dressing. Fill apple or orange skins with mixture. Arrange on a bed of watercress or lettuce leaves. Sprinkle with paprika.

NUT SALAD
Make a plain grapefruit salad. When you have it ready to serve, cover the top thickly with finely chopped almonds or pecans mixed. Pour over French dressing.

RUSSIAN FRUIT SALAD
Peel and pit some peaches, cut in slices and add as much sliced pineapple, some apricots, strawberries and raspberries, put these in a dish. Prepare a syrup of juice of two lemons, two oranges, one cup of water and one pound of sugar, a ½ teaspoon of powdered cinnamon, grated rind of lemon, add one cup red wine and a half glass of Madeira, arrak or rum. Boil this syrup for five minutes, then pour over the fruit, tossing the fruit from time to time until cool. Place on ice and serve cold.

FISH SALAD
Take one pound cold boiled fish left over from the day previous, or boil fresh fish and let cool, then skin, bone and flake. If fresh fish is used, mix two tablespoons of vinegar, a pinch of salt and pepper with the fish. Make a mayonnaise dressing (French mayonnaise preferred), and mix half with the fish, leaving other half to spread over top of salad, after it is put in bowl. Serve either with or without lettuce leaves.

FISH SALAD FOR TWENTY PEOPLE
Boil four pounds of halibut, cool and shred fish. Marinate the fish as directed. When ready to serve add six hard-boiled eggs chopped, and one pint bottle of pickles or chow-chow. The pickle may be omitted and celery cut fine be added. When these are well mixed serve on lettuce leaves with mayonnaise dressing, of which one pint will be required.

MAYONNAISE OF FLOUNDER
Put some fillets of flounder into boiling water with a little salt and lemon juice, and cook until tender, then drain thoroughly. When cold, put them in the center of some chopped lettuce, cover with mayonnaise sauce and garnish with slices of tomatoes and hard-boiled eggs.

HERRING SALAD, No. 1

Soak four herrings in cold water overnight, and then rinse several times in fresh cold water. Skin, bone, and cut in ½ inch pieces. Peel two apples, and cut in dice. Mix with herring, then add ½ cup of coarsely chopped almonds and one onion chopped fine. Remove the milsner or soft egg from the inside of herring, and mash perfectly smooth. Add ½ cup vinegar, one teaspoon of sugar, pinch of pepper. Mix well, and then pour over herring, stirring with a fork to prevent mashing. Set in icebox until ready to serve. Put sliced lemons on top. Herring can be left whole, dressing made and poured over whole herrings.

HERRING SALAD, No. 2

Soak three nice herrings in cold water three hours. Then remove the head and tail and bones. With a scissors cut in pieces as small as dice, add one-half cup of English walnuts cut fine, one tablespoon of boiled beets cut fine, two tablespoons of capers, one large apple cut in small pieces and one dill pickle cut up. Then take the soft egg, and mix with two cups of white vinegar until soft, add one teaspoon of sugar, three cloves and allspice and pour the sauce over the ingredients. The sauce should not be too thick. Mix all well together, and serve a spoonful on a lettuce leaf for each person. This salad will keep for weeks.

HUNGARIAN VEGETABLE SALAD

Mix together one cup each of cold cooked peas, beans, carrots, and potatoes. Cover with French dressing and let stand for twenty minutes. Add one cup of smoked salmon or haddock, cut in small pieces, the chopped whites of four hard-boiled eggs and two stalks of celery. Mix thoroughly, garnish top with yolk of egg pressed through a wire sieve, and with cucumbers and beets, cut in fancy shapes.

SALMON SALAD

Either cold boiled salmon or the canned variety may be used. In the latter event wash the fish in cold water, drain and expose to the outside air for at least one hour, as this removes any suggestion of the can. Flake the fish into small particles and to each cupful of the fish add the same quantity of shredded lettuce, one coarsely chopped hard-boiled egg, three slices of minced cucumber and six chopped olives. Mix the ingredients well, moisten with either a mayonnaise or boiled dressing and serve in individual portions in nest of heart lettuce leaves. Mask each portion with a tablespoon of dressing, and garnish with capers and grated egg yolk.

MAYONNAISE ESPECIALLY FOR SALMON
Rub the yolks of two hard-boiled eggs to a powder, then add eight tablespoons of cream very gradually to them, also white pepper, a pinch of salt and a mere suspicion of cayenne pepper. Lastly, add two tablespoons of white vinegar. It is very important that this last ingredient be put in drop by drop, otherwise the mixture will curdle.

MACKEREL SALAD
Procure a nice fat mackerel, boil, and when cold, proceed same as for "Salmon Salad," only do not cut the pieces quite as small.

MONTEREY SALAD
Select fine lemons, wipe carefully, scoop out the pulp, remove the tough inner skin and seeds, and to the rest add one box of boneless sardines, finely chopped, one teaspoon of prepared mustard, two hard-boiled eggs chopped, some Tabasco sauce, and mayonnaise. Fill each cup with the mixture. Cut a small slice from the bottom of the lemon, so that it will stand firmly. Garnish with chopped egg and chopped parsley, and serve on lettuce leaves.

RUSSIAN SALAD
Cut up all kinds of pickled cucumbers, small and large, sweet and sour, also mustard pickles, into very small lengths, also pickled beans and capers. Add six herrings, which you have soaked in water for twenty-four hours; skin and take out every bone, cut up as you did the pickles. Add half a pound of smoked salmon, also cut into lengths, six large apples chopped very fine, and one onion grated; mix all thoroughly and pour a rich mayonnaise dressing over all. Next day line a salad bowl with lettuce leaves, fill in the salad and garnish with hard-boiled eggs, nuts, and capers.

NIAGARA SALAD

Chop one thick slice of cold, cooked salmon. Make a dressing of mayonnaise, to which add one tablespoon of prepared mustard, one green onion chopped fine, one tablespoon of small Mexican peppers, one tablespoon of pimentos. Mix this dressing into the picked salmon.

CHICKEN SALAD

Place the chicken in boiling water, add one onion, a bay leaf and six cloves. Bring to a boil and let it boil rapidly for five minutes. Reduce the heat to below the boiling point, and let it cook until tender. Let chicken cool in the broth. By cooking it in this manner the dark meat will be almost as white as the meat of the breast. When the chicken is cold, cut into ½ inch cubes, removing all the fat and skin. To each pint allow one tablespoon of lemon juice, sprinkle the latter over the prepared chicken and place on ice. When ready to serve, mix the chicken with two-thirds as much white celery, cut into corresponding pieces: meanwhile prepare the following mayonnaise: Rub the yolks of two hard-boiled eggs as fine as possible, add one teaspoon of salt, then add, a drop at a time, one teaspoon of the finest olive oil. Stir constantly, add one teaspoon of prepared mustard and white pepper, and two teaspoons of white sugar; whip the white of one egg to a froth and add to the dressing; add about ½ cup of vinegar last, a spoonful at a time. Put the salad into the dressing carefully, using two silver forks; line the salad bowl with lettuce leaves, and garnish the top with the whites of hard-boiled eggs chopped up, or cut into half-moons. Garnish this salad with the chopped yolks and whites of hard-boiled eggs, being careful to have the whites and yolks separate. A few olives and capers will add to the decoration.

CHICKEN SALAD FOR TWENTY PEOPLE

Boil two large chickens in enough water to cover them, add salt while boiling; when very tender remove from the fire and allow the chickens to cool in the liquor in which they were boiled, when cold skim off every particle of fat, and reserve it to use instead of oil. If possible boil the chickens the day previous to using. Now cut the chickens up into small bits (do not chop), cut white, crisp celery in half inch pieces, and sprinkle with fine salt, allowing half as much celery as you have chicken, mixing the chicken and celery, using two silver forks to do this. Rub the yolks of six hard-boiled eggs as fine as possible, add ½ teaspoon salt, white pepper, four tablespoons of chicken-fat that has been skimmed off the broth, adding one at a time, stirring constantly, one tablespoon of best prepared mustard, two teaspoons each mustard seed and celery seed, and two tablespoons of white sugar; add gradually, stirring constantly, one cup of white wine vinegar. Pour this dressing over the chicken and celery and toss lightly with the silver forks. Line a large salad bowl with lettuce leaves, pour in the salad and garnish the top with the chopped whites of six hard-boiled eggs; pour a pint of mayonnaise over the salad just before serving. A neat way is to serve the salad in individual salad dishes, lining each dish with a lettuce leaf, garnish the salad with an olive stuck up in the center of each portion. The bones of the chicken may be used for soup, letting them simmer in water to cover for three hours.

BRAIN SALAD
Scald brains with boiling hot water to cleanse thoroughly. Boil until tender, in fresh cold salt water, being careful to remove from water while it is yet firm. Slice lengthwise and lay in dish. Pour over ½ cup of vinegar, which has been sweetened with a pinch of sugar to remove sharp taste, pinch of salt and pepper. Garnish with parsley and serve cold. Can also be served with mayonnaise.

SWEETBREAD SALAD
Take cucumbers and cut lengthwise to serve the salad in; scrape out the inside and salt well, then squeeze and use this to mix with the filling. Take a pair of sweetbreads, or calf's brains, wash well, and boil; when done, throw in cold water at once and skim them; chop fine, add bunch of celery, one can of peas, scraped part of cucumber; mix all together and season. Make a mayonnaise, mix with it, and fill the cucumber shells; keep all cold, and serve on lettuce leaf.

VEAL SALAD
Cut cold veal in ½ inch slices, season with two tablespoons of vinegar, pinch of salt and pepper. Make a dressing using the yolks of three hard-boiled eggs, mashed smooth, add gradually two tablespoons of melted cold chicken or turkey grease, stir until smooth and thick, then add one teaspoon of prepared mustard, large pinch of salt and pepper, one tea-

spoon of sugar, one teaspoon each of mustard and celery seed, and five tablespoons of white vinegar. Mix the dressing well with the veal, and serve with or without lettuce leaves.

NEAPOLITAN SALAD

Take some white meat of a turkey, cut up fine, cut up a few pickles the same way, a few beets, one or two carrots, a few potatoes (the carrots and potatoes must be parboiled), also a few stalks of asparagus; chop up a bunch of crisp, white celery; a whole celery root (parboiled), sprinkle all with fine salt and pour a mayonnaise dressing over it. Line the salad bowl with lettuce leaves or white cabbage leaves. Add a few hard-boiled eggs and capers; garnish with sprigs of fresh parsley.

POLISH SALAD, OR SALAD PIQUANT

Lay half a dozen or more large salt pickles in water for about six hours, then drain off all the water. Chop up two sour apples, one large onion or two small ones, chop the pickles and mix all thoroughly in a bowl and sprinkle over them a scant ½ teaspoon of pepper (white) and a tablespoon of sugar (either white or brown), adding a pinch of salt if necessary. Pour enough white wine vinegar over all to just cover. Do not make more at a time than you can use up in a week, as it will not keep longer.

FRESH FRUITS AND COMPOTE

Always select the best fruit, as it is the cheapest, and requires less sugar; and where every piece of fruit or every berry is perfect, there is no waste.

BLUEBERRIES
Wash and pick over carefully, drain off all the water, sprinkle powdered sugar over them and serve with cream or milk.

RASPBERRIES
Pick over carefully, set on ice, and serve in a dish un-sugared. Strawberries may be served as above.

RASPBERRIES AND CURRANTS
These berries, mixed, make a very palatable dish. Set on ice until ready to serve. Then pile in a mound, strewing plenty of pulverized sugar among them. As you do this, garnish the base with white or black currants (blackberries look pretty also) in bunches. Serve with cream or wine.

STRAWBERRIES
Pick nice ripe berries, pile them in a fruit dish. Strew plenty of pulverized sugar over them and garnish with round slices or quarters of oranges, also well sugared.

BANANAS
May be sliced according to fancy, either round or lengthwise. Set on ice until required. Then add sugar, wine or orange juice. In serving, dish out with a tablespoon of whipped cream.

CHILLED BANANAS
Cut cold bananas down lengthwise, and lay these halves on a plate with a quarter of a lemon and a generous teaspoon of powdered sugar. Eat with a fork or spoon after sprinkling with lemon juice and dipping in sugar.

GRAPEFRUIT

Cut in half, with a sharp knife, remove seeds, and sprinkle with sugar, or loosen pulp; cut out pithy white center; wipe knife after each cutting, so that the bitter taste may be avoided. Pour in white wine or sherry and sprinkle with powdered sugar, and let stand several hours in refrigerator to ripen. Serve cold in the shell. Decorate with maraschino cherry.

ORANGES

Cut an orange in half cross-wise. Place on an attractive dish, scoop out the juice and pulp with a spoon and sweeten if necessary.

PINEAPPLE

Peel the pineapple, dig out all the eyes, then cut from the core downward, or chop in a bowl, and set on ice until ready to serve. Then sugar the fruit well, and form into a mound in a dish. Garnish the base well with leaves or small fruit of any kind. You may squeeze the juice of one orange over all.

PEACHES

Peel fine, ripe freestone peaches. Cover plentifully with pulverized sugar, and serve with whipped cream. The cream should be cold. Peaches should not be sliced until just before dining, or they will be very apt to change color.

WATERMELONS

Use only those melons that are perfectly ripe. Do not select those that are very large in circumference; a rough melon with a bumpy surface is the best. Either cut in half or plug and fill with the following: Put on to boil some pale sherry or claret and boil down to quite a thick syrup with sugar. Pour this into either a plugged melon or over the half-cut melon, and lay on ice for a couple of hours before serving. If you use claret you may spice it while boiling with whole spices.

SNOWFLAKES

Grate a large coconut into a fruit dish, and mix it thoroughly and lightly with pulverized sugar. Serve with whipped or plain sweet cream.

TUTTI-FRUTTI
Slice oranges, bananas, pineapples and arrange in a glass bowl; sprinkle with pulverized sugar, and serve either with wine or cream. You may use both.

RIPE TOMATOES
Select nice, large, well-shaped tomatoes, pare, slice and put on ice. When ready to serve sprinkle each layer thickly with pulverized sugar.

PINEAPPLE SOUFFLÉ
Take a nice ripe pineapple, grate it and sweeten to taste. Beat the whites of two eggs stiff and mix with the pineapple. Before serving, whip half a pint of cream and put on the pineapple.

FROSTED APPLES
Pare and core six large apples. Cover with 2 cups water and three tablespoons of sugar; simmer until tender. Remove from the syrup and drain. Wash the parings and let simmer with a little water for thirty minutes. Beat the white of one egg to a stiff froth and add one tablespoon of sugar. Coat the top of the apples lightly with the meringue and place in a cool oven to dry. Strain the juice from the parings, add two tablespoons of sugar, return to the heat and let boil for five minutes; add a few drops of lemon juice and a little nutmeg, cool and pour around the apples.

APPLE FLOAT
Peel six big apples and slice them. Put them in a saucepan with just enough water to cover them and cook until tender. Then put them through a colander and add the grated rind and juice of half a lemon, sweeten to taste and stir in a trace of nutmeg. Fold in the stiffly beaten whites of four eggs and put the dish on ice. Serve with whipped or plain cream.

APPLE DELIGHT
Put a layer of apple sauce in a buttered pudding dish, dot with butter, add a layer of chopped peaches and apricots, sprinkle with blanched almonds ground rather coarsely, repeat until the pan is full; pour the peach juice over the mixture and bake at 325° for one hour.

APPLE COMPOTE

Take six apples, pare, quarter, core and lay them in cold water as soon as pared. Then take the parings and seeds, put in a dish with a cup of water and a cup of white wine, and boil for about fifteen minutes. Strain through a fine sieve, then put on to boil again, and add ½ cup white sugar and the peel of half a lemon. Put in the apples and let them stew for fifteen minutes longer. When the apples are tender, take up each piece carefully with a silver spoon and lay on a platter to cool. Let the syrup boil down to about half the quantity you had after removing the apples, and add to it the juice of half a lemon. Lay your apples in a fruit dish, pyramid shape, pour the syrup over them, serve.

BAKED APPLES

Take large, juicy apples, wash and core them well, fill each place that you have cored with brown sugar, cinnamon and raisins, and put a clove in each apple. Lay them in a deep dish, pour a teacup of water in the dish, and put a little sugar on top of each apple. When well done the apples will be broken. Then remove them carefully to the dish they are to be served in and pour the syrup over them. To be eaten cold. If you wish them extra nice, glaze them with the beaten white of an egg, ½ cup of pulverized sugar and serve with whipped cream.

STEAMED SWEET APPLES

For this dish use sweet apples, and steam in a closely covered iron pot for three-quarters of an hour. Quarter and core five apples without paring. Put into the pot, and melt beef drippings; when hot, lay a layer of apples in, skin down, sprinkle with brown sugar, and when nearly done, turn and brown; place on a platter and sprinkle with sugar.

FRIED APPLES

Quarter and core five apples without paring. Put into a frying pan one cup of sugar, one tablespoon of butter and three tablespoons of water. Let this melt and lay in the apples with the skin up. Cover and fry slowly until brown.

APPLE SAUCE VICTORIA

Pare, quarter and core the apples. Set on to boil in cold water, and boil them over a very brisk fire; when they are soft mash with a potato masher and pass the mashed apples through a sieve. Sweeten to taste and flavor with a teaspoon of vanilla. This way of seasoning apples is highly recommended, especially if they are tasteless.

PEACH COMPOTE

Pare the fruit, leave it whole and put on to boil with sweetened water. Add a few cloves (remove the heads), also a stick of cinnamon bark. Boil the peaches until tender, then take up with a perforated skimmer and lay them in your fruit dish. Boil the syrup until thick, then pour over the peaches. Eat cold with sweet cream. Peaches make a very nice dessert, cooked in the above manner, clings especially, which cannot be used to cut up.

COMPOTE OF RASPBERRIES

Make a syrup of ½ pound of sugar, and ½ cup of water, put into it one quart of berries which have been carefully picked and washed. Boil up once. Serve cold.

COMPOTE OF PINEAPPLE

Cut off the rind of a pineapple, core and trim out all the eyes. Cut into desired slices. Set on to boil with half a pound of sugar, and the juice of one or two tart oranges. When the pineapple is tender and clear, put into a compote dish and boil the syrup until clear. Pour over all and cool. The addition of a wineglass of brandy improves this compote very much.

COMPOTE OF PEARS

It is not necessary to take a fine quality of pears for this purpose. Pare the fruit, leaving on the stems, and stew in sugar and a very little water. Flavor with stick cinnamon and a few cloves (take out the head of each clove) and when soft place each pear carefully on a platter until cold. Then arrange them nicely in a glass bowl or flat glass dish, the stems all on the outer rim. Pour over them the sauce, which should be boiled thick like syrup. Eat cold.

HUCKLEBERRY COMPOTE

Pick over a quart of huckleberries or blueberries, wash them and set to boil. Do not add any water to them. Sweeten with ½ cup sugar, and spice with ½ teaspoon cinnamon. Just before removing from the fire, add a teaspoon of cornstarch which has been wet with a little cold water. Do this thoroughly in a cup and stir with a teaspoon so as not to have any lumps in it. Pour into a glass bowl. Eat cold.

RHUBARB SAUCE

Strip the skin off the stalks with care, cut them into small pieces, put into a saucepan with very little water, and stew slowly until soft. Sweeten while hot, but do not boil the sugar with the fruit. Eat cold. Very wholesome.

BAKED RHUBARB

Peel and cut into two-inch lengths three bunches of rhubarb. Dredge with flour and put in baking dish with one cup of sugar sprinkled over. Bake in 350° oven three-quarters of an hour. Very nice served hot as a vegetable, or cold as a sauce.

FIG SAUCE

Stew figs slowly for two hours, until soft; sweeten with loaf sugar, about two tablespoons to a pound of fruit; add a glass of port or other wine and a little lemon juice. Serve when cold.

DRIED FRUITS

To cook dried fruits thoroughly they should after careful washing be soaked overnight. Next morning put them over the heat in the water in which they have been soaked; bring to a boil; then simmer slowly until the fruit is thoroughly cooked but not broken. Sweeten to taste. Very much less sugar will be needed than for fresh fruit.

STEWED PRUNES

Cleanse thoroughly, soak in water ten or twelve hours, adding a little granulated sugar when putting to soak, for although the fruit is sweet enough, yet experience has shown that the added sugar changes by chemical process into fruit sugar and brings out better the flavor of the fruit. After soaking, the fruit will assume its full size, and is ready to be simmered on the back of the stove. Do not boil prunes, it will what spoils them. Simmer. Keep lid on. Shake gently, do not stir, and never let boil. When tender they are ready for table. Serve cold, and a little cream will make them more delicious. A little claret or sauterne poured over the prunes just as cooking is finished adds a flavor relished by many. Added just before simmering, a little sliced lemon or orange gives a rich color and flavor to the syrup.

BAKED PRUNES
Cook prunes in an oven-safe dish in the oven. Wash and soak the prunes and put them in the pot with a very little water; let them cook slowly at 300° for two hours. They will be delicious, thick and rich, without any of the objectionable sweetness. Lemon, juice and peel, may be added if desired.

PRUNES WITHOUT SUGAR
Wash prunes thoroughly, pour boiling water over same and let them stand for ten minutes. Then drain and pour boiling water over them again; put in sealed jar; see that prunes are all covered with water. Ready for use after forty-eight hours. Will keep for a week at a time and the longer they stand the thicker the syrup gets.

STEAMED PRUNES
Steam until the fruit is swollen to its original size and is tender. Sprinkle with powdered sugar and squeeze lemon juice over them.

PRUNE SOUFFLÉ
Remove the pits from a large cup of stewed prunes and chop fine. Add the whites of three eggs and ½ cup sugar beaten to a stiff froth. Mix well, turn into a buttered dish and bake thirty minutes in a 350° oven. Serve with whipped cream. If it is desired to cook this in individual cups, butter the cups, fill only two-thirds full, to allow for puffing up of the eggs, and set the cups in a pan of water to bake. Some like a dash of cinnamon in this.

SWEET ENTRÉE OF RIPE PEACHES
Take large, solid peaches, pour boiling water over them so that the skin may be removed smoothly. Have ready thick syrup made of sugar and water.

When boiling hot add peaches and boil about five minutes; remove and place in ice chest. When ready to serve have a sweet cracker on dish, place peach on same and pour over this a raspberry jelly slightly thinned and cover all with salted almonds or walnuts. Other fruits may be treated in like manner.

PASTA or MEHLSPEISE (FLOUR FOODS)

THIN NOODLES
Beat three whole eggs very light and sift in sufficient flour to make a stiff paste. Work until smooth, break off a piece and roll out on board very thin. Break off another piece and roll and continue until all is used. Let rolled-out dough dry, then cut all into very fine noodles of desired shape, size, and length. Boil noodles in pot of salted boiling water, drain in colander when tender and stir in two tablespoons of butter. Heat a tablespoon of butter in the frying pan and brown fine noodles in this butter.

BROAD NOODLES
Beat three whole eggs very light and sift in sufficient flour to make a stiff paste. Work until smooth, break off a piece and roll out on board very thin. Break off another piece and roll and continue until all is used. Let rolled-out dough dry, then cut all noodles as above in long strips one inch wide, trim to lengths desired. Boil noodles in pot of salted boiling water, drain in colander when tender. Put into bowl and stir in two tablespoons of butter. Or, if so desired, a cup of soup stock may be added and noodles browned in an oven-safe dish at 400°. Serve hot.

NOODLES WITH BUTTER
Plunge one pound of noodles into two quarts of boiling water and cook for fifteen minutes. Drain well, replace in the same pan, season with ½ teaspoon of salt, two teaspoons of white pepper, adding one ounce good butter. Gently mix without breaking the noodles until the butter is thoroughly dissolved, and serve.

NOODLES WITH CHEESE
If you make the noodles at home, use two eggs for the dough; if you buy macaroni use ¼ pound, cut up and boil in salt water; boil as directed; drain off the water and let cold water run through them; grate a cup of cheese; melt a piece of fresh butter, about the size of an egg, in a saucepan, stir in a heaping tablespoon of flour, add gradually to this 2 cups of rich milk, stirring constantly; take from the heat as it thickens. Butter a pudding dish, lay

in a layer of noodles, then cheese, then sauce, then begin with noodles again until all is used up. Sprinkle cheese on top, few cracker crumbs and flakes of butter here and there. Bake until brown.

NOODLES AND APPLES
Peel and cut six apples. Take broad noodles made out of three eggs, boil them fifteen minutes, drain, then mix with two tablespoons of fresh butter. Add some cinnamon and sugar to noodles. Put a layer of noodles, then apples and so on until pan is filled, being careful to have noodles on top. Put bits of fresh butter on top. Bake until apples are tender. If so desired, a milchig pie crust may be made and used as an under crust and when apples are tender and crust done, turn out on a large platter with crust side on top.

SCALLOPED NOODLES AND PRUNES
Make broad noodles with three eggs. Boil until tender, drain, pouring cold water through colander. Stew prunes, sprinkle with sugar and cinnamon. In a well-greased baking dish place one-quarter of the noodles, bits of butter or other fat, add half of the prunes, then another layer of the noodles, butter or fat, the remaining prunes, the rest of the noodles. Pour over the prune juice and spread crumbs over top and bake in a moderate oven until crumbs are brown.

NOODLES AND MUSHROOMS
Make broad noodles, boil and serve with melted butter spread over the noodles and this sauce: Brown a tablespoon of butter in the skillet, add ½ tablespoon of flour, then liquor of mushrooms, pinch of salt and pepper. When smooth, add mushrooms. Let boil and serve in a separate dish. When serving, a spoon of mushrooms is to be put over each portion of noodles.

GERÖSTETE FERVELCHEN PFARVEL (EGG BARLEY)
Make just as you would a noodle dough, only stiffer, by adding and working in as much flour as possible and then grate on a coarse grater. Spread on a large platter to dry; boil one cup of egg barley in salt water or milk, which must boil before you put in the egg barley until thick. Serve with melted butter poured over them. (A simpler and much quicker way is to sift a cup

or more of flour on a board; break in two eggs, and work the dough by rubbing it through your hands until it is as fine as barley grains.)

PFARVEL - FLEISCHIG

Make as much egg barley as required. Heat two tablespoons of oil, add ¼ cup of onions, fry until golden brown, add the dried egg barley and brown nicely. Place in a pudding-dish, add three cups of hot soup stock or water to more than cover. Bake in a 350° oven about one hour, or until the water has nearly all evaporated and the egg barley stands out like beads and is soft. The onion may be omitted. Serve hot in place of a vegetable.

KÄSEKNÖPFLI (CHEESE KREPLICH)

Make a dough of one egg with a tablespoon of water; add a pinch of salt; work this just as you would noodle dough, quite stiff. Sift the flour in a bowl, break in the egg, add the salt and water, mix slowly by stirring with the handle of a knife, stirring in the same direction all the time. When this dough is so stiff that you cannot work it with the knife, flour your noodle board and work it with the hollow of your hands, always toward you, until the dough is perfectly smooth; roll out as thin as paper and cut into squares three inches in diameter. Fill with pot cheese or Schmierkäse (cream cheese) that has been prepared in the following manner: Stir up a piece of butter the size of an egg, adding one egg, sugar, cinnamon, grated peel of a lemon and pinch of salt, pounded almonds, which improve it; fill the Knöpfli with a teaspoon, wet the edges with beaten egg, fold into triangles, pressing the edges firmly together; boil in boiling milk; when done they will swim to the top. Eat with melted butter or cream.

BOILED MACARONI

Break the macaroni into small pieces; boil for thirty minutes; drain and blanch in cold water. Reheat in tomato or cream sauce and serve. Grated cheese may be sprinkled over the dish if desired.

SPAGHETTI

Spaghetti is a small and more delicate form of macaroni. It is boiled until tender in salted water and is combined with cheese and with sauces the same as macaroni, and is usually left long. It makes a good garnish.

BAKED MACARONI WITH CHEESE

Cook one cup of broken macaroni in two quarts of boiling salted water for twenty or thirty minutes, drain and pour cold water through the colander. Put the macaroni in a pudding-dish in layers, covering each layer with cream sauce and grated cheese, one cup will be sufficient, and on the top layers sprinkle one cup of buttered breadcrumbs. Bake in oven until the crumbs are brown.

SAVORY MACARONI

After baking some flour to a pale fawn color pass it through a sieve or strainer to remove its gritty particles. Break a ½ pound of macaroni into short pieces, boil them in salted water until fairly tender, then drain. In a little butter in a saucepan brown a level tablespoon of very finely chopped onion, then add three or four sliced tomatoes, ½ teaspoon powdered mixed herbs, a little nutmeg, salt and pepper. When the tomatoes are reduced to a pulp add one pint of milk and allow it to come to the boiling point before mixing with it two tablespoons of the browned flour moistened with water. Stir and boil till smooth, press the whole through a strainer and return to the saucepan. When boiling, add the macaroni and a few minutes later stir in two tablespoons of grated or finely chopped cheese. It may be served at once, but is vastly improved by keeping the pan for half an hour by the side of the fire in an outer vessel of water. Or the macaroni may be turned into a casserole and finished off in the oven. For a meat meal the onions may be browned in sweet drippings or olive oil and soup stock substituted for the milk.

DUMPLINGS FOR STEW

Mix two teaspoons of baking powder with two cups of flour, one egg, one cup of cold water and a little salt. Stir all lightly together and drop the batter from the spoon into the stew while the water continues to boil. Cover closely and do not uncover for twenty minutes, boiling constantly, but not too hard. Serve immediately in the stew.

SPÄTZLEN OR SPATZEN

Sift two cups of flour into a bowl, make a depression in the center and break into it two eggs, add a ¼ teaspoon salt, and enough water or milk to form a smooth, stiff dough. Set on some water to boil, salt the water and when the water boils drop the Spätzle into it, one at a time. Do this with the spoon with which you cut the dough, or roll it on a board into a round roll and cut them with a knife. When the Spätzle are done, they will rise to the surface, take them out with a perforated skimmer and lay them on a platter. Now heat two tablespoons of butter and add breadcrumbs, let them brown for a minute and pour all over the Spätzle. If you prefer you may put the Spätzle right into the sauce pan in which you have heated the butter. Another way to prepare them is after having taken them out of the water, heat some butter in a sauce pan and put in the Spätzle, and then scramble a few eggs over all, stirring eggs and Spätzle together. Serve hot.

SOUR SPATZEN
Brown three tablespoons of flour with one tablespoon of sweet drippings, add a small onion finely chopped, then cover the sauce pan and let the onion steam for a little while; do this over a low heat so there will be no danger of the onion getting too brown; add vinegar and soup stock and two tablespoons of sugar. Let this boil until the sauce is of the right consistency. Serve with Spätzlen made according to the foregoing recipe, using water in place of the milk to form the dough. Pour the sauce over the Spätzlen before serving. By adding more sugar the sauce may be made sweet sour.

LEBERKNÖDEL (CALF LIVER DUMPLINGS)
Chop and pass through a colander ½ pound of calf's liver; rub to a cream four ounces of marrow, add the liver and stir hard. Then add a little thyme, one clove of garlic grated, pepper, salt and a little grated lemon peel, the yolks of two eggs and one whole egg. Then add enough grated breadcrumbs or rolled crackers to this mixture to permit its being formed into little marbles. Drop in boiling salt water and let cook fifteen minutes; drain, roll in fine crumbs and fry in hot fat.

MILK OR POTATO NOODLES
Boil seven or eight potatoes, peel and let them stand several hours to dry; then grate them and add two eggs, salt, and enough flour to make a dough thick enough to roll. Roll into long, round noodles as thick as two pencils and cut to length of baking pan. Butter pan and lay noodles next to each

other; cover with milk and lumps of butter and bake fifteen minutes, till yellow; serve immediately with breadcrumbs browned in butter.

KARTOFFELKLÖßE (POTATO DUMPLINGS)

Boil about eight potatoes in their jackets and when peeled lay them on a covered platter in refrigerator overnight. When ready to use them next day, grate, add two eggs, salt, a little nutmeg if desired, 4 tablespoons of farina, a tablespoon of oil, or chicken fat, one scant cup of flour gradually, and if not dry enough add more flour, but be sure not to make the mixture too stiff as this makes the balls heavy. Place balls in salted boiling water, cook until light and thoroughly done, serve just as they are or fried in chicken fat until brown. The dumplings may be made of the same mixture and in the center of each dumpling place strips of bread one inch long and one-fourth inch thick which have been fried in chicken fat and onions. Flour your hands well and make into dumplings. Put into boiling salted water, boil about twenty-five minutes. Serve at once with chopped onions browned, or browned breadcrumbs and chicken fat.

WIENER KARTOFFELKLÖßE

Boil eight potatoes. When they are very soft drain off every drop of water, lay them on a clean baking board and mash them while hot with a rolling pin, adding about one cup of flour. When thoroughly mashed, break in two eggs, salt to taste, and flavor with grated nutmeg. Now flour the board thickly and roll out this potato dough about as thick as your little finger and spread with the following: Heat some fresh goose fat in a sauce pan, cut up part of an onion very fine, add it to the hot fat together with one-half cup of grated breadcrumbs. When brown, spread over the dough and roll just as you would a jelly-roll. Cut into desired lengths (about three or four inches), put them in boiling water, slightly salted, and boil uncovered for about fifteen minutes. Pour some hot goose grease over the dumplings.

BAYRISCHE DAMPFNUDELN, No. 1

Soak one cake of compressed yeast in a cup of lukewarm milk with a teaspoon of sugar, a teaspoon of salt, and sift a pint of flour in a bowl, in which you may also stir a small cup of milk and one egg. Pour in the yeast and work all thoroughly, adding more flour, but guarding against getting the dough too stiff. Cover up the bowl of dough and let it rise until it is as high again, which will take at least four hours. Flour a baking board and mold small biscuits out of your dough, let them raise at least thirty minutes. Then butter large, round, deep pan and set in your dumplings, brushing each with melted butter as you do so. When all are in, pour in enough milk to reach just half way up to the dumplings. Bake at 350° until a light brown. Eat hot, with vanilla sauce.

BAYRISCHE DAMPFNUDELN, No. 2

Make the dough just as you would in the above recipe, adding a tablespoon of butter, and after they have risen - steam instead of baking them. If you have no steamer improvise one in this way: Put on a kettle of boiling water, set a colander on top of the kettle and lay in your dumplings, but do not crowd them; cover with a close-fitting lid and put a weight on top of it to keep in the steam, when done they will be as large again as when first put in. Take up one at first to try whether it is done by tearing open with two forks. If you have more than enough for your family, bake a pan of biscuits out of the remaining dough. Serve dumplings hot with prune sauce.

APPLE SLUMP

Pare, core and quarter apples, add a little water and sugar to taste, stew until tender and cover with the following mixture: Sift one pint of flour and one teaspoon of baking powder, add a pinch of salt, and two cups of milk, mix and turn out onto a lightly floured board. Roll to ½ inch thickness and place over the stewed apples, cover and cook for ten minutes without lifting the lid. Serve hot with cream and sugar or soft custard.

BOILED APPLE DUMPLINGS

Beat well, without separating, two eggs, add a pinch of salt, two cups of milk and one cup of flour. To a second cup of flour, add two teaspoons of baking powder; add this to the batter and as much more flour as is necessary to make a soft dough. Roll out quickly ½ inch thick. Cut into squares, lay two or three quarters of pared apples on each, sprinkle with sugar and pinch the dough around the apples. Have a number of pudding cloths ready, wrung out of cold water, and sprinkle well with flour. Put a dumpling in each, leave a little room for swelling and tie tightly. Drop into a kettle of rapidly boiling water and keep the water at a steady boil for an hour. Serve hot with hard sauce. Have a saucer in the bottom of kettle to prevent burning.

FARINA DUMPLINGS
Beat yolks of four eggs with three tablespoons of oil, or goose, turkey or chicken fat, or clear beef drippings. Put in enough farina to make a good batter. Beat whites of eggs to a stiff froth with pinch of salt, and stir in batter. Put on in large boiler sufficient water to boil dumplings and add one tablespoon of salt. When boiling drop in by tablespoons. Boil one hour. This quantity makes twenty dumplings.

HUCKLEBERRY DUMPLINGS
Take a loaf of stale bread; cut off the crust and soak in cold water, then squeeze dry. Beat three eggs light, yolks and whites together, add one quart berries and mix all together with a little brown sugar and a pinch of salt. Boil steadily one hour, serve with hard sauce.

PLUM KNÖDEL (HUNGARIAN)
Boil several potatoes, mash, mix with one egg yolk, a little salt and enough flour to make a dough soft enough to hold the impress of the finger. Roll out and cut into four-cornered pieces; in each square place a German plum which has had the pits removed and a mixture of sugar and cinnamon; put in in place of the pit. Roll each square into a round dumpling; put these into a pan with boiling salted water and let them cook covered for six or eight minutes. When done, serve with some breadcrumbs browned in butter or Schmalz and spread over the Knödel.

PEAR DUMPLING (BIRNE KLÖßE)
Take half a loaf of white bread or as much stale white bread, soak the white part and grate the crust, add one cup of suet chopped very fine, one cup of flour, one egg, salt and spices to taste, and ½ teaspoon of baking powder. Make this into a dumpling, put it on a tiny plate in a large kettle. Lay prunes and pears around, about a pound of each, one cup of brown sugar, two pieces of stick cinnamon, dash of claret and cold water to almost cover; then cover kettle tightly and boil four hours. Serve hot. Prunes and dried apples may be used as well.

PEACH DUMPLINGS

Make a dough of a quart of flour and a pint of milk, or water, a tablespoon of shortening, a pinch of salt, one egg and a spoon of sugar; add a piece of compressed yeast, which has previously been dissolved in water. Let the dough raise for three hours. In the meantime make a compote of peaches by stewing them with sugar and spices, such as cinnamon and cloves. Stew enough to answer for both sauce and filling. Then raised, flour the baking board and roll out the dough ½ inch thick. Cut cakes out of it with a tumbler, brush the edges with white of egg, put a teaspoon of peach compote in the center of a cake and cover it with another layer of cake and press the edges firmly together. Steam over boiling water and serve with peach sauce. A delicious dessert may also be made by letting the dough rise another half hour after being rolled out, and before cutting. Compote of huckleberries may be used with these dumplings instead of peaches, if so desired.

CHERRY ROLEY-POLEY

Make a rich baking powder biscuit dough, and roll it out until it is about ⅔ inch thick. Pit and stew enough cherries to make a thick layer of fruit and add sugar to taste. Spread them over the dough thickly and roll it up, taking care to keep the cherries from falling out. Wrap a cloth around it, and sew it up loosely with coarse thread, which is easily pulled out. Allow plenty of room for the dough to rise. Lay the roley-poley on a plate, set it in a steamer and steam for an hour and a half. Serve in slices, with cream or sauce.

SHABBAS KUGEL

Soak five wheat rolls in water, then press the bread quite dry, add one cup of drippings or oil, a pinch of salt, two eggs well beaten, one teaspoon of cinnamon, one grated lemon rind, ½ cup of sugar, one tablespoon of water. Stir all together thoroughly, grease the kugel pot well with warm melted fat, pour in the mixture and send it Friday afternoon to the bakery where it will remain till Saturday noon; it will then be baked brown. If one has a stove that will retain the heat for the length of time required, it will be baked nicely. The kugel must be warm, however, when served.

KUGEL (SCHARFE)
If one desires an unsweetened kugel omit the sugar and cinnamon in the recipe above and season with salt and pepper. When required for any other meal but Shabbas, a kugel can be baked brown in two hours.

KUGEL
Soak five ounces of white bread - it may be stale bread - in cold water; then squeeze out every bit of water, put it in a bowl, add ¾ cup of oil, or soft goose fat in small pieces, five whole eggs, one cup of flour, ½ cup of sugar, ¼ cup of cracker meal, three apples and two pears cut in small pieces, two dozen raisins with the seeds removed, salt to taste, a tiny pinch of pepper, ¼ teaspoon each of cinnamon and allspice. Mix all well together, and pour into an iron pan that has the bottom well covered with oil or goose fat; stick a few pieces of cut apple or pear in the top of the pudding. Pour a cup of cold water over all, place in the oven to bake. Bake slowly for five or six hours. If the water cooks out before it is ready to brown, add more. Bake brown, top and bottom.

NOODLE KUGEL
Cook three cups of broad noodles in salted boiling water ten minutes. Drain and add ¾ cup of chicken or goose fat and four eggs, well beaten. Place in a well-greased iron pot and bake until the top of the kugel is well browned. Serve hot with raspberry jelly or stewed fruit of any kind.

PEAR KUGEL
Cream one cup of rendered fat with one cup of sugar, add ½ loaf of bread, previously soaked and pressed dry, a little salt, ¼ cup of flour. Grease pudding dish and put in alternate layers of the mixture and pears that have been boiled with water, sugar and claret. Bake slowly at 325° three hours.

KRAUT KUGEL
Chop up cabbage, and let stew in fat slowly until quite brown. Do this the day previous to using. Next day mix in with the stewed cabbage ¼ of a loaf of bread soaked in water and squeezed dry, ½ cup of flour, ½ cup of brown sugar, ⅛ pound of raisins, some finely chopped citron, ¼ pound of almonds (mixed with a few bitter almonds), ½ teaspoon of salt, some cin-

namon and allspice about a teaspoon, juice and peel of one lemon and four eggs. Mix all thoroughly, pour into well-greased iron pan (kugel pot) and bake slowly at 325° for several hours.

APPLE KUGEL

Soak half a loaf of bread in water and squeeze dry, shave a cup of suet very fine and cut up some tart apples in thin slices. Add sugar, raisins, cinnamon, about one-quarter cup of pounded almonds and the yolks of three eggs. Mix all thoroughly. Add whites beaten to a stiff froth last. Bake one hour at 325°.

RICE KUGEL

Boil one cup of rice in water until done, then let it cool. In the meanwhile rub ¼ cup of oil, or chicken fat to a cream, add a scant cup of powdered sugar, a little cinnamon, the grated peel of one lemon, the yolks of three eggs, adding one at a time; ½ cup of raisins seeded, ½ pound of stewed prunes pitted, then add the cold rice. ½ cup of pounded almonds mixed with a few bitter ones improves this pudding. Serve with a pudding sauce, either wine or brandy. This pudding may be eaten hot or cold and may be either baked or boiled. If baked, one hour is required; if boiled, two hours; the water must be kept boiling steadily. Leftover rice may be used, butter instead of the fat, and the rice may be boiled in milk.

APPLE SCHALET, No. 1

Take one pound of fresh beef heart fat, shave it as fine as possible with a knife. Sift one quart of flour into a deep bowl, add two tumblers of ice-cold water, one tablespoon of brown sugar, a ¼ of a teaspoon of salt, then add the shaved heart fat and work well into the sifted flour. Put it on a pie board and work as you would bread dough, with the palm of your hand, until it looks smooth enough to roll. Do not work over five minutes. Now take half of this dough, flour your pie board slightly and roll out as you would pie dough, about once as thick. Grease a deep pudding dish (an iron one is best), one that is smaller at the bottom than the top, grease it well, line the pudding-dish, bottom and sides, clear to the top, fill this ⅓ full with chopped tart apples, raisins, part of a grated lemon peel, citron cut quite fine, pounded almonds and melted drippings here and there. Sprinkle thickly with sugar, half brown and half white, and a little ground cinnamon. Moisten each layer with 2 tablespoons of wine. Now put another layer of dough, rolling out half of the remaining dough and reserving the other half for the top covering, fill again with apples, raisins, etc., until full, then put on top layer. Press the dough firmly together all round the edge, using a beaten egg to make sure of its sticking. Roll the side dough over the top with a knife and pour a cup of water over the pudding before setting it in the oven. Bake at 325° for two hours. If the top browns too quickly, cover. The advantage of this pudding is, it may be baked the day previous to using, in fact, it is better the oftener it is warmed over - always adding a cup of water before setting it in the oven. Before serving the pudding turn it out carefully on a large platter, pour 4 tablespoons of brandy which has been slightly sweetened over the pudding and light it, carry to the table in flames. A novice had better try this pudding plain, omitting the wine, brandy, almonds and citron, moistening with water instead of wine before baking. Almost as nice and very good for ordinary use. Some apples require more water than others, the cook having to use her own judgment regarding the amount required.

APPLE SCHALET, No. 2
Line an iron pudding dish with schalet dough, greasing it well before you do so. Chop up some apples quite fine, put on the crust, also some raisins, sugar and cinnamon, then put another layer of pie and another layer of chopped apples, and so on until filled, say about three layers, the last being crust. Bake at 325° until a nice dark brown.

SCHALET DOUGH (MERBERDECK)
Cream four tablespoons of drippings or oil, add a pinch of salt, two tablespoons of granulated sugar, beat in well one egg, add one cup of sifted flour and enough cold water to moisten dough so that it can be rolled out - about three tablespoons will be sufficient; it depends on the dryness of the flour how much is required.

NOODLE SCHALET
Make the quantity of noodles desired, then boil. When done, drain through colander, pouring cold water over the noodles. When all the water has

drained off, beat up three eggs in a large bowl, mix the noodles with the beaten eggs. Grease an iron pudding dish with plenty of goose grease or drippings (or oil), put in a layer of noodles, then sprinkle ¼ cup of sugar, some pounded almonds, the grated peel of one lemon and a few raisins; sprinkle some melted fat over this, then add another layer of noodles, some more sugar and proceed as with the other layer until all the noodles are used. Bake two hours. Broad or fine noodles are equally good for this schalet. If desired, one tart apple chopped very fine may be added with the almonds.

CARROT SCHALET

Boil one pound of carrots, let them get perfectly cold before grating them. In the meanwhile cream a heaping tablespoon of drippings or chicken fat (or oil) and four tablespoons of sugar, add gradually the yolks of four eggs, the grated peel of one lemon, one teaspoon of cinnamon, a little grated nutmeg, three tablespoons of flour, one teaspoon of baking powder, pinch of salt, and the beaten whites last. Heat a few tablespoons of fat in a pudding dish, pour in the mixture and bake in a 375° oven one hour, then sprinkle sugar and cinnamon and return to oven for a few moments to brown. Serve hot.

SEVEN LAYER SCHALET

Take two cups of flour, one egg, three tablespoons of fat, one cup of water, a little sugar, pinch of salt, and knead lightly. Put dough aside in a cold place while you prepare a mixture of one cup of sugar, 1½ teaspoons of cinnamon and three tablespoons of breadcrumbs. Cut dough in seven pieces and roll out each piece separately. Place one layer on a greased baking tin and spread the layer with melted fat and sprinkle with sugar and cinnamon; place upon this the second layer, sprinkle on this two ounces of sweet and bitter almonds which have been grated and mixed with sugar; over this place the third layer and spread with oil, sprinkle with cinnamon and sugar and ½ pound of cleaned, seedless raisins. Place the fourth layer on and spread with jelly, and ½ pound of citron cut up very small. Cover over with another layer, spread fat and sprinkle with cinnamon and sugar and grated lemon peel and juice of lemon. Place the sixth layer and spread and sprinkle with sugar and cinnamon. Put on the last layer and spread with fat and sprinkle with sugar and cinnamon. Cut in four-cornered pieces and bake thoroughly and until a nice brown. This schalet may be made and left whole, with a frosting put on top.

BOILED POTATO PUDDING

Stir the yolks of four eggs, with ½ cup of sugar, add ½ cup of blanched and pounded almonds; grate in the peel, also the juice of one lemon, ½ pound of grated potatoes that have been boiled the day before. Lastly add the stiffly beaten whites, some salt and more potatoes, if necessary. Grease your pudding pan well, pour in the mixture and bake. Set in a pan of water in oven; water in pan must not reach higher than half way up the pudding form. Bake thirty minutes. Turn out on platter and serve with a wine, chocolate, or lemon sauce. One can bake in an iron pudding-form without the water.

POTATO SCHALET

Peel and grate five or six large potatoes and one onion. Soak some bread and two or three crackers. Press out the water and add to the potatoes and onion, salt to taste. Add two tablespoons of boiling fat and one beaten egg. Have plenty of hot fat in pan, put in the pudding, pour over it one cup of cold water. Bake in 400° oven one hour. Two slices of white bread, one inch thick, will be sufficient bread for this schalet.

SWEET POTATO PUDDING

Take one quart of grated, raw sweet potatoes, one tablespoon each of meat fat and chicken fat, ½ pound of brown sugar, 1 cup of molasses, 2 cups cold water, ¼ teaspoon of salt and a little black pepper, grated orange peel, ginger, nutmeg and cinnamon to taste. Pour into greased baking-pan and bake until it jellies. Bake in moderate oven. May be eaten as a dessert, warm or cold.

APPLE STRUDEL, No. 1

Sift two cups of flour, add pinch of salt and one teaspoon of powdered sugar. Stir in slowly one cup of lukewarm water, and work until dough does not stick to the hands. Flour board, and roll as thin as possible. Do not tear. Place a tablecloth on table, put the rolled out dough on it, and pull gently with the hands, to get the dough as thin as tissue paper. Have ready six apples chopped fine, and mixed with cinnamon, sugar, ½ cup of seedless raisins, ½ cup of currants. Spread this over the dough with plenty of chicken-fat or oil, all over the apples. Take the tablecloth in both hands, and roll the strudel, over and over, holding the cloth high, and the strudel will almost roll itself. Grease a baking-pan, hold to the edge of the cloth, and roll the strudel in. Bake brown, basting often with fat or oil.

APPLE STRUDEL, No. 2

Into a large mixing bowl place 1½ cups of flour, and ¼ teaspoon salt. Beat one egg lightly and add it to ⅓ cup warm water, and combine the two mixtures. Mix the dough quickly with a knife; then knead it, place on board, stretching it up and down to make it elastic, until it leaves the board clean. Now toss it on a well-floured board, cover with a hot bowl and keep in a warm place. While preparing the filling lay the dough in the center of a well-floured tablecloth on the table; roll out a little, brush well with some melted butter, and with hands under dough, palms down, pull and stretch the dough gently, until it is as large as the table and thin as paper, and do not tear the dough. Spread one quart of sour apples, peeled and cut fine, ¼ pound of almonds blanched and chopped, ½ cup of raisins and currants, one cup of sugar, and one teaspoon of cinnamon, evenly over ¾ of the dough, and drop over them a few tablespoons of melted butter. Trim edges. Roll the dough over apples on one side, then hold cloth high with both hands and the strudel will roll itself over and over into one big roll, trim edges again. Then twist the roll to fit the greased pan. Bake in a 400° oven until brown and crisp and brush with melted butter. If juicy small fruits or berries are used, sprinkle breadcrumbs over the stretched dough to absorb the juices. Serve slightly warm.

RAHM STRUDEL

Prepare the dough as for Apple Strudel as directed in the foregoing recipe, drip one quart of thick sour milk on it lightly, with a large spoon, put one cup of grated breadcrumbs over the milk, add two cups of granulated sugar, one cup of chopped almonds, one cup of raisins, and one teaspoon of cinnamon, roll and place in well-buttered pan in a 400° oven, put small pieces of butter over the top, basting frequently - until brown and crisp. Serve warm with vanilla sauce. Half this quantity may be used for a small strudel.

CHERRY STRUDEL

Make a dough of two cups of flour, a pinch of salt and a little lukewarm water; do not make it too stiff, but smooth. Slap the dough back and forth. Do this repeatedly for about fifteen minutes. Now put the dough in a warm, covered bowl and set it in a warm place for thirty minutes. In the meantime, stem and pit two quarts of sour cherries. Grate into them some stale bread (about a plateful); also the peel of half a lemon, and mix. Add one cup of sugar, some ground cinnamon and about four ounces of pounded sweet almonds, mix all thoroughly. Roll out the dough as thin as possible, lay aside the rolling-pin and pull, or rather stretch the dough as thin as tissue paper. In doing this you will have to walk all around the table, for when well stretched it will cover more than the size of an ordinary table. Pull off all of the thick edge, for it must be very thin to be good (save the pieces for another strudel). Pour a little oil or melted butter over this, and sprinkle the bread, sugar, almonds, cherries, etc., over it; roll the strudel together into a long roll. Have ready a long baking-pan well greased with butter; fold the strudel into the shape of a pretzel. Butter or grease top also and bake at 400° until a light brown; baste often while baking. Eat warm.

MANDEL (ALMOND) STRUDEL

Prepare the dough as for Apple Strudel No. 2. Blanch ½ pound of almonds and grind, when dried beat the yolks of four eggs light with ¼ pound of granulated sugar, add the grated peel of one lemon and mix in the almonds. Spread over the dough with plenty of oil, butter or fat and roll. Bake; baste very often.

CABBAGE STRUDEL

Heat ½ cup of oil, add one medium-sized cabbage and let it simmer until done, stirring constantly to keep from burning. While cooling prepare strudel dough, fill with cabbage and one cup of raisins and currants mixed, two cups of granulated sugar, ½ cup of chopped almonds and one teaspoon cinnamon, roll and put little pieces of grease on top; bake in 425° oven and baste frequently. The pans in which the strudel is baked must be greased generously. Serve this strudel hot. This strudel may be made for a milk meal by substituting butter for fat.

QUARK STRUDEL (DUTCH CHEESE)

Make a strudel or roley-poley dough and let it rest until you have prepared the cheese. Take ½ pound of cheese, rub it through a coarse sieve or colander, add salt, the yolks of two eggs and one whole egg, sweeten to taste. Add the grated peel of one lemon, two ounces of sweet almonds, and about four bitter ones, blanched and pounded, four ounces of sultana raisins and a little citron chopped fine. Now roll out as thin as possible, spread in the cheese, roll and bake, basting with sweet cream.

STRUDEL AUS KALBSLUNGE

Wash the lung and heart thoroughly in salt water, and put on to boil in cold water, adding salt, one onion, a few bay leaves and cook until very tender. Make the dough precisely the same as any other strudel. Take the boiled lung and heart, chop them as fine as possible and stew in a saucepan with some fat, adding chopped parsley, a little salt, pepper and mace, or nutmeg, the grated peel of half a lemon and a little wine. Add the beaten yolks of two eggs to thicken, and remove from the stove to cool. Roll out the dough as thin as possible, fill in the mixture and lay the strudel in a well-greased pan; bake at 400° until nicely brown, and baste often. Eat hot.

RICE STRUDEL

Prepare the dough same as for Apple Strudel. Leave it in a warm place covered, until you have prepared the rice. Wash a quarter of a pound of rice in hot water--about three times--then boil it in milk until very soft and thick. Let it cool, and then add two ounces of butter, the yolks of four eggs, four ounces of sugar and one teaspoon of vanilla, some salt and the beaten whites of two eggs, mix thoroughly. When your dough has been rolled out and pulled as thin as possible, spread the rice over it and roll. Add pounded almonds and raisins if desired. Put in a greased pan and bake at 400° until brown, basting with sweet cream or butter.

CEREALS

The cereals are the most valuable of the vegetable foods, including as they do the grains from which is made nearly all the bread of the world. For family use, cereals should be bought in small quantities and kept in glass jars, tightly covered. Variety is to be found in using the different cereals and preparing them in new ways. Many cereals are improved by adding a little milk during the latter part of the cooking. Boiling water and salt should always be added to cereals, one teaspoon salt to one cup of cereal. Long cooking improves the flavor and makes the cereal more digestible.

OATMEAL PORRIDGE
As oatmeal is ground in different grades of coarseness, the time for cooking varies and it is best to follow the directions given on the packages. The meal should be cooked until soft, but should not be mushy. The ordinary rule is to put a cup of meal into two cups of salted boiling water (a teaspoon of salt), and let it cook in a double boiler the required time. Keep covered until done; then remove the cover and let the moisture escape.

COLD OATMEAL
Oatmeal is very good cold, and in summer is better served in that way. It can be turned into fancy molds or into small cups to cool, and will then hold the form and make an ornamental dish.

OATMEAL WITH CHEESE
Cook one cup of oatmeal overnight and just before serving add one tablespoon of butter and one cup grated cheese. Stir until the cheese is melted and serve at once.

BAKED APPLE WITH OATMEAL
Pare and core the apples and fill the core space with leftover oatmeal mush. Put the apples in a baking dish; sprinkle with sugar; pour a little water into the bottom of the pan and bake in a moderate oven until the apples are tender. Serve warm with cream for breakfast or luncheon.

WHEAT CEREALS
Wheat cereals, like oatmeal, are best cooked by following the directions on the package. Most of them are greatly improved by the addition of a little milk or by a few chopped dates or whole sultana raisins.

CORNMEAL MUSH
Mix together one cup of cornmeal and one teaspoon of salt, and add one cup of cold water gradually, stirring until smooth. Pour this mixture into two cups of boiling water in a double boiler and cook from three to five hours. Serve hot with cream and sugar.

SAUTÉED CORNMEAL MUSH
Put leftover mush into a dish and smooth it over the top. When cold cut into slices one-half inch thick. Dip each slice into flour. Melt ½ teaspoon of drippings in a frying pan and be careful to let it get smoking hot. Brown the floured slices on each side. Drain if necessary and serve on a hot plate with syrup.

FARINA
To ½ cup of farina take one teaspoon of salt; pour gradually into three cups of boiling water and cook the mixture in a double boiler for about one hour.

HOMINY
Get the unbroken hominy and after careful washing soak it twenty-four hours in the water. Cook one cup of hominy slowly in the same water in a covered vessel for eight hours or until all the water has been absorbed by the hominy; add two tablespoons of butter, one teaspoon of salt and two tablespoons of cream and serve as a vegetable or as a cereal with sugar and cream.

MARMELITTA
Take two cups of coarse cornmeal and four cups of cold water, put on to boil; add ½ teaspoon of salt. Stir the cornmeal continually and when done place on platter, spread with butter, cheese or any cheese such as pot or cream cheese. To be eaten warm.

POLENTA

Place one cup of yellow cornmeal and three cups of cold water in a double boiler, add one teaspoon of salt, one-half teaspoon of pepper and cook for forty minutes. While still hot add one and one-half cups of grated cheese to the mixture and heat until it melts. Turn the mixture into a greased bowl and allow it to set. The meal may be sliced an inch thick or cut with a biscuit cutter and then fried in hot vegetable oil. Serve with white or tomato sauce as desired.

BARLEY, TAPIOCA, SAGO, ETC.

Add one teaspoon of salt to one quart of boiling water and pour gradually on ½ cup of barley or other hard grain and boil until tender, from one to two or more hours, according to the grain, and have each kernel stand out distinct when done. Add more boiling water as it evaporates. Use as a vegetable or in soups. Pearl barley, tapioca and sago cook quicker than other large grains.

BOILED RICE

Put ½ cup of rice in a strainer; place the strainer over a bowl nearly full of cold water; rub the rice; lift the strainer from the bowl and change the water. Repeat this until the water in the bowl is clear. Have two quarts of water boiling briskly, add the rice and one tablespoon of salt gradually so as not to stop the boiling; boil twenty minutes or until soft, do not stir; drain through a colander and place the colander over boiling water for ten minutes to steam. Every grain will be distinct. Serve as a vegetable or as a cereal with cream and sugar.

RICE IN MILK

Clean the rice as for boiling in water; and cook ½ cup of rice with 1½ cups of hot milk, and ½ teaspoon salt, adding a few seeded or sultana raisins if desired. Serve hot like boiled rice or press into small cups, cool and serve with cream and sugar.

RICE WITH GRATED CHOCOLATE

Cook ½ cup of rice, place in hot serving dish, sprinkle generously with grated sweet chocolate, set in oven one minute and serve.

STEAMED RICE
Wash two cups of rice carefully, put in double boiler; add eight cups of cold water and a pinch of salt and steam for two hours; do not stir. Serve with any kind of stewed fruit or preserve.

APPLES WITH RICE
Boil one cup of rice in water or milk; rub the kettle all over with a piece of butter before putting in the rice, season with salt and add a lump of butter. When cooked, add about six apples, pared, quartered and cored, sugar and cinnamon. This makes a nice side dish, or dessert, served with cream.

BOILED RICE WITH PINEAPPLE
Boil as much rice as desired and when done slice up the pineapple and add, with as much sugar as is required to sweeten to taste.

BAKED RICE
Arrange two cups of boiled rice in a baking dish in layers, covering each with grated cheese, a little milk, butter, salt and red pepper. Spread one cup of grated breadcrumbs over all and bake in a 350° oven until the crumbs are browned.

SWEET RICE
Clean and wash one cup of rice. Put on to boil with cold water, add a pinch of salt. When done drain off the water, if any; add two cups of milk, stir in and let boil for five minutes. Dish up, then sprinkle sugar and cinnamon generously over the top. The yolk of an egg can be added just before serving if desired.

EGGS BAKED IN RICE
Line a buttered dish with steamed rice. Break the eggs in the center, dot with butter, sprinkle with salt, pepper and bake in a moderate oven.

RICE AND NUT LOAF
Boil ½ cup of rice (brown preferred); drain and dry it. Mix with an equal quantity of breadcrumbs. Add level teaspoon of salt, and ¼ of a teaspoon of black pepper. Stir in one cup of chopped nuts - pecans or peanuts. Add

one tablespoon of chopped parsley and one egg. Mix thoroughly and pack in bread-pan to mold it. Turn it from pan into baking pan and bake in a 325° for forty-five minutes. Serve with cream sauce or purée of peas.

PILAF
Put two cups of water on to boil, add juice of two tomatoes and a pinch of salt. When boiling, add one cup of rice and let cook until the water has evaporated. Then add melted butter, mix well, and keep in warm place, covered, until ready to serve.

SPANISH RICE
Put one cup of washed rice in frying-pan with four or five tablespoons of oil; add three onions chopped and two cloves of garlic minced fine. Fry ten minutes; add one chopped red pepper, one teaspoon of paprika, and three ripe tomatoes or two cups of canned tomatoes, and one teaspoon of salt. Cook slowly about one hour, and as the water evaporates, add more boiling water to keep from burning.

LEFT-OVER CEREALS
Oatmeal, hominy, cracked wheat, and other cereals which are left over can be added next day to the fresh stock, for they are improved by long boiling and do not injure the new supply, or such as is left can be molded in large or in small forms, and served cold with cream, or milk and sugar. In warm weather, cereals are nicer cold than hot. Cold hominy and mush, cut into squares and fried, so that a crisp crust is formed on both sides, also hominy or farina, rolled into balls and fried, are good used in place of a vegetable or as a breakfast dish. Any of the cereals make good pancakes, or a small amount added to the ordinary pancake batter improves it.

EGGS

Eggs and the foods into which they enter are favorite articles of diet in most households. They are an agreeable substitute for meat and even when high in price make a cheaper dish than meat. A fresh egg should feel heavy, sink in water, and when held to a bright light show a clear round yolk.

TO KEEP EGG YOLKS
The yolks may be kept several days and be as if just separated from the whites if they are placed in a cup previously rinsed with cold water and a pinch of salt added to them. The cup must be closely covered with a wet cloth, and this must be changed and well rinsed in cold water every day. When whites are left over make a small angel cake or any of the cookies which require the whites of egg only. When yolks are left over use for making mayonnaise.

POACHED OR DROPPED EGGS
Fill a pan with boiling, salted water. Break each egg into a wet saucer and slip it into the water; set the pan back where water will not boil. Dip the water over the eggs with a spoon. When the white is firm and a film has formed over the yolk, they are cooked. Take them up with a skimmer, drain and serve hot, on toast. Season with salt.

BOILED EGGS
Soft-boiled eggs may be prepared in two ways. The eggs may be dropped carefully into boiling water and boiled three minutes, or they may be placed in a covered vessel of boiling water and allowed to stand in a warm place (but not on the stove) for ten minutes. Eggs prepared in this way are sometimes called "Coddled Eggs." They are much more delicate and digestible than the usual "Boiled Eggs." Hard-boiled eggs should be cooked in boiling water for fifteen or twenty minutes and then dropped in cold water to prevent the yolk from turning dark.

SCRAMBLED EGGS
Break into a bowl as many eggs as required, add salt and pepper. Have some very hot butter in the frying pan on the stove; pour in the eggs, stir constantly until set, not stiff, and serve on a hot platter at once.

FRIED EGGS
Melt in a frying pan a piece of butter, or fat for a meat meal. When hot, drop in the eggs, one at a time, being careful not to break the yolk. When the white of the egg is set they are done, though some persons like them turned over and cooked on the other side. Remove from the pan with a cake turner.

BAKED EGGS
Butter individual baking dishes and break an egg in each, being careful to keep the yolk whole. Put on each egg a bit of butter, a little pepper and salt. Bake in 350° oven from four to six minutes.

BAKED EGGS WITH CHEESE
Butter a baking dish of a size necessary for number of eggs desired, break eggs into dish, add salt, paprika, pepper to taste, one tablespoon of cream, and two tablespoons of grated cheese. Place dish in a pan of hot water in 350° oven for five minutes until eggs are set.

TOMATO WITH EGG
Cut top from tomatoes, remove seeds, put a raw egg in each tomato, dust with salt, pepper, and finely chopped parsley. Place in 350° oven until egg is set. Serve with cream sauce.

BAKED EGG WITH TOMATOES
Remove the skin from six fresh tomatoes, or take ½ can of tomatoes, chop them and put them on stove and cook for twenty minutes; season with one tablespoon of chopped parsley, ½ onion chopped, salt and pepper; thicken at the end of that time with one teaspoon of melted butter mixed with one tablespoon of flour. Put aside to cool. Then mix in the yolks of four eggs well beaten, and lastly cut and fold in the four whites. Butter a pudding dish and set this mixture in the oven in a pan of lukewarm water and bake in a350° oven until a golden brown.

PLAIN OMELET

To make an omelet for breakfast or luncheon for two persons, take three eggs, three tablespoons of sweet milk, and a ¼ teaspoon of salt. Whip the yolks of the eggs, the milk and salt to a light foam with an egg whip. Slowly add the yolk mixture to the whites of the eggs, which should be beaten to a stiff froth in a big bowl. After the yolks and milk are well whipped through the whites, beat the whole together for a few minutes with the egg beater. In an omelet pan or a large frying pan put a tablespoon of good butter. When the butter is bubbling hot, pour in the omelet mixture. Stir it lightly for the first minute with a broad-bladed knife, then stop stirring it; and, as the mixture begins to stiffen around the edge, fold the omelet toward the center with the knife. As soon as it is properly folded, turn it over on a hot platter. Decorate with sprigs of parsley and serve.

SWEET OMELET

Six eggs, two tablespoons of flour, one cup of cold milk. Wet the flour with a little of the milk, then add the rest of the milk and the yolks of the eggs. Beat the whites of the eggs to a stiff froth and pour into the flour, milk and yolks. Put a piece of butter into a sauce pan and let it get hot, but not so hot that the butter will burn. Then pour the mixture in and put in a 350º oven to bake in the sauce pan. It takes about ten minutes to bake. Then slip a knife under it and loosen it and slip off on a large plate. Sift powdered sugar on top and serve with a slice of lemon.

SWEET OMELET FOR ONE

One egg, beat white separately, two tablespoons of cold sweet milk, a pinch of salt. Brown on both sides or roll, spread with compote or sprinkle powdered sugar thickly over it. Serve at once.

SPANISH OMELET

In a chopping bowl place two nice large ripe tomatoes, first peeling them; one large or two medium-sized white onions, two sprigs of parsley, and one large green-bell pepper, first removing most of its seeds.Chop these ingredients well together quite fine, turn them into a saucepan and let them cook over rather a brisk heat until quite soft. Put no water in this mixture. Add a tablespoon of olive oil or of butter before it begins to cook and season well with salt and red pepper. Make the omelet the same as the plain one, but use water instead of milk in mixing it, and only use two tablespoons of water for the six eggs required. After the eggs are sufficiently beaten, mixed, and in the pan over the heat and when the edges begin to stiffen, cover the surface of the omelet to within an inch of the edge with the cooked vegetables. Fold the omelet quickly and turn it on a hot platter. Pour around it all the vegetables left in the pan and serve.

RUM OMELET

Take six eggs, beat whites and yolks well, add a pinch of salt and a teaspoon of brandy. Fry in a sauce pan quickly and spread with a compote of huckleberries or any other fruit. Roll up the omelet, pour a very small wineglass of rum over it, light it and serve at once.

SWEET ALMOND OMELET

Prepare ½ cup of sweet almonds, blanched, chopped fine and pounded smooth. Beat four eggs slightly, add four tablespoons of cream, and turn it into a hot omelet pan on which you have melted one tablespoon of butter. Cook carefully, drawing the cooked portion into the center and tilting the pan to allow the liquid part to run over the bare pan. When nearly all set, sprinkle the almonds over the surface and turn the edges over until well rolled. Then slip it out on a hot dish and dredge with powdered sugar, and scatter several salted almonds over the top. Serve immediately.

CORN OMELET

Take ½ cup of canned corn and chop it very fine (or the same amount cut from the cob). Add to that the yolk of one egg, well beaten with pepper and salt to taste, and two tablespoons of cream. Beat the white of the egg very stiff and stir in just before cooking. Have the pan very hot and profusely buttered. Pour the mixture on, and when nicely browned, turn one half over the other, as in cooking other omelets.

HERB OMELET

Take six eggs and beat well in a bowl. Add two tablespoons of cold water, and ¼ teaspoon of salt, a pinch of pepper, a teaspoon of chopped parsley, a quarter of a teaspoon of grated onion and a teaspoon of fine butter, shaved in little pieces. Mix well with a wooden spoon. Dissolve in the sauce pan the butter and add at once the beaten eggs, etc., inclining the sauce pan to the handle for an instant and then shaking the omelet into the center and turn up the right edge, then the left and fry briskly five minutes and serve.

POACHED EGGS WITH FRIED TOMATOES
Fry tomatoes (cut ½ inch thick) in butter, pepper and salt. Have prepared slices of bread cut round, and fried in butter. Put on a hot platter with a slice of tomato on each. Poach as many eggs as are required, in boiling salt water. Lift out very carefully, placing one egg on each tomato. Add to the gravy in which tomatoes were fried, two tablespoons of cream, one teaspoon of any pungent sauce, one teaspoon of mushroom catsup, juice of ½ a lemon, and a teaspoon of flour to thicken. Cook up once and pour over eggs. Serve very hot.

EGGS POACHED IN TOMATO SAUCE
Make a sauce of one tablespoon of butter, one tablespoon of flour, 1½ cups of canned tomatoes rubbed through a strainer, a pinch of soda, salt, pepper and sugar to taste. When sufficiently cooked drop in the required number of eggs, cook until the white is firm, basting the eggs often with the sauce. When done, lift the eggs carefully to squares of toast and pour the sauce around them.

EGGS PIQUANT
Set to boil the following mixture: Pour into the kettle water to the depth of about one inch, adding a little salt and half a cup of vinegar. When this boils, break in as many fresh eggs, one at a time, as you desire to have. Do this carefully so as not to break the yolks. As soon as the whites of the eggs are boiled, take up carefully with a perforated skimmer and lay in cold water. Then remove to a large platter and pour over the following sauce: Strain the sauce the eggs were boiled in and set away until you have rubbed or grated two hard-boiled eggs, yolks only. Add a tablespoon of butter, rubbed very hard and add also some sugar and part of the strained sauce. Boil up once and pour over the eggs. Garnish with parsley.

OMELET SOUFFLÉ
Yolks of six eggs and six tablespoons of powdered sugar, added gradually, and both beaten together until thick and smooth; juice of one lemon and a little grated rind; whites beaten as stiff as possible, stirred together. Put into a warm well-buttered dish; bake in quick oven ten minutes.

WHITE SAUCE OMELET
Make a white sauce of one tablespoon of butter blended with two tablespoons of flour, one-half teaspoon of salt, pinch of pepper and one teaspoon of sugar, adding one-half cup each of milk and cream. Beat the yolks of five eggs and stir them into the sauce, then add the stiffly beaten whites of the eggs, folding them in carefully. Melt two tablespoons of butter in the omelet pan, when it is hot put in the mixture and let it stand in a moderate heat for two minutes, place in a hot oven and cook until set. Remove from the oven, turn on a hot platter and serve.

EGGS WITH CREAM DRESSING
Blend two tablespoons of butter with three tablespoons of flour. Place on stove and stir until the butter is melted. Add one and one-half cups of milk, stirring all the time until the mixture is thick; season with one teaspoon of salt and a few grains of pepper. Separate the whites of six hard-boiled eggs from the yolks. Chop the whites fine and add to the dressing. Arrange slices of toast on a hot platter, pour the dressing over them; force the yolks through a ricer onto the toast and dressing; serve hot.

SCALLOPED EGGS
Use above recipe and mix one cup of breadcrumbs with one tablespoon of butter, sprinkle this over dish and bake fifteen minutes in a hot oven.

EGGS Á LA MEXICANA
Boil six dried Spanish peppers twenty minutes. Drain, remove the seeds, and chop fine. Chop ½ an onion, and one clove of garlic, and fry in butter. Add one cup of uncooked rice, cover with one cup of water and cook until tender. Add a lump of butter, salt, and, when done, cover with six eggs; then scramble all together. Serve on a hot dish.

EGGS SPANISH

Boil eggs hard; after cooling, remove shells and halve lengthwise. Cook for thirty minutes fresh or canned tomatoes with minced green onions, garlic, parsley, a laurel leaf, salt, pepper, and cayenne pepper to taste. Strain. Melt a slice of butter, add a little flour, and then add sauce gradually. Cook ten minutes; place eggs carefully in sauce and serve.

FRESH MUSHROOMS WITH EGGS

Peel nine good-sized mushrooms without using the stems and chop very fine; fry two tablespoons of butter and two finely chopped onions without browning. Add the mushrooms and steam them by covering the pan after seasoning with salt, pepper and paprika. Before serving, beat six whole eggs, and scramble with the mushrooms. Serve on hot buttered toast.

EGG RAREBIT

Make a cream sauce. Grate ½ pound American and Swiss cheese mixed, or American alone; add to the sauce. Chop three hard-boiled eggs, add to the sauce, season with salt and pepper, and serve on buttered toast.

KROSPHADA

Place two sliced onions with two ounces each of sugar and spices, pepper and salt to taste, in a pint of pure malt vinegar and boil gently until the onions are nearly done. Let it cool a little and then stir in six beaten eggs and sufficient crumbled gingerbread to make the whole quite thick. Place again over the fire for a few minutes, stirring frequently and mashing the mixture into a uniform paste, but be very careful that it does not boil.

CURRIED EGGS

Melt four tablespoons of butter in a frying pan, add one onion chopped fine and cook until straw colored. Then add one tablespoon of curry powder. Make a smooth paste of ¼ cup of water and two tablespoons of flour; add one tablespoon of lemon juice and ½ teaspoon salt. Add to the first mixture; boil five minutes. Arrange six hard-boiled eggs in a border of rice and pour the dressing over all.

FRICASSEED EGGS

Take six hard-boiled eggs, remove shells. Roll them in flour, then in egg to which has been added ½ teaspoon oil, ½ teaspoon vinegar, a few drops of onion juice, one teaspoon chopped parsley, a little nutmeg and salt. When quite covered, roll in vermicelli that has been broken into fine bits and fry in oil. Serve with the following sauce: One tablespoon of oil; one tablespoon of flour, browned together; add ½ cup of white wine and a cup of bouillon. Season with salt and cayenne and boil five minutes. Add one teaspoon each of chopped chives and parsley, some chopped olives and mushrooms; bring to a boil again and pour over the eggs.

EGGS EN MARINADE

Mix equal quantities of water and good meat gravy, two tablespoons each, with a teaspoon of vinegar and a seasoning of pepper and salt. Put in a stew pan and stir in gradually two well-beaten yolks of eggs. When it thickens and before it boils, have ready a half dozen nicely poached eggs and pour the sauce over them. Garnish with parsley.

SCALLOPED EGGS (FLEISCHIG)

Make a force-meat of chopped tongue, breadcrumbs, pepper, salt, a little parsley, one tablespoon of melted fat, and soup stock enough to make a soft paste. Half fill patty-pans with the mixture. Break an egg carefully on the top of each, sprinkle with a little salt, pepper and cracker dust. Put in the oven and bake about ten minutes. Serve hot.

SCRAMBLED EGGS WITH BRAINS

Scald brains with hot water, clean and skin, and boil a few minutes in fresh water. Melt a little fat in skillet, put in brains, finely chopped, and stir well until dry and done. Add one teaspoon of chopped parsley, pinch of salt, and three eggs well beaten. Stir with a fork until eggs are evenly cooked, put on hot platter, and serve immediately.

SCRAMBLED EGGS WITH SAUSAGE

Take one pound of cold, boiled sausage, skin and slice in ½ inch pieces. Place in a frying pan with two tablespoons of hot oil; brown on both sides a few minutes and just before serving add three eggs, beaten slightly; mix and cook until the eggs are set and serve immediately. Chopped tongue root may be used instead of sausage.

SMOKED BRISKET OF BEEF AND EGGS
Take slices of smoked breast of beef, brown in frying pan; place on hot platter. Slip as many eggs as are needed in frying pan and cook gently by dripping the hot fat over them until done. Place carefully on the beef slices and serve at once.

CHEESE

Cheese should not be tightly covered. When it becomes dry and hard, grate and keep covered until ready to use. It may be added to starchy foods. Care should be exercised in planning meals in which cheese is employed as a substitute for meat. As cheese dishes are inclined to be somewhat "heavy," they should be offset by crisp, watery vegetables, watercress, celery, lettuce, fruit salads and light desserts, preferably fresh or cooked fruit. Another point, too, is to be considered. Whether raw or cooked, cheese seems to call for the harder kinds of bread - crusty rolls or biscuits, zwieback, toast, pulled bread or hard crackers. A soft, crumbly cheese is best for cooking. Cheese is sufficiently cooked when melted, if cooked longer it becomes tough and leathery. Baking soda in cheese dishes which are cooked makes the casein more digestible.

COTTAGE CHEESE (POT CHEESE)
Heat sour milk slowly until the whey rises to the top; pour it off, put the curd in a bag and let it dry for six hours without squeezing it. Pour it into a bowl and break it fine with a wooden spoon. Season with salt. Mold into balls and keep in a cool place. It is best when fresh.

KOCH KÄSE (BOILED CHEESE)
Press one quart of fine cottage cheese through a coarse sieve or colander and set it away in a cool place for a week, stirring it once or twice during that time; when it has become quite strong, stir it smooth with a wooden or silver spoon; add a ¼ teaspoon of salt, and a few caraway seeds, yolks of two eggs and an even tablespoon of flour which has been previously dissolved in about one-half cup of cold milk; stir the flour and milk until it is a smooth paste, adding a lump of butter, about the size of an egg; add all to the cheese. Put the cheese on to boil until quite thick, stirring occasionally; boil altogether about one-half hour, stirring constantly the last ten minutes; the cheese must look smooth as velvet. Pour it into a dish which has been previously rinsed in cold water. Set it away in a cool place; to keep it any length of time, cover it with a clean cloth which has been dipped in and wrung out of beer. This cheese is excellent for rye bread sandwiches.

A DELICIOUS CREAM CHEESE

Sweet milk is allowed to stand until it is like a jelly, but does not separate. Then it is poured into a cheesecloth bag and hung up to drain until all the water is out of it and only the rich creamy substance remains. Sometimes it takes from twelve to twenty-four hours. At the end of this time, the cheese is turned from the bag into a bowl; then to every pint of the cheesy substance a tablespoon of butter is added and enough salt to season it palatably. Then it is whipped with a fork until it is a smooth paste and enough put on a plate to make a little brick, like a Philadelphia cheese. With two knives, one in each hand, lightly press the cheese together in the shape of a brick, smooth it over the top and put it away to cool. One quart of rich sour milk will make a good-sized cheese.

CHEESE BALLS, No. 1

Take one cake of cream cheese, one-quarter of a pound of chopped figs, one-quarter of a pound of chopped walnuts, roll into balls and serve on lettuce leaves.

CHEESE BALLS, No. 2

Mix one cake Neufchatel cheese, a piece of butter the size of the cheese, one tablespoon of cream, ¼ teaspoon of salt and six dashes of Tabasco Sauce and form one large ball or several small ones and roll in chopped pecan nuts.

CHEESE SOUFFLÉ

Melt 1½ tablespoons of butter, add one tablespoon of flour, stir until it loosens from the pan; add one and one-half cups of rich milk, pepper and salt. Take from the fire, add gradually four egg yolks and three-quarters of a cup of grated cheese, then the stiffly beaten whites of eggs. Bake at 400° in oven-safe ramekins about fifteen minutes and serve immediately.

CHEESE TIMBALS FOR TWELVE PEOPLE

Take 2 cups milk, four tablespoons of flour, and use enough of the milk to dissolve the flour, the balance put in double boiler; when it boils, add the dissolved flour, then add ¼ pound grated Swiss cheese. Let these two boil for fifteen minutes; when cool, add the yolks of four eggs; drop one in at a time and beat, then strain through a fine sieve about ten minutes before you put in the pans; beat the whites of two eggs and put in the above and mix; grease timbal forms, fill ¾ full only; bake in pan of boiling water twenty minutes. Let them stand about two minutes, turn out on little plates, and serve with tomato sauce, a sprig of parsley put on top of each one.

WELSH RAREBIT
Melt one tablespoon of butter, add two cups finely cut American cheese, when it melts add ½ cup of milk or stale beer, keep stirring until it is smooth. Add ½ teaspoon of prepared mustard, two beaten eggs. Cook one minute longer and salt to taste. Serve on toast.

GOLDEN BUCK
One pound of cheese, ½ stick of butter, ½ cup ale, one teaspoon of mustard, one egg (well beaten), and salt and paprika. Put butter in pan, and when melted add cheese cut up or grated; stir, and as cheese melts, add ale. When it begins to bubble, add egg well beaten. Stir continually to keep from getting stringy. In two or three minutes it will be ready to serve. Pour over hot buttered toast. This quantity is sufficient for four persons.

CHEESE BREAD
Take six thick slices of stale bread, well buttered; cut them in two; dip into milk; then place in a baking dish, with alternating layers of thinly sliced cheese, having cheese for top. Add ½ cup of milk, into which ½ teaspoon dry mustard has been put in. Bake in 425° oven fifteen minutes. Serve at once.

GREEN CORN, TOMATOES AND CHEESE
Into one tablespoon of melted butter stir two cups of grated cheese until it, too, is melted. Add ¾ cup of canned or grated fresh corn, one ripe green pepper, stir them, add one egg yolk mixed with ½ cup of tomato purée, one teaspoon of salt, ½ teaspoon of paprika. Toast five slices of bread and pour this mixture over it. Serve hot.

RICE AND CHEESE
Melt two ounces of butter in a pan; fry in the butter a finely minced onion. When this is of a nice golden color stir into it ¼ pound of well-boiled rice.

Work it well with a fork and then pour all into a buttered pie dish. Dredge over with a good coating of grated cheese, sprinkle the surface with melted butter and bake at 400° until nicely browned.

MACARONI AND CHEESE

Break three ounces of macaroni - noodles or spaghetti answer equally well - into small pieces, boil in rapidly boiling salted water; when tender drain off the water and add 1 cup milk; cook slowly till the macaroni has absorbed most of the milk. To 1 cup of thick white sauce add two ounces of grated cheese and mix with the macaroni; last of all add two well-beaten eggs. Butter a pudding mold, sprinkle it with browned breadcrumbs and pour in the macaroni mixture; steam gently for about half an hour, turn out and fill the center with stewed tomatoes and mushrooms.

CHEESE OMELET

Cook in double boiler one cup of milk, add one tablespoon of butter, one tablespoon of flour blended together and cook until thick; one cup of cheese cut up added, and stir until dissolved. Remove from fire and stir in yolks of four eggs beaten, ½ teaspoon of salt (pepper). Fold in whites of four eggs beaten stiff and a pinch of baking powder. Bake in a buttered dish 400° for thirty minutes.

CHEESE AND SWEET GREEN PEPPERS

Cheese and peppers make a very nice combination. Melt two ounces of cheese, add a tablespoon of chopped peppers and the same amount of butter, a little paprika, salt, and if liked, mustard. When the ingredients have been well-blended pour the mixture on hot buttered toast and serve.

CHEESE FONDUE

Soak ½ cup of breadcrumbs in one scant cup of milk; dissolve a speck of bicarbonate of soda in a drop of hot water and add to the milk, one egg, yolk and white beaten separately, ½ cup of dry cheese grated, one tablespoon of butter, salt and pepper to taste, beat well, pour into a well buttered baking dish, strew dry crumbs moistened with butter over the top, and bake in a hot oven until light brown. Serve at once in the dish in which it is baked.

TOMATOES, EGGS AND CHEESE (HUNGARIAN)
Place two tablespoons of butter in a pan (after having the water boil to heat the pan). Let butter melt, add one small onion chopped fine and cook until soft, 2 cups of tomatoes strained and let come to a boil; add ½ pound mild cheese cut fine, and stir until smooth. Break in three eggs and stir hard until eggs are done. Serve on buttered toast.

CRACKERS AND CHEESE
Split in two some Bent's water biscuits; moisten them with hot water and pour over each piece a little melted butter and prepared mustard; then spread with a thick layer of grated cheese; sprinkle with paprika or cayenne. Place them in a hot oven until the cheese is soft and creamy.

RAMEKINS OF EGG AND CHEESE
Beat three new-laid eggs and blend thoroughly with two ounces of grated cheese and one ounce of partly melted butter. Place the mixture in little pans or saucers and bake at 400° in the oven about 15 minutes.

BREAD

Homemade bread is very much more palatable and more nutritious than baker's bread and it is worthwhile to spend time and effort in its preparation. To make good bread, it is necessary to have good flour, fresh yeast and the liquid used in moistening must be neither too hot nor too cold or the bread will not rise properly.

FLOUR

The housekeeper should know about the different kinds of flour. We get the bread flour from the spring wheat; the pastry flour from the winter wheat. Bread flour contains more gluten than pastry flour and is used for bread on that account. Pastry flour having less gluten and slightly more starch is more suitable for pastry and cake mixtures and is used wherever softness and lightness are desired. Graham flour is the whole kernel of wheat ground. Entire wheat flour is the flour resulting from the grinding of all but the outer layer of the wheat. Rye flour is next best to wheat flour for bread making, but is generally combined with wheat flour, since by itself it makes a sticky bread. Cornmeal is also combined with wheat flour. Variety bread is composed of bread flour, rye flour and cornmeal combined in one loaf. If flour is musty, it is not kosher and must be destroyed. Keep flour either in tins or barrels in a dry atmosphere.

YEAST

In cities where fresh compressed yeast can be obtained, it is not worth while to prepare one's own. Compressed yeast is always in proper condition to use until it becomes soft, often the yeast cakes are slightly discolored, but this does not affect the yeast, being caused by the oxidation of the starch in the cake. Keep yeast in cool place.

WHITE BREAD

Set the dough at night and bake early in the morning; take ½ cake of compressed yeast, set in a cup of lukewarm milk or water adding a teaspoon of salt and a tablespoon of sugar. Let this rise, if it does not, the yeast is not fresh or good. Measure eight cups of sifted flour into a deep bread bowl, add one teaspoon of salt; make a depression in the center, pour in the risen yeast and one cup of lukewarm milk or water. In winter be sure that the bowl, flour, milk, in fact everything has been thoroughly warmed before mixing. Mix the dough slowly with a wooden spoon and then knead as directed. This amount will make two loaves, either twisted or in small bread pans. Bake forty-five minutes in a 350° oven. If the bread is set in the morning use a cake of compressed yeast and bake the loaves in the afternoon.

INDIVIDUAL LOAVES
Make dough according to the above recipe. Work small pieces of dough into strands a finger long, and take three strands for each loaf. Make small as possible, brush with beaten egg or sweetened water and sprinkle with poppy seed (Mohn). Allow them to rise before setting them in the oven. These are called "Vienna loaves" and are used at weddings, parties and for the Succoth festival in the Succah. If ½ cake of yeast has been used, the ½ cake of yeast which is left over, can be kept in good condition several days by rewrapping it in the tinfoil and keeping it in a cool, dry place.

BUTTERBARCHES
Dissolve one cake of compressed yeast in ½ cup of lukewarm milk, add a teaspoon of salt, and a tablespoon of sugar and let it rise. Then make a soft dough of eight cups of sifted flour and as much milk as is required to work it, about two cups; add the yeast, ½ cup of sugar, four tablespoons of butter dissolved in the warm milk, the grated peel of a lemon, two or three dozen raisins seeded, and two eggs well beaten. Work this dough perfectly smooth with the palm of your hand, adding more flour if necessary. It is hardly possible to tell the exact amount of flour to use; experience will teach you when you have added enough. Different brands of flour vary, some being drier than others. Work the dough as directed, set it aside covered until it is double the bulk of the original piece of dough. Then work again and divide the dough into two parts, and divide each of the pieces of dough into three parts. Work the six pieces of dough thoroughly and then roll each piece into a long strand; three of which are to be longer than the other three. Braid the three long strands into one braid (should be thicker

in the center than at the end), and braid the shorter strands into one braid and lay it on top of the long braid, pressing the ends together. Butter a long baking-pan, lift the barches into the pan and set in a warm place to rise again for about one-half hour. Then brush the top with beaten egg and sprinkle poppy seed all over the top. Bake in a 350° oven one hour.

BARCHES
These are to be used for a meat meal and are made in the same manner as butter barches, omitting the milk and butter; use water and a little shortening of dripping or rendered fat or a vegetable oil; grate a dozen almonds (blanched) and add with two well-beaten eggs, ½ cup of sugar, salt, raisins and the grated peel of one lemon. Work just as you would butter barches. Bake one hour in 350° oven. Wrap in a damp, clean towel as soon as baked to prevent the crust from becoming too hard.

POTATO BREAD
Add one medium-sized mashed boiled potato to any of the foregoing recipes. This will give a moister bread, which retains its freshness longer.

GRAHAM BREAD
Dissolve one cake of compressed yeast and four tablespoons of light brown sugar or molasses in one cup of lukewarm water and one cup of milk which has been scalded and cooled to lukewarm. Add two tablespoons of melted butter, then four cups of Graham flour and one cup of white flour (sifted), adding flour gradually, and one teaspoon of salt. Knead thoroughly, being sure to keep dough soft. Cover and set aside in a warm place to rise for about two hours. When double in bulk, turn out on kneading board, mold into loaves, and place in well-greased pans, cover and set to rise again--about one hour or until light. Bake one hour, in a 325° oven than for white bread. If wanted for overnight use ½ cake of yeast and an extra half teaspoon of salt.

GLUTEN BREAD
Dissolve one cake of compressed yeast and one tablespoon of sugar in one cup of milk, scalded and cooled, and one cup of lukewarm water; add one level tablespoon of butter then three cups of gluten flour gradually, and one teaspoon of salt. Knead thoroughly until smooth and elastic; place in

well-greased bowl; cover and set aside in a warm place, free from draught, to rise until light, which should be in about two hours. Mold into loaves; place in greased pans, filling them half full. Cover, let rise again, and when double in bulk, which should be in about one hour, bake in moderate oven forty-five minutes. This will make two one-pound loaves. For diet use omit shortening and sugar.

RAISIN BREAD

Make dough as directed for Butterbarches, using ¼ cup of raisins and omitting the lemon and egg. Form in loaves, fill well-greased pans half full; cover and let rise until light; about one hour. Glaze with egg diluted with water, and bake at 350° for forty-five minutes.

ROLLED OATS BREAD

Pour two cups of boiling water over two cups of rolled oats, cover and let stand until lukewarm. Dissolve one cake of compressed yeast and one-fourth cup of brown sugar in ½ cup of lukewarm water, add two tablespoons of shortening, the oatmeal and the water in which it has been swelling. Beat well, add about three cups of flour to make a dough, also add one teaspoon of salt. Let rise until it doubles in bulk. Mold into two loaves in pan and bake at 350° for forty-five minutes.

POTATO-RYE BREAD

Cook one quart of potatoes diced, in boiling water until tender. Strain, reserving potato water. Measure and add enough more water to make three cups. Let come to a boil, add ¼ cup of salt, and very gradually one and ¼ cup of cornmeal. Cook two minutes, stirring constantly until thick. Remove from fire, add two tablespoons of any kind of fat, the potatoes riced or mashed and when cooled two cups of flour; then one tablespoon of sugar and one cake of yeast dissolved in one cup of lukewarm water. Mix and knead to a stiff dough adding wheat flour to keep it from sticking. Cover, set aside in a warm place overnight, or until double its bulk. Shape into four loaves, let rise again; bake in a 350° oven one hour or more, until well done. Glaze with egg diluted with water before putting in the oven. These loaves will keep moist one week.

RYE BREAD (AMERICAN) No. 1

Dissolve one cake compressed yeast in two cups of lukewarm water and one cup of milk which has been scalded and cooled; or if so desired the milk may be omitted and all water used; add 2½ cups of rye flour or enough to make a sponge. Beat well; cover and set aside in a warm place, free from draught, to rise about two hours. When light add 1½ cups of sifted white flour, one tablespoon of melted butter or oil, 2½ cups of rye flour to make a soft dough and last one tablespoon of salt. Turn on a board and knead or pound it five minutes. Place in greased bowl; cover and let rise until double in bulk - about two hours. Turn on board and shape into loaves; place in floured shallow pans; cover and let rise again until light - about one hour. Brush with white of egg and water, to glaze. With sharp knife cut lightly three strokes diagonally across top, and place in oven. Bake in slower oven than for white bread. Caraway seeds may be used if desired. By adding ½ cup of sour dough, left from previous baking, an acid flavor is obtained, which is considered by many a great improvement. This should be added to the sponge. Bake in a 350° oven.

RYE BREAD, No. 2

Sift three cups of rye flour, three cups of wheat flour and two teaspoons of salt in a bowl. Dissolve one-half cake of compressed yeast or any other yeast in two cups of lukewarm water. When the yeast is dissolved pour it into the flour and make into a dough. Lay it on a kneading board, and knead until smooth and elastic, put it back into the bowl, cover with a towel, and set aside overnight to rise. Next morning, lay the dough on a biscuit or kneading board again and knead well. Make into a loaf, put into a pan, and when well risen, moisten the top with a little cold water and bake in a 350° oven.

ZWIEBELPLATZ

Take a piece of rye bread dough. After it has risen sufficiently roll out quite thin, butter a long cake pan and put in the rolled dough. Brush with melted butter; chop some onions very fine, strew thickly on top of cake, sprinkle with salt, put flakes of butter here and there. Another way is to chop up parsley and use in place of onions. Then called "Petersilien Platz." Bake in a 350° oven.

VARIETY BREAD

Dissolve one cake of compressed yeast in two cups of lukewarm water or milk, add two teaspoons of salt, three cups of bread or wheat flour, one cup of cornmeal, one cup of rye flour and one-half cup of dark molasses, and mix very thoroughly. Let rise, shape into loaves, let rise again and bake in a 350° oven for forty-five minutes

ROLLS

Take bread dough, when ready to shape into loaves and make a long even roll. Cut into small even pieces, and shape with thumb and fingers into round balls. Set close together in a shallow pan, let rise until double the bulk, and bake in a 425° oven from ten to twenty minutes. If crusty rolls are desired, set apart in a shallow pan, bake well, and cool in draft.

TEA ROLLS

Scald one cup of milk and when lukewarm dissolve one cake of compressed yeast and add one and one-half cups of flour. Beat thoroughly, cover and allow to stand until light. Add ¼ cup of sugar, 1½ teaspoons of salt, two eggs, ⅓ cup of butter and enough flour to knead. Allow to rise again until light. Shape into round or small oblong finger rolls, and place in buttered pans close together, when light bake in 425° oven.

CRESCENT ROLLS

Take bread or Kuchen dough, and when well risen, toss on floured baking board, roll into a square sheet, ¼ inch thick. Spread with melted butter, and cut into six-inch squares, then cut each square into two equal parts through opposite corners, thus forming two triangles. Roll over and over from the longest side to the opposite corner and then shape the rolls into half moons or crescents. Place in floured or greased pans, rather far apart; brush with beaten yolk to which a little cold water has been added and sprinkle tops ofcrescents or horns with poppy seed. Set in warm place to rise and when double its bulk, bake in 425° oven until brown and crusty.

BUNS
Make same as tea rolls. When well risen mold into small round buns; place in well-greased pans, one inch apart. Cover set aside to rise until light - about one hour. Brush with egg diluted with water; bake at 400° for twenty minutes. Just before removing from the oven, brush with sugar moistened with a little water.

RAISIN OR CURRANT BUNS
Boil two large potatoes and strain the water into a pitcher dissolve ⅔ cake of yeast in a cup. Put potatoes in a pan with a cup of sugar; large lump of butter, and teaspoon of salt. The heat of potatoes will melt the sugar and butter. Mash with large masher to a cream; pour in rest of potato water, add 2 cups flour and mix together. Then cover and set in a warm place all night. In the morning add more flour mix quickly and put currants or raisins in as you turn the dough. This will keep them from settling in the bottom of the bread. Put in hot pans and bake in a 400° oven. This makes a delicious holiday bread. Eat with butter, hot or cold.

BREAD STICKS
Take pieces of raised bread dough, roll ⅜ inch thick and four or five inches long. Place in floured pan, far apart, brush tops with beaten yolk and poppy seed. Let rise bake in a hot oven until brown.

FRENCH ROLLS
Prepare the yeast as for bread and work just the same; add ¼ cup of butter, ¼ cup of sugar, one whole egg and one egg yolk beaten very light, flavor with mace or a few gratings of lemon peel; work until it leaves the hands perfectly clean, then form into rolls, let raise, brush with beaten egg, place rolls in pan close together and bake at 400°.

BUTTERED TOAST
Slice even slices of baker's bread, not too thin, put in biscuit pan on the top rack of a 425° oven, brown nicely on one side, then turn and brown on the other, spread with butter, and a little powdered sugar, if desired, and serve at once.

MILK OR CREAM TOAST

Toast as many slices of stale light bread as desired a light brown. Heat milk or cream, allowing ½ cup for each slice, add small lump of butter. When just at the boiling point, pour over bread that has been placed in dish, sprinkle with sugar and cinnamon, cover, and serve immediately.

CINNAMON TOAST FOR TEA

Bread cut thin and browned, but not dried. Butter the toast while very hot, thinly and evenly, and sprinkle over each piece some powdered cinnamon and sugar.

ARME RITTER

Beat two eggs slightly, add ½ teaspoon of salt, and ⅔ cup of milk; dip six slices of stale bread in the mixture. Have a griddle hot and well buttered; brown the bread on each side. Serve hot with cinnamon and sugar or a sauce.

COFFEE CAKES (KUCHEN)

RENDERED BUTTER
Procure as much country or Western butter as desired, you may get several pounds of it when it is cheap during the summer; or any butter unfit for table use may be made sweet and good for cooking purposes and will last for months, if prepared in the following manner: Place the butter in a deep, iron kettle, filling only half full to prevent boiling over. Set it on the stove to simmer slowly for several hours. Watch carefully that it does not boil over. Do not stir it, but from time to time skim it. When perfectly clear, and all the salt and sediment has settled at the bottom, the butter is done. Set aside a few minutes, then strain into stone jars through a fine sieve, and when cold tie up tightly with paper and cloth. Keep in a cool, dry place.

COFFEE CAKE (KUCHEN) DOUGH for following recipes
Soak ½ ounce of yeast in ½ cup of lukewarm milk; when dissolved put in a bowl, or round agate pan, and stir in one cup of sifted flour, one teaspoon of sugar and ¼ teaspoon of salt, mix thoroughly, and put in a warm place (not hot) to rise, from one to two hours. When well risen, cream well together one cup of sugar and ¾ cup of butter, then add three eggs, five cups of sifted flour, one cup of milk and one teaspoon of salt, mix together until light, then stir in the risen yeast, and with a spoon work well for ten minutes, and set aside to rise again, five or six hours or all night. Dough should not be very stiff. When well risen it can be used for cinnamon cake, pies or pocket books. This recipe makes one large cinnamon cake, three pies, and about one dozen pocket books.

KAFFEEKUCHEN (CINNAMON)
Butter long and broad cake pans thoroughly, roll out enough dough to cover them, and let it rise about thirty minutes before baking, then brush it well with melted butter. Sprinkle sugar and cinnamon on top and some chopped almonds. Take a small lump of butter, a very little flour, some sugar and cinnamon and rub it between the hands until it is like lumps of almonds, then strew on top of cakes. Bake ten to twenty minutes in a 400° oven to a golden brown.

CINNAMON ROLLS OR SCHNECKEN

Take half the Kuchen dough. Roll ½ inch thick and spread well with melted butter. Sprinkle generously with scraped maple, brown or granulated sugar and cinnamon, then roll. Cut the roll into equal parts about one inch thick, place close together endwise in a sauce pan, generously buttered, spread with one-fourth inch layer of brown or maple sugar. Let rise until light, and bake ten to twenty minutes in a 400° oven, a golden brown. Invert the sauce pan, remove rolls and serve caramel side up.

ABGERUEHRTER KUGELHOPF

Soak ½ ounce of yeast or one cake compressed yeast in a very little lukewarm milk; add a pinch of salt and one tablespoon of sugar, stir it up smooth and set back of the stove to rise. In the meantime rub a scant cup of butter and a scant cup of powdered sugar to a cream, add gradually the yolks of four eggs, one at a time and add also the grated peel of a lemon. Sift two cups of flour into a bowl, make a depression in the center, pour in the yeast, one cup of lukewarm milk, and make a light batter of this. Add the creamed butter and eggs and stir until it forms blisters and leaves the bowl clean. Take ½ cup of cleaned and seeded dark raisins and cut up some citron very fine. Dredge flour over them before adding, and if necessary, add more flour to the dough, which should be of the consistency of cup cake batter. Last, add the stiffly beaten whites of the eggs. Place in a well-greased long or round pan with tube in center; let rise until double in bulk, and bake in 375° oven until browned and thoroughly done.

PLAIN BUNT OR NAPF KUCHEN

Take one cake compressed yeast, add a pinch of salt, one tablespoon of sugar, and about two tablespoons of lukewarm water. Stir the yeast until it is a smooth paste and set it in a warm place to rise. Sift 2½ cups of flour (use the same size cup for measuring everything you are going to use in your cake), make a depression in the center, stir in the yeast and a scant cup of lukewarm milk, make batter, and let it rise until you have prepared the following: Rub ½ cup of butter and ¾ cup of powdered sugar to a cream, just as for cup cake, then add gradually one egg at a time, using three altogether, and stirring all the time in one direction. Work in the risen batter two or three spoons at a time between each egg. Grate in the peel of a lemon or an orange. Butter the bunt-form well (do this always before you begin to work). Blanched almonds may be set in the grooves of the cake-form after buttering it. Put in the dough, set it in a warm place and let it rise for an hour and a half or two hours. Bake in a 350° oven one full hour, covered at first.

CHOCOLATE COFFEE CAKE
Pour a bunt Kuchen dough into long, well-buttered tins, and when baked remove from the oven and cover thickly with boiled chocolate icing.

POCKET BOOKS
Take as much of the coffee cake dough as you desire, lay it on a well-floured biscuit board and mix just enough more flour with it to enable you to roll it out without sticking to the board. Roll out about ¼ inch thick and cut the dough in squares about as long as your finger. Beat the yolk of one egg and two tablespoons of milk together; wet each square well with the mixture, lay one raisin in the center, sprinkle thickly with sugar and cinnamon mixed together, then put a small dab of butter on top. Catch the four corners of each square together, so that the inside is protected. Lay the pocket books, not too closely together, in a greased pan and set aside to rise. When well risen bake in a 350° oven until well baked and browned nicely.

BOLA
Make a good, rich bread dough. Let it rise overnight; next morning mix with dough two eggs, ½ pound of butter well kneaded; put in warm place until well risen. When risen, roll out into thin sheets and sprinkle with chopped almonds, citron, cinnamon and plenty of brown sugar and lumps of butter all through; roll up like jelly-roll, cut in pieces a finger long, grease pan, stand pieces in center, others around and let rise before baking at 350° until golden brown. Watch it well while baking.

FRENCH COFFEE CAKE (SAVARIN)
Soak one cake of compressed yeast in a little lukewarm water or milk. Put the yeast in a cup, add two tablespoons of lukewarm water, a pinch of salt and one tablespoon of sugar, stir it up well with a spoon and set back of the stove to rise. Rub ½ cup of butter to a cream, add ⅓ cup of powdered sugar and stir constantly in one direction. Add the yolks of four eggs, one

at a time, and the grated peel of a lemon. Sift two cups of flour into a bowl, make a depression in the center of the flour, pour in the yeast and one cup of lukewarm milk. Stir and make a light batter of this. Add the creamed butter and eggs, stir until it forms blisters and leaves the bowl clean; ½ cup of dark raisins, ½ cup of pounded almonds and a little citron, cut up very fine, and last the stiff-beaten whites of the eggs. Fill your cake forms that have been well-greased, set in a warm place to rise until double in bulk, about forty-five minutes, and bake in a 350° oven for forty-five minutes. Fill the center with whipped cream and serve with rum sauce.

BABA Á LA PARISIENNE
Prepare the yeast as above; cream a scant cup of butter with four tablespoons of sugar, the grated peel of a lemon, add five eggs, one at a time, stirring each egg a few minutes before you add the next. Have ready two cups of sifted flour and add two spoonfuls between each egg until all is used. Make a soft dough of the yeast, a scant cup of lukewarm milk, add two spoonfuls between each egg until all is used up, a pinch of salt, and one cup of flour. Let it rise for fifteen minutes. Now mix all well, rub the form with butter, and blanch ½ cup of almonds, cut into long strips and strew all over the form. Fill in the mixture or cake batter, let it rise two hours and bake at 325° until golden brown.

MOHN (POPPY SEED) ROLEY POLEY
Roll out a piece of dough large enough to cover your whole baking-board, roll thin. Let it rise until you have prepared the filling; grind one cup of black poppy seed in a coffee-mill as tight as possible and clean it well, throw away the first bit you grind so as not to have the coffee taste; put it on to boil with one cup of milk, add two tablespoons of butter, ½ cup of raisins, ½ cup of walnuts or almonds chopped up fine, two tablespoons of molasses or syrup, and a little citron cut up fine. When thick, set it away to cool, and if not sweet enough add more sugar and flavor with vanilla. When this mixture has cooled, spread on the dough which has risen by this time. Take up one corner and roll it up into a long roll, like a jelly-roll, put in a greased pan and let it rise an hour, then spread butter on top and bake at 325° until quite brown, so as to bake through thoroughly. When cold cut up in slices, as many as you are going to use at one time only.

MOHN WACHTEL

Take coffee cake dough. Let the dough rise again for an hour, spread with a poppy seed mixture, after cutting into squares, fold into triangles and pinch the edges together. Lay in well-buttered pans, about two inches apart, and let them rise again, spread with poppy seed filling. Take ½ pound of poppy seed (mohn) that have previously been soaked in milk and then ground, add ¼ pound of sugar, and the yolks of three eggs. Stir this all together in one direction until quite thick and then stir in the beaten whites to which you must add two ounces of sifted flour and ¼ of a pound of melted butter. Fill the tartlets and bake at 400° until golden brown. The poppy seed filling in Mohn Roley Poley may be used in the Mohn Wachtel if so desired.

MOHNTORTE

Line a deep pie plate with a thin sheet of Kuchen dough, let it rise about half an hour, then fill with a poppy seed filling same as used with Mohn Wachtel. Fill the pie plates and bake at 400° until golden brown.

SMALL MOHN CAKES

Roll coffee cake dough out quite thin, spread with melted butter (a brush is best for this purpose). Let it rise a little while, then sprinkle well with one cup of sugar, add ½ pound of ground poppy seed moistened with ½ cup of water, cut into strips about an inch wide and four inches long; roll and put in a well-buttered pan to rise, leaving enough space between each and brush with butter. Bake in 375° oven at first, then decrease the heat to 325°; bake slowly until golden brown.

BERLINER PFANNKUCHEN (PURIM KRAPFEN)

Take 1½ cups of flour, a pinch of salt sifted into a deep bowl, one cup of lukewarm milk and ¾ cake of compressed yeast which has been dissolved in a little warm water and sugar. Stir into a dough, cover with a towel and set away in a warm place to rise. When well risen, take ½ cup of butter, one cup of sugar, a little salt and rub to a cream. Add two eggs well beaten, stir all well and add the risen dough, one teaspoon of salt and work in gradually five cups of sifted flour and the grated peel of a lemon. Stir the dough until it blisters and leaves the dish perfectly clean at the sides. Let the dough rise slowly for about two hours (all yeast dough is better if it rises slowly). Take a large baking-board, flour well and roll out the dough on it as thin as a double thickness of pasteboard. When it is all rolled out, cut with a round cutter the size of a tumbler. When all the dough has been cut out, beat up an egg. Spread the beaten egg on the edge of each cake (spread only a few at a time for they would get too dry if all were done at once). Then put one-half teaspoon of marmalade, jam or jelly on the cake. Put another cake on top of one already spread, having cut it with a cutter a little bit smaller than the one used in the first place. This makes them stick better and prevents the preserves coming out while cooking. Set all away on a floured board or pan about two inches apart. Spread the top of each cake with melted butter and let them rise from one to two hours. When ready to fry, heat at least two pounds of rendered butter or any good vegetable oil in a deep iron kettle. Try the butter with a small piece of dough. If it rises immediately, put in the doughnuts. In putting them in, place the side that is up on the board down in the hot butter. Do not crowd them in the kettle as they require room to rise and spread. Cover them with a lid. In a few seconds uncover. If they are light brown, turn them over on the other side but do not cover them again. When done they will have a white stripe around the center. Take them up with a perforated skimmer, lay on a large platter, sprinkle with pulverized sugar. If the butter gets too hot take from the fire a minute. These are best eaten fresh. The doughnuts may be baked in moderately hot oven and when half done glazed with sugar and white of egg.

TOPFA DALKELN - CHEESE CAKES (HUNGARIAN)
Take ½ ounce of yeast, mix with a little scalded milk that has cooled to lukewarm, ½ cup of flour and put aside in a warm place to rise. Allow two cups of scalded milk to become lukewarm. Add one pound of flour (four cups sifted flour) to the risen sponge, then the two cups of milk, mix these very well, cover with a cloth and put aside in a warm place to rise. Take one pound of sweet pot cheese, a pinch of salt, three egg yolks, rind of one lemon, one-half cup of light colored raisins and sugar to taste; mix very well and add the beaten whites and mix thoroughly. When the dough is very well risen, place on a pastry board, roll out and spread with melted butter, fold these edges over to the middle, then the top and bottom over,

roll again and spread with butter, fold all sides in once more, roll, spread with butter, repeat the folding, roll out to one-half inch thickness, cut in three-inch squares, place a tablespoon of the cheese mixture in the center of each square, fold over opposite corners, spread egg white over the top of each pocket, let rise fifteen to thirty minutes and bake in a 400° oven; when they are well risen, lower heat and bake to a golden brown. This will make about thirty cakes. The dough in the above may be used with the following filling: Boil ½ pound of prunes, mash to a pulp, sweeten, add the grated peel of a lemon, some cinnamon, etc., and put one teaspoon of this into each square. Take up the corners, fasten them firmly, also pinch all along the edges and lay in a buttered pan, let them rise half an hour before baking. Spread them with melted butter, and bake a nice brown.

PUFFS (PURIM)
Make the dough same as for Berliner Pfannkuchen, and when well risen roll out on a floured board ½ inch thick, cut in triangles, lay on floured dishes or board to rise. When well risen, drop into a deep kettle of boiling butter and with a spoon baste with the butter until brown; remove with a perforated skimmer and sprinkle with powdered sugar.

KINDLECH
Into a large bowl sift one pound of fine flour. Make a depression in the center and pour into it one yeast cake dissolved in a little milk. Let this remain until the milk and yeast have risen a little. Stir in the surrounding flour together with three well-beaten eggs, a ¼ pound of butter, six ounces of sugar, a pinch of salt and two cups of lukewarm milk. Knead the whole into a smooth dough. Roll this out very lightly on a well-floured board, brush over with a feather dipped in melted butter and strew thickly with chopped almonds, sultanas and currants. Next fold over about three fingers' width of the dough. Brush the upper surface of this fold with melted butter and strew with mixed fruit and almonds. Fold over again and repeat the operation until the whole of the dough is folded up in layer somewhat resembling a flattened roley poley pudding. Brush the top well with another feather dipped in beaten egg and cut the whole into thick slices or fingers. Let them stand for thirty minutes and then bake for an hour in a 325° oven.

A CHEAP COFFEE CAKE

This German coffee cake is made by kneading into a pint of bread dough one well-beaten egg, ½ cup of sugar, and a generous tablespoon of butter. The mixture is rolled flat, placed in a shallow pan, let rise again until very light, sprinkled with finely chopped nuts, dusted over with sugar and cinnamon and baked in a 400° oven.

BOHEMIAN KOLATCHEN

Make Kuchen dough. Add a little cinnamon and mace and one teaspoon of anise seed, well pounded, or flavor to taste. Let rise till very light, then take out on mixing board and roll out to about ½ inch in thickness. Cut in rounds three inches in diameter and lay on a well-buttered pan, pressing down the center of each so as to raise a ridge around the edge. When well risen, brush the top over with stiffly beaten white of an egg and sprinkle with granulated sugar. Bake in a 375° oven until golden brown.

ZWIEBACK

Scald ½ cup of milk and when lukewarm add to one cake of compressed yeast. Add ¼ cup of sugar, one-fourth cup of melted butter, one-half teaspoon of salt and three eggs unbeaten, ½ teaspoon of powdered anise and enough flour to handle. Let rise until light. Make into oblong rolls the length of middle finger and place together in a buttered pan in parallel rows, two inches apart. Let rise again and bake twenty minutes. When cold, cut in ½ inch slices and brown evenly in a 375° oven.

SOUR CREAM KOLATCHEN

Cream ½ cup of butter, add five yolks, two tablespoons of sugar, grated rind of a lemon, one cup of thick sour cream and one ounce or two cakes of yeast dissolved with a little sugar in two tablespoons of lukewarm milk. Stir all together and add three cups of flour; mix and drop from end of teaspoon on well-greased pans. Let rise until light in a warm place. Place a raisin or cherry on the top of each cake, spread with beaten white of egg, sprinkle with sugar and bake ten minutes in a 400° oven.

RUSSIAN TEA CAKES

Mix one cup of sugar, one cup of eggs (about five), and one cup of sour cream with enough flour to roll. Toss on board, roll out ¼ inch thick, spread with a thin layer of butter, fold the dough over, roll and spread again; repeat three or four times, using altogether three-fourths pound of brick butter. Then place dough in a bowl, cover, and let stand on ice to harden. Then roll as thin as possible, strew with one cup of chopped almonds, sugar and cinnamon, and cut into seven-inch strips. Roll each strip separately into a roll, cut into squares and strew top with chopped almonds, sugar and cinnamon. Bake in a 400° oven until evenly browned.

WIENER KIPFEL

Dissolve one ounce of yeast in ½ cup of lukewarm milk, a pinch of salt and one tablespoon of sugar, set away in a warm place to rise. Sift one pound of flour into a deep bowl and make a dough of one cup of lukewarm milk and the yeast. Set it away until you have prepared the following: Rub a ¼ pound of butter and four ounces of sugar to a cream, adding yolks of three eggs and one whole egg. Add this to the dough and work well. Let it rise about one hour, then roll out on a well-floured board, just as you would for cookies and let it rise again for at least thirty minutes. Spread with beaten whites of eggs, raisins, almonds and citron. Cut dough into triangles. Pinch the edges together. Lay them in well-buttered pans about two inches apart and let then rise again. Then spread again with stiff-beaten whites of eggs and lay a few pounded almonds on each one. Bake at 400° until a light yellow.

SPICE ROLL

Roll out coffee cake dough quite thin and let it rise thirty minutes, brush with melted butter and make a filling of the following: Grate some Lebkuchen or plain gingerbread; add ½ cup of almonds or nuts, one cup of raisins and one cup of cleaned currants. Strew these all over the dough together with some brown sugar and a little syrup. Spice with cinnamon and roll. Spread with butter and let it rise for an hour. Bake at 400° until brown.

WIENER STUDENTEN KIPFEL

Make dough same as for Wiener Kipfel. Roll it out quite thin on a well-floured board and let it rise. Cut also into triangles (before you cut them, spread with melted butter). Mix one cup of chopped fresh walnuts with one cup of brown sugar, juice of a lemon, or grind the nuts; add cream to make a paste, sugar to taste and flavor with vanilla, and fill the triangles with the mixture. Take up the three corners and pinch together tightly. Set in well-buttered pans and let them rise again and spread or brush each one with melted butter. Bake at 400° until a light brown.

YEAST KRANTZ
Take coffee cake dough, add ¼ cup of currants. Let rise in warm place, then toss on floured board. Divide into three or four equal parts, roll each part into a long strand and work the strands together to form one large braid. Place braid in form of a circle in greased baking-pan or twist the braid to resemble the figure eight, pretzel shape. Let rise again in a warm place and bake in a 350° oven for thirty minutes, or until thoroughly done. Brush with beaten eggs and sugar, sprinkle with a few chopped almonds. Brown slightly.

STOLLEN
Sift two pounds of flour into a bowl and set a sponge in it with one cake of compressed yeast, one teaspoon of salt, one pint of lukewarm milk and one tablespoon of sugar. When this has risen, add ½ pound of creamed butter, a ¼ pound of raisins, and ¼ pound of sugar, yolks of four eggs, four ounces of powdered almonds, and the grated peel of a lemon. Work all well, beating with the hands, not kneading. Let this dough rise at least three hours, roll, press down the center and fold over double, then form into one or two long loaves, narrow at the end. Brush the top with melted butter, let rise again and bake forty-five minutes in a 350° oven.

APPLE CAKE (KUCHEN)
After the pan is greased with butter, roll out a piece of dough quite thin, lay it in the pan, press a rim out of the dough all around the pan and let it rise for about ten minutes. Pare five large apples, core and quarter them, dipping each piece in melted butter before laying on the cake, sprinkle bountifully with sugar (brown being preferable to white for this purpose) and cinnamon. See that you have tart apples. Leave the cake in the pans and cut out the pieces just as you would want to serve them. If they stick to the pan, set the pan on top of the hot stove for a minute and the cake will then come out.

CHEESE CAKE OR PIE

Take 1½ cups of cream cheese, rub smooth with a silver or wooden spoon through a colander or sieve, then rub a piece of sweet butter the size of an egg to a cream, add gradually ½ cup of sugar and the yolks of three eggs, a pinch of salt, grate in the peel of a lemon, ½ cup of currants and a little citron cut up very fine. Line two pie plates with some Kuchen dough or pie dough (see recipe), roll it out quite thin, butter the pie plates quite heavily, and let the dough in them rise at least thirty minutes before putting in the cheese mixture, for it must be baked immediately after the cheese is put in, and just before you put the cheese into the plates whip up the whites of the eggs to a very stiff froth and stir through the cheese mixture. Bake at 350° about an hour.

CHERRY CAKE

Line a cake-pan, which has been well buttered, with a thin layer of Kuchen dough. Stone two pounds of cherries and lay them on a sieve with a dish underneath to catch the juice. Sprinkle sugar over them and bake. In the mean time beat up four eggs with a cup of sugar, beat until light and add the cherry juice. Draw the Kuchen to the oven door, pour this mixture over it and bake.

PEACH KUCHEN

Grease your cake-pans thoroughly with good clarified butter, then line them with a rich coffee cake dough which has been rolled very thin and set in a warm place to rise. Then pare and quarter enough peaches to cover the dough. Lay the peaches in rows and sweeten and set in oven to bake. Make a meringue quickly as possible and pour over the cakes and bake at 350° until a light brown.

FRESH PRUNE CAKE (KUCHEN)

Line a greased biscuit-pan with some of the coffee cake dough. Roll the dough thin and let it come up on the sides of the pan, then set aside to rise. When risen, cut the prunes in halves (they must be the fresh ones, not dried), lay in rows thickly and close together all over the bottom of the pan, do not leave any space between the prunes. Sprinkle very thickly with sugar, lightly with cinnamon, and lay bits of fresh butter all over the top. Bake until done in a 375° oven.

PRUNE CAKE (KUCHEN)

Line one or two plates with a thin roll of Kuchen dough and let it rise again in the pans which have been heavily greased. Have some prunes boiled very soft, take out the kernels, mash them until like mush, sweeten to taste, add cinnamon and grated peel of a lemon or lemon juice, put in the lined pie plates and bake immediately at 350°. Serve with whipped cream, sweetened and flavored.

HUCKLEBERRY KUCHEN

Line your cake-pans, which should be long and narrow, with a rich Kuchen dough, having previously greased them well. Make a paste of cornstarch, one cup of milk, one tablespoon of butter and one teaspoon of cornstarch wet with cold milk. Boil until thick, sweeten and flavor with vanilla and spread on top of the cake dough, then sprinkle thickly with huckleberries which have been carefully picked, sugared and sprinkled with ground cinnamon. Bake in a 400° oven.

HUCKLEBERRY PIE

Clean, pick and wash two cups of huckleberries, then drain them. Beat yolk of one egg and two tablespoons of sugar until light, add one tablespoon of milk, then the drained berries. Line one pie plate with rich pastry or cookie dough, pour on it the berry mixture, put in the oven and bake light brown; remove from the oven, spread with a meringue made of the white of the egg beaten stiff, and two tablespoons of sugar added. Brown nicely at 375°. The white can be beaten with the yolk and sugar, if preferred.

MUFFINS AND BISCUITS

BAKING POWDER BATTERS
Batter is a mixture of flour with sufficient liquid to make it thin enough to be beaten. Pour-batter requires one measure of liquid to one measure of flour. Drop-batter requires one measure of liquid to two measures of flour. To make a batter. Sift flour before measuring. Put flour by spoonfuls into the cup; do not press or shake down. Mix and sift dry ingredients. Measure dry, then liquid ingredients, shortening may be rubbed or chopped in while cold, or creamed; or it may be melted and then added to dry ingredients, or added after the liquid. Use two teaspoons of baking powder to one cup of flour. If eggs are used, less baking powder will be required.
When sour milk is used, take one level teaspoon of soda to a pint of milk; when molasses is used, take one teaspoon of soda or baking powder to each cup of molasses. Mix dry materials in one bowl and liquids in another, combine them quickly, handle as little as possible and put at once into the oven. The oven for baking biscuits should be hot enough to brown a teaspoon of flour in one minute.

BROWN BREAD
Mix and sift together one cup each of rye, graham flour, cornmeal and one teaspoon of salt. Dissolve one teaspoon of soda in one cup of molasses. Add alternately to flour with two cups of sour milk. Grease one-pound baking powder cans, put in the dough and boil 2½ hours, keeping the water always ¾ up around the tins. Turn out on baking tins and place in the oven fifteen minutes to brown. To be eaten warm, whatever is left over can be steamed again or toasted.

CORN BREAD
Mix and sift one cup of cornmeal, one cup of flour, two tablespoons of sugar, ½ teaspoon of salt, three teaspoons of baking powder. Melt one tablespoon of butter and add to one egg; mix milk and egg and beat this into the dry ingredients, pour this mixture into well-greased tins and bake in a 400° oven for thirty minutes. Cut in squares and serve hot. Bake in gem tins if preferred.

BRAN BREAD

Sift four teaspoons of baking soda, two teaspoons of salt with four cups of white flour, add four cups of bran flour and mix well. Add one cup of molasses and four cups of sweet milk. Use chopped nuts or raisins or both as desired. This will make three or four flat loaves. Place in greased pans (four and a half by nine inches), and bake one hour in a 350° oven.

JOHNNIE CAKE

Mix one cup flour and two cups corn-meal, one heaping teaspoon of baking soda, ½ cup sugar, add two eggs beaten with 1½ cups of buttermilk, ½ cup of molasses and ½ cup of shortening, melted. Beat all ingredients as fast as possible for a minute. Pour the dough into a warm, well-buttered pan and bake at 375° for half an hour. The dough should be as soft as gingerbread dough. Serve hot.

EGGLESS GINGERBREAD WITH CHEESE

Sift two cups of flour, one teaspoon of baking soda, ½ teaspoon of salt and two teaspoons of ginger. Melt ¾ cup of grated cheese in ½ cup of hot water, add ½ cup of molasses and blend perfectly. Add the flour and seasonings very gradually and beat thoroughly. Bake in muffin tins at 375° for fifteen minutes and serve while warm.

GINGERBREAD

To one cup of molasses add one cup of milk, sour or sweet, dissolve one teaspoon of baking soda in the milk, one tablespoon of butter, one or two eggs, one teaspoon of ginger and one of ground cinnamon, add enough sifted flour to make a light batter. Bake in a shallow pan at 350° until knife comes clean.

WHITE NUT BREAD

Mix 2½ cups of flour, four teaspoons of baking powder, ½ teaspoon of salt, ½ cup of sugar and ½ cup of walnut meats, broken; add one egg beaten with one cup of milk and let this mixture stand for about twenty minutes in well-greased bread pan before placing in a 350° oven to bake. Bake about an hour. Better day after it is made.

BAKING POWDER BISCUITS

Sift two cups of flour with ½ teaspoon of salt, four teaspoons of baking powder, and four tablespoons of butter; cut butter in with two knives and mix with ½ to ⅔ cup of water or milk, stir this in quickly with a knife, when well mixed place on a well-floured board and roll out about one inch thick, work quickly, cut with a biscuit cutter or the cover of a ½ pound baking powder can; place on a greased pan and bake quickly in a well-heated 400° oven for ten to fifteen minutes. Butter substitutes may be used in place of butter.

DROP BISCUIT

Add to ingredients for baking powder biscuit enough more milk or water to make a thick drop batter, about two tablespoons; mix as directed for biscuit, drop by spoonfuls an inch apart on a greased baking-sheet or into greased gem pans, small size. The more crust the more palatable these biscuits are. The mixture should not be soft enough to run. Bake in a 400° oven ten to twelve minutes.

SOUR MILK BISCUITS

Mix and sift two cups of flour, ½ teaspoon of salt and ½ teaspoon of baking soda; cut in one tablespoon of butter, stir in with a knife enough sour milk to make a soft dough. Roll ½ inch thick; cut in small rounds and bake in a 400° oven about twenty minutes.

BRAN MUFFINS

Sift ½ cup of white flour with one teaspoon of baking soda; mix three tablespoons of molasses with one tablespoon of butter, add two cups of bran, 1½ cups of sweet milk, then add the flour and ½ teaspoon of salt, stir all together; ½ cup of chopped dates or raisins may be added if so desired. Bake in muffin pans in a 350° oven thirty minutes.

CORN MUFFINS, No. 1

Beat the yolks and whites of two eggs separately. Add to this two cups of flour, of which one is a full cup of white and ¾ of the cornmeal. This must be sifted three times. Put into this flour two teaspoons of baking powder, together with a pinch of salt. Mix the prepared flour with a little boiling water, adding the eggs; also a little sugar may be put in, if desired. Then add enough tepid milk to make the mixture into a batter, after which pour into your pans; or, if cornbread is desired, into the plain pan (thin). Bake in a 400° oven. This quantity makes a dozen muffins. Butter your pan well, or the small gem-pans, according to which is used, and in so doing heat the pan a little.

CORN MUFFINS, No. 2
Mix one cup of white flour, ½ cup of cornmeal, one tablespoon of sugar, ½ teaspoon of salt and ½ teaspoon of baking soda, add one egg beaten into one cup of sour milk and one tablespoon of melted butter. Beat thoroughly and bake at 400° in well-greased tins until knife comes out clean.

GRAHAM MUFFINS
Mix one cup of Graham flour, one cup of wheat flour, ½ teaspoon of salt, two teaspoons of baking powder, add to this one tablespoon of melted butter creamed with ½ cup of sugar and one well-beaten egg, moisten with 1½ cups of milk. Beat all well and bake in muffin-tins in 375° oven one-half hour.

WHEAT MUFFINS
Mix two cups of flour, ½ teaspoon of salt, three teaspoons of baking powder, two tablespoons of sugar and sift these ingredients twice, rub in one tablespoon of butter. Separate one egg. Beat the yolk and add it to one cup of milk and one teaspoon of molasses. Mix with the dry ingredients and stir until smooth. Fold in the beaten white of egg and pour into hot, well-greased muffin-tins. Bake fifteen to twenty minutes in 400° oven.

RICE MUFFINS
Beat one cup of cold rice, two eggs, one cup of sweet milk, one teaspoon of salt, one tablespoon of sugar, two teaspoons of baking powder, enough flour to make a stiff batter and lastly one tablespoon of melted butter. Bake in muffin tins at 400° about fifteen minutes.

RYE FLOUR MUFFINS
Sift 1½ cups of rye flour with one-half teaspoon of salt and one teaspoon of baking soda; add ½ cup of molasses and one well-beaten egg or ½ cup of

water if the egg is omitted, ¼ cup of chopped raisins and four tablespoons of melted shortening - butter, or any good butter substitute will do. Bake in muffin pans in 400° oven twenty-five minutes. Fill pans three-fourths full.

GLUTEN GEMS

Beat the yolks of two eggs, add one cup of milk; then 1½ cups of gluten flour, two teaspoons of baking powder; beat well, stir in the whites of the two eggs, and bake at 400° in hot buttered gem pans about twenty minutes.

EGGLESS GINGER GEMS

Mix ½ cup of molasses, ½ cup of sugar, one tablespoon of butter, and warm slightly; beat up well and stir at least ten minutes. Add the following spices: ½ teaspoon each of ginger and cinnamon; and gradually ½ cup of milk and 2½ cups of sifted flour in which has been sifted two teaspoons of baking powder. ¼ cup of currants or raisins may be added. Bake at 400° in well-greased gem pans and eat warm for tea or lunch.

POPOVERS

Mix to a smooth batter two cups each of milk and well-sifted flour, the yolks of three fresh eggs and a teaspoon of salt. Butter well the inside of six or eight deep earthen popover cups and stand them in a pan in a 400° oven. While the cups are heating, beat to a froth the whites of the three eggs and stir them quickly in the batter. Open the oven door, pull the pan forward, pour the batter in the hot buttered cups up to the brim. Push the pan back, close the oven door, and bake the popovers till they rise well and are brown at the sides where they part from the cups. Serve them hot, folded lightly in a napkin.

ONE-EGG WAFFLES

Mix 1½ cups of flour, one teaspoon of baking powder, one-quarter teaspoon of salt; add 1¾ cups of milk, add the milk slowly, then one well-beaten egg and two tablespoons of melted butter; drop by spoonfuls on a hot buttered waffle iron, putting one tablespoon in each section of the iron. Bake and turn, browning both sides carefully; remove from the iron; pile one on top of the other and serve at once.

THREE-EGG WAFFLES

Mix two cups of flour, one teaspoon of baking powder, one-half teaspoon of salt, and sift these ingredients; add the yolks of three eggs beaten and stirred into 1¼ cups of milk; then add one tablespoon of melted butter and fold in the whites of the eggs. Bake and serve as directed under One-Egg Waffles.

DOUGHNUTS

Mix 2½ tablespoons of melted butter, one cup of granulated sugar, two eggs, one cup of milk, ½ nutmeg grated, sifted flour enough to make a batter as stiff as biscuit dough; add two teaspoons of baking powder and one teaspoon of salt to the sifted flour. Flour your board well, roll dough out about ½ inch thick, and cut into pieces three inches long and one inch wide. Cut a slit about an inch long in the center of each strip and pull one end through this slit. Fry quickly in hot Crisco. Sprinkle powdered sugar on top of each doughnut.

FRENCH DOUGHNUTS

French doughnuts are much daintier than the ordinary ones, and are easily made. Take one cup water, one cup of milk, 12 tablespoons butter, ½ pound of flour, and six eggs. Heat the butter, milk, and water, and when it boils remove from the stove and stir in the flour, using a wooden spoon. When well mixed, stir in the eggs, whipping each one in separately until you have a hard batter. Now pour your dough into a pastry bag. This is an ordinary cheesecloth bag, one corner of which has a tiny tin funnel, with a fluted or fancy edge. (These little tins may be purchased at any tinware store.) It should be very small, not over two inches high at the most, so the dough may be easily squeezed through it. Pour the paste on buttered paper, making into ring shapes. Fry in hot oil or butter substitute. Dust with powdered sugar.

CRULLERS

Cream two tablespoons of butter with one-half cup of sugar, then beat in one at a time two whole eggs. Mix well, then add ½ cup of milk, two teaspoons of baking powder, and sufficient flour to make a soft batter to roll out. (Try three cups and then add as much more flour as necessary.) Last, add ½ teaspoon cinnamon. Roll ½ inch thick, cut in strips one inch wide, three inches long and fry in hot Crisco.

STRAWBERRY SHORTCAKE (BISCUIT DOUGH)
Mix two cups of flour, four teaspoons of baking powder, ½ teaspoon of salt, one tablespoon of sugar; work ¼ cup of butter with tips of fingers, and add ¾ cup of milk gradually. Toss on floured board, divide in two parts. Pat, roll out and bake twelve minutes in 400° oven in layer-cake tins. Split and spread with butter. Pick, hull, and drain berries. Sweeten one box of strawberries to taste. Crush slightly and put between and on top of short cake. Allow one box of berries to each short cake. Serve with cream, plain or whipped. Strawberries make the best short cake, but other berries and sliced peaches are also good.

DOUGH FOR OPEN FACE PIES
The directions for making the dough for Cinnamon Buns may be followed in making the under crust for fruit pies, such as apple, plum, huckleberry and peach. Enough for two pies. Drippings and water may be substituted for butter and milk respectively.

CINNAMON BUNS
Sift together one pint of flour, one tablespoon of sugar, ½ teaspoon of salt, two teaspoons of baking powder. Rub in two tablespoons of butter, mix with milk to soft dough. Roll out ½ inch thick, spread with soft butter, granulated sugar, and powdered cinnamon. Roll up like jelly roll, cut in inch slices, lay close together in greased pan, and bake in 400° oven for about 15 minutes.

FRUIT WHEELS
Sift together two cups of flour, two teaspoons of baking powder, ½ teaspoon of salt, one tablespoon of sugar. Rub in two large tablespoons of butter. Mix to soft dough with milk; roll out ½ inch thick. Spread thickly with soft butter, dust with one teaspoon of flour, four tablespoons of granulated sugar, one teaspoon of cinnamon; sprinkle over ½ cup each of raisins, chopped citron, and cleaned currants. Roll up, cut in ½ slices, put one inch apart on greased, flat pans, and bake in 400° oven about 15 minutes.

PANCAKES, FRITTERS, Etc.

BUCKWHEAT CAKES
Dissolve one cake of compressed yeast and two level teaspoons of brown sugar in two cups of lukewarm water and one cup of milk, scalded and cooled; add two cups of buckwheat and one cup of sifted white flour gradually and 1½ teaspoons of salt. Beat until smooth; cover and set aside in a warm place, free from draft, to rise about one hour. When light stir well and cook on a hot griddle.

GERMAN PANCAKES, No. 1
Beat two eggs very thoroughly without separating the yolks and whites; add ½ teaspoon of salt, sift in 2½ tablespoons of flour, add one cup of milk gradually at first, and beat the whole very well. Melt one tablespoon of butter in a large frying pan, turn mixture in and cook slowly until brown underneath. Grease the bottom of a large pie plate, slip the pancake on the plate; add the other tablespoon of butter to the frying-pan; when hot, turn uncooked side of pancake down and brown. Serve at once with sugar and lemon slices or with any desired preserve or syrup. This pancake may be served rolled like a jellyroll.

GERMAN PANCAKES, No. 2
Beat two eggs until very light, add ½ cup of flour and ½ teaspoon of salt and beat again; then add one cup of milk slowly, and beat thoroughly. Heat a generous quantity of butter in a frying pan, and pour all the batter into this at one time; place on a hot stove for one minute; then remove to a 375° oven; the edges will turn up on sides of pan in a few minutes; then reduce heat and cook more slowly until light, crisp and brown, about seven minutes. Take it out, slide it carefully on a hot plate, sprinkle plentifully with powdered sugar and send to the table with six lemon slices.

GERMAN PANCAKES, No. 3
Beat the yolks of four eggs until very light, then add ½ cup of milk and stir in ¾ cup of sifted flour, ⅛ teaspoon of baking powder, a pinch of salt, and lastly, just before frying, add the stiffly beaten whites of eggs and mix well together. Put on stove an iron skillet with a close-fitting top; heat in two

tablespoons of rendered butter; when very hot, pour in enough of the batter to cover the bottom of the skillet, cover at once with the top, and when the pancake is brown on one side, remove the top and let it brown on the other side. Take it up with a perforated skimmer, lay on a plate and sprinkle with powdered sugar and some lemon juice. Serve at once. Pancakes must only be made and fried when ready to be eaten, as they fall from standing.

BREAD PANCAKES

Soak stale bread overnight in sour milk, mash the bread fine in the morning, and put in ½ teaspoon of salt, two eggs, two teaspoons of baking soda, dissolved in hot water, and thicken with finely sifted flour. Mix all thoroughly together, then pour, by spoonfuls, on hot buttered griddle. Let the cakes brown on one side, and turn over and brown on the other.

RICE PANCAKES OR GRIDDLE CAKES

Boil in a double boiler 2 cups milk, three tablespoons of rice and two tablespoons of granulated sugar. It will take from fifty to sixty minutes for the rice to be thoroughly cooked, and the mixture to thicken. Remove from the fire and when a little cool, add one tablespoon of vanilla and the yolk of egg into which one tablespoon of flour has been smoothly stirred. Mix all thoroughly together, then pour, by spoonfuls, on hot buttered griddle. Let the cakes brown on one side, and turn over and brown on the other.

GRIMSLICH

Half a loaf of bread, which has been soaked and pressed, two eggs, ½ cup of sugar, ¼ cup raisins, one tablespoon of cinnamon, and ¼ cup of almonds pounded fine. Beat whites to a froth and add last. Drop by tablespoonful and fry. Serve with stewed fruit. Pieces of stale bread can be used. Soak in tepid water. Squeeze water thoroughly from bread and make as directed.

POTATO PANCAKES

Peel six large potatoes and soak several hours in cold water; grate, drain, and for every pint allow two eggs, about one tablespoon of flour, ½ teaspoon of salt, a little pepper; a little onion juice may be added if so desired. Beat eggs well and mix with the rest of the ingredients. Drop by spoonfuls on a hot greased sauce pan in small cakes. Turn and brown on both sides. Serve with applesauce. When eggs are very expensive the cakes can be made with one egg. When required for a meat meal, the pancakes may be fried in drippings; the edges will be much more crisp than when fried in butter, which burns so readily.

POTATO CAKES
Made just as pancakes, only baked in the oven in a long cake pan with plenty of butter or drippings under and above.

SOUR MILK PANCAKES
Mash fine and dissolve one level teaspoon of baking soda in three cups of sour milk; beat one egg well; then put in a little salt and ½ cup of flour; stir in the milk, make a smooth batter, and last stir in one tablespoon of syrup. Bake on a hot griddle.

FRENCH PANCAKE
Stir three egg-yolks with ½ teaspoon of salt and ¼ cup of flour, until smooth; add one cup of cold milk gradually, then fold in the beaten whites. Heat pan, add two tablespoons of butter and when hot pour in pancake; let cook slowly and evenly on one side, finish baking in oven.

CHEESE BLINTZES
With a fork beat up one egg, ½ teaspoon of salt, add one cup of water and one cup of sifted flour, beat until smooth. Grease a frying pan very slightly with butter or oil, pour in two tablespoons of the batter, tilting the pan so as to allow the batter to run all over the pan. Fry over a low heat on one side only, turn out the semi-cooked cakes on a clean cloth with the uncooked side uppermost; let cool. Prepare a filling as for cheese kreplich, using ½ pound of pot cheese, a piece of butter size of an egg, add one egg, pinch of salt, a little cinnamon and sugar to taste and grated peel of a lemon. Spread this mixture on the cooled dough, fold over and tuck the edges in well. Then sprinkle with powdered sugar and cinnamon, and fry in plenty of oil or butter. These blintzes are served hot.

SWEET BLINTZES
These little pancakes may be filled with the fruit filling in following recipe; or with a poppy seed filling, using one cup of seed and adding one cup of

sugar, moistening with one-half cup of water. The recipe given for the dough makes only six blintzes and where more are required double or triple the quantities given to make amount desired. For Purim, fold blintzes in triangular shapes. Fry as directed.

BLINTZES
Make dough as directed for cheese blintzes. Filling may be made of force meat, highly seasoned; fry in hot fat, or filling may be made of ½ pound of apples, peeled and cored and then minced with one ounce of ground sweet almonds, one ounce of powdered sugar, a pinch of cinnamon, juice of ½ lemon; mix well and bind with the beaten white of egg. Spread either of these mixtures on the dough, fold over and tuck edges in well. Fry in plenty of oil or fat. Sprinkle those containing the fruit mixture with sugar and cinnamon. These may be served either hot or cold.

FRITTER BATTER
Mix and sift 1⅓ cups of flour, two teaspoons of baking powder, ¼ teaspoon of salt, and add ⅔ cup of milk or water gradually, and one egg well beaten. For fruit batter add a little sugar, for vegetables pepper and salt.

BELL FRITTERS
Stir three eggs until very light, then stir in one cup of sweet milk, then sift in three cups sifted flour; beat for ten minutes, then add three teaspoons of baking powder, and fry by spoonfuls in hot oil. Half this amount will be sufficient for three persons. Serve with any sweet sauce.

APPLE FRITTERS
Choose four sour apples; pare, core and cut them into small slices. Stir into fritter batter and fry in boiling hot fat or oil. Drain on paper; sprinkle with powdered sugar and serve.

PINEAPPLE FRITTERS
Soak slices of pineapple in sherry or white wine with a little sugar and let stand one hour. Drain and dip slices in batter and fry in hot oil. Drain on brown paper and sprinkle with powdered sugar. Fresh pears, apricots and peach fritters made the same as pineapple fritters. Bananas are cut in slices or mashed and added to batter.

ORANGE FRITTERS

Yolks of two eggs beaten with two spoons of sugar, stir into this the juice of ¼ lemon and just enough flour to thicken like a batter; add the beaten whites and dip in one slice of orange at a time, take up with a large kitchen spoon and lay in the hot oil or butter and fry a nice brown. Sprinkle pulverized sugar on top.

MATRIMONIES

Sift three cups of flour in a bowl, pour in two scant cups of sour milk, beat very thoroughly, add one teaspoon of salt, the well-beaten yolks of three eggs, mix well, then add the stiffly beaten whites of the eggs and one level teaspoon of soda sifted with one teaspoon of flour. Mix well and fry at once in very hot butter. Baste the grease over them with a spoon until they are nicely browned. Serve with preserves.

QUEEN FRITTERS

Put in a deep skillet on the fire one cup of water, one-fourth cup of fresh butter; when it comes to a boil, stir in one cup of sifted flour and continue stirring until the dough leaves the side of the skillet clean. Remove from the fire and when cool break in three eggs, one at a time, stirring continually. Add a little salt. Mix all well, then drop pieces about the size of a walnut into plenty of boiling butter or Crisco and fry a light brown. Drain, make an opening in each, fill with preserves and sprinkle with sugar; serve at once.

VEGETABLE FRITTERS

Cook the vegetables thoroughly; drain them, chop fine and add to the batter. Drop in boiling hot fat, drain and dry on paper.

CORN FRITTERS

Grate two cups of corn from the cob. Ears that are too old for eating in the ordinary method will serve very well for this. Mix with the corn one egg, beaten light, a cup of sweet milk into which has been stirred a bit of soda the size of a pea, two teaspoons of melted butter, a pinch of salt and enough flour to make a thin batter. Beat well together and fry on a griddle as you would cakes for breakfast.

ERBSEN LIEVANZEN (DRIED PEA FRITTERS)
Boil one cup of dried peas, pass through a hair sieve, pour into a bowl, add two ounces of butter rubbed to a cream, add also some soaked bread (soaked in milk), stir all into a smooth paste. Add salt, one teaspoon of sugar, one yolk and one whole egg, one ounce of blanched and pounded almonds. If too thick add more egg, if too thin more bread. Fry a nice brown.

SQUASH FRITTERS
Two cups of boiled squash, ½ cup of flour, one teaspoon of baking powder, one egg and two tablespoons of milk. It is assumed that the squash has been prepared as a vegetable, with seasoning and a little butter, and what is here used is a cold, left over portion of the same. Mix baking powder with the flour and add to the squash; add milk and stir all together. Beat egg and stir in. Have hot fat in pan and drop fritters from spoon into pan. When browned on both sides remove to hot platter.

FRENCH PUFFS (WINDBEUTEL)
Put one cup of water and ¼ pound of butter on to boil. When it begins to boil stir in ¼ pound of sifted flour. Stir until it leaves the kettle clean, take off the heat and stir until lukewarm, then stir in four eggs, one at a time, stirring until all used up. Flavor with the grated peel of a lemon. Put on some rendered butter in a kettle. When the butter is hot, dip a large teaspoon in cold water and cut pieces of dough with it as large as a walnut, and drop into the hot butter. Try one first to see whether the butter is hot enough. Do not crowd - they need plenty of room to raise. Dip the hot butter over them with a spoon, fry a deep yellow and sprinkle powdered sugar over them.

SHAVINGS (KRAUS GEBACKENES)
Sift about 2 cups flour in a bowl, make a depression in the center; break in five eggs, a pinch of salt, one teaspoon of ground cinnamon and one tablespoon of pulverized sugar. Mix this as you would a noodle dough, though not quite as stiff. Roll out very thin and cut into long strips with a jagging iron. Fry a light yellow. Roll on a round stick as soon as taken up from the fat or butter, sprinkle with sugar and cinnamon or grated peel of a lemon. Mix both thoroughly. Do not let the butter get too brown; if the fire is too strong take off a few minutes.

SNIP NOODLES, FRIED

Sift two cups of flour with three teaspoons of salt in it, make into a dough by adding enough sweet milk to make soft as biscuit dough. Break off small pieces and roll between the hands in the shape of croquettes. Now put ½ cup of rendered butter in a skillet that has a top to it; when the butter is hot, lay in the pieces of dough (do not put too many in at one time), add ½ cup of cold water, put on the cover and let cook until the water is cooked out and noodles are brown on one side. Remove the cover and brown on the other side.

NOODLE PUFFS

Make a noodle dough with as many eggs as desired, roll out somewhat thin, cut in strips four inches long by one inch wide. Have a skillet half full of boiling hot chicken fat; drop in the strips, a few at a time, baste with the hot grease until brown on both sides. Remove to a platter, sprinkle generously with powdered sugar and cinnamon, and serve.

SNOWBALLS (HESTERLISTE)

Mix one teaspoon of butter, ¼ teaspoon of salt, one tablespoon of sugar with one egg. Add one tablespoon of cream, one teaspoon of brandy and flour to make stiff dough. Work the whole together with a spoon until the flour is mixed with the other ingredients and you have a dough easily handled. Break the dough in pieces about the size of a walnut; roll each piece out separately just as thin as possible without tearing (the thinner the better), make three lengthwise slashes in the center of each piece of dough after rolling out. Heat a large deep skillet about half full with boiling hot butter or oil, drop in the snowballs, not more than three at one time, brown quickly on one side, then on the other, turn carefully with a perforated skimmer as they are easily broken. Remove to a platter, sprinkle with powdered sugar and cinnamon and a few drops of lemon juice.

MACROTES

Blend one pound of good light dough with two eggs, 12 tablespoons butter, and add as much flour as may be needed to make the whole sufficiently dry. Make it into the shape of a French roll, and cut off rather thin slices, which should be placed before the fire to rise, and then fried in oil. Let them drain carefully, and when nearly cold dip each in very thick syrup flavored with essence of lemon.

CAKES

GENERAL DIRECTIONS FOR MAKING CAKES

Use only the best material in making cake.
Gather together all ingredients and utensils that are required. If tins are to be greased, do so the first thing; some cakes require greased or buttered paper, if so, have paper cut the size that is needed and butter the paper.
Use pastry flour. Sift flour twice at least and measure after sifting.
Measure or weigh the sugar, butter, milk and flour. In measuring butter always pack the cup so as to be sure to get the proper quantity. Use the half-pint measuring cup.
If fruit is to be used, wash and dry it the day before it is needed. Dust with flour just before using, and mix with the hand till each piece is powdered so that all will mix evenly with the dough instead of sinking to the bottom.
A few necessary implements for good cake making are a pair of scales, a wooden spoon, two wire egg whips, one for the yolks and the other for the whites of eggs.
A ten-inch mixing-bowl, and two smaller bowls.
Two spatula or leveling knives.
A set of aluminum spoons of standard sizes.
For convenience, cakes are divided into two classes: Those containing butter or a butter substitute and cake containing no shortening.
The rules for mixing cakes with butter are:
Break the eggs, dropping each in a saucer or cup. If the whites and yolks are to be used separately divide them as you break the eggs and beat both well before using; the yolks until light and the whites to a stiff froth, so stiff that you can turn the dish upside down and the eggs will adhere to the dish.
Rub the butter to a cream that should be done with a wooden spoon in a deep bowl, add the sugar gradually. In winter set the bowl over hot water for a few minutes as the butter will then cream more easily. Add the yolks or the whole eggs, one at a time, to creamed butter and sugar. Sift the baking powder with the last cup of flour, add flour and milk alternately until both are beaten thoroughly into the mixture, add beaten whites of eggs last to the dough and then set in the oven immediately.
Sponge cakes and cakes that do not contain butter and milk must never be

stirred, but the ingredients beaten in, being careful to beat with an upward stroke. Separate the yolks of the eggs from the whites, and beat the yolks with an eggbeater until they are thick and lemon-colored. Then add the sugar, a little at a time, beating constantly. Now beat the whites until they are stiff and dry; add them; the flour should be added last and folded lightly through. Every stroke of the spoon after flour is added tends to toughen the batter. Bake at once. All sponge cakes and Torten should be baked in ungreased molds.

TO BAKE CAKES
Make sure the oven is in condition, it can better wait for the cake than the other way around. Light your gas oven five or ten minutes before needed and reduce heat accordingly when cake is put in oven.

For the coal stove, have the oven the right temperature and do not add coal or shake the coals while cake is baking. If a piece of soft yellow paper burns golden brown in five minutes the oven is moderately hot; if it takes four minutes the oven is hot, if seven minutes is required the oven is fit for slow baking. Sponge cakes require a slow oven; layer cakes a hot oven, and loaf cakes with butter a moderate oven. Never look after your cake until it has been in the oven ten minutes. If cake is put in too cool an oven it will rise too much and be of very coarse texture. If too hot, it browns and crusts over the top before it has sufficiently risen. If, after the cake is put in, it seems to bake too fast, put a brown paper loosely over the top of the pan, and do not open the oven door for five minutes at least; the cake should then be quickly examined and the door carefully shut, or the rush of cold air will cause it to fall. Setting a small dish of hot water in the oven will also prevent the cake from scorching. When you think your cake is baked, open the oven door carefully so as not to jar, take a straw and run it through the thickest part of the cake, and if the straw comes out perfectly clean and dry your cake is done. When done, take it out and set it where no draft of air will strike it, and in ten minutes turn it out on a flat plate or board. Do not put it in the cake box until perfectly cold. Scald out the tin cake box each time before putting a fresh cake in it. Make sure it is airtight. Keep in a cool place, but not in a damp cellar or a refrigerator.

TIME-TABLE FOR BAKING CAKES
Sponge cake, three-quarters of an hour.
Pound cake, one hour.
Fruit cake, three and four hours, depending upon size.
Cookies, from ten to fifteen minutes. Watch carefully.
Cup cakes, a full half hour.
Layer cakes, twenty minutes.

ONE EGG CAKE
Cream ¼ cup of butter with one-half cup of sugar, add sugar gradually, and one egg, well beaten. Mix and sift 1½ cups of flour and 2½ teaspoons of baking powder, add the sifted flour alternately with ½ cup of milk to the first mixture; flavor with vanilla or lemon. Bake thirty minutes at 375° in a shallow pan. Spread with chocolate frosting.

LITTLE FRENCH CAKES
Beat ¼ cup of butter to a cream with ¼ cup of sugar and add one cup of flour. Stir well and then add one egg that has been beaten into one cup of milk, a little at a time. Fill buttered saucers with the mixture, bake at 375° and when done, place the cakes one on top of another with jam spread between.

GRAFTON CAKE. LAYERS AND SMALL CAKES
Cream four tablespoons of butter with 1½ cups of sugar, beat in separately two whole eggs, add one cup of milk alternately with two cups of flour in which has been sifted two teaspoons of baking powder, beat all thoroughly. This recipe will make two layer cakes that may be spread with any of the cake fillings or icings. To make small cakes omit one of the egg-whites, fill well-buttered gem pans a little more than half full, and bake in a 375° oven until a delicate brown. The white reserved may be beaten to a stiff froth and then gradually stir in four tablespoons of powdered sugar and the juice of half a lemon. When the cakes are cool, spread with the icing and decorate with raisins, nut meats, one on top of each or sprinkle with candied caraway seeds.

CUP CAKE

Cream one cup of butter with two cups of sugar and add gradually the yolks of four eggs, one at a time. Sift three cups of flour, measure again after sifting, and add two teaspoons of baking powder in the last sifting. Add alternately the sifted flour and one cup of sweet milk. Add last the beaten whites of the eggs. Flavor to taste. Bake at 350° in cupcake tins for about 20 minutes.

GOLD CAKE

Take one cup of powdered sugar, ½ cup of butter rubbed to a cream; add yolks of six eggs and stir until very light. Then sift two cups of flour with one and ½ teaspoons of baking powder sifted in well (sift the flour two or three times). Grate in the peel of a lemon or an orange, add the juice also, and add ¾ cup of milk alternately with the flour. Bake in 350° oven for about thirty minutes or until knife comes clean.

WHITE CAKE

Cream ¾ cup of butter and 1¼ cups of sugar very well. Stop stirring, pour ½ cup of cold water on top of butter mixture and whites of eight eggs slightly beaten on top of water; do not stir, add one teaspoon of vanilla. Sift 2½ cups of pastry flour, measure, then mix with two heaping teaspoons of baking powder, and sift three times. Add to cake mixture and then beat hard until very smooth. Turn into ungreased angel cake pan, place in 325° oven. Let cake rise to top of pan, then increase heat to 350° and bake until firm. Invert pan, when cool cut out.

MARBLE CAKE

Take two cups of sugar, one cup of butter, four eggs (yolks), one cup of milk, three cups of flour, and three teaspoons of baking powder (scant). Cream the butter and sugar, and add the yolks of eggs. Then add the milk, flour, baking powder, and the beaten whites of the eggs; flavor with lemon. To make the brown part; take a square of bitter chocolate and melt above steam, and mix with some of the white; flavor the brown with vanilla. Put first a tablespoon of brown batter in the pan, and then the white. Bake in quick oven thirty-five minutes.

LEMON CAKE

Rub to a cream ½ cup of butter with 1½ cups of pulverized sugar and add gradually the yolks of three eggs, one at a time, and ½ cup of sweet milk. Sift two cups of flour with one teaspoon of baking powder, add alternately with the milk and the stiffly beaten whites of three eggs. Add the grated peel of ½ lemon and the juice of one lemon. Bake in 350° oven for about thirty minutes or until knife comes clean.

ORANGE CAKE

Beat light the yolks of five eggs with two cups of pulverized sugar, add juice of a large orange and part of the peel grated, ½ cup of cold water and two cups of flour, sifted three times. Add two teaspoons of baking powder in last sifting and add last the stiff-beaten whites of three eggs. Bake about 25 minutes at 350° in layers, and spread the following icing between and on top. Icing: beat the whites of two eggs stiff, add the juice and peel of one orange and sugar enough to stiffen.

POTATO CAKE

Cream ⅔ cup of butter with two cups of granulated sugar; add ½ cup of milk, yolks of four eggs, one cup of hot mashed potatoes, one cup of chocolate, one teaspoon each of cinnamon, cloves, and nutmeg, one teaspoon of vanilla, one cup of chopped walnuts, two cups of flour, two teaspoons of baking powder, then beaten whites of four eggs. Bake at 325° in two pans for about 30 minutes, and cut in half when cold. Put jam between layers.

POUND CAKE

Rub one pound of butter and one pound of powdered sugar to a cream, add the grated peel of a lemon, a glass of brandy and the yolks of nine eggs, added one at a time, and last one pound and a quarter of sifted flour with ½ teaspoon of baking powder and the beaten whites of the eggs. Bake in 325° oven for about thirty minutes or until knife comes clean

BAKING POWDER BUNT KUCHEN

Beat two whole eggs for ten minutes with two cups of sugar, 2½ tablespoons of melted butter, add one cup of milk, three cups of flour in which have been sifted two teaspoons of baking powder, flavor with one teaspoon of vanilla; ¼ cup of raisins may be added. Bake one hour at 325°.

QUICK COFFEE CAKE

Cream ½ cup of butter with one cup of sugar, add three eggs, 1½ cups of flour, two teaspoons of baking powder, mixed with the flour, and ½ cup milk. Mix well together; bake at 350° about thirty minutes in a long bread or cake pan, and have on top chopped almonds, sugar and cinnamon.

BAKING POWDER CINNAMON CAKE

Cream ¾ cup of sugar with a piece of butter the size of an egg, beat together; then add two eggs, ½ cup of milk (scant), 1½ cups of flour, one teaspoon of vanilla and two teaspoons of baking powder. Put cinnamon, flour, sugar and a few drops of water together, and form in little pfarvel with your hand and sprinkle on top of cake; also sprinkle a few chopped nuts on top. Bake at 325° in flat pan until knife comes clean.

GERMAN COFFEE CAKE (BAKING POWDER)

Take three cups of flour sifted, one teaspoon of salt, three tablespoons of sugar, three teaspoons of baking powder, two eggs, two tablespoons of butter, and ⅔ cup of milk. Stir well together, adding more milk if necessary. Keep batter very stiff, sprinkle with melted butter (generously) sugar and cinnamon, and again with melted butter. Put into well-buttered shallow pans and bake at 350° about half an hour.

COVERED CHEESE CAKE

Cream one cup of sugar with butter the size of an egg, add two eggs well beaten and one cup of water alternately with 2½ cups of flour in which has been sifted two teaspoons of baking powder.

Filling.
Beat two eggs with ½ cup of sugar, add ½ pound of pot cheese, one tablespoon of cornstarch boiled in one cup of milk, cool this and add, flavor with lemon extract. Put ½ of the batter in cake pan, then the filling and the other half of batter. Bake in 325° oven for thirty-five minutes. Sift sugar on top when done.

BLITZKUCHEN

Take one cup of powdered sugar, ½ cup of butter, one cup of pastry flour, ¼ teaspoon of baking powder, peel and juice of one lemon, five or six eggs. Beat sugar with two whole eggs; add butter, beat until foamy; after that the flour mixed with baking powder, lemon and four yolks. Last the stiffly beaten whites of the eggs. Mix this well, bake in form in a 375° hot oven about 25 minutes

KÖNIGKUCHEN
Cream ¼ cup of butter with one cup of sugar, yolks of six eggs, one-quarter pound of raisins, one-quarter pound of currants, juice and peel of one lemon, one spoon of rum, twenty blanched and grated almonds, two cups of flour mixed with ½ teaspoon of baking powder, two stiffly beaten whites of eggs. Bake at 325° in an ungreased form about one hour.

NUT CAKE
Take ½ cup of butter, three eggs, 1½ cups of sugar, 2½ cups of flour, 2½ level teaspoons of baking powder, and one-half cup of milk. One cup of any kind of nuts. Rub the butter and sugar to a light white cream; add the eggs beaten a little; then the flour sifted with the powder. Mix with the milk and nuts into a rather firm batter. Bake in a paper lined tin in a 350° oven thirty-five minutes.

LOAF COCONUT CAKE
Rub one cup of butter and two cups of sugar to a cream. Add one cup of milk, whites of four eggs, three cups of flour (measure after sifting), and three teaspoons of baking powder added in last sifting. Add a grated coconut and last the stiffly beaten whites. Bake at 350° in a loaf about thirty minutes. Line tin with buttered paper.

FRUIT CAKE (WEDDING CAKE)
Take one pound of butter and one pound of sugar rubbed to a cream, yolks of twelve eggs, one tablespoon of cinnamon, one teaspoon of allspice, ½ teaspoon of mace, ½ teaspoon of cloves, ¼ pound of almonds pounded, two pounds of raisins (seeded and chopped), three pounds of currants (carefully cleaned), one pound of citron (shredded very fine), and ¼ pound of orange peel (chopped very fine). Soak all this prepared fruit in one pint of brandy overnight. Add all to the dough and put in the stiffly beaten whites last. Bake in a 300° oven for several hours, in cake pans lined with

buttered paper. When cold wrap in cloths dipped in brandy and put in earthen jars.

APPLE SAUCE CAKE

This applesauce cake will be found as delicious and tasty as the rich fruit cake, which is so difficult to prepare, and it is very much less expensive. In a big mixing bowl, beat to a creamy consistency four tablespoons of butter, one egg and one cup of sugar. Add a ¼ teaspoon of salt, one teaspoon of allspice, one teaspoon of vanilla and a little grated nutmeg. Beat and stir all these ingredients well together with the other mixture, then add one cup of chopped raisins, after dusting them with flour. Mix these well through the dough and then add one cup of unsweetened apple sauce which has been pressed through a fine wire sieve. After this is well mixed with the other ingredients, stir in one teaspoon of baking soda dissolved in one tablespoon of boiling water. Last of all, stir in one cup of flour, sifting twice after measuring it. Bake forty-five minutes in moderate oven. The tendency in making this cake is to get the dough too thin, therefore the apple sauce should be cooked quite thick, and then if the dough is still too thin add more flour. Bake one hour in 350° oven. This cake can be made with chicken Schmalz in place of butter. Ice with plain white frosting.

SPICE CAKE

This spice cake is economical, easy to make and delicious, three qualities which must appeal to the housewife. Cream one cup of brown sugar and ½ cup of butter (or a little less of any butter substitute). Add ½ teaspoon of ground cloves and ground cinnamon, one cup of sour milk, one teaspoon of baking soda, two cups of flour and one cup of raisins chopped. Have ready a 350° oven and bake forty-five minutes.

GREEN TREE LAYER CAKE AND ICING

One cup of granulated sugar, ½ cup of butter, three eggs, one cup of milk, 2½ scant cups of sifted flour, one teaspoon of vanilla extract, two teaspoons of baking powder. Cream the butter and sugar together as usual, and then break in three eggs and beat until very creamy. Add the flour and milk alternately, reserving a little of the flour to add after the vanilla and baking powder. Beat well and bake at 350° in layer cake tins until knife comes clean. The entire success and lightness of this cake depends upon the beating of the sugar, butter and eggs. If these are beaten long enough they will become as creamy and fluffy as whipped cream.

Icing for This Cake.
1½ cups of confectioner's sugar (not powdered), butter the size of a large egg, two tablespoons of cocoa, one teaspoon of vanilla, moisten to make the mixture the consistence of very thick cream. Cream or whipped cream may be used for the mixing, but many like this icing when made with lukewarm coffee. The sugar and butter are creamed together thoroughly and then the cocoa and vanilla are added, and lastly the cream or coffee. This is a good imitation of German tree cake. The icing on tree cake is an inch thick, and it is marked to represent the bark of a tree. The way it is served is with a little green candy on it, and it is really very delicious although extremely rich. The thicker or rather firmer this icing is, the better.

EGGLESS, BUTTERLESS, MILKLESS CAKE
One package of raisins, two cups of sugar, two cups of boiling water, one teaspoon of cinnamon, one teaspoon of cloves, two tablespoons of oil, chicken Schmalz or clarified drippings, ½ teaspoon of salt. Boil all together five minutes, cool, add one teaspoon of soda dissolved in water, three cups of flour. Bake at 325° for forty-five minutes, make two cakes in layer pans.

APPLE JELLY CAKE
Rub one cup of butter and two cups of sugar to a cream, add four eggs, whites beaten separately, one cup of milk, two teaspoons of baking powder and 3½ cups of flour. Bake at 350° in layer tins until knife comes clean.

Filling.
--Pare and grate three large apples ("Greenings" preferred), the juice and peel of a lemon, one cup of sugar and one well-beaten egg. Put in ingredients together and boil, stirring constantly until thick. Cool and fill in cake.

CREAM LAYER CAKE

Rub one cup of butter and two scant cups of sugar to a cream; the yolks of four eggs beaten in well, add gradually one cup of milk and three cups of sifted flour, and add three teaspoons of baking powder in last sifting; put whites in last. Bake at 350° in layers as for jelly cake until knife comes clean. When cold, spread with the following filling: Moisten two tablespoons of cornstarch with enough cold milk to work it into a paste. Scald 2 cups milk with ½ cup of sugar and a pinch of salt. Beat the yolks of two eggs light; add the cornstarch to this, and as soon as the milk is scalded pour in the mixture gradually, stirring constantly until thick. Drop in one teaspoon of sweet butter, and when this is mixed in, set away until cool. Spread between layers.

COCONUT LAYER CAKE

Rub to a cream ½ cup of butter and 1½ cups of pulverized sugar. Add gradually three eggs, ½ cup of milk and two cups of flour, adding two teaspoons of baking powder in last sifting. Bake at 350° in layers until knife comes clean.

Filling

One grated coconut and all of its milk, to half of which add the beaten whites of two eggs and one cup of powdered sugar. Lay this between the layers. Mix with the other half of the grated coconut five tablespoons of powdered sugar and strew thickly on top of cake, which has been previously iced.

CHOCOLATE LAYER CAKE

Stir one scant ½ cup of butter to a cream with one cup of sugar. Add alternately ½ cup of sweet milk, yolks of two eggs which you have previously beaten until quite light, add whites of two, and ½ cup of sifted flour. Make a custard of ½ cup of milk, with one cup of grated chocolate, ½ cup of granulated sugar; boil until thick, add the yolk of one egg, then remove from the fire; stir until cool, add this to the cake batter, add 1½ cups of sifted flour, two teaspoons of baking powder and one of vanilla flavoring. Bake at 350° in layers until knife comes clean, and ice between and on top with plain white icing flavored to taste. You may substitute almond or colored icing.

CARAMEL LAYER CAKE

Place ½ cup of sugar in pan over fire. Stir until liquid smokes and burns brown. Add ½ cup of boiling water and cook into syrup. Take one cup butter, 1½ cups of sugar, yolks of two eggs, over one cup of water and two cups of flour. Beat all thoroughly. Add enough of the burnt sugar to flavor, also one teaspoon of vanilla, another half cup of flour, two teaspoons of baking powder and whites of two eggs. Bake at 350° until knife comes clean in two layers, using remainder of burnt sugar for icing.

HUCKLEBERRY CAKE

Stir to a cream one cup of butter and two cups of powdered sugar and add gradually the yolks of four eggs. Sift into this three cups of flour, adding two teaspoons of baking powder in the last sifting and add one cup of sweet milk alternately with the flour to the creamed butter, sugar and yolks. Spice with one teaspoon of cinnamon and add the stiff-beaten whites of the eggs. Lastly, stir in two cups of huckleberries which have been carefully picked over and well dredged with flour. Be careful in stirring in the huckleberries that you do not bruise them. You will find a wooden spoon the best for this purpose, the edges not being so sharp. Bake in a 375° oven; try with a knife, if it comes out clean, your cake is baked. This will keep fresh for a long while.

CREAM PUFFS

One cup of hot water, ½ cup of butter; boil together, and while boiling stir in one cup of sifted flour dry; take from the stove and stir to a thin paste, and after this cools add three eggs unbeaten, and stir vigorously for five minutes. Drop in tablespoonfuls on a buttered tin and bake in a 400° oven twenty-five minutes, opening the oven door no oftener than is absolutely necessary, and being careful that they do not touch each other in the pan. This amount will make twelve puffs. Cream for puffs: one cup of milk, one cup of sugar, one egg, three tablespoons of flour, vanilla to flavor. Stir the flour in a little of the milk; boil the rest, turn this in and stir until the whole thickens. When both this and the puffs are cool open the puff a little way with a sharp knife and fill them with the cream.

CHOCOLATE ÉCLAIRS

To make Éclairs spread the batter, prepared as in foregoing recipe, in long ovals and when done cover with plain or chocolate frosting, as follows: Boil one cup of brown sugar with ½ cup of molasses, one tablespoon of butter and two tablespoons of flour. Boil for one-half hour, then stir in one-fourth pound of grated chocolate wet in ¼ cup of sweet milk and boil until it hardens on the spoon. Flavor with vanilla. Spread this upon the Éclairs.

DOBOS TORTE
Cream yolks of six eggs with ½ pound of powdered sugar; add ¾ cup of flour sifted three times; then add beaten whites of six eggs lightly and carefully into the mixture. Butter pie plates on under side and sprinkle with flour lightly over the butter and spread the mixture very thin. This amount makes one cake of twelve layers. Bake each layer at 400° about 8 minutes. Remove layers at once with a spatula.

Filling.
Cream ½ pound of sweet butter and put on ice immediately; take ½ pound of sweet chocolate and break it into a cup of strong liquid coffee; add ½ pound of granulated sugar and let it boil until you can pull it almost like candy; remove from fire and stir the chocolate until it is quite cold. When cold add the chocolate mixture to the creamed butter. This filling is spread thin between the layers, spread the icing thicker on top and sides of the cake. This is very fine, but care must be taken in baking and removing the layers, as layers are as thin as wafers. Bake and make filling a day or two before needed.

SPONGE CAKE
Weigh any number of eggs; take the same weight of sugar and half the weight of flour; the grated rind and juice of one lemon to five eggs. The mixture should be very light and spongy, great care being used not to break down the whipped whites. The oven should be 350° at first, and the heat increased to 400° after a time. The cake must not be moved or jarred while baking. The time will be forty to fifty minutes, according to size of cake. Use powdered sugar for sponge cake. Rosewater makes a good flavoring when a change from lemon is wanted.

SMALL SPONGE CAKES

Separate the whites and yolks of four eggs, beat the whites stiff, and beat into them ½ cup of granulated sugar. Beat the yolks to a very stiff froth and beat into them ½ cup of granulated sugar. This last mixture must be beaten for exactly five minutes. Add the juice and grated rind of one small lemon; beat yolks and whites together well, then stir in very gently one scant cup of flour that has been sifted three times. Remember that every stroke of the spoon after the flour is added toughens the cake just that much, so fold the flour in just enough to mix well. If baked in small patty pans they taste just like lady fingers. Bake twenty or twenty-five minutes in moderate oven.

DOMINOES

Make a sponge cake batter, and bake in long tins, not too large. The batter should not exceed the depth of ¼ of an inch, spread it evenly and bake it in a 400° oven (line the tins with buttered paper) until knife comes clean. As each cake is taken from the oven, turn it upside down on a clean board or paper. Spread with a thin layer of currant or cranberry jelly, and lay the other cake on top of it. With a hot, sharp knife cut into strips like dominoes; push them with the knife about an inch apart, and ice them with ordinary white icing, putting a tablespoonful on each piece, the heat of the cake will soften it, and with little assistance the edges and sides may be smoothly covered. Set the cakes in a warm place, where the frosting will dry. Make a horn of stiff white paper with just a small opening at the lower end. Put in one spoon of dark chocolate icing and close the horn at the top, and by pressing out the icing from the small opening, draw a line of it across the center of each cake, and then make dots like those on dominoes. Keep the horn supplied with the icing.

LADYFINGERS

Beat the yolks of three eggs until light and creamy, add ¼ pound of powdered sugar (sifted) and continue beating; add flavoring to taste, vanilla, lemon juice, grated rind of lemon or orange. To the whites of the three eggs add ¼ of a teaspoon of salt and beat until very stiff. Stir in lightly ½ cup of flour and then fold in the beaten whites very gently. Press the mixture through a pastry tube on a baking-tin, covered with paper in portions ½ inch wide by four inches long, or drop on oblong molds; sift a little powdered sugar on top of each cake, and bake at 400° from ten to fifteen minutes. Do not let brown. Remove immediately from pan, brush the flat surface of one cake with white of egg and press the underside of a second cake upon the first.

JELLY ROLL

Take three eggs creamed with one cup of granulated sugar, one cup of flour sifted with two teaspoons of baking powder, add ½ cup of boiling water. Bake at 400° in broad pan for about 15 minutes - while hot, remove from pan and lay on cloth wet with cold water. Spread with jelly and roll quickly. Sprinkle with powdered sugar.

ANGEL FOOD

Sift one cup of pastry flour once, then measure and sift three times. Add a pinch of salt to the whites of eight or nine eggs or just one cup of whites, beat about one-half, add ½ teaspoon of cream of tartar, then beat the whites until they will stand of their own weight; add 1¼ cups of sugar, then flour, not by stirring but folding over and over until thoroughly mixed in; flavor with ½ teaspoon of vanilla or almond extract. Bake at 350° in an ungreased pan, patent tube pan preferred. Place the cake in an oven that will just warm it enough through until the batter has raised to the top of the mold, then increase the heat to 400° until the cake is well browned over; if by pressing the top of the cake with the finger it will spring back without leaving the imprint of the finger the cake is done through. Great care should be taken that the oven is not too hot to begin with as the cake will rise too fast and settle or fall in the baking. Bake thirty-five to forty minutes. When done, invert the pan; when cool remove from pan.

SUNSHINE CAKE

Beat yolks of five eggs lightly, add one teaspoon of vanilla, or grated rind of one lemon. In another bowl beat seven whites to a froth with a scant ½ teaspoon of cream of tartar, then beat until whites are very stiff. Gradually add one cup of granulated sugar, sifted three times, to the beaten whites. Fold whites and sugar, when beaten, into the beaten yolks. Sift one cup of flour three times, then put into sifter and shake lightly, fold into the cake. Bake at 375° for forty minutes in ungreased cake pan. As directed for sponge cake invert pan. Remove cake when it has cooled.

MOCHA TORTE

Beat one cup of powdered sugar with the yolks of four eggs; when very light, add one cup of sifted flour in which has been mixed one teaspoon of baking powder, add three tablespoons of cold water, ½ teaspoon of vanilla, one tablespoon essence of mocha, add the stiffly beaten whites and bake at 400° for fifteen to twenty minutes in two layer pans. Spread when cold with 2 cups cream to which has been added one tablespoon of mocha essence, 1½ tablespoon powdered sugar and then well whipped. Garnish with pounded almonds.

PEACH SHORTCAKE

Make a sponge cake batter of four eggs, one cup of pulverized sugar, a pinch of salt and one cup of flour. Beat the eggs with the sugar until very light. Beat until the consistency of dough and add the grated peel of a lemon, and last the sifted flour. No baking powder necessary. Bake at 400° in jelly tins. Cut the peaches quite fine and sugar bountifully. Put between layers. Eat with cream. The same recipe may be used for Strawberry Shortcake.

BREMEN APPLE TORTE

Take seven peeled and cored apples, six tablespoons of sugar, two tablespoons of butter, and cook together until apples are soft. Cream six eggs; add to them one pint of sour cream, one tablespoon of vanilla, ½ teaspoon of cinnamon, and sugar to taste; then pour into the cooked apples and let all boil together till thick. Remove from stove. Take three cups of finely rolled zwieback, and in the bottom of a well-greased pan put a layer of two cups of crumbs, then a layer of the apple mixture, a layer of the remaining crumbs, and lastly lumps of butter over all. Bake at 325° one hour.

VIENNA PRATER CAKE

Cream the yolks of six eggs with one cup of granulated sugar. Add ¾ cup of sifted chocolate, ¾ cup of flour (sifted twice), 1½ teaspoon of vanilla. Add the beaten whites. Bake at 375° for thirty minutes. When cold, cut in half and fill with the following: One cup of milk, two egg yolks, one cup of chopped walnuts. Boil, stirring constantly to prevent curdling. Sweeten to taste, and after removing from the fire add one tablespoon of rum. Spread while hot.

SAND TORTE

Cream ½ pound of butter with ½ pound of sugar; drop in, one at a time, the yolks of six eggs. Add one small wine glass of rum, ¼ pound of cornstarch, and ¼ pound of flour that have been thoroughly mixed; one teaspoon of baking powder, the beaten whites of six eggs. Bake one hour in a 350° oven.

ALMOND CAKE OR MANDELTORTE, No. 1

Take ½ pound of almonds and blanch by pouring boiling water over them, and pound in a mortar or grate on grater (the latter is best). Beat yolks of eight eggs vigorously with one cup of sugar, add ½ lemon, grated peel and juice, one tablespoon of brandy, and four ladyfingers grated, the almonds, and fold in the stiffly beaten whites of eggs. Bake in 350° oven one hour.

ALMOND CAKE OR MANDEL TORTE, No. 2

Take ¼ pound of sweet almonds and ⅛ pound of bitter ones mixed. Blanch them the day previous to using and then grate or pound them as fine as powder. Beat until light the yolks of nine eggs with eight tablespoons of granulated sugar. Add the grated peel of one lemon and ½ teaspoon of mace or vanilla. Beat long and steadily. Add the grated almonds and continue the stirring in one direction. Add the juice of the lemon to the stiff-beaten whites. Grate four stale ladyfingers, add and bake at 325° for one hour at least.

BRODTORTE

Take six eggs, seven tablespoons of granulated sugar, seven tablespoons of breadcrumbs, ⅛ pound of chopped almonds, ½ teaspoon of allspice, one tablespoon of jelly, grated rind and juice of one lemon, one teaspoon of cinnamon, ½ teaspoon of cloves, ½ wine glass of brandy. Beat yolks of eggs well and add sugar and beat until it blisters, add breadcrumbs, almonds, jelly, spice, lemon, and brandy. Then add beaten whites, and bake at 325° about forty minutes.

RYE BREAD TORTE

Beat the yolks of four eggs very light with one cup of sugar; add one cup of sifted dry rye breadcrumbs to which one teaspoon of baking powder and a pinch of salt have been added. Moisten ½ cup of ground almonds with two tablespoons of sherry, add and lastly fold in the beaten whites of eggs. Bake in ungreased form in 350° oven until knife comes out clean.

ZWIEBACK TORTE
Beat the yolks of six eggs with 1⅛ cups of sugar, add ½ box of zwieback, which has been rolled very fine, add one teaspoon of baking powder, season with one tablespoon of rum or sherry wine and ½ teaspoon of bitter almond extract. Lastly, fold in the stiffly beaten whites of the six eggs and bake in ungreased form in 350° oven for forty-five minutes.

CHOCOLATE BRODTORTE
Separate the yolks and whites of ten eggs. Beat the yolks with two cups of pulverized sugar. When thick add 1¾ cups of sifted dry rye breadcrumbs, ½ pound of sweet almonds, also some bitter ones, grated or powdered as fine as possible, ¼ pound of citron shredded fine, one cake of chocolate grated, the grated peel of one lemon, the juice of one orange and one lemon, one tablespoon of cinnamon, one teaspoon of allspice, ½ teaspoon of cloves, and a wine glass of brandy. Bake at 325° in ungreased form until knife comes out clean. Frost with a chocolate icing, made as follows: Melt a small piece of chocolate. Beat the white of an egg stiff with scant cup of sugar, and stir into the melted chocolate and spread with a knife.

BURNT ALMOND TORTE
Beat up four eggs with one cup of sifted powdered sugar. Beat until it looks like a heavy batter. When you think you cannot possibly beat any longer stir one cup of sifted flour with ½ teaspoon of baking powder. Stir it into batter gradually and lightly, adding three tablespoons of water. Bake in jelly tins at 325°.

Filling:
Scald ¼ pound of almonds (by pouring boiling water over them), remove skins, put them on a pie plate and set them in the oven to brown slightly. Meanwhile, melt three tablespoons of white sugar, without adding water, stirring it all the while. Stir up the almonds in this, then remove them from the fire and lay on a platter separately to cool. Make an icing of the whites of three eggs, beaten very stiff, with one pound of pulverized sugar, and flavor with rosewater. Spread this upon layers and cover each layer with almonds. When finished frost the whole cake, decorating with almonds.

CHOCOLATE TORTE

Take nine eggs, ½ pound of pulverized sugar, ½ pound of almonds, half cut and grated; ½ pound of finest vanilla chocolate grated, ½ pound of raisins, cut and seeded; seven soda crackers, rolled to a powder; one teaspoon of baking powder, juice of three lemons and ¼ glass of wine. Beat whites of eggs to a stiff froth and stir in last. Beat yolks with sugar until very light; then add chocolate, and proceed as with other Torten.

DATE TORTE

Beat ½ pound of pulverized sugar with the yolks of six large eggs. Beat long and steadily until a thick batter. Add ½ pound of dates, cut very fine, one teaspoon each of allspice and ground cinnamon, one-fourth pound of chocolate grated, juice and peel of one lemon, 3½ soda crackers, rolled to a fine powder, one teaspoon of baking powder, and last the stiff-beaten whites. Bake at 325° until knife comes out clean. Cake can be cut in half and put together with jelly.

GERMAN HAZELNUT TORTE

Beat together for twenty minutes until very light the yolks of eight eggs with ½ pound of granulated sugar, then add the very stiffly beaten whites of eggs, place the bowl in which it has been stirred over a boiler in which water is boiling on the stove, stir continually but slowly until all the batter is well warmed but not too hot, add a small pinch of salt, and ½ pound of grated hazelnuts, add the nuts gradually, mix well and pour into a greased spring form. Bake at 325° until knife comes out clean. The grated rind of ½ lemon can be added if desired. Ice with boiled icing.

LINZERTORTE

Cream one pound of butter with one pound of sugar until foamy, then add one by one four whole eggs. Mix well, then stir in ¾ pound of pounded almonds or walnuts, one teaspoon of cinnamon, ¼ teaspoon of cloves, one pound of flour, one teaspoon of baking powder, and a few drops of bitter almond essence. Put in four layer pans and bake in 325° oven until knife comes out clean. Put together with apricot, strawberry, or raspberry jam and pineapple marmalade, each layer having a different preserve. Ice top and sides. If only two layers are desired for home use, half the quantity of ingredients can be used. This is a very fine cake. It is better the second day.

RUSSIAN PUNCH TORTE
Bake three layers of almond tart and flavor it with a wine glass of arrack. When baked, scrape part of the cake out of the thickest layer, not disturbing the rim, and reserve these crumbs to add to the following filling: Boil ½ pound of sugar in one-fourth cup of water until it spins a thread. Add to this syrup a wine glass of rum, and the crumbs, and spread over the layers, piling one on top of the other. Another way to fill this cake is to take some crabapple jelly or apple marmalade and thin it with a little brandy.

WALNUT TORTE, No. 1
Grate eight ounces of walnuts and eight ounces of blanched almonds. Beat light the yolks of twelve eggs and ¾ pound of sugar. Add the grated nuts and ¼ pound of sifted flour, fold in the whites beaten to a stiff froth. Bake at 325° until knife comes out clean, in layers and fill with sweetened whipped cream.

WALNUT TORTE, No. 2
Separate the yolks and whites of six eggs, being very careful not to get a particle of the yolks into the whites. Sift ½ pound of granulated sugar into the yolks and beat until thick as batter. Add a pinch of salt to the whites and beat very stiff. Have ready ¼ pound of grated walnuts, reserve whole pieces for decorating the top of cake. Add the pounded nuts to the beaten yolks, and two tablespoons of grated ladyfingers or stale sponge cake. Last, add the stiffly beaten whites of the eggs. Bake at 350° in layers and fill with almond or plain icing.

CHESTNUT TORTE
Boil one pound of chestnuts in the shells, peel them while warm, put nuts through potato ricer or colander. Beat well the yolks of six eggs with six tablespoons of sugar, add all the chestnut purée but two or three tablespoons reserved for top of torte, then add three teaspoons of baking powder and the well-beaten whites of the six eggs; bake in 350° oven fifteen to twenty minutes. Whip ½ pint of cream, add to this the chestnut purée which was reserved, and a little sugar; garnish torte with this mixture. Enough for twelve persons.

NUT HONEY CAKE

Mix two cups of brown sugar, two cups of honey, six egg yolks and beat them thoroughly. Sift together three cups of flour, one-quarter teaspoon of salt, three teaspoons of ground cinnamon, one-half teaspoon each of ground cloves, ground nutmeg and allspice, and one and one-half teaspoons of soda; add one cup of chopped raisins, one-half ounce of citron cut in small pieces, one-half ounce of candied orange peel cut in small pieces, one-half pound of almonds coarsely chopped. Beat the whites of three eggs very stiff and add them last. Pour the dough to the depth of about half an inch into well-buttered tins and bake in a slow oven for one-half hour.

ICINGS AND FILLINGS FOR CAKES

BOILED ICING
One cup of sugar, ⅓ cup of boiling water, white of one egg beaten stiff. Pour water on sugar until dissolved, heat slowly to boiling point without stirring; boil until syrup will thread when dropped from tip of spoon; as soon as it threads, pour slowly over beaten white, then beat with heavy wire spoon until of proper consistency to spread. Flavor.

WHITE CARAMEL ICING
Put on to boil two cups of brown sugar, one cup of milk and a small lump of butter. Boil until it gets as thick as cream, then beat with a fork or egg whip until thick and creamy. Spread quickly on cake.

MAPLE SUGAR ICING
Boil two cups of maple sugar with ½ cup of boiling water until it threads from the spoon. Pour it upon the beaten whites of two eggs and beat until cold. Spread between layers and on top of cake. Do not make icings on cloudy or rainy days.

UNBOILED ICING
Take the white of one egg and add to it the same quantity of water (measure in an egg shell). Stir into this as much confectioner's sugar to make it of the right consistency to spread upon the cake. Flavor with any flavoring desired. You may color it as you would boiled frosting by adding fruit coloring.

COCONUT ICING
Mix coconut with the unboiled icing. If you desire to spread it between the cakes, scatter more coconut over and between the layers.

NUT ICING
Mix any quantity of finely chopped nuts into any quantity of cream icing (unboiled) as in the foregoing recipes. Ice the top of cake with plain icing, and lay the halves of walnuts on top.

ORANGE ICING

Grate the peel of ½ orange, mix with two tablespoons of orange juice and one tablespoon of lemon juice and let stand fifteen minutes. Strain and add to the beaten yolk of one egg. Stir in enough powdered sugar to make it the right consistency to spread upon the cake.

CHOCOLATE GLAZING

Grate two sticks of bitter chocolate, add five tablespoons of powdered sugar and three tablespoons of boiling water. Put on the stove, over moderate heat, stir while boiling until smooth, glossy and thick. Spread at once on cake and set aside to harden.

CHOCOLATE ICING, UNBOILED

Beat the whites of three eggs and 1½ cups of pulverized sugar, added gradually while beating. Beat until very thick, then add four tablespoons of grated chocolate and two teaspoons of vanilla. This quantity is sufficient for a very large cake.

INSTANTANEOUS FROSTING

To the white of an unbeaten egg, add 1¼ cups of pulverized sugar and stir until smooth. Add three drops of rosewater, ten of vanilla, and the juice of ½ a lemon. It will at once become very white, and will harden in five or six minutes.

PLAIN FROSTING

To one cup of confectioner's sugar add some liquid, either milk or water, to make it the right consistency to spread, flavor with vanilla. Instead of the water or milk, orange juice can be used. A little of the rind must be added. Lemon juice can be substituted in place of vanilla. Chocolate melted over hot water and added to the sugar and water makes a nice chocolate icing; flavor with vanilla.

ALMOND ICING

Take the whites of two eggs and ½ pound of sweet almonds, which should be blanched, dried and grated or pounded to a paste. Beat the whites of the eggs, add ½ pound of confectioner's sugar, one tablespoon at a time, until all is used, and then add the almonds and a few drops of rosewater. Spread between or on top of cake. Put on thick, and when nearly dry cover with a plain icing. If the cakes are well dredged with a little flour after baking, and then carefully wiped before the icing is put on, it will not run and can be spread more smoothly. Put the frosting in the center of the cake, dip a knife in cold water and spread from the center toward the edge.

MOCHA FROSTING
One cup of pulverized sugar into which sift two dessertspoons of dry cocoa, two tablespoons of strong hot coffee in which is melted a piece of butter the size of a walnut. Beat well and add a little vanilla.

MARSHMALLOW FILLING
Melt ½ pound marshmallows over hot water, cook together one cup of sugar and ¼ cup of cold water until it threads thoroughly. Beat up the white of an egg and syrup and mix, then add to the melted marshmallows and beat until creamy and cool. Can be used for cake filling or spread between two cookies.

FIG FILLING
One pound of figs chopped fine, one cup of water, ½ cup of sugar; cook all together until soft and smooth.

BANANA FILLING
Mash six bananas, add juice of one lemon and three or more tablespoons of sugar; or add mashed bananas with whipped cream or boiled icing.

CREAM FILLING
Scald two cups of milk. Mix together ¾ of a cup of sugar, one-third cup of flour and one-eighth teaspoon of salt. Add to three slightly beaten eggs and pour in scalded milk. Cook twenty minutes over boiling water, stirring constantly until thickened. Cool and flavor. This can be used as a foundation for most fillings, by adding melted chocolate, nuts, fruits, etc.

COFFEE FILLING
Put three cups of warmed-over or freshly made coffee in a small casserole, add two tablespoons of powdered sugar, one-half teaspoon of vanilla. When at boiling point (do not let it boil), add one cup of milk or cream. Then add one tablespoon of cornstarch that has been moistened with cold water. Stir

in while cooking until it is smooth and glossy. When the cake is cool, pour mixture over the layers.

LEMON JELLY FOR LAYER CAKE
Take one pound of sugar, yolks of eight eggs with two whole ones, the juice of five large lemons, the grated peel of two, and ¼ pound of butter. Put the sugar, lemon and butter into saucepan and melt over a gentle heat. When all is dissolved, stir in the eggs that have been beaten, stir rapidly until it is thick as honey, and spread some of this between the layers of cake. Pack the remainder in jelly glasses.

PIES AND PASTRY

PUFF PASTE OR BLÄTTERTEIG

To make good puff paste one must have all the ingredients cold. Use a marble slab if possible and avoid making the paste on a warm, damp day. It should be made in a cool place as it is necessary to keep the paste cold during the whole time of preparation. This recipe makes two pies or four crusts, and requires ½ pound of butter and ½ teaspoon of salt, ½ pound of flour and ½ cup of ice water.

Cut off ⅓ of the butter and put the remaining ⅔ in a bowl of ice water. Divide this into four equal parts; pat each into a thin sheet and set them away on ice. Mix and sift flour and salt; rub the reserved butter into it and make as stiff as possible with ice water. Dust the slab with flour; turn the paste upon it; knead for one minute, then stand it on ice for five minutes. Roll the cold paste into a square sheet about ⅓ of an inch thick; place the cold butter in the center and fold the paste over it, first from the sides and then the ends, keeping the shape square and folding so that the butter is completely covered and cannot escape through any cracks as it is rolled. Roll out to ¼ inch thickness, keeping the square shape and folding as before, but without butter. Continue rolling and folding, enclosing a sheet of butter at every alternate folding until all four sheets are used. Then turn the folded side down and roll in one direction into a long narrow strip, keeping the edges as straight as possible. Fold the paste over, making three even layers. Then roll again and fold as before. Repeat the process until the dough has had six turns. Cut into the desired shapes and place on the ice for twenty minutes or longer before putting in the oven.

If during the making the paste sticks to the board or pin, remove it immediately and stand it on the ice until thoroughly chilled. Scrape the board clean; rub with a dry cloth and dust with fresh flour before trying again. Use as little flour as possible in rolling, but use enough to keep the paste dry. Roll with a light, even, long stroke in every direction, but never work the rolling pin back and forth as that movement toughens the paste and breaks the bubbles of air.

The baking of puff paste is almost as important as the rolling, and the oven must be very hot, with the greatest heat at the bottom, so that the paste will rise before it browns. If the paste should begin to scorch, open the drafts at once and cool the temperature by placing a pan of ice water in the oven.

FLEISCHIG PIE CRUST

For shortening use drippings and mix with goose, duck or chicken fat. In the fall and winter, when poultry is plentiful and fat, save all drippings of poultry fat for piecrust. If you have neither, use rendered beef fat.

Take ½ cup of shortening, 1½ cups of flour. Sifted pastry flour is best. If you have none at hand take two tablespoons of flour off each cup after sifting; add a pinch of salt. With two knives cut the fat into the sifted flour until the shortening is in pieces as small as peas. Then pour in six or eight tablespoons of cold water; in summer use ice-water; work with the knife until well mixed (never use the hand). Flour a board or marble slab, roll the dough out thin, sprinkle with a little flour and put dabs of soft drippings here and there, fold the dough over and roll out thin again and spread with fat and sprinkle with flour, repeat this and then roll out not too thin and line a pie plate with this dough. Always cut dough for lower crust a little larger than the upper dough and do not stretch the dough when lining pie-pan or plate.

If fruit is to be used for the filling, brush over top of the dough with white of egg slightly beaten, or sprinkle with one tablespoon of breadcrumbs to prevent the dough from becoming soggy.

Put in the filling, brush over the edge of pastry with cold water, lay the second round of paste loosely over the filling; press the edges together lightly, and trim, if needed. Cut several slits in the top crust or prick it with a fork before putting it in place.

Bake from thirty-five to forty-five minutes until crust is a nice brown.

A gas stove is more satisfactory for baking pies than a coal stove as pies require the greatest heat at the bottom.

The recipe given above makes two crusts. Bake pies having a cooked filling in a quick oven and those with an uncooked filling in a moderate oven. Let pies cool upon plates on which they were made because slipping them onto cold plates develops moisture that always destroys the crispness of the lower crust.

TO MAKE AND BAKE A MERINGUE

To beat and bake a meringue have cold, fresh eggs, beat the whites until frothy; add to each white one level tablespoon of powdered sugar. Beat until so stiff that it can be cut with a knife. Spread on the pie and bake with the oven door open until a rich golden brown. Too much sugar causes a meringue to liquefy; if not baked long enough the same effect is produced.

PIE CRUST (MERBERTEIG)

Rub one cup of butter to a cream, add four cups of sifted flour, a pinch of salt and a tablespoon of brown sugar; work these together until the flour looks like sand, then take the yolk of an egg, a wine-glass of brandy, ½ cup of ice-water and work it into the flour lightly. Do not use the hands; knead with a knife or wooden spoon, knead as little as possible. If the dough is of the right consistency no flour will be required when rolling out the dough. If it is necessary to use flour use as little as possible. Work quickly, handle dough as little as possible and bake in a hot oven. Follow directions given with Fleischig Pie Crust. Fat may be substituted for butter in the above recipe.

PARVE, COOKIE AND PIE DOUGH

Sift into a mixing bowl 1½ cups of flour and ½ teaspoon of baking powder. Make a depression in the center; into this pour a generous half cup of oil and an exact half cup of very cold (or ice) water; add pinch of salt, mix quickly with a fork, divide in two portions; do not knead, but roll on a well-floured board, spread on pans, fill and bake at once in a quick oven. No failure is possible if the formula is accurately followed and these things observed; ingredients cold, no kneading or re-rolling; dough must not stand, but the whole process must be completed as rapidly as possible. Do not pinch or crimp the edge of this or any other pie. To do so makes a hard edge that no one cares to eat. Instead, trim the edges in the usual way, then place the palms of the hand on opposite sides of the pie and raise the dough until the edges stand straight up. This prevents all leakage and the crust is tender to the last morsel.

TARTLETS

Roll puff paste ⅛ inch thick; cut it into squares; turn the points together into the middle and press slightly to make them stay. Bake at 400° until thoroughly done; place a spoonful of jam in the center of each; cover the jam with meringue and brown the meringue in a quick oven. By brushing the top of the paste with beaten egg, diluted with one teaspoon of water, a glazed appearance may be obtained.

BANBURY TARTS

Cut one cup of raisins and one cup of nuts in small pieces, add one cup of sugar, one well-beaten egg, one tablespoon of water, the juice and grated rind of one lemon. Mix well. Line patty-pans with pie dough, fill with mixture and bake at 400° until crust is brown.

FRUIT TARTLETS

If canned fruit is used, take a large can of any kind of fruit, drain all the syrup off and put in a saucepan with an equal quantity of sugar. Cook until it forms a syrup, then pour in the fruit, which has been stoned (if necessary), and cook until the whole is a syrupy mass. If fresh fruit is used, put on two parts of sugar to one of water and cook until syrupy, then add the fruit, which has been peeled, sliced and stoned, and cook until the whole is a thick, syrupy mass. Line the patty cases or plain muffin rings with the puff paste. Put a spoonful or two of the fruit in each one and bake at 400° until a nice brown. Peaches, white cherries, Malaga grapes, huckleberries and apples make nice tartlets. One large can California fruit fills twelve tartlets.

APPLE FLADEN (HUNGARIAN)

Rub together on a pastry-board ½ pound of sweet butter with one pound (four cups sifted) of flour, add four tablespoons of powdered sugar, a little salt, four egg yolks and moisten with one-half cup of sour cream; cover and set aside in the ice-box for thirty minutes. Take two pounds of sour apples, peel, cut fine, mix with ½ cup of light-colored raisins, sugar and cinnamon to taste. Cut the dough in two pieces, roll out one piece and place on greased baking-pan, spread over this four tablespoons of breadcrumbs and the chopped sugared apples, roll out the other half of dough, place on top and spread with white of one egg, sprinkle with two tablespoons of powdered almonds. Bake in 375° oven.

LINSER TART

Make a dough of ½ pound each of flour, sugar and almonds that are grated with peel on, two eggs, a little allspice, a little citron, pinch of salt. Flavor with brandy. Take a little more than half, roll it out and line a pie-pan, put strawberry jam on and then cut rest of dough in strips and cover the same as you would prune pie. Brush these strips with yolk of egg and bake in moderate oven.

MACAROON TARTS

Line a gem or muffin pan with rich pie dough; half fill each tart with any desired preserve, and bake in a 400° oven. Beat the whites of three eggs to a stiff froth and add ½ pound of powdered sugar and stir about ten minutes or until very light, and gradually ½ pound of grated almonds. Divide this macaroon paste into equal portions. Roll and shape into strips, dusting hands with powdered sugar in place of flour. Place these strips on the baked tarts in parallel rows to cross each other diagonally. Return to 325° oven about fifteen minutes. Let remain in pans until almost cold.

LEMON TART (FLEISCHIG)

Make a rich crust and bake in small spring form. Beat three whole eggs and yolks of three very light with one cup of sugar. Add juice of three lemons and grated rind of one, and juice of one orange. Put whole on stove and stir until it comes to a boil. Put on baked crust, spread a meringue made of the remaining three whites and three tablespoons of sugar on top, and put in 350° oven to brown. May be used as a filling for tartlets.

VIENNA PASTRY FOR KIPFEL

Take ½ pound of pot cheese and ½ pound of butter and two cups of flour sifted four times, add a pinch of salt and work these ingredients into a dough; make thirty small balls of it and put on a platter on the ice overnight. In the morning, roll each ball separately into two-inch squares. These squares may be filled with a teaspoon of jelly put in the center and the squares folded over like an envelop; or fill them with ½ pound of walnuts, ground; ½ cup of sugar and moisten with a little hot milk. Roll and twist into shape. Brush with beaten egg and bake in a 375° oven.

CHEESE STRAWS

½ cup of flour, two tablespoons of butter, four tablespoons of grated cheese, yolk of one egg, dash of cayenne pepper, enough ice water to moisten. Mix as little as possible. Roll out about ¼ inch thick and cut into long, narrow strips. Shake a little more cheese on top and bake in 400° oven. This is also an excellent piecrust for one pie, omitting pepper and cheese. Serve cheese straws with salads.

LAMPLICH

Make a mincemeat by chopping finely eight medium-sized apples, ½ pound each of raisins, currants and sugar, a little citron peel, two or three cloves and one teaspoon of powdered cinnamon. Cut some good puff paste into little triangles and fill with the mince, turning the corners of the paste over it so as to make little puffs. Place these closely together and on a buttered baking dish until it is full. Now mix two tablespoons of melted butter with one teacup of thick syrup flavored with essence of lemon, and pour it over the puffs. Bake until done in a 325° oven.

MIRLITIOUS

Pound and sift six macaroons; add one tablespoon of grated chocolate and one pint of hot milk. Let stand ten minutes, and then add yolks of three eggs well beaten, one tablespoon of sugar, one teaspoon of vanilla. Line patty-tins with puff paste; fill with the mixture and bake at 400° twenty minutes.

APPLE PIE, No. 1
Pare, core and slice four apples. Line a pie plate with plain pastry. Sprinkle with breadcrumbs. Lay in the apples, sprinkle with ½ cup of sugar, flavor with cinnamon, nutmeg or lemon juice or two tablespoons of water if apples are not juicy. Cover with upper crust, slash and prick and bake in 350° oven until the crust is brown and the fruit is soft.

APPLE PIE, No. 2
Put in saucepan ½ cup of sugar and ¼ cup of water, let it boil a few minutes, then lay in five large apples or six small ones, which have previously been peeled and quartered; cover with a lid and steam until tender but not broken. Line pie plate with rich milchig pastry, lay on the apples, sprinkle with sugar and cinnamon and bits of butter, drop a few drops of syrup over all and bake at 375°.

INDIVIDUAL APPLE DUMPLINGS
Butter six muffin rings and set them on a shallow agate pan that has been well buttered. Fill the rings with sliced apples. Make a dough of 1½ cups of pastry flour sifted several times with ½ teaspoon of salt and three level teaspoons of baking powder. Chop into the dry ingredients ¼ of a cup of shortening, gradually add ¾ of a cup of milk or water. Drop the dough on the apples on the rings. Let bake at 350° about twenty minutes. With a spatula remove each dumpling from the ring, place on dish with the crust side down. Serve with cream and sugar, hard sauce or with a fruit sauce.

WHIPPED CREAM PIE
Make a crust as rich as possible and line a deep tin. Bake in a 400° oven and spread it with a layer of jelly or jam. Next whip one cup of sweet cream until it is thick. Set the cream in a bowl of ice while whipping. Sweeten slightly and flavor with vanilla, spread this over the pie and put in a cool place until wanted.

GRATED APPLE PIE
Line a pie plate with a rich puff paste. Pare and grate four or five large tart apples into a bowl into which you have stirred the yolks of two eggs with about ½ cup of sugar. Add a few raisins, a few currants, a few pounded

almonds, a pinch of ground cinnamon, and the grated peel of a lemon. Have no top crust. Bake in a 400° oven. In the meantime, make a meringue of the whites of the eggs by beating them to a very stiff froth and add about three tablespoons of pulverized sugar. Spread this over the pie when baked and set back in the oven until brown. Eat cold.

APPLE CUSTARD PIE
Line your pie plates with a rich crust. slice apples thin, half fill your plates and pour over them a custard made of four eggs and two cups of milk, sweetened and seasoned to taste. Bake at 375° until set.

CHERRY PIE, No. 1
Line a pie plate with rich paste, sprinkle cornstarch lightly over the bottom crust and fill with cherries and regulate the quantity of sugar you scatter over them by their sweetness. Bake at 375° with an upper crust, secure the edges well by pinching firmly together. Eat cold.

CHERRY PIE, No. 2
Pick the stems out of your cherries and put them in an earthen crock, then set them in the oven until they get hot. Take them out and seed them. Make tarts with or without tops and sugar to your taste. The heating of the fruit gives the flavor of the seed, which is very rich, but the seeding of them while hot is not a delightful job. Made this way they need no water for juice.

SNOWBALLS
Pare and core nice large baking apples, fill the holes with some preserves or jam, roll the apples in sugar and cover with a rich piecrust and bake at 375°.

BLACKBERRY AND CURRANT PIE
When ready to make the pie, mix as much fruit in a bowl as required, sweeten, stirring the sugar through the berries and currants lightly with a spoon. Dust in a little flour and stir it through the fruit. Cut one of the pieces of pastry in halves, dust the pastry-board with flour and roll the lump of pastry out very thin, cover the pie plate, a big deep one, with the pastry, trim off the edges with a knife, cutting from you. Fill the dish with the fruit, dust the surface well with flour. Roll out the other piece for the top crust, fold it over the rolling pin, cut a few gashes in it for a steam vent. Carefully put on the top

crust, trim it well about the edge of the pie plate. press it closely together with the end of your thumb or with a pastry knife and stand the pie in a 350° oven and bake till the surface is a delicate brown. Then remove the pie and let it stand until it is cool. The top crust may be made lattice fashion by cutting the pastry in strips, but it will not be as good as between two closed crusts.

CUSTARD PIE

Line the pie plate with a rich crust. Beat up four eggs light with one-half cup of sugar, a pinch of salt, one pint of milk and grated nutmeg or grated lemon peel, and pour in shell and bake in 325° oven until lightly browned.

CREAM PIE

First line a pie plate with puff paste and bake, and then make a cream of the yolks of four eggs, a little more than a pint of milk, one tablespoon of cornstarch and four tablespoons of sugar, and flavor with two teaspoons of vanilla. Pour on crust and bake at 350°; beat up the whites with two tablespoons of powdered sugar and half a teaspoon of cream of tartar. Spread on top of pie and set back in the oven until baked a light brown.

COCONUT PIE

Line a pie plate with puff paste and fill with the following custard: Butter size of an egg, creamed with one cup of granulated sugar, one tablespoon of flour, ¾ cup of grated coconut, one tablespoon of milk, vanilla, pinch of salt, and the beaten whites of three eggs. Bake at 350° until lightly browned.

COCONUT LEMON PIE

Beat the yolks of six eggs and one cup of sugar until very light, squeeze in the juice of three lemons and the rind of two of them, stir well, then add ½ of a coconut grated, and lastly add the whites of six eggs, beaten to a stiff froth. Line a deep pie plate with rich pastry, sprinkle a little flour over it, pour in the lemon mixture and bake at 375° until lightly browned. This makes one pie in deep pie plate.

LEMON PIE, No. 1

Cover the reverse side of a deep pie plate with a rich puff paste, and bake a light brown. Remove from the oven until the filling is prepared. Take a large juicy lemon, grate and peel and squeeze out every drop of juice. Now take the lemon and put it into a cup of boiling water to extract every particle of juice. Put the cup of water on to boil with the lemon juice and grated peel, and a cup of sugar; beat up the yolks of four eggs very light and add to this gradually the boiling lemon juice. Return to the kettle and boil. Then wet a teaspoon of cornstarch with a very little cold water, and add also a teaspoon of butter and when the boiling mixture has thickened remove from the fire and let it cool. Beat up the whites of the eggs to a very stiff froth, add half of the froth to the lemon mixture and reserve the other half for the top of the pie. Bake the lemon cream in the baked pie crust at 350°. Add a few tablespoons of powdered sugar and ½ teaspoon of cream of tartar to the remaining beaten whites. If you desire to have the meringue extra thick, add the whites of one or more eggs. When the pie is baked take from the oven just long enough to spread the meringue over the top, and set back for two or three minutes, leaving the oven doors open just the least bit, so as not to have it brown too quickly.

LEMON PIE, No. 2

Line a deep pie plate with nice crust, then prepare a filling as follows: After removing the crust from two slices of bread about two inches thick, pour over it one cup of boiling water; add one dessertspoon of butter, and beat until the bread is well soaked and smooth; then add the juice and rind of one lemon, one cup of sugar, the yolks of two eggs, well beaten, and a little salt; mix well; fill pie with mixture and bake at 375° until firm. Beat white of two eggs to a stiff froth, add four tablespoons of powdered sugar and spread on top and brown.

MOCK MINCE PIE

Pare, core, and chop fine eight tart apples. Add one cup of raisins, ½ cup of currants, one ounce of chopped citron, ½ teaspoon each of cinnamon, cloves, spice and mace, a tiny bit of salt and grated nutmeg. Pour over whole one tablespoon of brandy, and juice and rind of one lemon. Line bottom and sides of plate with crust, fill in with mixture, and put strips of dough across. Bake at 375° until lightly browned.

MINCE PIE

Boil two pounds lean, fresh beef. When cold, chop fine. Add ½ pound chopped suet, shredded very fine, and all gristle removed. Mix in a bowl two pounds of raisins, two pounds of currants, ½ pound of citron, chopped very fine. Two tablespoons of cinnamon, two tablespoons of mace, one grated nutmeg, one tablespoon of cloves, allspice, and salt. Mix this with meat and suet. Then take two cups of white wine, 2½ pounds of brown sugar. Let stand. Chop fine four apples, and add meat to fruits. Then mix wine with whole, stir well, and put up in small stone jars. This will keep all winter in a cool place. Let stand at least two days before using. Line pie plates with a rich crust, fill with mincemeat mixture, put a rich paste crust on top, or strips if preferred, prick slightly and bake at 375°. Serve warm, not hot.

PUMPKIN PIE

Press through a sieve one pint of stewed pumpkin, add four eggs and a scant cup of sugar. Beat yolks and sugar together until very thick and add 2 cups milk to the beaten eggs. Then add the pressed pumpkin, ½ teaspoon of cinnamon, less than ½ teaspoon of mace and grated nutmeg. Stir the stiffly beaten whites in last. Bake at 350° in a very rich crust without cover.

GRAPE PIE

Squeeze out the pulps and put them in one vessel, the skins into another. Then simmer the pulp a little and press it through a colander to separate the seeds. Then put the skins and pulps together and they are ready for the pies.

HUCKLEBERRY PIE

Line a pie plate with rich pastry. Pick, clean and wash one pint of huckleberries, drain and lay them thickly on the crust. Sprinkle thickly with sugar, lightly with cinnamon, and drop bits of butter over the top. Bake at 350° until a nice even brown.

PEACH CREAM TARTS

One cup of butter, and a little salt; cut through just enough flour to thoroughly mix, a cup of ice-water, one whole egg, and the yolks of two eggs mixed with a tablespoon of brown sugar. Add to the flour in which you have previously sifted two teaspoons of baking powder. Handle the dough as little as possible in mixing. Bake in round rings in a 400° oven until a light brown. When baked, sift pulverized sugar over the top and fill the hollow center with a compote of peaches. Heap whipped cream or ice cream on top of each one, the latter being preferable.

MOCK CHERRY PIE
Cover the bottom of pie plate with rich crust; reserve enough for upper crust. For filling use two cups of cranberries, cut in halves; one cup of raisins, cut in pieces; two cups of sugar, butter the size of walnut. Dredge with flour, sprinkle with water. Bake thirty minutes in a 350° oven.

PEACH CREAM PIE
Line a pie plate with a rich crust and bake, then fill with a layer of sweetened grated peaches. Whip one cup of rich cream, sweeten and flavor and spread over the peaches. Set in ice chest until wanted.

PEACH PIE, No. 1
Line a pie plate with a rich pie crust, cover thickly with peaches that have been pared and sliced fine (canned peaches may be used when others are not to be had), adding sugar and cover with strips of dough; bake at 400°.

PEACH PIE, No. 2
Pare, stone, and slice the peaches. Line a deep pie plate with a rich paste, sprinkle a little flour over the bottom crust and lay in your fruit, sprinkle sugar liberally over them in proportion to their sweetness. Bake at 350° with crossbars of paste across the top. If you want it extra fine, with the whites of three eggs to a stiff froth and sweeten with about four tablespoons of pulverized sugar, adding ¼ teaspoon of cream tartar, spread over the pie and return to the oven until the meringue is set. Eat cold.

PINEAPPLE PIE, No. 1
Line your pie plate with a rich paste, slice pineapples as thin as possible, sprinkle sugar over them abundantly and put flakes of sugar here and there. Cover and bake at 350° until lightly browned. You may make pineapple pies according to any of the plain apple pie recipes.

PINEAPPLE PIE, No. 2

Pare and core the pineapple and cut into small slices and sprinkle abundantly with sugar and set it away in a covered dish to draw enough juice to stew the pineapple in. Bake two shells on perforated pie plates of a rich pie dough. When the pineapple is stewed soft enough to mash, mash it and set it away to cool. When the crust is baked and cool whip 1 cup sweet cream and mix with the pineapple and fill in the baked shell.

PRUNE AND RAISIN PIE

Use ½ pound of prunes, cooked until soft enough to remove the stones. Mash with a fork and add the juice in which they have been cooked; ½ cup of raisins, cooked in a little water for a few minutes until soft; add to the prune mixture with ½ cup of sugar; a little ground clove or lemon juice improves the flavor. Bake at 350° with two crusts until lightly browned.

PRUNE PIE

Make a rich pie paste. After the paste is rolled out thin and the pie plate lined with it, put in a layer of prunes that have been stewed the day before, with the addition of several slices of lemon and no sugar. Split the prunes in halves and remove the pits before laying them on the pie crust. After the first layer is in sprinkle it well with sugar, then pour over the sugar three or four tablespoons of the prune juice and dust the surface lightly with flour. Repeat this process until there are three layers, then cut enough of the paste in strips to cover the top of the fruit with a lattice crust and bake the pie in a 400° oven until golden brown. Few pies can excel this in daintiness of flavor.

PLUM PIE

Select large purple plums, about fifteen plums for a good-sized pie; cut them in halves, remove the kernels and dip each half in flour. Line your pie-tin with a rich paste and lay in the plums, close together, and sprinkle thickly with a whole cup of sugar. Lay strips of paste across the top, into bars, also a strip around the rim, and press all around the edge with a pointed knife or fork, which will make a fancy border. Bake at 350° until crust is golden brown. Sift powdered sugar on top. Damson pie is made in the same way. Eat cold.

RHUBARB PIE

Make a very rich crust, and over the bottom layer sprinkle a large tablespoon of sugar and a good teaspoon of flour. Fill half-full of rhubarb that has been cut up, scatter in ¼ cup of strawberries or raspberries, sprinkle with more sugar and flour, and then proceed as before. Over the top dot bits of butter and another dusting of flour. Use a good cup of sugar to a pie. Pinch the crusts together well after wetting them, to prevent the juice, which should be so thick that it does not soak through the lower crust at all, from cooking out. Bake at 375° until crust is golden.

STRAWBERRY PIE

Make a rich fleishchig pie crust and bake on the reverse side of pie-pan. Pick a quart of berries, wash and drain, then sugar. Take the yolks of four eggs beaten well with ½ cup of sugar and stir the beaten whites gently into this mixture. Pour over strawberries. Put in pie crust and bake at 350° until brown. This mixture with most all fruit pies will be found delicious.

SWEET POTATO PIE

Measure one cup of mashed, boiled sweet potatoes. Thin with one pint of sweet milk. Beat three whole eggs very light with ½ cup of sugar. Mix with sweet potatoes. Season with ¼ teaspoon of grated nutmeg, one teaspoon of cinnamon, and ½ teaspoon of lemon extract. Line pie plate with crust, fill with mixture, and bake in 400° oven until crust is golden.

VINEGAR PIE

Line a pie plate with a rich crust and fill with the following mixture: One cup of vinegar, two of water and two cups of sugar, boil; add a lump of butter and enough cornstarch to thicken; flavor with lemon essence and put in a shell and bake at 375° until crust is golden.

MOHNTORTE

Line a form with a rich puff paste, fill with ½ pound of white Mohn (poppy seed) which has been previously soaked in milk and then ground. Add ¼ pound of sugar and the yolks of six eggs; stir all together in one direction until quite thick. Then stir the beaten whites, to which add two ounces of sifted flour and a ¼ pound of melted butter. Fill and bake at 375° until crust is golden. When done, frost either with vanilla or rose frosting.

RAISIN PIE
Line pie pan with rounds of rich pastry, fill with same mixture as for Banbury Tarts; cover with a round of pastry and bake at 375° until a light brown.

RAISIN AND RHUBARB PIE
Chop one cup of rhubarb and one cup of raisins together, add two tablespoons of melted butter or chicken fat, grated rind and juice of one lemon, one cup of sugar, one well beaten egg, ¼ cup of bread or cracker crumbs, ½ teaspoon of salt; mix all ingredients thoroughly. Bake at 375° between two rounds of pastry until golden. Canned rhubarb may be used.

COOKIES

In baking small cakes and cookies, grease the pans. If the pans cool before you can take off the cookies, set back on stove for a few moments. The cakes will then slip off easily. Sponge, drop cakes, anise cakes, etc., are better baked on floured pans. A whole raisin, an almond blanched, a piece of citron or half a walnut may be used to decorate. A good way to glaze is, when cookies are about baked, rub over with a brush dipped in sugar and water and return to oven a moment.

FILLED BUTTER CAKES (DUTCH STUFFED MONKEYS)

Make a paste by working ¾ pound of butter into one pound of flour, with three-fourths pound of light brown sugar, one egg, one teaspoon of cinnamon, and a pinch of salt. Next mix ½ pound of finely chopped citron peel with ½ pound of ground almonds, and three ounces of butter. Then flavor with ½ teaspoon of vanilla and bind with the yolks of two eggs. Roll out the dough and divide into two parts. Place ½ on a well-buttered flat pan and spread the mixture over it and cover with the other half of the paste. Brush with beaten egg, sprinkle with poppy seed and bake in a 375° oven for thirty minutes. When done let cool and then cut into square or oblong pieces. The butter cakes may be made of one layer of dough sprinkled with citron and almonds and some poppy seed.

SUGAR COOKIES

In a mixing bowl put a cup of sweet butter and two cups of granulated sugar; beat these ingredients to a cream, then add three eggs, grated lemon rind, and four tablespoons of brandy. Beat the added ingredients thoroughly with the others until the mixture is smooth and creamy. Sift three cups of flour in a big bowl with a teaspoon of salt and three teaspoons of baking powder; stir this a little at a time in the bowl with the other ingredients, until the mixture is a light dough, just stiff enough to roll out. If there is not enough flour, sift more in to make the dough the desired stiffness; then dust the pastry board well with flour, put part of the dough on the board, toss it lightly with your hands from side to side till the dough is covered with flour. Then dust the rolling-pin well with flour and roll the dough very thin; cut it in shapes with a cookie cutter, lift each cookie up carefully with a pancake turner, slip them quickly in a big baking-pan, the inside of which has been well rubbed with flour, and bake them in a 350° oven till light brown. Just a moment before taking the pan out of the oven sprinkle the surface of the cookies lightly with granulated sugar. When a little cool take the cookies out of the pan with the pancake turner and lay them on a big platter. When they are cold put the cookies in a stone crock. It is a good plan to have two or three baking-pans so, while one panful is baking, another may be filled and be ready to put in the oven when the other is removed. Only put enough dough on the pastry board at a time to roll out nicely on it.

MOTHER'S DELICIOUS COOKIES (MERBERKUCHEN)
Take ten boiled eggs and two raw ones, one pound of best butter, ½ pound of almonds, one lemon, some cinnamon, one wineglass of brandy, one pound of pulverized sugar and about 1½ pounds flour. This quantity makes one hundred cookies, and like fruitcake, age improves them, in other words, the older the better. Now to begin with: Set a dish of boiling water on the stove, when it boils hard, break the eggs carefully, one at a time, dropping the whites in a deep porcelain dish, and set away in a cool place. Take each yolk as you break the egg and put it in a half shell, and lay it in the boiling water until you have ten boiling. When boiled hard take them up and lay them on a plate to cool. In the meantime, cream the butter with a pound of pulverized sugar, add the grated peel of a lemon, a teaspoon of cinnamon and half of the almonds, which have been blanched and pounded or grated (reserve the other half for the top of the cookies, which should not be grated, put pounded). Add the hard-boiled yolks, which must be grated, and the two raw eggs, sift in the flour, and add the brandy. Beat up the whites of the twelve eggs very stiff, add half to the dough, reserving the other half, but do not make the dough stiff, as it should be so rich that you can hardly handle it. Flour the baking-board well, roll out about ⅛ inch thick. Now spread with the reserved whites of eggs, reserving half again, as you will have to roll out at least twice on a large baking-board. Sprinkle well with the pounded almonds after you have spread the beaten whites of the eggs on top, also sugar and cinnamon. Cut with a cookie-cutter. Have at least five large pans greased ready to receive them. See that you have a good fire. Time to bake, five to ten minutes. Pack them away when cold in a stone jar or tin cake-box. These cookies will keep a long time.

VANILLA COOKIES

Rub one cup of butter and one cup of sugar to a cream; add two eggs and two level teaspoons of baking powder, flour enough to make a dough. Flavor with vanilla, roll very thin, spread with beaten white of egg and sugar. Proceed as for sugar cookies.

OLD-FASHIONED MOLASSES COOKIES

Put in a mixing bowl one generous cup of butter which has stood in a warm place until quite soft; add two cups of New Orleans molasses; whip these ingredients to a foam; then add two teaspoons of powdered ginger, one teaspoon of powdered cinnamon and grate in half a large nutmeg; stir these spices well through the mixture; then dissolve two teaspoons of baking-soda in ½ cup of hot water; stir it through the mixture, and last, stir in enough sifted flour to make a light dough just stiff enough to roll out. Dust the pastry board well with flour and rub the rolling-pin well with flour; then flour the hands well, take out some of the dough, put it on the pastry board, quickly roll it out to the thickness of ¼ inch; cut the dough out with a round cutter, with or without scallops, and put them in well-floured baking-pans and bake in a 325° oven till a golden brown.

SOUR MILK COOKIES

Take one cup of butter, one cup of sugar, two or three eggs, and ⅔ cup of sour milk. Dissolve a teaspoon of soda in a little hot water; add part of it at a time to the milk until it foams as you stir it. Be careful not to get in too much. Mix up soft, only using flour sufficient to roll out thin. A teaspoon of cardamom seed may be sprinkled into the dough.

HUNGARIAN ALMOND COOKIES

Scant ¼ pound of almonds, blanched and grated; scant ½ pound of sweet butter; not quite ¾ pound of flour; a little sugar and a pinch of salt, and two yolks. Mix this well, pound the dough well with the rolling-pin, then roll out not too thin. Bake at 350° until golden.

NUTMEG CAKES (PFEFFERNUESSE)

Sift one pound of flour and one pound of pulverized sugar into a large bowl, four eggs, a piece of citron grated or chopped very fine, also the peel of a lemon, one whole nutmeg grated, one tablespoon of ground cinnamon, ½ teaspoon of ground cloves, and ½ teaspoon of allspice. Mix all thoroughly in a deep bowl. Sift a heaping teaspoon of baking powder in with the flour. Work into little balls as large as hickory nuts with buttered or floured hands. Bake at 350° on buttered tins, an inch apart.

ANISE SEED COOKIES (SPRINGELE)
Four eggs, not separated, but thoroughly beaten, then add 1½ cups of granulated sugar, and beat for thirty minutes; add two heaping cups of flour and fourteen drops of anise seed oil; drop from a teaspoon on well-buttered pans, and bake in a 350° oven. It will improve them to let them stand from two to three hours in the pans before baking.

CARDAMOM COOKIES
Boil six eggs hard. When cold shell and grate the yolks (reserve the whites for salads or to garnish vegetables), add ½ pound of sugar, the grated peel of a lemon and ½ wineglass of brandy. Stir in ½ pound of butter which has been worked to a cream. Sift in as much flour as you think will allow you to roll out the dough; take as little as possible, a little over ½ pound, and flour the board very thick. Put in about two cents worth of cardamom seed (good luck with that!) and a little rosewater. Cut out with a fancy cake-cutter and brush with beaten egg. Sprinkle pounded almonds and sugar on top. Bake at 350°

PURIM CAKES
Take two cups of flour, one tablespoon of sugar, add four eggs and two tablespoons of oil; knead all these together, roll out not very thin, cut in squares, close two sides, prick with a fork so they will not blister; put on tins and bake well. Then take one pound of honey, boil, and put the squares in this and let boil a bit; then drop in ¼ pound of poppy seeds and put back on fire. When nice and brown sprinkle with a little cold water, take off and put on another dish so they do not stick to each other.

PARVE COOKIES
To one pound of flour take one teaspoon of baking powder, four eggs, ¼ pound of poppy seeds, three tablespoons of oil, two pounds of sugar and a little salt; knead not too stiff and put on tins and bake in 400° oven till a nice brown. (Do not let burn.)

TEIGLECH

Mix one pound of flour, one teaspoon of baking powder, three tablespoons of oil, and four eggs; knead very well. Roll out in strips three inches long, place on tins and bake. Take a pound of chopped nuts, ½ pound of honey, and ½ pound of sugar; mix thoroughly with wooden spoon and boil with the cakes until brown. Take off the stove, wet with cold water, spread out on board. When cold, pat with the hands to make thin and sprinkle with dry ginger.

HONEY CORN CAKES

Boil one pound of pure honey. Take one pound of cornmeal mixed with a little ground allspice, cloves, and pepper, add the boiled honey, make a loose batter, add one wineglass of brandy; mix all, and cool. Wet the hands with cold water, take pieces of the dough and knead until the dough comes clear from the hand; afterwards knead with white flour so it is not too hard; add one pound of chopped nuts, sprinkle flour on tins, spread dough, not too thin; leave the stove door open till it raises; then close door, and when done take out. Spread with brandy and cut in thin slices.

CROQUANTE CAKES (SMALL CAKES)

Blanch and cut in halves ¾ pound of shelled almonds, and slice ½ pound citron; mix well together and roll in a little flour; add to them ¾ pound of sugar, then six eggs well beaten, and last the rest of the flour (¾ pound). Butter shallow pans, and put in the mixture about two inches thick; after it is baked in a 400° oven slice cake in strips ¾ inch wide and turn each piece. Put back in oven and bake a little longer. When cold put away in tin box.

KINDEL

Two pounds of soup fat rendered a day or two before using, three pints of flour, one teaspoon of salt, ⅔ cup of granulated sugar, one teaspoon of baking powder, two teaspoons of vanilla, flour. Knead well, add enough beer to be able to roll. Let it stand two hours. Roll, cut in long strips three inches wide. Fill with the following: 1½ cups of brown sugar, two tablespoons of honey, two pounds of walnuts chopped fine, one pound of stewed prunes chopped fine, two cups of sponge cake crumbs, juice of one lemon, spices to taste, few raisins and currants, and a little citron chopped fine; add a little wine, a little chicken Schmalz; heat a few minutes. You may use up remnants of jellies, jams, marmalades, etc. Put plenty of filling in center of strips, fold over, with a round stick (use a wooden spoon), press the dough firmly three inches apart, then with a knife cut them apart. They will be the shape of the fig bars you buy. Grease the pan and the top of cakes, and bake in 350° oven. They will keep - the longer the better.

ALMOND MACAROONS, No. 1

Blanch ½ pound of almonds, pound in mortar to a smooth paste, add one pound of pulverized sugar and the beaten whites of four eggs, and work the paste well together with the back of a spoon. Dip your hands in water and roll the mixture into balls the size of a hickory nut, and lay on buttered or waxed paper an inch apart. When done, dip your hands in water and pass gently over the macaroons, making the surface smooth and shiny. Set in a 325° oven for forty-five minutes.

ALMOND MACAROONS, No. 2

Prepare the almonds by blanching them in boiling water. Strip them of the skins and lay them on a clean towel to dry. Grate or pound ½ pound of almonds, beat the whites of five eggs to a stiff, very stiff froth; stir in gradually ¾ pound of pulverized sugar (use confectioner's sugar if you can get it), and then add the pounded almonds, to which add a tablespoon of rosewater or a teaspoon of essence of bitter almonds. Line a broad baking-pan with buttered or waxed paper and drop upon this half a teaspoon of the mixture at a time, allowing room enough to prevent their running together. Sift powdered sugar over them and bake in a 400° oven to a delicate brown. If the mixture has been well beaten they will not run. Try one on a piece of paper before you venture to bake them all. If it runs add a little more sugar.

ALMOND MACAROONS WITH FIGS

Beat stiff the whites of three eggs, add ½ pound of sugar, and ½ pound of finely cut figs, ½ pound of either blanched almonds cut into long slices, or cut up walnuts. Heat a large pan, pass ironing-wax over surface, lay in waxed paper, and drop spoonfuls of mixture on paper, same distance apart. Bake very slowly in very moderate oven. Remove and let cool; then take paper out with the macaroons, turn over and place hot cloths on wrong side, when cakes will drop off.

ALMOND STICKS - FLEISCHIG
Take ½ glass of fat, two eggs, four cups of flour, two teaspoons of baking powder, one cup of water, ½ cup of sugar; knead lightly, and roll out not too thin. Two cups of sugar, mix with two teaspoons of cinnamon; one-half pound of grated almonds, ½ pound of small raisins (washed). Reserve ½ of the sugar and cinnamon, the nuts and raisins; brush the dough with melted fat and sprinkle with almonds and sugar. Put a little of the almond and raisin mixture around the edge and roll around twice. Cut in small pieces, brush every piece with fat, and roll in the sugar and almonds which has been reserved for this purpose. Place in greased pan and bake in 400° oven.

ALMOND STICKS
Grind two cups of almonds and reserve ¼ cup each of sugar and nuts, and an egg yolk for decorating. Cream one cup of butter, add ¾ cup of sugar, then two whole eggs, almonds and two cups of flour. Roll thin and cut in strips or squares, with fluted cookie cutter. Brush with yolk, sprinkle with nuts and sugar, set aside, and bake in 350° oven.

PLAIN WAFERS
Sift one cup of flour and one teaspoon of salt together. Chop in one tablespoon of butter, and add milk to make a very stiff dough; chop thoroughly and knead until smooth; make into small balls and roll each one into a thin wafer. Place in shallow greased and floured pans and bake in a 400° oven until they puff and are brown.

POPPY SEED COOKIES (MOHN PLÄTZCHEN)
Take an equal quantity of flour, sugar and butter, and mix it well by rubbing with the hollow of the hands until small grains are formed. Then add one cup of poppy seed, two eggs, and enough Rhine wine to hold the dough together. Roll out the dough on a well-floured board, about half a finger in thickness, cut into any shape desired. Bake at 400°.

CARAWAY SEED COOKIES

Beat ¾ pound of butter and a pound of sugar to a cream; add three eggs, one ¼ teaspoon of salt, a gill of caraway seeds and a teaspoon of powdered mace, stirring all well together to a cream; then pour in a cup of sour milk in which a level teaspoon of baking-soda is stirred. Hold the cup over the mixing bowl while stirring in the soda, as it will foam over the cup. Last of all stir in enough sifted flour to make a light dough, stiff enough to roll thin. Roll on a pastry board well dusted with flour. Cut in round shapes and place in baking-tins well rubbed with flour. Sprinkle a little sugar over the cookies and bake them in a 350° oven till a light brown. When cool, carefully lift the cookies from the pans with a pancake turner.

CITRON COOKIES

Take ½ cup of butter and 1½ cups sugar, and rub to a cream. Add two eggs, ¾ cup of milk, ½ cup of citron, cut up very fine, one teaspoon of allspice and one of cloves. Sift one heaping teaspoon of baking powder into enough flour to thicken. Make stiffer than ordinary cup cake dough; flavor to suit taste, and drop on large tins with a teaspoon. Grease the pans, and bake in a 400° oven. The best plan is to try one on a plate. If the dough runs too much add more flour.

GINGER WAFERS

Take one cup of butter, one cup of sugar, one cup of molasses, ½ cup cold coffee, with two teaspoons of soda, one teaspoon of ginger, and flour enough to make a dough stiff enough to roll out thin. Shape with cutter and bake in 400° oven.

ANISE ZWIEBACK

Take the yolks of five eggs, ½ pound of sugar, one tablespoon of water, vanilla, ½ pound of flour, one teaspoon of baking powder, ½ of five cents worth anise seeds [good luck with that!], and the beaten whites of the eggs. Butter square tins and bake. When cooled cut in strips one inch wide and toast on both sides.

HURRY UPS (OATMEAL)

Sift one cup of flour with two teaspoons of baking powder, one teaspoon of salt, add one cup of rolled oats, one tablespoon of sugar and two tablespoons of melted butter, mix with ½ cup of milk. Drop by teaspoons onto a greased pan, press well into each two or three raisins, or a split date and bake for twenty minutes in a 400° oven. Can be served with butter, honey, or maple sugar.

PECAN, WALNUT, OR HICKORY NUT MACAROONS

Take one cup of pulverized sugar, and one cup of finely pounded nut meats, the unbeaten whites of two eggs, two heaping teaspoons of flour, and one scant teaspoon of baking powder. Mix these ingredients together and drop from a teaspoon that you have previously dipped in cold water, upon buttered paper. Do not put them too near each other, for they always spread a great deal. Bake at 400° about fifteen minutes.

DATE MACAROONS

Stone thirty dates; chop them fine. Cut ½ pound of almonds lengthwise in slices, but do not blanch them. Beat the whites of two eggs until foamy, add one cup of powdered sugar, and beat until stiff; add the dates, then the almonds, and mix very thoroughly. Drop mixture with teaspoon in small piles on tins, ½ inch apart. Bake thirty minutes in a 325° oven or until dry. They are done when they leave the pan readily.

MANDELCHEN

Blanch two cups of almonds and dry them overnight. Grind very fine, add ½ cup of sugar and enough butter to knead into a very stiff paste. Roll very thin, cut in small rounds, place in baking-tin in 350° oven. When done, roll in grated almonds and powdered sugar.

COCONUT KISSES

Beat the white of one egg; add ½ cup of sugar with a flavoring of vanilla, fold in one cup of shredded coconut, drop by teaspoonfuls on a well-greased baking-pan, inverted, and bake at 400° for about ten or twelve minutes in a slow oven. Remove from pan when cookies are cold.

CORNFLAKE COCONUT KISSES

Mix the whites of two eggs, beaten stiff, with ½ cup of sugar, add ½ cup of shredded coconut, fold in two cups of corn flakes, a pinch of salt, one-half teaspoon of vanilla. Make and bake same as kisses above.

CHOCOLATE COOKIES

Beat whites of three eggs to a snow, add ¾ cup of powdered sugar, one cup of ground sweet chocolate, one cup of walnuts chopped, three tablespoons of flour. Drop by teaspoonful on greased baking-tin. Bake in 325° oven about 15 minutes.

BASELER LOEKERLEIN (HONEY CAKES)

Take ½ strained honey, ½ pound of sifted powdered sugar, ½ pound of almonds (cut in half lengthwise), ½ pound of finest flour, one ounce of citron (cut or chopped extremely fine), peel of a lemon, a little grated nutmeg, also a pinch of ground cloves and a wineglass of brandy. Set the honey and sugar over the fire together, put in the almonds, stir all up thoroughly. Next put in the spices and work into a dough. Put away in a cold place for a week, then roll about as thick as a finger. Bake in a 400° oven and cut into strips with a sharp knife after they are baked (do this while hot), cut three inches long and two inches wide.

HONEY CAKES, No. 1

One pound of real honey, not jar; one cup of granulated sugar, four eggs, one tablespoon of allspice, three tablespoons of salad-oil, four cups of flour, well sifted; three teaspoons of baking powder. Warm up or heat honey, not hot, just warm. Rub yolks well with sugar, beat whites to a froth, then mix ingredients, add flour and bake in 350° oven for one hour.

HONEY CAKES, No. 2

Three eggs, not separated, beaten with one cup of sugar, one cup of honey, one cup of blanched almonds chopped finely, one teaspoon each of allspice, cloves, and cinnamon, one cup of chocolate and flour enough to make a thick batter; one teaspoon of baking-soda. Spread very thin on square, buttered pans, bake in a hot oven, and when done, spread with a white icing, cut into squares, and put a half blanched almond in the center of each square.

LEKACH

This recipe is one that is used in Palestine. It makes a honey cake not nearly as rich as those in the foregoing recipes for honey cakes, but will very nicely take the place of a sweet cracker to serve with tea. Take three cups of sifted flour, ¼ teaspoon of salt, add three eggs, one teaspoon of allspice, one teaspoon of soda, the grated rind and juice of ½ lemon and three tablespoons of honey, mix all ingredients well. Roll on board to one-fourth inch in thickness and cut with form. Brush with white of egg or honey diluted with water. On each cake put an almond or walnut. Bake in 350° oven from fifteen to twenty minutes.

LEBKUCHEN

Four eggs, one pound of brown sugar; beat well. Add ⅛ pound of citron shredded, ⅛ pound of shelled walnuts (broken), 1½ cups of flour, one teaspoon of baking powder, two teaspoons of cinnamon, ¼ teaspoon of allspice. Spread the dough in long pans with well-floured hands, have about 1½ inches thick. Bake in 375° oven. When baked, cut in squares and spread with icing. Set in a cool stove or the sun to dry. It is best to let these cakes and all honey cakes stand a week before using.

OLD-FASHIONED LEBKUCHEN

Heat one cup of molasses, mix it with two cups of brown sugar and three eggs, reserving one white for the icing; add one level teaspoon of baking-soda that has been dissolved in a little milk, then put in alternately a little flour and a cup of milk; now add one tablespoon of mixed spices, ½ cup of brandy, one small cup each of chopped nuts and citron, and lastly, flour enough to make a stiff batter. Place in shallow pans and bake at 325°. When done, cover with icing and cut in squares or strips.

Icing for Lebkuchen.

One cup of powdered sugar added to the beaten white of one egg; flavor with one teaspoon of brandy or lemon juice.

DESSERTS

BOILED CUSTARD

Take two cups of milk, two eggs or the yolks of three eggs, two tablespoons of sugar and ½ teaspoon of vanilla. Put the milk on to heat in a double boiler. Beat the eggs thoroughly with the sugar; into them pour the hot milk, stirring to prevent lumps. Return all to the double boiler and cook until the custard coats the spoon, but no longer. If the mixture should curdle, set the boiler in a pan of cold water and beat with a wire egg-beater until smooth. When the steam passes off add the vanilla or other flavoring. In the winter, when eggs are expensive, the custard may be made with one egg and one heaping teaspoon of cornstarch dissolved in a little cold milk. If desired, the whites of the eggs may be beaten separately and added to the custard after it is cold or beaten with sugar into a meringue.

CARAMEL CUSTARD

Melt ½ cup of sugar until it is light brown in color, add four cups of scalded milk. Beat the eggs, add the milk and sugar, one-quarter teaspoon of salt, one teaspoon of vanilla and bake in cups as directed for cup custard. Serve with caramel sauce.

CUP CUSTARD FOR SIX

Stir until quite light four eggs, yolks and whites, and four tablespoons of sugar; have ready four cups of scalded milk; mix, add pinch of salt and one teaspoon of good vanilla; pour into cups and place cups into pan of boiling water. Put into oven and bake at 350° exactly twenty-five minutes.

CHOCOLATE CUSTARD

Beat yolks of three eggs, three tablespoons of sugar till light, dissolve one heaping tablespoon of grated unsweetened chocolate, one tablespoon of sugar and one of hot water. When dissolved, add slowly one pint of milk heated to boiling, pour this hot mixture over the beaten eggs and sugar, cook in double boiler, stirring constantly till it thickens; when cool, flavor with vanilla, and place on ice. When ready to serve, half-fill small punch glasses with the custard, heap over them sweetened whipped cream, flavored; putting on top of each glass, and serve cold.

CHOCOLATE CORNSTARCH PUDDING
Take one quart of milk, 1½ cups of sugar, seven heaping tablespoons of cocoa, six level tablespoons of cornstarch, one tablespoon of vanilla; place milk and sugar up to boil, when boiling, add cocoa, dissolved to a smooth paste; then add cornstarch dissolved in cold water, let come to a boil, remove from heat and add the vanilla; then place in mold and allow to get cold. Serve with whipped cream.

BLANC MANGE
Heat one quart of milk to boiling point. Dissolve four large tablespoons of cornstarch in a quarter cup of cold milk. Beat two whole eggs with one-half cup of sugar until light, and add a tiny pinch of salt. When the milk begins to boil, add a piece of butter, size of a hickory nut, then pour it over the well-beaten eggs and sugar, mix well, and put back on the stove. Stir until it begins to boil, then stir in the dissolved cornstarch until the custard is very thick. Remove from the heat, flavor with vanilla or lemon, pour into a mold, and set on ice until very cold and firm. Serve with cream.

FLOATING ISLAND
Beat light the yolks of three eggs with ¼ cup of sugar. Scald a pint of milk, beat up the whites of three eggs very stiff and put them into the boiling milk, a spoonful at a time. Take out the boiled whites and lay them on a platter; now pour the hot milk gradually on the beaten yolks, when thoroughly mixed, return to the heat to boil. When it begins to thicken remove. When cool, flavor with vanilla or bitter almond. Pour into a deep glass dish; put the whites on top, and garnish with jelly or candied fruit. Eat cold.

RED RASPBERRY OR CURRANT FLOAT
Take a ½ pint glass of red raspberry or currant juice and mix it with ¼ cup of sugar. Beat the whites of four eggs to a stiff froth and add gradually ¼ cup of powdered sugar. press the raspberries through a strainer to avoid seeds and by degrees beat the juice with the sugar and eggs until so stiff that it stands

in peaks. Chill it thoroughly and serve in a glass dish half filled with cold whipped cream. Heap on the mixture by the spoonful, like floating island. If currant juice is used it will require a pint of sugar.

ROTE GRITZE
Take one cup of currant juice, sufficiently sweetened, and a pinch of salt. Let this boil and add to it enough cornstarch to render it moderately thick and then boil again for ten minutes. It should be eaten cold with cream. (About ¼ cup of cornstarch dissolved in cold water will be sufficient to thicken.)

APPLE SNOW
Peel and grate one large sour apple, sprinkling over it ¾ cup of powdered sugar as it is grated to keep it from turning dark. Add the unbeaten whites of two eggs; beat constantly for half an hour; arrange mound fashion on a glass dish with cold boiled custard around it.

BOHEMIAN CREAM
Stir together and whip one pint of double cream and one pint of grape juice or grape jelly melted, this must be whipped to a froth. Drain if needed. Put in cups and set on ice for several hours. Serve with ladyfingers.

PRUNE WHIP
Soak ½ pound of prunes in cold water overnight. In the morning let them simmer in this water until they are very soft. Remove stones and rub through strainer. Add ½ cup of sugar and cook five minutes or until the consistency of marmalade. When the fruit mixture is cold, add the well-beaten whites of three eggs and ½ teaspoon of lemon juice; add this gradually, then heap lightly in buttered dish and bake twenty minutes in a 325° oven. Serve cold with thin custard or cream.

RICE CUSTARD
Beat four eggs light with one cup of sugar. Add one cup of cooked rice, two cups of sweet milk, juice and rind of one lemon, ½ teaspoon of cinnamon. Pour in pudding-pan and place in a pan filled with hot water; bake until firm in 350° oven. Serve with lemon sauce.

PRUNE CUSTARD
Heat a little more than a pint of sweet milk to the boiling point, then stir in gradually a little cold milk in which you have rubbed smooth a heaping tablespoon of butter and a little nutmeg. Let this just come to a boil, then pour into a buttered pudding-dish, first adding one cup of stewed prunes with the stones taken out. Bake at 350° for fifteen to twenty minutes. A little cream improves it when it is served in the saucers.

TAPIOCA CUSTARD
Soak four tablespoons of tapioca overnight in one quart of sweet milk. In the morning beat the yolks of three eggs with one cup of sugar. Put the milk and tapioca on in a double boiler, adding a pinch of salt; when this comes to boiling point stir in the eggs and sugar. Beat the whites to a stiff froth and stir quickly and delicately into the hot mixture. Flavor with vanilla. Eat cold.

WHIPPED CREAM
To one pint of rich thick cream add ¼ of a pound of powdered sugar and ½ teaspoon of vanilla. Put in a large platter in a cool place and whip with a wire egg-whip until perfectly smooth and velvety. Set on ice until wanted. In the summer set the cream on ice before whipping. A good plan is to set the bowl in another one filled with ice while whipping.

DESSERT WITH WHIPPED CREAM
Line the edges of a mold or a large glass dish with ladyfingers and fill up with whipped cream. Ornament with macaroons and candied fruit. Serve cold.

AMBROSIA
Cut up into small pieces different kinds of fruit; then chop up nuts and marshmallows (not too fine). Mix these and sugar, not allowing it to draw too much juice. Flavor with sherry, if you like. Serve individually, putting whipped cream on the top with a cherry.

MACAROON ISLAND
Fill a glass bowl with alternate layers of macaroons and ladyfingers, sprinkle a layer of finely-chopped nuts over the cake, then a layer of crystallized cherries. Boil one cup of wine, one cup of sugar and ½ cup of water together until

syrupy and thick, pour it over the contents of the bowl, let this cool, then place a thick layer of thickly-whipped sweetened and flavored cream over all. Serve very cold.

PISTACHIO CREAM
Take out the kernels of half a pound of pistachio nuts and pound them in a mortar with one tablespoon of brandy. Put them in a double boiler with a pint of rich cream and add gradually the yolks of three eggs, well beaten. Stir over the fire until it thickens and then pour carefully into a bowl, stirring as you do so and being careful not to crack the bowl. (Put a silver spoon into the bowl before pouring in the cream, as this will prevent it cracking). When cold, stick pieces of the nuts over the cream and serve.

TIPSY PUDDING
Cut stale sponge cake into thin slices, spread with jelly or preserves, put two pieces together like sandwiches and lay each slice or sandwich on the plate on which it is to be served. Wet each piece with wine, pour or spread a tablespoon of rich custard over each piece of pudding, and then frost each piece with a frosting and put in a 350° oven for a few minutes. Eat cold.

APPLE AND LADYFINGER PUDDING
Core and peel apples, take top off, chop the top with almonds, citron and raisins; butter your pan, fill apples, sugar them and pour over a little wine, bake until tender; when cool add four yolks of eggs beaten with one cup of sugar, then last, add beaten whites and eight lady fingers rolled, and juice of one whole lemon; pour over apples, bake at 350°. Eat cold.

FIG DESSERT
Soak two cups white figs overnight. In the morning, boil slowly until tender, add two cups of sugar and boil until a thick syrup is formed. Line a dish with sponge cake or ladyfingers; pour the figs in the center and cover with whipped cream that has been sweetened and flavored. Decorate with candied cherries or angelica.

STRAWBERRIES Á LA "BRIDGE"
Into a champagne-glass put large strawberries, halved and sugared, and an equal amount of marshmallows halved. Place on top a mass of whipped cream, already sweetened and flavored; then a single strawberry, sprinkle with shelled pecans.

QUEEN OF TRIFLES
Make a rich custard of four eggs, one cup of granulated sugar and one quart of milk to which has been added one teaspoon of cornstarch. Let this cook in double boiler, stirring constantly, until the custard is very thick. Cool. Soak ½ pound of macaroons in sherry wine, blanch and chop ¼ pound of almonds, cut fine ¼ pound of dried figs; ¼ pound of crystallized cherries and ½ pound of lady fingers are required as well. Line a deep glass bowl with the ladyfingers cut in half, add macaroons, fruit and almonds in layers until all are used. Then pour the boiled custard over all. Set on ice and when cold, fill the bowl with whipped cream that has been sweetened and flavored with vanilla. Decorate with a few cherries.

ICEBOX CAKE
Mix ½ cup of butter creamed with ½ cup of confectioner's sugar, three whole eggs added, one at a time, beat these all for twenty minutes, add ½ pound of chopped nuts, one tablespoon mocha essence or one square of bitter chocolate melted, or one teaspoon of vanilla. Grease a spring form, put two dozen ladyfingers around the edge, at the bottom put one dozen macaroons, then add the filling and let this all stand for twenty-four hours in icebox. When ready to serve, pour 2 cups cream, whipped, over all and serve.

AUFLAUF
Boil one cup of milk and when boiling stir in quickly ½ cup of sifted flour and work smooth until all lumps are out and it is the consistency of soft mashed potatoes. Stir all the while over fire. When smooth remove from stove and while yet warm break in, one by one, yolks of three eggs, a pinch of salt, then the beaten whites of three eggs. Bake in well-buttered hot square pans, in a 425° oven, from fifteen to twenty minutes. Serve as soon as done with jelly or preserves. If batter is not thick enough a little more flour must be added to the milk.

LEMON PUFFS
Beat the yolks of four eggs until very light, add the stiffly beaten whites and then stir in two cups of milk, add a pinch of salt, three tablespoons of fresh butter melted, and five level tablespoons of flour that have been wet with a little of the milk from the pint, stir well together and divide equally between cups. Butter the cups before pouring in the mixture. Bake in 400° oven until brown (generally twenty minutes). Turn out carefully in the dish in which they are to be served, and pour over them the following:

LEMON SAUCE
Put on to boil 1½ cups of water with juice of two lemons, sweeten to taste, add a few small pieces of cinnamon bark; when boiling stir in three teaspoons of cornstarch that have been dissolved in a little cold water. Boil a few minutes, then pour over the well-beaten yolks of two eggs, stirring all the time. Stir in stiffly beaten whites of eggs, and pour over and around puffs when cold. Serve cold.

LEAF PUFFS
Cream one cup of butter until soft, add two cups of sifted flour, mix well, and add just enough sweet cream to make a nice dough, not too soft. Roll thin, cut in long strips or squares, bake in long pans in a moderately hot oven. When light brown, draw to the door of the oven, sprinkle with powdered sugar and let stand a few minutes longer in the oven.

SAGO PUDDING WITH STRAWBERRY JUICE
Prepare one cup berry juice and sweeten to taste. Have ready a scant half teacup of sago soaked one hour in water enough to cover. Boil the sago in the fruit juice until thick like jelly. Beat up the whites of two eggs and add to the sago while hot and remove immediately from the stove. Mold and serve with cream or berry juice. This mold can be made with any kind of fruit juice preferred.

APPLE TAPIOCA PUDDING
Soak ¾ cup of tapioca and boil it in one quart of water until clear, sweetening to taste. Pare and core six apples and place them in a baking dish. Fill the cores with sugar, pour the tapioca around them and grate a little nutmeg over the top. Cover and bake until the apples are soft. Serve with cream.

RHUBARB PUDDING

Grate some stale rye bread and take a bunch of rhubarb; cut fine without peeling, put the cut rhubarb in a pan with a big pinch of baking-soda, and pour boiling water over to cover. While that is steeping, grate the rye bread and butter pudding-form well, and put crumbs all over the pan about one-quarter inch deep, then add one-half the rhubarb that has been well drained of the water; season with brown sugar, cinnamon, nuts and any other seasoning you like; then some more crumbs, and other one-half of rhubarb, and season as before the top crumbs, put flakes of butter all over top; bake at 350° until done.

SCALLOPED PEACHES

Pare a number of peaches and put them whole into a baking tin, together with layers of breadcrumbs and sugar and add a few cloves. Bake at 350° until the top is brown. Serve with hot butter sauce or cream.

CHESTNUT PUDDING

Boil one pound of chestnuts fifteen minutes. Shell and skin them, then put back on stove with a cup of milk and boil until tender. Rub through a colander. Butter a mold, line it with the pulp, then add a layer of applesauce that has been colored with currant jelly, then another layer of chestnuts, and again apple sauce. Squeeze lemon juice over all, and bake in a moderate oven. Turn out on a platter and serve with whipped cream colored with currant jelly.

FARINA PUDDING WITH PEACHES

To one quart of milk add ½ cup of farina, salt, and a small piece of butter. Boil in a double boiler until thick. Beat the yolks of four eggs with four tablespoons of white sugar, and add this just before taking off the fire. Stir it thoroughly, but do not let it boil any more. Flavor with vanilla. Beat the whites of the eggs to a stiff froth with pulverized sugar. After the eggs have been whipped, butter a pudding dish, put in part of the custard, in which you have mixed the whites (if you have any extra whites of eggs beat and use them also), then a layer of stewed or canned peaches; cover with the remaining custard and bake. Eat with rum sauce.

FARINA PUDDING, No. 2

1½ pints of milk with nine level tablespoons of sugar, five bitter and five sweet almonds chopped fine, brought to boiling point, and twelve level tablespoons of farina dropped in slowly and stirred constantly. Cook for twelve minutes, add vanilla to taste, then add slowly the beaten whites of five eggs. Put it in a form and when cold serve with a fruit sauce.

RICE PUDDING

To three cups of milk, add half a cup of rice, which you have previously scalded with hot water. Boil in a double boiler until quite soft. Beat the yolks of three eggs with three tablespoons of white sugar, add this just before taking it off the fire. Stir it thoroughly with a wooden spoon, but do not let it boil any more. Add salt to the rice while boiling, and flavor with vanilla. Beat the whites of the eggs with powdered sugar to a stiff froth, and after putting the custard into the pudding dish in which you wish to serve it, spread with the beaten whites and let it brown slightly at 400° in the oven.

PRUNE PUDDING

Take one quart of milk, one teaspoon of salt, one cup of sugar and two well-beaten eggs. Heat this and then pour in slowly one cup of cream of wheat or farina, stirring constantly. Boil fifteen minutes; then butter a deep pudding dish and put in a layer of stewed prunes - that have been cut up in small pieces with a scissors; on the bottom, over this, pour a layer of the above, alternating in this order until all has been used. Bake ten minutes in a 400° oven. Plain cream, not whipped or sweetened, is a delicious sauce for this.

BROWN BETTY

Pare, quarter, core and slice four medium-sized apples. Melt ¼ cup of butter and pour it with the juice of half a lemon over one cup of breadcrumbs. Mix ½ teaspoon of cinnamon, grated rind of ½ lemon and ¼ cup of sugar together. Butter a baking dish; put in alternate layers of apple and breadcrumbs, sprinkling the apples with the sugar mixture, and making the last layer of crumbs. Pour ¼ cup of boiling water on before adding the last layer of crumbs; cover and bake for thirty minutes or until the apples are soft;

then uncover and brown the crumbs. Serve with cream or with soft custard or lemon sauce. If desired for a meat meal, substitute chicken-fat for butter and use lemon sauce.

APPLE AND HONEY PUDDING

Take four cups of raw apples cut in small pieces, two cups of breadcrumbs, ½ cup of hot water, two teaspoons of butter, two teaspoons of cinnamon, ½ cup of honey. Put a layer of the apple in a well-buttered pudding dish; then a layer of crumbs. Mix the honey and hot water. Pour part of this over the crumbs, sprinkle with cinnamon and dot with a few bits of butter. Fill the dish with alternate layers of apples, crumbs, honey, etc., having a layer of crumbs on top. Cover and bake at 350° forty-five minutes. Serve with cream.

QUEEN BREAD PUDDING

Take one cup of grated breadcrumbs, soak it in one pint of sweet milk; then break three eggs; separate the whites, add to the yolks one cup of sugar and a small piece of butter; beat it well, and squeeze the breadcrumbs out of the milk, and add this to the yolks and flavor with vanilla. Grease the pans with butter, put the mixture in the pan, and pour the milk over it; set in the oven to bake at 350° until nearly dry, then add a layer of fresh fruit (apricots or peaches are the best or strawberry preserves); add the whites of eggs that were beaten stiff. Serve cold with cream or milk. This can also be served hot.

BREAD PUDDING

Soak 1½ cups of breadcrumbs in a pint of sweet milk for half an hour; separate the whites and yolks of two eggs, setting the whites in a cool place until needed. Beat the yolks with ½ cup of sugar and add the grated peel of one lemon and stir into the breadcrumbs. Put in some raisins and pour into a greased pudding dish and bake in a 350° oven, about half an hour. Beat the whites of the eggs to a stiff froth, adding ½ cup of powdered sugar; and spread this on top of pudding and return to the oven and brown delicately. May be eaten hot or cold, with jelly sauce or whipped cream. Stale cake of any kind may be used instead of bread; and ginger bread also is particularly nice, adding raisins and citron, and spreading a layer of jelly on the pudding before putting on the icing.

CORNMEAL PUDDING

Bring one pint of milk to the boiling point; pour it gradually on ½ cup of Indian meal, stirring all the while to prevent lumps. When cool add three eggs well beaten, and one tablespoon of flour, ½ cup of sugar, ½ teaspoon of ginger, one teaspoon of cinnamon, pinch of salt and one pint cold milk. Pour into buttered pudding dish and bake at 325° about 90 minutes. Serve with hot maple sugar or cream.

BLACK BREAD PUDDING

Yolks of three eggs beaten with one cup of sugar; add one teaspoon of cinnamon, pinch of cloves, and pinch of allspice; one cup of stale rye bread-crumbs added gradually. Mix well and add beaten whites. Bake at 325°. Half an hour before serving, add one cup of claret or white wine. Serve with sherry wine sauce or whipped cream.

DIMPES DAMPES (APPLE SLUMP)

Mix ½ cup of sugar, ¼ teaspoon of salt, two cups of flour and gradually two cups of milk to make a smooth batter. Melt ½ cup or a little less of butter in a large shallow dripping-pan and let it spread all over the pan to grease it well, then pour ½ cup of butter and one quart of sliced apples to the batter. Mix and pour into pan or pans not more than ¾ inch deep and bake in a 350° oven, thirty to forty-five minutes, until a golden brown. This quantity serves ten people.

BIRD'S NEST PUDDING

Pare four or five large tart apples and cut off the top of each apple to use as a cover. Now scrape out all the inside, being careful not to break the apples; mix scrapings with sugar, cinnamon, raisins, a few pounded almonds and add a little white wine and the grated peel of one lemon. Fill up the apples with this mixture and put back the top of each apple, so as to cover each well. Grease a deep dish, set in the apples and stew a few minutes. In the meantime make a sponge cake batter of four eggs, one cup of pulverized sugar, one cup of flour and pour over the apples and bake at 350° for thirty minutes. Eat warm or cold, with or without sauce. Plain baked apples can be substituted for the filled apples.

SUET PUDDING WITH PEARS

Take ½ pound of suet and chop it to a powder. Soak a loaf of stale bread, squeeze out the water and add to the suet. Work bread and suet well with your hands and add two eggs, one cup of sugar, one teaspoon of salt, allspice, cloves, cinnamon and grated peel of a lemon. Add flour enough to work into a huge ball; sift two teaspoons of baking powder in flour. Pare about half a peck of cooking pears and cut in halves, leaving the stems on. Lay half the pears in a large kettle, put the pudding in center of the pears, and lay the rest of the pears all around. Add sugar, sliced lemon, a few cloves, some cinnamon bark and three tablespoons of syrup. Fill up with cold water and boil half an hour on top of stove. Then bake at 325° for at least three hours, adding water if needed.

CORN PUDDING

Scrape with a knife six ears of green corn, cutting each row through the middle. Add two cups of milk, ½ cup of butter, three eggs - the whites and yolks beaten separately - a little salt and white pepper. Stir the yolks into the milk and corn, pour into a baking dish, stir in the whites and bake at 325° for 1½ hours.

CHERRY PUDDING

Scald a pint of crackers or breadcrumbs in a quart of boiling milk; add a piece of butter the size of an egg, a good pinch of salt, four eggs, 1½ cups sugar, a little ground cinnamon and a quart of stoned cherries. Bake in 400° oven.

HUCKLEBERRY PUDDING

Sprinkle four tablespoons of flour over 1½ pints huckleberries and set aside for half an hour. Soak one pint crumbled bread in one quart milk; add three tablespoons of sugar, pinch of salt, and the huckleberries. Put all into a greased pudding dish with flakes of butter on top. Bake at 350° for forty-five minutes. Serve with hard sauce.

PUDDING Á LA GRANDE BELLE

This pudding is economical and dainty if nicely made. Brush small molds with butter, fill with crumbled bread and dried English currants. Beat three eggs without separating; add one pint of milk and four tablespoons of sugar. Pour carefully over the bread and let stand five minutes. Place molds in baking-pan of boiling water and bake at 350° for thirty minutes, or steam half an hour. Serve with liquid pudding sauce.

STEAMED PUDDINGS

The tin molds are best for this purpose, either melon, round, or brick. If the mold is buttered first, then sprinkled with granulated sugar, a nice crust will form. Have a large, deep pan filled with boiling water. Place mold in, let water come up to rim, put a heavy weight on top of mold to keep down, and boil steadily. The pan must be constantly replenished with boiling water, if the pudding is to be done in time. Always place paper in top of mold to prevent water from penetrating. When puddings are boiled in bags, a plate must be placed in bottom of pan to prevent burning. Only certain puddings can be boiled in bags. Always grease inside of bag, so puddings will slip out easily. A bag made of two thicknesses of cheesecloth, stitched together, will do. Always leave room in mold or bag for pudding to rise, using a smaller or larger mold according to quantity of pudding. If not boiled steadily, and emptied as soon as done, puddings will fall and stick.

ALMOND PUDDING

Beat the yolks of four eggs very light with ½ cup sugar; then add ½ cup grated walnuts or almonds, ½ cup grated white breadcrumbs, then the stiffly beaten whites of four eggs. Put in pudding form and steam from 1½ to two hours. Serve with wine or fruit sauce.

RYE BREAD PUDDING

Dry ½ cup of rye breadcrumbs in oven. Beat the yolks of four eggs very light with ½ cup sugar, then add a pinch of cloves and allspice, ½ teaspoon cinnamon, grated rind of ½ lemon, and ¼ pound chopped almonds. Moisten crumbs with three tablespoons of whiskey or brandy, add to eggs, then add stiffly beaten whites of four eggs. Put in mold and boil three hours. Serve with a brandy or whiskey sauce.

NAPKIN PUDDING

Soak ½ loaf of stale white bread in water until moist, squeeze perfectly dry. Put in skillet two tablespoons of clear fat or butter, and when hot add bread, and stir until smooth and dry. Beat five eggs light with one cup of sugar, stir bread in, mix well, and flavor with rind (grated) and juice of one lemon. Grease a bag or very large napkin, place pudding in this, tie, leaving plenty room to rise, place in boiling water and boil two hours. Make a jelly sauce, not as thin as usual, and pour over just before serving. If desired ½ cup of currants can be added to pudding.

STEAMED BERRY PUDDING

Take one tablespoon of butter (or other shortening), ¼ cup of sugar, yolk of one egg, ½ cup milk, one cup flour, one teaspoon baking powder, ¼ teaspoon salt, ½ cup berries or pitted cherries rolled in flour. Put in a well-greased melon mold and cook in boiling water steadily for two hours. Serve with hard sauce.

CARROT PUDDING

Take one cup of sugar, ⅓ cup butter, one cup grated carrots, one cup grated potatoes, one cup raisins, one cup currants, two cups breadcrumbs, ½ teaspoon baking soda stirred in the potatoes, one teaspoon each of cloves, cinnamon, and allspice. Mix all these and add a little syrup and four tablespoons of whiskey. Steam four hours. Serve with hard sauce.

CHERRY PUDDING

Grate ½ pound of stale rye bread and wet this with a wineglass of red wine. Pound two tablespoons of almonds, stir the yolks of four eggs with ½ cup powdered sugar, flavor with cinnamon, and add the grated bread and almonds. Stone ½ pound each of sweet and sour cherries. Mix all thoroughly with the beaten whites added last. Do not take the juice of the cherries. Butter the pudding mold well before you put in the mixture. To be eaten cold.

DATE PUDDING

Melt three tablespoons of butter, add ½ cup molasses, ½ cup milk, 1⅔ cups flour sifted with ½ teaspoon of baking soda, ¼ teaspoon salt, ¼ teaspoon each of cloves, cinnamon, and nutmeg. Add to the above ½ pound dates, stoned and cut. Turn into a well-buttered mold. Butter the cover also and steam 2½ hours. Keep at a steady boil. Serve with any kind of sauce.

PRINCE ALBERT PUDDING
Rub to a cream ½ pound sweet butter and ½ pound sifted powdered sugar; add the yolks of six eggs, one at a time, and the grated peel of one lemon. Stone ½ pound raisins, and add also a little citron, cut very fine. Now add gradually ½ pound of the finest flour, sifted three or four times, and the stiffly beaten whites of the eggs. Pour this mixture into a well-buttered mold, into which you have strewn some blanched and pounded almonds. Boil fully three hours. Serve with sweet brandy or fruit sauce.

PEACH PUDDING
In a large mixing bowl whip to a cream two eggs, three tablespoons of sugar, and two tablespoons of butter. To this, after it is well beaten, add a ¼ of a teaspoon of salt and half a grated nutmeg. Stir these ingredients well into the mixture; then stir in a cup of milk. Last add, a little at a time--stirring it well in to make a smooth batter - 1½ cups flour and ¾ cup of corn meal, which have been sifted together, with three teaspoons of baking powder in another bowl. Butter well the inside of a two-quart pudding mold; put a layer of the pudding batter an inch deep in the mold; cover this with a layer of fine ripe peaches that have been peeled and cut in quarters or eighths - this depends upon the size of the peaches. Sprinkle the layer of peaches with a light layer of sugar; then pour in a layer of batter; then a layer of peaches. Repeat this process till all the material is in, leaving a layer of batter on top. Steam for two hours.

NOODLE PUDDING
Make noodles with two eggs. Boil in boiling salt water for ten minutes, drain, and set aside. Beat the yolks of four eggs with one cup of powdered sugar until light, add a ¼ cup of pounded almonds, a pinch of salt, the drained noodles, and the whites of the eggs beaten to a stiff froth. Mix well, pour into a greased pudding mold, and boil 1½ hours.

PRUNE PUDDING
Take the yolks of four eggs, a cup of granulated sugar, and stir to a cream. Chop fine thirty prunes (prunes being boiled without sugar), and add two tablespoons of sweet chocolate, two tablespoons of grated almonds, and the whites, which have been beaten to a snow. Boil 2½ hours in a pudding form and serve with whipped cream.

PLUM PUDDING (FOR THANKSGIVING DAY)

Soak a small loaf of bread; press out every drop of water, work into this one cup of suet shaved very fine, the yolks of six eggs, one cup of currants, one cup of raisins seeded, ½ cup of citron shredded fine, ¾ cup of syrup, one wineglass of brandy, one cup of sifted flour and the stiffly beaten whites of eggs last. Boil four hours in greased melon mold.

PLUM PUDDING, No. 2

Chop a half box of raisins and currants, ¼ pound of citron, ¼ pound of suet (chopped very fine), two eggs, 1½ cups of sugar, a wineglass of brandy, two cups of cider, one teaspoon of cinnamon and ground cloves. When all these are well mixed add enough flour (with a teaspoon of baking powder in it) to thicken well. Cook in a greased mold and allow to steam for three hours.

HONEY PUDDING

Mix ½ cup honey with six ounces of breadcrumbs and add ½ cup milk, ½ teaspoon ginger, grated rind of half a lemon and yolks of two eggs. Beat the mixture thoroughly and then add two tablespoons of butter and the whites of the eggs well beaten. Steam for about two hours in a pudding mold that is not more than three-quarters full.

PUDDING SAUCES

BRANDY SAUCE
Take one cup of water, a quarter glass of brandy, one cup of sugar, juice of half a lemon. Boil all in double boiler. Beat the yolks of two eggs light, and add the boiling sauce gradually to them, stirring constantly until thick.

CARAMEL SAUCE
Put one cup cut loaf sugar in a saucepan on the stove without adding a drop of water. Let it melt slowly and get a nice brown without burning. Beat the yolks of three eggs until light, stir in two cups milk, and when the sugar is melted, stir all into the saucepan and continue stirring until the sugar is dissolved and the sauce is somewhat thickened; then remove from the heat, add one teaspoon vanilla extract, put in a bowl and put the stiffly beaten whites of eggs on top. Serve with puddings, cakes or fritters.

CHOCOLATE SAUCE, No. 1
Dissolve ½ pound of chocolate in one cup of water and sugar to taste, boil somewhat thick and flavor with vanilla.

CHOCOLATE SAUCE, No. 2
Scald two cups milk, add two tablespoons cornstarch diluted with ½ cup cold milk, and cook ten minutes over boiling water. Melt three squares of chocolate over hot water, add three tablespoons of sugar, and three tablespoons of hot water; stir until smooth, then add to cooked mixture. Beat the whites of three eggs until stiff, add ¾ of a cup of powdered sugar; add the yolks and stir into cooked mixture; cool and add vanilla.

FOAM SAUCE
Cream ¼ cup of butter with one cup of powdered sugar, until very light. Add separately the unbeaten whites of two eggs, stirring briskly and beat again. Add one teaspoon of vanilla and ½ cup of hot water. Pour in sauceboat, and place boat in a pan of boiling water on stove, until it becomes frothy, then serve immediately.

FRUIT SAUCES

Wash the fruit well, then put on the stove in a saucepan without adding any more water. Cover with a lid, and let the fruit get thoroughly heated all through until it comes to a boil, but do not boil it. Stir occasionally. When well heated, mash the fruit well with a wooden potato masher, then strain through a fine sieve, being careful to get every drop of substance from the fruit. Sweeten the juice with sugar to taste, add a few drops of wine or lemon juice, put back on the stove, and cook until it thickens, stirring occasionally. Serve with cake, fritters or puddings. Blackberries, strawberries or raspberries, make a nice sauce.

HARD SAUCE

Take one cup sugar, ½ cup sweet butter and stir to a cream. Flavor with grated lemon peel or essence of lemon. Make into any shape desired and serve.

JELLY SAUCE

Take thin jelly, add one cup boiling water and brandy or wine (½ cup), add a little more sugar and thicken with one teaspoon cornstarch dissolved in a little cold water. The beaten white of egg may be added.

KIRSCH SAUCE

Put one cup sugar, and two cups water on to boil. Mix two tablespoons cornstarch in ¼ cup of cold water, and when the water in the saucepan is boiling, add cornstarch and stir for two minutes. Remove from stove and add one cup of Kirsch wine and stir again. Strain and serve with pudding.

LEMON SAUCE, No. 1

Boil one cup sugar with ½ cup water, rind of one lemon, juice of one lemon, and 2½ teaspoon of butter. When boiling stir in a scant teaspoon of cornstarch dissolved in a little cold water. Serve hot. Serve with puddings or fritters.

LEMON SAUCE, No. 2

Boil the strained juice of two lemons, and the grated peel of one, with 1 cup sugar, and one glass of white wine or water. When boiled to a syrup add the yolks of three eggs well beaten, also half of the whites beaten to a froth.

Use the other half of the stiffly beaten whites, sweetened with powdered sugar, to decorate the sauce. Serve immediately.

PRUNE SAUCE

Take about one pound of Turkish prunes, wash them in hot water, and put on to boil in cold water. Boil until they are very soft. Remove the pits or kernels, and strain over them the water they were boiled in, sweeten to taste. Flavor with ground cinnamon, then mash them until a soft mush. If too thick, add the juice of an orange.

WINE SAUCE, No. 1

Take ½ cup of white wine, and 1½ cups of water, put on to boil in double boiler, and in the meantime beat up the yolks of two eggs very light, with two teaspoons white sugar, some grated nutmeg, or three small pieces of cinnamon bark, or the grated rind of half a lemon, and add a teaspoon of flour to this gradually. When perfectly smooth add the boiling wine, pouring very little at a time and stirring constantly. Return to boiler and stir until the spoon is coated.

WINE SAUCE, No. 2

Melt one tablespoon of butter in a saucepan, stir in one tablespoon of flour, then add ½ cup of cold water, stirring constantly until smooth. Then add one cup of white wine, one ounce of chopped citron. Remove from fire, let cool, flavor with one teaspoon each of pistachio and vanilla extract. If desired, one teaspoon of red Curaçao or Maraschino liquor can be added for flavoring.

VANILLA OR CREAM SAUCE

Mix one teaspoon cornstarch and one tablespoon of sugar thoroughly; on them slowly pour one cup of scalding milk, stirring all the time. Cook and stir in a double boiler for ten minutes; then set aside to cool. When ready to use stir in one teaspoon of vanilla and the white of one egg, stiffly beaten. Serve in place of whipped cream.

FROZEN DESSERTS

In making frozen desserts attention to detail is the essential thing to perfect success.

PREPARING SALT
The smaller the ice is broken the better, while the salt should never be too fine. A salt prepared especially for the purpose is known as "ice cream salt." This salt and the finely broken ice are put in alternate layers about the cream can. Begin with a layer of ice, making this about three inches deep. Then put in a layer of salt about an inch in depth, and continue in this way up to the top of the cream can. The ice can be put in a gunny sack and then broken up with a heavy hammer or hatchet.

FREEZING CREAMS AND WATER ICES
Fill the cream can ¾ full. Cover; place in wooden bucket; adjust the top and pack, as directed above. Turn crank slowly and steadily. After freezing drain off water, remove dasher; with a spoon pack hard. Put cork in top of lid. Repack freezer. Cover top with heavy pieces of carpet and paper. When time comes to serve, wipe top of can carefully before opening. In very hot weather renew the salt and ice three times, and keep the blanket cold and wet with the brine from the freezer.

VANILLA ICE CREAM, No. 1
Take one pint milk, two cups sugar, one large tablespoon flour rubbed smooth in cold milk, two eggs beaten light, one teaspoon vanilla extract, and one quart sweet cream, well beaten. Heat the milk in a double boiler, and when it is at boiling point add the flour, eggs and one cup of sugar. Cook about twenty minutes, stirring very often. Let the mixture get cold, then add the remaining sugar and the vanilla and cream, and freeze. A more novel flavoring is made with a mixture of vanilla, lemon and almond extracts. The quantities given in this recipe make about two quarts of ice cream.

VANILLA ICE CREAM, No. 2
Beat three whole eggs very light with one cup of granulated sugar until all grain is dissolved and mass is a light yellowish color. Whip one pint of cream

until stiff, add to eggs and sugar, then add one cup of sweet milk, flavor with vanilla to taste, and put in freezer and turn until hard. This is a basis for almost any kind of cream.

CHOCOLATE ICE CREAM, No. 1

Make same as Vanilla Ice Cream, No. 2, only omitting the milk. Dissolve on stove ½ pound sweet chocolate, in one cup sweet milk, rub smooth and thick, let get cold, and add to the eggs, just before putting in cream. Flavor with vanilla.

CHOCOLATE ICE CREAM, No. 2

Take one quart cream, one pint milk, two eggs, one teacup of grated chocolate (double vanilla), two cups of pulverized sugar, one teaspoon of cornstarch and one of extract of vanilla. Beat the yolks of the eggs, and sugar and let them come to a boil. Then take them quickly from the heat, dissolve the chocolate in a little milk over the heat, stir it all the time. When smooth mix with the milk and eggs, add the cream and vanilla. Freeze when cold.

COFFEE ICE CREAM

Make same as Vanilla Ice Cream No. 2. Flavor with 1½ tablespoons of mocha extract, add one cup of grated walnuts. Freeze.

FROZEN CUSTARD

One quart milk, five egg yolks, sweeten to taste, and flavor with vanilla to taste. Boil the milk first, and after the yolks of eggs are beaten stir into the milk. When cold add the beaten whites and vanilla; put in freezer and turn. Canned strawberries are very nice in this.

APRICOT, PEACH, STRAWBERRY, BANANA OR PINEAPPLE CREAM

Make same as Vanilla Ice Cream No. 2, omitting the milk. If canned fruit is to be used, drain off the juice, and add it to the eggs and cream. Mash the fruit through a sieve, add it to rest of mixture, and freeze the whole. If fresh fruits are used, one pint is required. Mash fine, strain and sweeten before adding to the cream. For peach and strawberry a few drops of pink coloring may be added Bananas must be mashed smooth, but not sweetened. Chop all fruits very fine. For pineapple, the sliced is preferred to the grated. Either canned or fresh can be used.

TUTTI-FRUTTI ICE CREAM
Take three pints cream, one pound pulverized sugar and 9 egg yolks. Prepare just like the other creams. When half frozen add ½ pound of crystallized fruit, peaches, apricots, cherries, citron, etc., chopped very fine. Put in also a wineglass of pale sherry and the juice of an orange or lemon. Finish freezing.

FROZEN PUDDINGS
For frozen puddings ice must be crushed and mixed with rock-salt, the same way as for freezing cream. Pudding-mold must have a tight cover; have a receptacle sufficiently large to line bottom and sides with a thick layer of mixed salt and ice. Put the mold in the center, fill with the pudding, cover tightly, then put ice on top and all around. Put a sheet of plain tissue paper in top of mold to prevent salt from penetrating. Cover whole with a cloth and let freeze from three to four hours.

BISCUIT TORTONI, No. 1
Take ½ cup granulated sugar, ¼ pound stale macaroons grated, ½ pint heavy cream (whipped), three eggs, vanilla or sherry wine. Stir yolks of eggs until thick and add sugar and stir again; add whipped cream, and whipped whites of eggs, and grated macaroons; flavor to taste. Put this all into freezer and pack outside with ice and salt alternately. Do not turn. Let stand five or six hours, adding ice from time to time. When serving put grated macaroons on top.

BISCUIT TORTONI, No. 2
Take 2 egg yolks, one pint cream, eight macaroons, vanilla and flavor, ½ cup of sugar, ½ cup of milk. Beat yolks of eggs and the sugar very light. Put on milk to a boil, and when it comes to a boil stir into the beaten eggs and sugar and set away to cool. Beat cream and add macaroons, leaving just enough to put in the bottom of your form. When your custard is cool, add cream, put all in forms, pack and freeze two hours or longer.

MOCHA MOUSSE
Cream yolks of three eggs with ½ cup granulated sugar. Add ½ pint cream, whipped; ½ cup grated macaroons, two tablespoons of mocha extract, one teaspoon vanilla, lastly beaten whites. Put in a mold and pack in salt and ice for three hours.

MAPLE MOUSSE
Whip one pint of cream until quite thick. Break two eggs into another bowl, beat until light and add gradually, ½ cup maple syrup. When the two are well mixed, whip them gradually into the cream. Pour the whole into a freezer can, without the dasher; cover; pack in ice and salt, and let stand for three hours.

MAPLE BISQUE
Boil one cup of maple syrup until quite thick; beat 3 egg yolks; add to syrup while hot, stirring constantly until well mixed. Let cool. Beat whites of eggs to a froth. Whip one pint cream, mix all together; add ½ cup chopped nuts. Have a pudding-mold buttered; see that the edges fit close. Pack in rock salt and ice four hours.

FROZEN CREAM CHEESE WITH PRESERVED FIGS
Take three Neufchatel cheeses. Mash the cheese to a smooth paste and add ½ cup thick cream, ½ teaspoon salt, one rounding teaspoon of sugar. Place in a small square mold, bury in salt and ice and let stand several hours. When ready to serve unmold, cut in squares, place each on a lettuce leaf, decorate the center of the cheese square with a preserved fig and serve at once.

RUM PUDDING
Beat 2 egg yolks with ½ cup of sugar until light, then add stiffly beaten whites. Flavor with one tablespoon of rum. Whip one pint of cream very stiff, stir into beaten eggs. Line a melon mold with lady fingers, split in half. Then put a layer of whipped cream over. Chop one-half pound of marron glacé fine and sprinkle some over cream. Put another layer of ladyfingers, cream and marrons, and so on until mold is filled. Close tightly and pack in rock salt and ice, from three to four hours.

CHERRY DIPLOMATE

Line a mold with white cake, thinly sliced, which you have previously dipped in maraschino or some other fine brandy. Then fill in with plain white ice cream, then a layer of cherry ice, next a layer of candied cherries, next a layer of cherry ice, then a layer of strawberry ice cream or the plain white vanilla. Finish it up with a layer of cake again and be sure to dip the cake in the maraschino. Cover all up tight and pack in ice until wanted.

NESSELRODE PUDDING

Put on ½ pound of shelled and skinned chestnuts in cold water, and let them boil until very tender, then press them through a purée sieve. Beat 5 egg yolks with ½ pound of sugar until light, then add the mashed chestnuts, then stir in one pint of sweet cream. Put on to boil in a double boiler, add a few grains of salt, and stir until the mixture begins to boil, then remove at once from heat and set aside to cool. In a bowl, put ¼ pound crystallized pineapple cut up, one ounce citron cut fine, ¼ cup raisins, and ½ cup maraschino cordial. Put the chestnut cream in a freezer, freeze ten minutes, then add one pint cream that has been whipped stiff with two tablespoons of powdered sugar, turn until it begins to get stiff, then add the fruits and turn awhile longer. Pack in a pudding-mold in rock salt and ice two hours.

CANNED FRUIT FROZEN

Without opening, pack a can of pears in ice and salt, as for ice cream. Let it remain for three or four hours. When taken out, cut the can open around the middle. If frozen very hard, wrap around with a towel dipped in hot water; the contents can then be clipped out in perfect rounds. Cut into slices and serve with a spoonful of whipped cream on each slice. This will serve six or eight persons. Canned peaches may be used if desired.

PETER PAN DESSERT

Cut a banana in four strips, cross two over two in basket-shape, fill center square with a tablespoon of ice-cream and sprinkle over all some chopped walnuts, pistachio nuts and marshmallows, cut in strips.

FRUIT SHERBETS

There is no form in which ices are more palatable or healthful than in the form of sherbet. This is made of fruit juice, sugar and water. The simplest sherbet is made by mixing the sugar, water and fruit juice together. A richer and smoother ice is obtained by boiling the sugar and water together, then adding the fruit juice, and when the mixture is cool, freezing it. It takes nearly twice as long to freeze the preparation made in this way as when made with the uncooked mixture. Sherbets are usually served at the end of a dinner, but they are sometimes served before the roast.

APRICOT ICE
Pare and grate one dozen apricots, and blanch a few of the kernels. Then pound them and add to the grated fruit. Pour a pint of water over them, adding the juice of a lemon also. Let them stand for an hour and strain, adding ½ pound of sugar just before freezing.

LEMON ICE
Take six large, juicy lemons and grate peel of three lemons; two oranges, juice of both, and peel of one; squeeze out every drop of juice and steep the grated peel of lemon and orange in juice for an hour. Strain and mix in one pint of sugar. Stir until dissolved and freeze.

LEMON GINGER SHERBET
Shave very thin bits of the yellow peel from two lemons, being careful not to get any of the white. Cut eight lemons (using the first two) into halves, extract seeds and press out the juice. Cut ¼ pound of ginger in strips. Boil until clear, four cups sugar, two quarts boiling water, ginger and shaved lemon peel. Add lemon juice and strain through a cheesecloth. Freeze until thick and add the stiff-beaten whites of two eggs. Mix well; finish freezing, and pack.

ORANGE ICE
Make a syrup of two cups of sugar and four cups of water. Boil fifteen minutes and add two cups orange juice, ½ cup of lemon juice and the grated rind of one orange and one lemon. Freeze and serve in glasses.

PINEAPPLE ICE

Make a syrup of four cups of water, two cups of sugar and boil fifteen minutes. Add one can grated pineapple and juice of six lemons. Cool and add four cups of ice water. Freeze until mushy, using half ice and half salt.

PUNCH ICES

To the juice of two lemons take three-quarters of a pound of loaf sugar, two or three tablespoons of rum and one pint of water. Rub the rind of the lemons onto the sugar, then boil the sugar and water together for fifteen minutes, add the lemon juice and rum, mix well, strain, and set aside to cool. Then put the mixture into the freezing can and freeze until set.

RASPBERRY ICE

Make a strong lemonade, add raspberry juice to taste, and some grated pineapple. Put into freezer and turn like ice cream and pack, and let stand five hours.

WATERMELON SHERBET

Take good, pale sherry and boil down to quite a thick syrup, with loaf sugar; and then allow to cool. When cold mix with the chopped meat of a very fine, sweet melon, use only the heart of the soft red part, not any near the white rind. Freeze in a freezer as you would ice, but do not allow it to get too hard. Serve in glasses. You may use claret instead of the sherry. If you do, spice it while boiling with whole spices, such as cloves and cinnamon. Strain before adding to the melon.

CAFÉ Á LA GLACÉ

Take five tablespoons of fresh-roasted and ground coffee. Pour four cups of boiling water over it; cover quickly and put on the back of the stove, and add one-half pound of sugar. When cold, press through a sieve, and fill in the can to be frozen. Let it remain in freezer five minutes longer before you begin to turn the freezer. Serve in glasses, and put sweetened whipped cream on the top.

CANDIES AND SWEETS

WHITE FONDANT
Used as a foundation for all cream candies.
Put 2½ cups granulated sugar in a saucepan, add ¾ cup hot water, and ½ of a teaspoon of tartar. Stir until sugar is dissolved, but no longer. Boil without stirring until, when tried in cold water, it will form a soft ball. Wash down the edges of the pan with the finger first dipped in cold water, as the sugar boils up. Pour slowly on greased pan or marble slab. Cool slightly; beat with a wooden spoon until white and creamy. As soon as large lumps appear, it should be kneaded with the hands until smooth. Place in bowl and cover with waxed paper, let it stand overnight in a cool place. If covered and kept in a cool place this will keep for days. Form into bonbons, color and flavor any desired way; dip in melted chocolate, to which has been added a small piece of wax or paraffin. In fact, the bonbons may be used in any desired way.

DIVINITY
Boil two cups of granulated sugar, ½ cup corn syrup, and ½ cup water until it will thread. Beat into the stiff whites of two eggs; add one cup of nuts. Beat until cool and thick. Pour out, cool, and when set, cut into squares.

FUDGE
Boil together two cups granulated sugar, ⅛ teaspoon salt, and one cup milk or cream, until when tried in cold water, it will form a soft ball (about eight minutes). Add ½ a cake of Baker's chocolate, two tablespoons of butter and one teaspoon of vanilla. Beat until smooth and creamy; pour into greased pans; cool and cut in squares.

PINOCHE
Take one cup of (packed) medium brown sugar, ¼ cup cream, ⅓ cup nut meats, ¼ pound pecans, and ⅓ pound hickory nuts. Cook sugar and cream to soft ball test. Cool until you can bear your hand on bottom of pan. Stir until it begins to thicken, add chopped nuts; and when it is too thick to pour easily, spread quickly on a buttered pan, cut in squares and cool.

FRUIT LOAF
Chop coarsely ½ cup of raisins, ½ cup of nuts, ½ cup figs or dates, add enough honey or corn syrup to make a stiff loaf, about two tablespoons. Place in ice box for one hour, slice and serve in place of candy, rolling each slice in cornstarch.

GLACÉ FOR CANDIES
Boil one pound of sugar with ½ pint of water until it ropes; then add ½ cup of vinegar and boil until it hardens. Dip in fruit, orange slices, nuts or green grapes with stems on, and put aside on a buttered platter to set.

ORANGE CHIPS
Can be made after the fruit has been used. Halve, scoop out, then scrape inside; lay the peel in salt water overnight. Make syrup of two cups of sugar and one cup of water. When boiled thick, cut orange-peel in small strips and drop them into boiling liquid, letting them remain about ten minutes. Remove strips carefully, spreading them on waxed paper to dry. Grapefruit rind may be used as well as that of oranges.

CANDIED CHERRIES, PINEAPPLE AND OTHER FRUITS
Boil, but do not stir, ½ pound of loaf sugar in one breakfast cup of water. Pit some cherries, or prepare any desired fruit, and string them on a thread, then dip them in the syrup; suspend them by the thread. When pineapples are used, slice them crosswise and dry them on a sieve or in the open air; oranges should be separated into sections and dried like pineapple.

STUFFED DATES
Make a cut the entire length of dates and remove stones. Fill cavities with English walnuts, blanched almonds, pecans or with a mixture of chopped nuts, and shape in original form. Roll in granulated sugar or powdered sugar and serve on small plate or bonbon dish.

DATES STUFFED WITH GINGER AND NUTS
Remove the stones from choice dates, and chop together equal measures of preserved ginger and blanched nuts chopped, (hickory, pecan, or almond). Mix with fondant or a paste of confectioner's sugar and ginger syrup. Use only enough fondant or paste to hold the ingredients together. With this mixture fill the open space in the dates, cover securely, and roll in granulated sugar.

DATES STUFFED WITH FONDANT
Fill with fondant, letting it project slightly, and insert in it a pecan or half a walnut. Roll in granulated sugar.

STUFFED FIGS
Cut a slit in the side of dried figs, take out some of the pulp with the tip of a teaspoon. Mix with ¼ cup of the pulp, ¼ cup of finely-chopped crystallized ginger, a teaspoon of grated orange or lemon rind and a tablespoon of lemon juice. Fill the figs with the mixture, stuffing them so that they look plump.

STUFFED PRUNES
Take one pound of best prunes, stone and soak in sherry for about an hour (do not cover with the wine). Fill prunes with one large browned almond and one-half marshmallow or with another prune, roll in granulated sugar, and when all are finished, put in oven for two or three minutes.

FROSTED CURRANTS
Pick fine, even, large bunches of red currants (not too ripe) and dip each bunch, one at a time, into a mixture of frothed white of egg, then into a thick, boiled sugar syrup. Drain the bunches by laying on a sieve, and when partly dry dip again into the boiled syrup. Repeat the process a third time; then sprinkle powdered sugar over them and lay on a sheet of paper in a slightly warm oven to dry. Used on extra occasions for ornamenting charlottes, cakes, creams, etc.

BEVERAGES

All drinks contain a large proportion of water which is the beverage nature has provided for man. Water for hot drinks should be freshly boiled, freshly drawn water should be used for cold drinks.

COFFEE

Coffee should be bought in small quantities and kept in airtight cans, and freshly ground as needed. To have perfect coffee, use an earthen or china pot, and have the water boiling when turned onto the coffee. Like tea, the results will not be right if the water is allowed to fall below the boiling point before it is used. Have the coffee ground to a fine powder in order to get its full flavor as well as strength.

BOILED COFFEE

Allow one tablespoon of coffee to each cup of boiling water. Mix coffee with two tablespoons of cold water. Clean egg shells and put in the pot. Allow this to come to a boil and add boiling water, bring to a boil, and boil for one minute; add a tablespoon of cold water to assist the grounds in settling. Stand the pot where it will keep hot, but not boil, for five minutes; then serve at once, as coffee allowed to stand becomes flat and loses its aroma. Most cooks use a clean shell or a little of the white of an egg if they do not use the whole. Others beat the whole egg, with a little water, but use only a part of it, keeping the rest for further use in a covered glass in the ice chest. Cream is usually served with coffee, but scalded milk renders the coffee more digestible than does cream. Fill the cup one-fourth full of hot scalded milk; pour on the freshly made coffee, adding sugar.

FILTERED COFFEE

Place one cup of finely ground coffee in the strainer of the percolater; place the strainer in the pot and place over the heat. Add gradually six cups of boiling water and allow it to filter. Serve at once.

TURKISH COFFEE

For making this the coffee must be pulverized, and it should be made over an alcohol lamp with a little brass Turkish pot. Measure into your pot as many after-dinner coffee cups of water as you wish cups of coffee. Bring the water to a boil and drop a heaping teaspoon of the powdered coffee to each cup on top of the water and allow it to settle. Add one, two or three coffeespoons of powdered sugar, as desired. Put the pot again over the flame; bring the coffee to a boil three times, and pour into the cups. The grounds of the coffee are of course thick in the liquid, so one lets the coffee stand a moment in the cup before drinking.

FRENCH COFFEE
Have your coffee ground very fine and use a French drip coffee pot. Instead of pouring through water, pour milk through, brought just to the boiling point. The milk passes through slowly, and care must be taken not to let scum form on the milk.

COFFEE FOR TWENTY PEOPLE
Add and mix one pound of coffee finely ground, with one egg and enough cold water to thoroughly moisten it, cover and let stand several hours. Place in thin bag and drop in seven quarts of boiling water. Boil five minutes, let stand ten minutes. Add cream to coffee and serve. After-dinner coffee is made double the strength of boiled coffee and is served without cream or milk.

BREAKFAST COCOA
Mix two tablespoons prepared cocoa with two tablespoons of sugar and a few grains of salt, dilute with one-half cup of boiling water to make a smooth paste, then add ½ cup of boiling water and boil five minutes, turn into three cups of scalded milk and beat two minutes, using Dover beater and serve.

RECEPTION COCOA
Stir one cup of boiling water gradually onto two tablespoons of cocoa, two tablespoons of sugar and one teaspoon of cornstarch, a few grains of salt (that have been well mixed) in a saucepan; let boil five minutes, stirring constantly. Heat three cups of milk in a double boiler, add the cocoa mixture and ½ teaspoon of vanilla; beat with egg-beater until foamy and serve hot in chocolate cups, with a tablespoon of whipped cream on top of each

cup, or take the cheaper marshmallows, place two in each cup and fill cups two-thirds full of hot cocoa.

HOT CHOCOLATE
Scrape two ounces of unsweetened chocolate very fine, add three tablespoons of sugar, small piece of stick cinnamon and one cup of boiling water; stir over moderate heat until smooth, then add three cups of hot milk. Return to the fire for a minute, do not let it boil, remove, add one teaspoon of vanilla. Beat with an eggbeater and serve.

CHOCOLATE SYRUP
Dissolve two cups of sugar in one cup of water and boil five minutes. Mix one cup of cocoa with one cup of water and add to the boiling syrup. Boil slowly for ten minutes, add salt; cool and bottle for further use. This syrup will keep a long time in the ice chest in summer and may be used for making delicious drinks.

CHOCOLATE NECTAR
Put into a glass two tablespoons of chocolate syrup, a little cream or milk and chopped ice, and fill up the glass with soda water, or milk. Drop a little whipped cream on top.

ICED CHOCOLATE
Follow recipe for boiled chocolate, but do not beat, add one egg, finely chopped ice and ¾ cup of milk, put in a bowl and beat thoroughly or pour into jar with cover and shake thoroughly. Serve in tall glasses.

ICED COFFEE
Take boiled coffee, strain, add sugar to taste and chill. When ready to serve, add one quart of coffee, ½ cup of cream and pour in pitcher. Serve in tall glasses. Have ready a small bowl of whipped cream and, if desired, place a tablespoon on top of each glass.

TEA
Scald the teapot. Allow one teaspoon of tea to each person, and one extra. When the water boils, pour off the water with which the pot was scalded,

put in the tea, and pour boiling water over it. Let it draw three minutes. Tea should never be allowed to remain on the leaves. If not drunk as soon as it is drawn, it should be poured off into another hot teapot, or into a hot jug, which should stand in hot water.

TEA (RUSSIAN STYLE)
Use a small earthenware teapot, thoroughly clean. Put in two teaspoons of tea leaves, pour over it boiling water to one-fourth of the pot, and let it stand three minutes. Then fill the pot entirely with boiling water and let it stand five minutes. In serving dilute with warm water to suit taste, or serve cold, but always without milk. A thin slice of lemon or a few drops of lemon juice is allowed for each cup. Preserved strawberries, cherries or raspberries are considered an improvement.

RUSSIAN ICED TEA
Make tea for as many cups as desired, strain and cool. Place in icebox, chill thoroughly and serve in tall glass with ice and flavor with loaf sugar, one teaspoon of rum or brandy, one slice of lemon or one teaspoon preserved strawberries, raspberries, cherries or pineapple, or loaf sugar may be flavored with lemon or orange and packed and stored in jars to be used later to flavor and sweeten the tea. Wash the rind of lemon or orange and wipe dry, then rub over all sides of the sugar.

HOT WINE (GLÜHWEIN)
Mix one quart claret, one pint water, two cups of sugar, ½ teaspoon of whole cloves, one teaspoon of whole cinnamon, lemon rind cut thin and in small pieces. Boil steadily for fifteen minutes and serve hot.

FRUIT DRINKS
The success of lemon-, orange- and pineapple-ades depends upon the way they are made. It is best to make a syrup, using one cup of granulated sugar to one cup of water. Put the sugar in cold water over the fire; stir until the sugar is dissolved; then cook until the syrup spins a fine thread. Take from the fire and add the fruit juices while the syrup is hot. If lemonade is desired, lemon should predominate, but orange or pineapple juice or both should be added to yield the best result. Small pieces of fresh pineapple,

fresh strawberries and maraschino cherries added at time of serving will make the drink look pretty and will improve the flavor. Shaved or very finely cracked ice should be used.

PINEAPPLE LEMONADE
Pare and grate a ripe pineapple; add the juice of four lemons and a syrup made by boiling together for a few minutes two cups of sugar and the same quantity of water. Mix and add a quart of water. When quite cold strain and ice. A cherry in each glass is an agreeable addition, as are a few strawberries or raspberries.

QUICK LEMONADE
Wash two lemons and squeeze the juice; mix thoroughly with four tablespoons of sugar, and when the sugar is dissolved add one quart of water, cracked ice, and a little fresh fruit or slices of lemon if convenient. If the cracked ice is very finely chopped and put in the glasses just before serving it will make a better looking lemonade. When wine is used take two-thirds water and one-third wine.

LEMONADE IN LARGE QUANTITIES
Take one dozen lemons, one pound of sugar and one gallon of water to make lemonade for twenty people.

FRUIT PUNCH FOR TWENTY PEOPLE
Take one pineapple, or one can of grated pineapple, one cup of boiling water, two cups of freshly made tea (one heaping tablespoon of Ceylon tea, steep for five minutes); one dozen lemons, three oranges sliced and quartered, one quart bottle Apollinaris water, three cups of sugar boiled with 1½ cups of water six to eight minutes, one quart of water, ice. Grate the pineapple, add the one cup of boiling water, and boil fifteen minutes. Strain through jelly-bag, pressing out all the juice; let cool, and add the lemon and orange juice, the tea and syrup. Add Apollinaris water just before serving. Pieces of pineapple, strawberries, mint-leaves or slices of banana are sometimes added as a garnish.

MILK LEMONADE
Dissolve in one quart of boiling water two cups of granulated sugar, add ¾ cup of lemon juice, and lastly, 1½ pints of milk. Drink hot or cold with pounded ice.

EGG LEMONADE
Break two eggs and beat the whites and yolks separately. Mix juice of two lemons, four tablespoons of sugar, four cups of water and ice as for lemonade; add the eggs; pour rapidly back and forth from one pitcher to another and serve before the froth disappears.

MARASCHINO LEMONADE
Take the juice of four lemons, twelve tablespoons of sugar, eight cups of water, one cup of maraschino liquor and a few cherries.

ORANGEADE
Take four large, juicy oranges and six tablespoons of sugar. Squeeze the oranges upon the sugar, add a very little water and let them stand for fifteen minutes; strain and add shaved ice and water, and a little lemon juice.

CLABBERED MILK
One of the most healthful drinks in the world is clabbered milk; it is far better in a way for every one than buttermilk, for it requires no artificial cult to bring it to perfection. The milk is simply allowed to stand in a warm place in the bottles just as it is bought, and when it reaches the consistency of a rich cream or is more like a jelly the same as is required for cheese, it is ready to drink. Pour it into a glass, seasoning it with a little salt, and drink it in the place of buttermilk.

COLD EGG WINE
To each glass of wine allow one egg, beat up, and add sugar to taste. Add wine gradually and grated nutmeg. Beat whites separately and mix.

SODA CREAM
Take three pounds of granulated sugar and 1½ ounces of tartaric acid, both dissolved in one quart of hot water. When cold add the well-beaten whites of three eggs, stirring well. Bottle for use. Put two large spoonfuls of this syrup in a glass of ice-water, and stir in it one-fourth of a teaspoon of bicarbonate of soda. Any flavor can be put in this syrup.

MULLED WINE
Put cinnamon and allspice (to taste) in a cup of hot water to steep. Add three eggs well beaten with sugar. Heat to a boil a pint of wine, then add spice and eggs. Stir for three minutes and serve.

STRAWBERRY SHERBET
Crush a quart of ripe strawberries, pour a quart of water over them, and add the juice of two lemons. Let this stand about two hours, then strain over a pound of sugar, stir until the sugar is dissolved, and then set upon ice. You may add one tablespoon of rose-water. Serve with chopped ice.

DELICIOUS AND NOURISHING SUMMER DRINK
Pare thinly the rind of three large lemons, put it into a large jug with one pound of raisins stoned and finely chopped, one pound of sugar, and the juice of the lemons. Add one gallon of boiling water, leave to stand for five days, stirring well every day. Then strain and bottle for use.

SHERRY COBBLER
It is best to mix this in a large bowl and fill in glasses just before serving, and put a little of each kind of fruit in each goblet with pounded ice. To begin with, cut pineapple in slices and quarters, a few oranges and a lemon, sliced thin; one cup of powdered sugar and one tumbler of sherry wine. A few berries, such as black and red raspberries, and blackberries are a nice addition. Cover the fruit with the sugar, laid in layers at the bottom of your bowl with pounded ice; add the wine and twice as much water as wine; stir all up well before serving.

CLARET CUP
Squeeze into a glass pitcher the strained juice of 1½ lemons, add two tablespoons of powdered sugar, one tablespoon of red Curaçao; then pour in three cups of claret, and one cup of Apollinaris water. Mix thoroughly, add a few slices of orange or pineapple, or both, and a few maraschino cherries. Cut the rinds from two cucumbers without breaking them, hang them on the inside of the pitcher from the top; drop in a good-sized lump of ice and serve at once in thin glasses. Place a bunch of mint at the top of the pitcher.

CORDIAL
Two quarts of water, and 2¾ pounds of sugar. Boil thirty minutes. Take off stove and add one quart of alcohol. Color and flavor to taste.

EGGNOG
Separate the whites and yolks of the eggs. To each yolk add one tablespoon of sugar and beat until very light. Beat whites to a stiff froth. One egg is required for each glass of eggnog. Add two tablespoons of brandy or rum, then ½ cup milk or cream to each glass, lastly the whites of the eggs. Pour in glass, put a spoon of whipped cream over and grated nutmeg on top.

UNFERMENTED GRAPE JUICE
Wash and stem ten pounds of Concord grapes, put them in a preserving kettle and crush slightly. Bring to the boiling point and cook gently for one-half hour. Strain through cheesecloth or jelly bag, pressing out all the juice possible; return to fire and with two pounds of sugar cook for fifteen minutes; strain again, reheat and pour into sterilized bottles thoroughly heated. Put in sterilized corks and dip the necks of the bottles in hot sealing wax. If you can get the self-sealing bottles, the work of putting up grape juice will be light. Sterilize bottles and corks.

OTHER FRUIT JUICES
Raspberry, blackberry and strawberry juice may be made by following the recipe for grape juice but doubling the quantity of sugar. For currant juice use four times as much sugar as for grape juice.

FRUIT SYRUPS

Fruit syrups may be made like fruit juices, only using more sugar--at least half as much sugar as fruit juice.

RASPBERRY VINEGAR

Put two quarts of raspberries in a bowl and cover them with two quarts of vinegar; cover and stand in a cool place for two days. Mash the berries; strain the vinegar through cheese-cloth; pour it over two quarts of fresh raspberries; let stand for another two days; strain and put in a preserving kettle with sugar, allowing a pound of sugar to a pint of juice. Heat slowly, skimming when the vinegar begins to boil. Boil twenty minutes and put in sterilized bottles. Serve as a drink, using two tablespoons to a glass of water

BLACKBERRY WINE

Measure your berries and bruise them; to every gallon add one quart of boiling water; let the mixture stand twenty-four hours (stirring occasionally), then strain off all the liquor into a cask; to every gallon add two pounds of sugar; cork tightly and let stand till the following October.

BLACKBERRY CORDIAL

Simmer the berries until they break, then strain and to each quart of juice add one pound of sugar. Let this dissolve by heating slowly, then add one tablespoon each of cinnamon, nutmeg, cloves, and if desired, allspice. Simmer altogether twenty minutes. Bottle and seal.

CHERRY SYRUP

Mash and pound the cherries until the stones are all broken, then press through a cloth. Use a pound of sugar to a quart of juice; boil, skim and bottle. When cold, seal.

CHERRY BRANDY

To one gallon of brandy allow two quarts of cherries. Mash and pound them until all the stones are broken, put in the brandy and add a pound of cut loaf sugar. Set in the sun for two or three weeks, shake daily, strain and bottle.

CHERRY BOUNCE

The little wild cherry is excellent for this purpose, as the stone kernels contain alcohol. Wash carefully, sugar plentifully, and add whole spice, cloves (with the heads removed) and stick cinnamon. Fewer cloves than the other spices. Get good whiskey and allow ½ as much cherries as whiskey. To a quart bottle allow scant half pint sugared cherries to 1½ pints of whiskey. Bottle and seal. Let stand at least two months. Open, shake bottle well and taste, and if necessary add more sugar. Seal again, and let stand another month. Is not good under three months and the older it gets the finer it becomes.

CIDER EGG NOG

Break six eggs, put the yolks in one dish, the whites in another. To each yolk add a tablespoon of granulated sugar, beat the yolks and sugar to a foam; then flavor with a little grated nutmeg, stirring it well through the mixture; then add a ½ pint of hot sweet cider to each egg, beat it well through and pour into a hot punch bowl. Beat the whites of the eggs to a stiff froth with a little sugar and cover the surface of the punch. Serve in cups.

TOM AND JERRY (Non-Alcoholic)

Beat six eggs and six tablespoons of sugar to a stiff froth, add four cups of unfermented grape juice and the same amount of sweet cider. Have two porcelain pitchers as hot as possible, pour the mixture into one of them. Then pour the mixture back and forth from one pitcher to the other five or six times, and pour the foaming beverage into hot cups and serve.

HOT MILK PUNCH

Beat one egg to a stiff froth with two tablespoons of sugar; add to it two tablespoons of home-made grape wine; stir all well together, put in a large drinking glass and fill with hot milk. Grate a little nutmeg on the top and serve.

FRUITS

BAKED CRANBERRIES OR CHERRY PRESERVES
Pick over, wash and drain four quarts of large, perfect cranberries; or stem and then stone four pounds of large cherries, use a cherry pitter so cherries remain whole. Place a tablespoon of hot water in a jar, then alternately in layers cherries or cranberries and sugar (with sugar on top), cover closely. This amount will require four pounds of sugar. Bake in a very slow oven two hours. Let stand. Then keep in a cool, dry place. The cranberries will look and taste like candied cherries, and may be used for garnishing.

BAKED CRAB-APPLE PRESERVES
Wash, wipe and remove the blossom ends of one-half peck of perfect red Siberian crab-apples. Pour one tablespoon of water in bottom of one gallon stone jar, then place in alternate layers of apples and sugar, using four pounds altogether (with sugar on top). Cover with two thicknesses of Manila paper, tied down securely or with close fitting plate. Bake in a very slow oven (that would only turn the paper a light brown), two or three hours; let stand to cool, keep in cool, dry place.

BAKED SICKEL PEARS
May be prepared the same way. Flavor, if desired, with ginger or lemon juice.

BAKED QUINCES
Quinces may be wiped, cored, and quartered; sugar filled in the cavities, and baked same as crab-apples, in a 325° oven three or more hours until clear and glassy.

JELLIES

CURRANT JELLY
Pick over half ripe currants, leaving stems on. Wash and place in preserving kettle. Pound vigorously with wooden masher until there is juice enough to boil. Boil slowly until fruit turns white and liquid drops slowly from the spoon. Stir to prevent scorching. Remove from fire. Take an enameled cup and dip this mixture into the jelly bags, under which large bowls have been placed to catch the drip. Drip overnight. Next morning measure the juice. For every pint allow a pint of granulated sugar, which is put in a flat pan. Juice is put in kettle and allowed to come to boiling point. Sugar is placed in oven and heated. When juice boils add sugar and stir until dissolved. When this boils remove from fire and skim. Do this three times. Now test liquid with syrup gauge to see if it registers 25° degrees. Without gauge let it drip from spoon. half cooled, to see if it jells. Strain into sterilized jelly glasses. Place glasses on a board in a sunny exposure until it hardens. Cover with melted paraffin one-fourth inch thick.

RASPBERRY AND CURRANT JELLY
Follow the recipe for Currant Jelly, using half raspberries and half currants.

RASPBERRY JELLY
Follow the recipe for Currant Jelly.

BLACKBERRY JELLY
Follow the recipe for Currant Jelly.

STRAWBERRY JELLY
To five quarts of strawberries add one quart of currants and proceed as with Currant Jelly; but boil fifteen minutes.

GRAPE JELLY

The Concord is the best all-round grape for jelly, although the Catawba grape makes a delicious jelly. Make your jelly as soon as possible after the grapes are sent home from the market. Weigh the grapes on the stems and for every pound of grapes thus weighed allow three-quarters of a pound of the best quality of granulated sugar. After weighing the grapes, place them in a big tub or receptacle of some kind nearly filled with cold water. Let them remain ten minutes, then lift them out with both hands and put them in a preserving kettle over a very low fire. Do not add any water. With a masher press the grapes so the juice comes out, and cook the grapes until they are rather soft, pressing them frequently with the masher. When they have cooked until the skins are all broken, pour them, juice and all, in a small-holed colander set in a big bowl, and press pulp and juice through, picking out the stems as they come to the surface. When pulp and juice are pressed out, pour them into a cheesecloth bag. Hang the bag over the preserving kettle and let the juice drip all night. In the morning put the kettle over the fire and let the grape juice boil gently for a half hour, skimming it frequently. While the juice is cooking put the sugar in pans in a moderate oven and let heat. As soon as the juice is skimmed clear stir in the hot sugar, and as soon as it is dissolved pour the jelly in the glasses, first standing them in warm water. Place glasses after filling them in a cool dry place until jelly is well set, then pour a film of melted paraffin over the top and put on the covers. Label.

CRABAPPLE JELLY

Take eight quarts of Siberian crabapples, cut up in pieces, leaving in the seeds, and do not pare. Put into a stone jar, and set on the back of the stove to boil slowly, adding four quarts of water. Let them boil, closely covered all day, then put in a jelly-bag and let them drip all night. Boil a pint of juice at a time, with a pound of sugar to every pint of juice. Boil five minutes steadily, each pint exactly five minutes. Now weigh another pound of sugar and measure another pint of juice. Keep on in this way and you will be through before you realize it. There is no finer or firmer jelly than this. It should be a bright amber in color, and of fine flavor. You may press the pulp that remains in the jelly-bag through a coarse strainer, add the juice of two lemons and as much sugar as you have pulp, and cook to a jam.

APPLE JELLY

Take sour, juicy apples, not too ripe, cut up in pieces, leave the skins on and boil the seeds also. Put on enough water to just cover, boil on the back of the stove, closely covered, all day. Then put in jelly-bag of double cheese-cloth to drip all night. Next morning measure the juice. Allow a wine-glass of white wine and juice of one lemon to every three pints of juice. Then boil a pint at a time, with a pound of sugar to every pint.

NEAPOLITAN JELLY

Take equal quantities of fully ripe strawberries, raspberries, currants and red cherries. The cherries must be stoned, taking care to preserve the juice and add to rest of juice. Mix and press through a jelly-press or bag. Measure the juice, boil a pint at a time, and to every pint allow a pound of sugar and proceed as with other fruit jellies.

QUINCE JELLY

Prepare the fruit and cook peels and cores as directed for preserving. Cut the quinces in small pieces and let them boil in the strained water for one hour with kettle uncovered. When cooked the desired length of time, pour the whole into a jelly-bag of white flannel or double cheesecloth; hang over a big bowl or jar and let the liquor all drain through. This will take several hours. When all the liquor is drained, measure it and return to the kettle. To each pint of liquor weigh a pound of sugar. While the liquor is heating put the sugar in the oven, then add to the boiling hot liquor and stir it until sugar is melted. When the whole is thick, and drops from the spoon like jelly, pour it through a strainer into the jelly glasses; and when the jelly is cool, put on the covers--first pouring a film of melted paraffin over the surface.

A WINTER JELLY

One-half peck of tart apples, one quart of cranberries. Cover with cold water and cook an hour. Strain through a jelly-bag without squeezing. There should be about three pints of juice. Use a bowl of sugar for each bowl of juice. When the juice is boiling add sugar which has been heated in oven and boil twenty minutes. Skim and pour into glasses. Will fill about seven. Cover with paraffin.

CRANBERRY JELLY

Wash and pick ripe cranberries and set on to boil in a porcelain-lined kettle closely covered. When soft strain the pulp through a fine wire sieve. Measure the juice and add an equal quantity of sugar. Set it on to boil again and let it boil very fast for about ten minutes--but it must boil steadily all the time. Wet a mold with cold water, turn the jelly into it and set it away to cool, when firm turn it into a glass salver. Pour into jelly glasses and cover with paraffin.

DAMSON JAM

Weigh three-quarters of a pound of sugar for each pound of fruit. After washing the plums carefully, put them in a preserving kettle with just enough water to keep them from sticking to the bottom. Set them over a moderate fire and let them simmer for half an hour; then turn them, juice and all, into a colander, filling the colander not more than half full. Have the colander set over a large earthen bowl. With a potato masher, press juice and pulp through the colander into the bowl, leaving skins and pits as dry as possible. Remove these from the colander and repeat the process until all the pulp and juice is pressed out; then pour it into the kettle and, while it is heating slowly, heat the sugar in the oven. As soon as the juice and pulp begins to simmer stir in the hot sugar, and when it drops from the spoon like a thick jelly pour it into the glasses. This is one of the most delicious fruit preserves made and is always acceptable with meat and poultry or as a sweetmeat at afternoon teas. Pour into jelly glasses and cover with paraffin.

RASPBERRY JAM

To five pounds of red raspberries (not too ripe) add five pounds of loaf sugar. Mash the whole well in a preserving kettle (to do this thoroughly use a potato masher). Add one quart of currant juice, and boil slowly until it jellies. Try a little on a plate; set it on ice, if it jellies remove from the fire, fill in small jars, cover with brandied paper and tie a thick white paper over them. Keep in a dark, dry, cool place. If you object to seeds, press the fruit through a sieve before boiling.

JELLIED QUINCES

Jellied quinces are made after the direction for preserved quinces, only the fruit is cut in tiny little pieces and when put in the syrup is allowed to cook twenty minutes longer, and is put in small glasses with the syrup and not skimmed out as for preserves. Leave the glasses open till the jelly sets, then cover.

CHERRY CONSERVE
Take 3½ pounds of large red cherries, stone them and cook for fifteen minutes. Heat 2½ pounds of sugar in the oven; add it to the cherries; also ¼ pound of seeded raisins and the juice and pulp of three oranges. Cook until the mixture is as thick as marmalade.

PICKLED PEACHES
Brush but do not peel the peaches. Select medium-sized ones. When all are well brushed, stick each peach quite full of cloves. Make a thick syrup of half a pound of sugar to a pound of fruit. Cook the peaches in the syrup until they may be easily pierced with a broom splint. Then carefully skim them from the syrup and after they have cooled on the platters put them in glass jars or stone crocks. To the syrup in the kettle add a few pieces of stick cinnamon and a few whole allspice. Add half a pint of good cider vinegar and a tablespoon of tarragon vinegar to each quart of syrup, and when the syrup just comes to a boil after adding the vinegar pour it over the peaches. Delicious with cold chicken.

SPICED GRAPES
Pulp seven pounds of Concord grapes; cook the pulp and skins until soft; put them through a fine sieve; then add 4½ pounds of granulated sugar, one pint of cider vinegar, two tablespoons of ground cinnamon, and two tablespoons of ground cloves. Bring to a boil; then cook slowly for 1½ hours. Put in an earthen crock when cool. This recipe may also be used with currants; use five pounds of sugar instead of four and one-half pounds.

PICKLED VEGETABLES

PREPARED MUSTARD
Rub together one teaspoon of sugar, ¼ teaspoon of fine salt and one tablespoon of best salad oil. Do this thoroughly. Mix two tablespoons of ground mustard with vinegar enough to thin it. Then add to the mixture of sugar, and if too thick, add a little boiling water.

BEET AND HORSERADISH RELISH
Take three cups of cold, boiled beets, grate, and add ½ cup of grated horseradish; season with ¼ teaspoon of pepper, one teaspoon of salt and two tablespoons of sugar. Add all the vinegar the horseradish and beets will absorb, and place in covered jar or glass and it is ready for use. Will keep a long time.

PICKLED RED CABBAGE (HUNGARIAN STYLE)
Select a medium-size, very hard head of red cabbage. Remove the outer leaves and cut the stalk off close to the head. Then cut the cabbage in quarters and take out the heart close to the leaves. With a very sharp, thin-bladed knife cut the cabbage in shreds as fine as possible. After the cabbage is all finely cut let cold water run over it through a colander; put the cabbage in a big kitchen bowl or a stone-crock in layers about two inches thick. Over each layer place two or three thin slices of red onions, and sprinkle about four generous tablespoons of salt. Repeat this process till all the sliced cabbage is in the jar or bowl. Let the last layer be one of salt. Pour a pint of cold water over this. Cover it with a plate that fits closely and lay a weight of some sort on the plate and stand the bowl in a cool place overnight. In the morning pour the cabbage, brine and all, in a large colander to drain; let the cold water from the tap run over it for about five minutes; then return the cabbage to the receptacle in which it was salted. A stone-crock is really the best, as the cabbage will keep in it all winter. In a kettle or saucepan over the fire add a pint of good cider vinegar, a gill of tarragon vinegar, a half pint of cold water, a half pound of granulated sugar, four bay leaves, a level tablespoon of allspice, a teaspoon of peppercorns and three ounces of stick cinnamon broken in ½-inch pieces. Let this all boil one

minute and while boiling hot pour it over the cabbage in the jar; place the plate which should be of porcelain, over it; then put the cover of the jar on and let this stand for twenty-four hours. Then pour off the vinegar, heat it again till it just boils, pour it over the cabbage, cover it and put it in a cool place. It will keep in perfect condition all winter, and is one of the most delicious relishes known.

SAUERKRAUT

Line the bottom and sides of a clean barrel or keg with cabbage leaves. Cut into fine shreds one or two dozen large heads of white, crisp cabbage. Do this on a large slaw-cutter. Now begin to pack: First put in a layer of cabbage, say about four inches deep, and press down firmly and sprinkle with about four tablespoons of salt. Put one or two tart apples, cut up fine, between each layer, or some Malaga grapes (which will impart a fine flavor to the kraut). When four layers have been put in, pound with a wooden beetle until the cabbage is quite compact and then add more cabbage, and so on until all has been salted, always pounding down each layer. Last, cover with cabbage leaves, then a clean cloth, a well-fitting board, and a heavy stone, to act as weight on top of all. It is now ready to set away in a cool cellar to ferment. In two weeks examine, remove the scum, if any; wash the cloth, board and stone, wash also the sides of the keg or jar, and place all back again. This must be done weekly.

PASSOVER DISHES
CAKES, PUDDINGS, SAUCES, WINES, ETC.

How to set the table for the service of the "Seder" on the eve of Pesach or Passover.

Set the table as usual, have everything fresh and clean; a wineglass for each person, and an extra one placed near the platter of the man who conducts the seder. Then get a large napkin; fold it into four parts, set it on a plate, and in each fold put a perfect matzoh; that is, one that is not broken or unshapely; in short, one without a blemish. Then place the following articles on a platter: One hard-boiled egg, a lamb bone that has been roasted in ashes, the top of a nice stick of horseradish (it must be fresh and green), a bunch of nice curly parsley and some bitter herb (the Germans call it lattig), and, also, a small vessel filled with salt water. Pare and chop up a few apples, add sugar, cinnamon, pounded almonds, some white wine and grated lemon peel, and mix thoroughly. Place these dishes in front of the one that conducts the seder, and to his left place two pillows, nicely covered, and a small table or chair, on which has been placed a wash-bowl with a pitcher of water and clean towel. In some families hard-boiled eggs are distributed after the seder.

ROSEL, BEET VINEGAR

Place beets in a stone crock, removing greens. Cover with cold water and put in a warm place and let stand for three or four weeks or until the mixture becomes sour. This is used as a vinegar during Pesach and to make beet soup, Russian style.

RAISIN WINE, No. 1

To two pounds of raisins (cut in half if desired), add three quarts of cold water. Either place the mixture on a corner of the stove and let it simmer for two or three days or boil it until ⅓ of the water has evaporated. A few tablespoons of sugar and a handful of stick cinnamon can be added if additional sweetness and flavoring are wished. When cold strain through a fine cloth. The strength of the wine depends largely upon the quality of the raisins.

RAISIN WINE, No. 2

Take two pounds of raisins, seeded and chopped, one pound of white loaf sugar, and one lemon. Put all into a stone jar, pour six quarts of boiling water over all and stir every day for a week. Then strain and bottle. Ready for use in ten or twelve days.

YOM-TOV SOUP

Take two pounds of ribs of beef and one chicken. Place in a large cooking vessel with plenty of water and add a split carrot and onion, a head of celery, a little parsley root, pepper and salt to taste, and a pinch of saffron. Let the whole simmer for two hours. The meat is then removed and can be used as a separate dish.

MATZOTH MEAL KLEIS, No. 1

This is an accompaniment of the Yom-tov soup described above. To each tablespoon of matzoth meal take one egg. Beat the egg separately, adding a very little ground ginger, powdered cinnamon, ground almond, pepper and salt. Now stir in the matzoth meal and make into a paste with chicken fat or clarified dripping. Form this paste into small balls and boil them for twenty minutes in the Yom-tov soup.

PALESTINE SOUP

Three pounds of Jerusalem artichokes, two quarts of stock, one onion, one turnip, one head of celery, pepper and salt to taste. Peel and cut the vegetables into slices and boil them in stock until tender, then rub through a hair sieve. Beat the yolks of three eggs, add to the soup, and stir over the heat until just to the boiling point. The soup should be about the thickness of rich cream. If not thick enough, a little potato flour may be added.

POTATO FLOUR NOODLES

Take three eggs, beat until a light yellow and add ½ cup of potato flour and ½ cup of water, beat well. Heat a frying pan, grease well and pour in the batter; fry in thin leaves or wafers. Cool, cut thin as noodles. Just before serving soup, strain, then let it come to a boil and add noodles and let soup again come to a boil and serve.

MATZOTH MEAL NOODLES

Add ⅛ teaspoon of salt to two eggs, beat slightly, stir in two tablespoons of matzoth meal. Heat a little fat in sauce pan, pour in egg mixture; when cooked on one side turn on the other. Roll the pancake and cut into noodles ⅛ inch wide. Drop into boiling soup before serving.

MARROW DUMPLINGS

One tablespoon marrow creamed . Add a pinch of salt, little nutmeg and the yolk of one egg mixed in gradually; some finely chopped parsley and then enough matzoth meal to hold; wet the hands and roll the mixture into small balls. Add to the boiling soup, and boil fifteen minutes.

ALMOND BALLS

One-eighth pound of almonds chopped fine. Yolk of one egg, well beaten. Add almonds to egg, pinch of salt, little grated rind of lemon. Beat white of egg stiff, then mix all together. Drop a little from end of teaspoon into boiling fat. Put in soup just before serving.

MATZOTH MEAL KLEIS, No. 2

Beat one tablespoon of chicken Schmalz till quite white; pour one cup of boiling water over one egg. Add it to the dripping; stir these together, then add the flour, seasoning, a little chopped parsley, ginger, pepper and salt, and enough matzoth meal to form into small balls the size of a marble. Drop these into the boiling soup and cook about fifteen minutes. Test one in boiling water and if it boils apart add more meal.

MATZOTH KLEIS, No. 1

Soak four matzoth in cold water and press them after being thoroughly saturated. Add a little pepper, salt, sugar, parsley, and a half onion chopped fine, first browning the onion. Beat four eggs and add all together. Then put in enough matzoth meal so that it may be rolled into balls. The less meal used the lighter will be the balls. They should boil for twenty minutes before serving. Serve matzoth kleis in place of potatoes and garnish with minced onions browned in three tablespoons of fat. All matzoth meal and matzoth kleis are lighter if made a few hours before required and put in the ice chest until ready to boil. When used as a vegetable make the balls considerably larger than for soup.

MATZOTH KLEIS, No. 2

Take six matzoth, three eggs, two cooking-spoons of chicken fat, parsley, onion, salt, pepper and ginger. Soak the matzoth in boiling water a minute, then drain every drop of water out of them. press through sieve. Fry about three onions in the two tablespoons of chicken fat, and when a light brown, put the matzoth in the sauce pan with the fat and onions to dry them. Add one teaspoon of salt, dash of pepper and ginger and one tablespoon of chopped parsley. Add the three yolks of eggs and beat all this together a few minutes; last, add the well-beaten whites. Form into balls by rolling into a little matzoth meal. Drop in boiling salt water and boil fifteen minutes; drain and pour over them hot fat with an onion, cut fine and browned.

FILLED MATZOTH KLEIS

Prepare a matzoth dough as for the soup kleis. Make round flat cakes of it with your hands, and fill with cooked prunes (having previously removed the kernels). Put one of the flat cakes over one that is filled, press the edges firmly together and roll until perfectly round. Boil them in salt water--the water must boil hard before you put them in. Heat some goose fat, cut up an onion in it and brown; pour this over the kleis and serve hot. The kleis may be filled with a cheese mixture. Use butter in that case.

ENGLISH LEMON STEWED FISH

Have washed and scraped clean the nape or head and shoulders of halibut, a shad, or any good firm fish; cut it up small and lay it in a stew-pan with one pint of water and three or four good sized onions, fried in oil a light brown; put them on top of the fish with a pinch of cayenne pepper, and a teaspoon of ground ginger, with two teaspoons of salt; let it all stew gently until it is done; if there should be too much gravy on it before adding the sauce, take some off. Prepare two eggs and six good sized lemons, squeezed and strained; then take some of the gravy from the fish while it is boiling, add it to the lemon, with the two eggs well beaten, and a tablespoon of potato flour; mix smoothly with some chopped parsley; when all is well mixed, add it to the fish, shake it gently for five minutes while it is boiling, taking care not to let it burn; when it is sufficiently cooked let it stand for an hour and serve it. Garnish with slices of lemon and parsley. To be eaten cold.

SOLE WITH WINE (FRENCH RECIPE)
Take a sole or fillets of any delicate fish. Lay on a fireproof dish, sprinkle with white pepper, salt and a little shallot, cover with claret or white wine, and let it cook in the oven till done. Draw off the liquor in a saucepan and let it boil up. Have ready the yolks of three eggs, well stirred (not beaten), the juice of a lemon, and two ounces of butter. Put all together in a bowl. Little by little add the hot sauce, stirring all the time. Pour it over the fish, and sprinkle with chopped parsley. Serve very hot. A few mushrooms are a palatable addition to this dish.

RED MULLET IN CASES
To four mullets allow one dozen button mushrooms, one tablespoon of finely chopped parsley, two shallots, the juice of a lemon, salt and pepper. Oil some pieces of foolscap paper, lay the fish on them and sprinkle over them the mushroom, parsley, shallot, lemon juice, pepper and salt. Fold them in the cases and cook on a well-greased baking sheet in a 350° oven for about twenty or thirty minutes. Send to the table in cases very hot.

CHRIMSEL, No. 1
Sift one cup of matzoth meal in a bowl, stir into it one cup of boiling soup stock or wine. When mixed add one tablespoon of chopped almonds, one teaspoon of sugar, a pinch of salt and the yolks of four eggs well beaten; then add the stiffly beaten whites of the four eggs and fry by tablespoonsfuls in boiling hot butter or goose grease. Sprinkle with powdered sugar and serve with wine sauce.

CHRIMSEL, No. 2

Soak about three matzoth. In the meantime seed a handful of raisins and pound as many almonds as you have raisins. Now press every drop of water out of the matzoth, put them in a bowl and stir them to a cream; add a pinch of salt, the peel of a lemon, yolks of four eggs and a cup of sugar, the raisins and almonds, and also a little cinnamon. Heat some oil in a sauce pan; the more fat the lighter the chrimsel will be. Last add the stiffly beaten whites to the dough. Then fry a light brown on both sides; use about a tablespoonful of batter for each chrimsel; serve with stewed prunes. Lay the chrimsel on a large platter and pour the prunes over all. Eat hot.

KENTUCKY CHRIMSEL

Two and one-half cups of meal, four eggs, two cups of sugar, one kitchenspoon of goose fat, one of beef fat, four apples, and spices according to taste. One glass of wine also, if convenient. Put the meal in a bowl with salt, pepper, ground, clove, allspice, and cinnamon mixed into it; peel and grate the apples, melt the fat and mix, put in eggs and then stir in the sugar which has been boiled with water to a thin syrup and cooled off. Hollow out two pieces, put cranberries or any fruit between them; form into balls the size of a medium apple, and bake them at 350° on a well-greased pie plate for about one hour.

MATZOTH WITH SCRAMBLED EGGS (ÜBERSCHLAGENE MATZOTH)

Break six matzoth in small pieces in a colander. Pour boiling water through them, drain quickly. They should be moist but not soggy. Beat three whole eggs well, fold the matzoth in lightly. Heat four tablespoons of goose fat or oil in a sauce pan, add the egg mixture; scrape and scramble carefully with spoon from the bottom of the pan and while scrambling add four tablespoons of sugar and cook gently until eggs are set. Serve at once. The sugar may be omitted if so desired.

SCRAMBLED MATZOTH

Soak six matzoth in water until soft. Squeeze out the water and mix with four beaten eggs. Add ½ teaspoon of salt and fry.

MATZOTH DIPPED IN EGGS, No. 1

Beat up as many eggs as are required; into these dip matzoth that have been soaked in milk. Fry quickly to a light brown on both sides, lay on a large platter, sprinkle with a mixture of sugar, cinnamon and grated peel of a lemon. The more eggs used the richer this will be. Fry in butter.

MATZOTH DIPPED IN EGGS, No. 2

Beat six eggs very light, add one-half tablespoon of salt. Heat two tablespoons of goose fat or olive oil in a sauce pan. Break four matzoth into large, equal pieces. Dip each piece in the egg mixture and fry a light brown on both sides. Serve hot, sprinkled with sugar, cinnamon and a little grated lemon rind.

ZWIEBEL MATZOTH

As an appetizer nothing is better than a cake of unleavened bread rubbed with a raw onion, sprinkled lightly with salt and placed in the oven for a few minutes to dry. Buttered and eaten hot, it adds a relish to breakfast or tea.

MATZOTH EIRKUCHEN

Pour ½ cup of water on ¼ cup matzoth meal, add one teaspoon of salt and beat the yolks of four eggs very light, add to the meal mixture, let stand five minutes. Beat whites of eggs very stiffly, fold lightly into the yolk mixture. Drop mixture by spoonfuls in small cakes on hot greased sauce pan. Turn when brown and brown on other side. Serve with sugar, jelly or preserves.

MATZOTH MEAL MACAROONS

Beat egg yolk separately. Add one teaspoon of matzoth meal and pinch of salt. Whip white to a snow, fold in the whites, and fry by tablespoonfuls in butter or fat and serve with prunes.

PIE CRUST

Soak 1½ matzoth and press dry; heat one tablespoon of fat and add the soaked matzoth. When dry add ½ cup of matzoth meal, two eggs, two tablespoons of sugar and ⅛ teaspoon of salt. Mix well and press into pie plate with hands, as it is impossible to roll the dough. Have dough ¼ inch thick.

MAMOURAS (TURKISH)
Dip in boiling salted water for one minute, one matzoth for each person to be served. Put the soaked matzoth in a dish, pour over it a little olive oil and grated cheese and repeat this until you have made as many layers as you have persons to serve; cut in slices and serve. Use Hashkeval - Greek Cheese.

GERMAN PUFFS
Into ½ pint of water put ¼ pound of melted fat; when boiling add one-quarter pound of meal, finely sifted; it will form a thick paste. Beat up four eggs, remove the mixture from the fire and stir in the eggs. Grease some cups and put a spoonful in each; bake in a 400° oven. When done sprinkle with cinnamon and cover with clarified sugar.

STEWED SWEETBREADS
Soak one pair of sweetbreads for two or three hours in sufficient warm water to cover them, then drain. Put them in a stew-pan, with boiling water to cover them, and then boil gently for seven or eight minutes. They are then ready for dressing. Lay the sweetbreads in a stew-pan, pour two cups of veal stock over them, add salt and cayenne pepper to taste, and simmer gently for one hour. Lift them out on to a very hot dish, add juice of ½ lemon and one teaspoon of potato flour to the gravy, stir smoothly, and boil up, pour over the sweetbreads and serve at once.

BEEFSTEAK PIE
Cut up two pounds of chuck steak; put it on to stew with salt, pepper and a little nutmeg and the juice of a lemon. Cook a few forcemeat balls, made very small, and a few potatoes cut in small pieces. Make ready a crust as follows: Boil four or five large floury potatoes; when done, strain and mash with salt and pepper, a little chopped parsley and a little melted fat; mix it with two well-beaten eggs; then put a layer of it

around the bottom and sides of a deep pie dish; lay in the stew, cover with the balance of the potato; brush it over with the yolk of an egg and bake in a quick oven till brown.

POTATO PLUM KNÖDEL (HUNGARIAN)
Peel and cook seven or eight large potatoes, place in a bowl, add salt, four whole eggs, one and one-half tablespoons of melted chicken fat and a little more than a cup of matzoth meal. Knead in bowl to smooth consistency. Take a handful at a time, pat smooth and flat, in the center put a tablespoon of prune jam, form into a dumpling, place dumplings in boiling salt water, kettle half covered and allow to cook twelve to fifteen minutes. Take out with strainer and serve hot. Have ready a cup of hot melted chicken fat and sugar and cinnamon. Serve over Knödel to taste.

BIRMOILIS (TURKISH)
Take some mashed potatoes, grated cheese, well-beaten eggs; make a good paste, take tablespoonfuls of this mixture and drop in boiling oil; fry until brown. Serve with a syrup made of sugar and water.

POTATO MARBLES
Mix ½ pound of plain mashed potatoes smoothly with a generous teaspoon of finely chopped parsley, pepper and salt to taste; beat one egg, add it to the potato, mix well and make it into little balls the size of a cherry. Lay a tiny sprig of parsley on each, arrange the balls on a greased tin and bake at 400° until a light brown.

MINA (TURKISH)
Place some matzoth in cold water to soak. Take the matzoth out and dry them on a towel; grease a pan with olive oil and put in matzoth enough to cover bottom of pan. Take chopped meat, bind with an egg, season with salt, pepper, and chopped parsley. Cover this with the matzoth, add some olive oil, cover with mashed potatoes and one or two well-beaten eggs and bake until brown. If so desired the meat may be omitted. Grated cheese may be used, covered with mashed potatoes and eggs.

PRUNE BLINTZES

Take three cups of potato flour mixed with three eggs, add a little water and mix well. Heat a small frying pan, grease with a little fat and pour into it enough batter to make thin pancakes. Chop prunes, add a little sugar and fill each cake with this mixture, fold into three-cornered pieces and fry. When done put in a pan, sprinkle with sugar and bake in oven. Do not let burn.

MEAT BLINTZES

The same pancakes can be used with meat taken from soup; fry two small onions with a little fat and chop with the meat. Add two eggs, salt and pepper to taste.

MATZOTH SPICE CAKE

To every egg add ½ tablespoon of matzoth meal and one tablespoon of sugar. Sift meal five times, mix with sugar, ½ tablespoon of ground ginger, ½ tablespoon of cinnamon, ¼ tablespoon of cloves; mix with the well-beaten yolks and cut and fold in gently the stiffly beaten whites.

MATZOTH MEAL CAKE

To the yolks of eight eggs add 1½ cups of pulverized sugar; stir until the consistency of batter, add the grated rind of a lemon, two teaspoons of ground cinnamon and two squares of chocolate grated, one teaspoon of allspice; add the juice of an orange, and ½ wine-glass of wine, and ¾ cup of matzoth meal finely sifted, and ¼ pound almonds finely pounded. Last, fold in the stiffly beaten whites of the eggs. Bake in a 350° oven for forty-five minutes; try with a straw.

MATZOTH CHARLOTTE, No. 1

Soak one matzoth; beat and add to the beaten yolks of two eggs, add ¼ teaspoon of salt, ¼ cup of chopped almonds, one-fourth cup of raisins, ¼ cup of currants, and mix thoroughly. Fold in the stiffly beaten whites of two eggs and bake in a greased baking dish.

MATZOTH CHARLOTTE, No. 2

Four eggs (yolks), one cup of sugar, pinch of salt, three matzoth (soaked in water and squeezed out), one grated apple, one lemon rind and juice, ¼ cup of almonds, and ¼ cup of raisins. Put the stiffly beaten whites of eggs in last, before putting into oven. Bake in an 350° oven about ½ to ¾ an hour. To be eaten warm.

MATZOTH KUGEL

Soak three matzoth, heat two tablespoons of fat in a sauce pan, press all the water out of the matzoth with your hands and dry them in the sauce pan of heated fat; add about ¼ pound of matzoth meal; stir the matzoth and matzoth meal well with a large spoon; add by degrees the yolks of five eggs and two ounces of pounded almonds, and the grated peel of ½ lemon. Add also one large sour apple, grated, a pinch of salt, and last the stiffly beaten whites of the eggs. Line a kugeltopf well with fat, and pour about a quarter pound of hot fat over the kugel. Bake immediately; serve with wine sauce.

MATZOTH SHALET

Four soaked matzoth, nine eggs, one cup of sugar, two grated apples, 1½ cups of seeded raisins, one tablespoon of cinnamon, grated rind of an orange or a lemon and a few pounded almonds. Beat the sugar, eggs, and cinnamon until light; then add all the ingredients, except the matzoth, mixing well. Now drain the matzoth, gradually adding them to the mixture, beating until very light. Melt ½ pound of rendered fat into the dish for baking, and then pour in the mixture. Bake in a 350° oven for one hour. Serve hot with wine, fruit, or prune sauce.

POTATO PUDDING

Stir the yolks of eight eggs with a cup of sugar, add four tablespoons of blanched and pounded almonds, and grate in the peel of a lemon. Add also its juice. Have ready ½ pound of grated potatoes that have been cooked the day previous. Last, add the stiffly beaten whites. Add one teaspoon of salt. Grease your pudding form well, pour in the mixture and bake. Set in a pan of boiling water in the oven. The water in the pan must not reach higher than half way up the pudding form. Time required, half an hour. When done turn out on a platter. Serve with a wine or chocolate sauce. You may bake this pudding in an iron pudding form without setting it in the boiling water.

MATZOTH PLUM PUDDING
One-half pound of chopped suet, ½ pound of moist sugar, ½ pound of raisins (stoned and chopped), ½ pound of currants, ½ pound of mixed peel, two matzoth soaked in cold water and then well drained and beaten, one-quarter pound of sifted meal, the rind of ½ lemon, one teaspoon of ground cinnamon, eight eggs and a wineglass of rum. Beat all these ingredients thoroughly together, and boil for eight hours in a pudding mold or basin. Serve with rum sauce.

BATTER PUDDING
One teacup of matzoth-meal, one pint of milk, two eggs, three ounces of brown sugar, two ounces of butter and the rind of a lemon. Mix the meal into a batter with the milk and eggs, add the sugar, butter (melted), grated rind of a lemon and a tablespoon of rum, if desired. Pour the mixture in a greased basin or mold, and boil for one hour or bake for ½ hour.

BEOLAS
Take six eggs. Beat them until very light. Add a little fine meal, just enough to give it consistency. Drop this from the point of a spoon into boiling olive oil or fat. When light brown, take out, and drain. Serve cold with a syrup made of water, cinnamon and sugar.

COCONUT PUDDING
One grated coconut, six eggs, grated rind and juice of two lemons, one cup of granulated sugar and the milk of the coconut; beat the yolks of the eggs with the sugar and the grated rind of lemon until light and creamy; add gradually the coconut and the beaten whites of the eggs, and lastly put in the milk of the coconut, to which has been added the juice of the lemons. Bake in a 350° oven for ½ hour and serve quite cold.

CARROT PUDDING

Beat 1½ cups of powdered sugar and the yolks of eight eggs; take 1½ cups peeled and grated raw carrots and stir all together. Add one cup of grated almonds, the rind of half a lemon chopped finely, one tablespoon of wine, and last the beaten whites of the eggs. Bake in a well-buttered and flour-sprinkled form at least one hour in a 325° oven.

ALMOND PUDDING, No. 1

Take the whites of seven eggs with the yolks of ten, ½ pound of pulverized sweet almonds with ½ ounce of pounded bitter almonds, ½ pound of powdered sugar and one tablespoon of orange-flower water. Beat the eggs well with the orange water, then add the sugar and almonds gradually; beat all for one hour or until it bubbles; then grease deep pie-dishes with olive oil and pour in the mixture. They must be baked in a 350° oven. When the mixture is set and browned place over them a paper greased with olive oil to prevent them getting dark. Serve cold. Powdered sugar should be sprinkled freely over the pudding before serving. If you wish to have them very rich boil ½ pound of sugar with ½ pint of water until it thickens; cool and pour over the pudding when you take it from the oven.

ALMOND PUDDING, No. 2

Take one pound blanched almonds pounded, eight eggs, cinnamon, and lemon rind. Beat the eggs for twenty minutes, then add 1½ cups of sugar gently, and then the almonds; mix all together thoroughly. Bake in shallow pans and serve cold.

ALMOND HILLS

Roast ¼ pound of sweet almonds, cut into strips lengthwise in a sauce pan of heated sugar, not too brown. Beat ½ pound of sifted powdered sugar and the whites of five eggs to a very stiff froth. Mix all thoroughly and place teaspoonfuls of this mixture on waxed paper, and bake a light brown, in 325° oven.

APPLE SPONGE PUDDING

Pare eight apples and cut off the tops carefully, so as to be able to use them as covers to the apples. Now scrape out the inside with a knife, being careful not to break the apple. Mix the scrapings with sugar, raisins, cinnamon, pounded almonds and a little white wine. Fill this mixture into the hollow of the apple and clap on a cover for each apple; then grease a pudding dish, lay in the apples and stew them for a few minutes, but not long enough to break them. Make a sponge cake batter of eight eggs and two scant cups of sugar and a pinch of salt and add the grated peel of a lemon and beat until thick, at least half an hour. Fold in a cup of matzoth flour, sifted very fine. Pour this batter over the apples and bake in a 350° oven. Serve with wine sauce. Half this quantity is sufficient for a small family.

GRATED APPLE PUDDING
Take six good-sized apples, six yolks of eggs, ½ cup of sugar (or to taste), ½ pound of grated almonds, or ½ cup of matzoth-meal, ½ teaspoon of salt, ½ teaspoon of cinnamon. Pare the apples and leave them whole. Then grate all the apple from the pulp. To this add the above, also about three tablespoons of chicken or goose grease. When all is well mixed, add the whites well beaten to a stiff froth. Mix very light. Bake in well-greased baking dish at 350°.

APPLE PUDDING
Soak three matzoth and squeeze the water out well; put them in a bowl with three good-sized apples cut in small thick pieces; add ¼ pound of currants, ¼ pound of raisins, a little cinnamon, some rind of lemon cut thin, ¼ pound of brown sugar and two ounces of melted fat; mix all well together with six beaten eggs; pour in a greased dish and bake in a 350° oven. This pudding can be boiled if preferred. Serve with rum sauce.

FOAM TORTE
Four egg whites, well beaten; add one tablespoon of vinegar drop by drop, one cup of sugar, one tablespoon of vanilla; beat for twenty minutes. Line spring form with this batter on all sides. Reserve a little of the mixture and drop by drops on top of torte. Let bake forty-five minutes in 350° oven; when baked remove. Serve with sliced bananas, peaches and cream or strawberries.

SPONGE CAKE, No. 1

Take eight eggs, one pound of granulated sugar, grated rind of a lemon, and six ounces of fine matzoth-meal. Beat the eggs, sugar and lemon rind together until very light, to about the thickness of a custard, then add the meal, stirring it in without much beating. Bake in a 375° oven one-half hour.

SPONGE CAKE, No. 2

Take eight eggs, 1½ cups of granulated sugar, one cup of mixed matzoth-meal and potato flour and flavoring to taste. Beat the yolks of the eggs and the sugar together until very light. Then add the flavoring, matzoth-meal and potato flour and last of all the whites of the eggs beaten to a stiff froth. Stir lightly and bake in a 375° oven.

POTATO FLOUR SPONGE CAKE

Separate the whites and yolks of nine eggs. Beat the whites of seven eggs very stiff. To the well-beaten yolks of nine eggs and the whites of two, add 1¾ cups of sugar and juice and rind of one lemon. Beat thoroughly, add one scant cup of potato flour, and beat again. Now fold in the beaten whites very carefully, and bake slowly in a 350° oven. Bake forty to fifty minutes.

STRAWBERRY SHORTCAKE WITH MATZOTH-MEAL

Beat until very light the yolks of four eggs and three-quarters of a cup sugar; add rind of ½ lemon, a pinch of salt, ½ cup of sifted matzoth meal, and last the stiffly beaten whites of the eggs. Bake in two shallow square pans in a 350° oven. When cold lay a cake on a platter, spread thickly with strawberries that have been well sugared. Put the other cake on top. Spread over the top and sides with cream that has been sweetened, flavored and whipped very stiff.

HASTY PUDDING

Take any kind of old cake, cut up in slices, dip in wine or sprinkle some wine over all. Make a custard with one pint of milk and four eggs. Put one tablespoon of potato flour with the yolks, sweeten to taste, boil the custard, flavor and pour over cake in pudding dish. Beat whites to a stiff froth, add sugar and spread over all. Put in oven to brown slightly. Eat cold.

POTATO FLOUR PUDDING
Take ¼ pound of goose oil, stir it to a cream and stir in gradually the yolks of ten eggs and three-quarters of a pound of sifted sugar, the grated peel of a lemon, also its juice and one-half teaspoon of salt. Add last ½ pound of potato flour and the stiffly beaten whites of the eggs. Have the pudding form well greased before putting in the mixture. Bake in a 350° oven. Serve with raspberry sauce, made of jelly. Take a glass of red raspberries, press them through a hair sieve, add a wineglass of red wine, add sugar to taste, and let it boil hard for about five minutes.

PESACH CAKE WITH WALNUTS
Cream together the yolks of nine eggs, and ½ pound of powdered sugar, weigh one pound of walnuts before shelling; when shelled, grind; to the creamed yolks and sugar add two tablespoons of well sifted matzoth flour, a pinch of salt, and one teaspoon of vanilla, then mix in the ground walnuts. Fold in gently the nine beaten whites. Bake three-quarters of an hour.

DATE CAKE
Eight eggs, 1¼ cups of pulverized sugar, two tablespoons of ground cinnamon and cloves mixed, one cup of matzoth-meal, ½ pound seeded dates, cut fine, and the juice of ½ lemon. Beat the yolks of the eggs and sugar together until very light, add the matzoth meal, spices, dates and lemon, and finally put in the whites of the eggs, beaten to a stiff froth. Bake in a 350° oven three-quarters of an hour.

CHOCOLATE CAKE
Beat the yolks of four eggs with ½ cup of sifted sugar, add ¼ pound of grated sweet almonds, ¼ pound of finely-grated vanilla chocolate, and ¼ pound of raisins, ½ cup of matzoth meal sifted fine, juice of an orange, ¼ cup of wine, and lastly the stiffly beaten whites. Bake one hour in a 325° oven, in a form lined with greased paper.

COOKIES

Sift together ½ cup of matzoth meal and ¼ cup of potato flour. Add ½ cup of sugar, ¼ cup of chopped almonds and two eggs. Roll out in potato flour mixed with sugar. Cut and bake on greased tins in a 400° oven.

ALMOND CAKE

One pound of almonds, pounded; one pound of sugar, one or two eggs and enough cinnamon to give a strong flavor. Bake in a shallow pan and cut into small sections.

ALMOND MACAROONS

One pound of almonds ground fine, 1½ pounds of powdered sugar, the whites of five eggs and the grated rind of two lemons. Beat the whites of eggs to a snow, add the sugar and the grated lemon rind and almonds; mix it well together. Grease a very thin paper with olive oil, sprinkle some powdered sugar over it, place on a tin. Form the cakes and place them a little distance from each other and bake in a 350° oven. When done let them cool before you touch them.

CINNAMON STICKS

Grate ½ pound of almonds, beat the whites of four eggs to a stiff froth, add gradually one pound of pulverized sugar and a tablespoon of cinnamon. Roll out this dough into half finger lengths and about as thick as your little finger. Bake, and when done ice each one with boiled frosting.

IMBERLACH

Take two cups of matzoth flour, ¼ pound of powdered ginger, mix together with three eggs. Set this dough aside until it dries. Take ½ pound of honey and ¾ pound of sugar and boil until it gets a reddish color. Beat in the ginger and matzoth dough, mix it with honey, set back on stove, stirring constantly; when the mixture is thick and a reddish color, place on the board so as to cool; roll and cut in two-inch lengths.

KREMSLEKH

To each tablespoon of matzoth-meal take one egg, a pinch of salt, ½ teaspoon of sugar, a teaspoon of ground almonds, a few stoned and chopped raisins, a pinch of ground cinnamon, a spoon of oil, or its equivalent of beef dripping, and just enough water to make the whole into a stiff paste. Mix the ingredients very thoroughly. Now take a large enameled saucepan and about half fill it with oil or fat. Bring this to boiling point but do not let it burn. Shape the paste into small pieces and drop them into boiling fat, turning them continually until well browned and then take out and drain carefully on a strainer. May be eaten hot or cold.

EGG MARMALADE
Make a thick syrup by dissolving one pound of sugar in ½ pint of water over the fire, adding one ounce of pounded almonds while the syrup is clarifying. Take the saucepan off the heat and when the contents have become moderately cool stir in carefully the well-beaten yolks of twenty eggs. It will need rather prolonged stirring to blend the eggs with the syrup. Now flavor with vanilla or wine and cook over a slow fire, stirring constantly and taking great care that the mixture does not burn.

RADISH PRESERVES (RUSSIAN STYLE)
Take black radishes, clean and cut them in strips. Weigh, and to three pounds of radishes take one pound of honey and 1½ pounds of sugar. Set the radishes on to boil with water, pour off this water, add fresh water and let cook awhile; pour off the second water, add the honey to radishes and let cook well. Then add the sugar and let cook again. When the radishes begin to get brown add one-quarter pound of white ginger, and some walnuts broken into quarters. Stir. When brown, remove from stove. Must come out of the pan dry; no syrup must remain.

BEET PRESERVES (RUSSIAN)
Cut beets in strips like noodles, wash, cook in water one-half hour. To three pounds of beets take one pound of honey and one pound of sugar. When the beets have cooked on slow fire until white, strain off and add the honey. Let cook well and add sugar; cook, add white ginger to taste, stirring continually, add ¼ pound of almonds, cut in slices; one-quarter of an hour before being done, mix, and when the beets brown put in jars.

PRUNES

Wash the prunes well, first in warm water, then in cold. Cut up half a lemon, some stick cinnamon and sugar to taste. Cook them in the oven, covered tight, allowing a liberal quantity of water; stew slowly for two hours; thicken with a teaspoon of potato flour, and wet the potato flour with the juice of an orange before adding. If the prunes are for chrimsel, leave out the thickening.

LEMON PRESERVES

Take seven lemons, slice thin and remove seeds. Draw string through slices, fasten ends, lay them in a pan with water; boil a short time, remove the lemon, pour off water; cook two pounds of sugar with two cups of water. When the sugar is syrupy add ½ pound of large raisins, put in the lemon and let cook until the syrup is thick.

CANDIED LEMON AND ORANGE PEEL

Lemon and orange peel if saved can be put to excellent use. Take out the greater portion of the white inside; throw the rinds into boiling water and simmer gently for twenty minutes. Drain, weigh, and take a pound of sugar to every pound of peel. Put a layer of sugar and a layer of fruit into the preserving kettle; stand it over a slow fire until the sugar melts. When melted, cook slowly until the rinds are transparent. Lift them out; drain them and when nearly dry roll in granulated sugar.

WINE SAUCE

One cup of white wine, ½ cup of water, grated peel of lemon, teaspoon of potato flour wet with cold water, add the yolks of two eggs, stirring constantly; when thick, add the beaten whites and serve.

RUM SAUCE

Beat yolks of two eggs with a tablespoon of sugar, and a small cup of cold water, a wineglass of rum and the juice of a lemon, and bring to boiling point, stirring all the time. The two whites of eggs may be whipped very firm and spread over the pudding just before serving.

SUGAR SYRUP
Two cups of brown sugar, one cup of boiling water, and cinnamon to taste. Stir the ingredients together in a saucepan until the sugar is dissolved and then let the mixture simmer slowly until it thickens.

MOCK WHIPPED CREAM FILLING
Use between and on top of layer cakes, or as a filling for torten. Peel and grate one large sour apple, three-quarters cup of white sugar, white of one egg; beat all together a long time, flavor with vanilla or grated rind of one-half lemon. Mix the apple with the sugar as soon as possible or it will turn dark.

LEMON CREAM FILLING
Put on to boil the yolks of five eggs, ½ cup of granulated sugar, the juice of three lemons and grated rind of one, and about a brandy glass of water. Stir constantly so as to prevent curdling. When it has thickened and comes to a boil take it from the stove and add the beaten whites of eggs.

FILLING FOR CHRIMSEL
This is made of unblanched, pounded almonds, grated apples, chopped raisins, brown sugar, plenty of cinnamon and the grated rind of a lemon. Mix the ingredients together and fill the hollowed out center of the chrimsel with them. Then place one chrimsel upon another, being careful not to let the filling escape from its hollow and fasten the edges securely together with the fingers, keeping the rounded shape uninjured. Fry them in boiling fat, turning them from one side to the other until a dark brown. Serve hot with sugar syrup.

STRAWBERRY DESSERT
Line a dish with macaroons, wet them with wine, put over this a box or quart of strawberries, and sugar them well. Beat the yolks of four eggs with one small cup of sugar, grated rind of lemon and half its juice . Beat the whites to a stiff froth, and half the yolks; pour over all in your pudding dish. When baked spread the other half of the whites on top, having previously sweetened the remaining whites with sugar. Bake a light brown. Eat cold with whipped or plain cream.

Notes

INDEX

ABGERUEHRTER KUGELHOPF.....220
AGRISTOGA SAUCE.....58
AHILADO SAUCE (TURKISH).....54
ALMOND
    BALLS.....344
    CAKE.....358
    CAKE OR MANDEL TORTE, No. 2.....260
    CAKE OR MANDELTORTE, No. 1.....260
    HILLS.....354
    MACAROONS.....358
    MACAROONS WITH FIGS.....289
    MACAROONS, No. 1.....289
    MACAROONS, No. 2.....289
    PUDDING.....307
    PUDDING, No. 1.....354
    PUDDING, No. 2.....354
    STICKS.....290
    STICKS - FLEISCHIG.....290
    CREAM SOUP.....35
    SALTED.....21
AMASTICH.....100
AMBROSIA.....20
AMBROSIA.....298
ANCHOVY
    CANAPÉS.....6
    CANAPÉS WITH TOMATOES.....16
    SANDWICHES.....22
    SAUCE.....66
ANISE SEED COOKIES (SPRINGELE).....287
ANISE ZWIEBACK.....291
APPETIZER.....18
APPLE
    AND HONEY PUDDING.....304
    AND LADYFINGER PUDDING.....299
    BAKED.....170
    BAKED WITH OATMEAL.....192
    CAKE (KUCHEN).....228
    COMPOTE.....170
    CUSTARD PIE.....276
    DELIGHT.....169
    DUMPLINGS.....275
    DUMPLINGS, BOILED.....181
    FLADEN (HUNGARIAN).....272
    FLOAT.....169
    FRIED.....170
    FRITTERS.....241
    FROSTED.....169

APPLE (continued)
    GRATED PUDDING.....355
    JELLY.....337
    KUGEL.....185
    PIE, GRATED.....275
    PIE, No. 1.....275
    PIE, No. 2.....275
    PUDDING.....355
    SAUCE.....68
    SAUCE VICTORIA.....171
    SCHALET, No. 1.....185
    SCHALET, No. 2.....186
    SLUMP.....181
    SLUMP.....305
    SNOW.....297
    SPONGE PUDDING.....354
    STEAMED SWEET.....170
    STRUDEL, No. 1.....188
    STRUDEL, No. 2.....189
    TAPIOCA PUDDING.....301
    TORTE, BREMEN.....259
    WITH RICE.....195
APRICOT ICE.....319
APRICOT, PEACH, STRAWBERRY, BANANA OR PINE APPLE CREAM.....315
ARDAY-INFLUS.....124
ARME RITTER.....218
ARTICHOKES (FRENCH OR GLOBE).....109
ASPARAGUS.....109
ASPARAGUS OR CAULIFLOWER (HUNGARIAN).....113
ASPARAGUS SALAD.....153
ASPARAGUS, CREAM OF SOUP.....35
ASPIC (SULZ).....81
AUFLAUF.....300

BABA Á LA PARISIENNE.....222
BAKED BEANS WITH BRISKET OF BEEF.....143
BAKED HASH.....91
BAKING POWDER BATTERS.....231
BAKING POWDER DUMPLINGS.....44
BANANA DAINTY.....160
BANANA FILLING.....267
BANANAS.....167
BANANAS, CHILLED.....167
BANBURY TARTS.....272
BARCHES.....213
BARLEY AND VEGETABLE SOUP.....41
BARLEY SOUP.....33
BARLEY, TAPIOCA, SAGO.....194

BASELER LOEKERLEIN (HONEY CAKES).....293
BASS Á LA WELLINGTON, BAKED.....58
BASS, BAKED BLACK.....57
BATTER PUDDING.....353
BAYRISCHE DAMPFNUDELN, No. 1.....180
BAYRISCHE DAMPFNUDELN, No. 2.....181
BEANS
- & BARLEY.....143
- BAKED WITH BRISKET OF BEEF.....143
- HARICOT AND BEEF.....143
- SPANISH.....146
- STRING OR GREEN SNAP.....134
- STRING SALAD.....154
- SWEET SOUR.....134
- SWEET SOUR AND LINZEN.....143
- WITH LAMB.....134
- WITH TOMATOES.....134

BEARNAISE SAUCE.....64
BEARNAISE SAUCE, QUICK.....64
BEEF
- PAN ROAST.....85
- ROLLED – POT ROASTED.....87
- SMOKED.....93
- SMOKED BRISKET OF AND EGGS.....205
- SPANISH SHORT RIB OF.....89
- STEAK PIE.....349
- STEAK, FRIED.....88

BEER SOUP.....39
BEER SOUP (PARVE).....41
BEET
- AND CAULIFLOWER SALAD.....154
- AND HORSERADISH RELISH.....340
- BAKED.....111
- BOILED.....111
- GREENS.....111
- PRESERVES (RUSSIAN).....359
- SALAD.....153
- SOUP - RUSSIAN (FLEISCHIG).....28
- SOUP (RUSSIAN).....41
- SOUR BUTTERED.....111

BELGIAN RED CABBAGE.....120
BELL FRITTERS.....241
BEOLAS.....353
BERLINER PFANNKUCHEN (PURIM KRAPFEN).....223
BIRD'S NEST PUDDING.....305
BIRMOILIS (TURKISH).....350
BIRNE KLÖßE.....182
BISCUIT TORTONI, No. 1.....316
BISCUIT TORTONI, No. 2.....316
BISCUIT, DROP.....233

BISCUITS, BAKING POWDER.....233
BISCUITS, SOUR MILK.....233
BITKI (RUSSIAN HAMBURGER STEAK).....91
BLACK BEAN SOUP.....40
BLACK BREAD PUDDING.....305
BLACK OLIVES.....16
BLACKBERRY AND CURRANT PIE.....276
BLACKBERRY CORDIAL.....332
BLACKBERRY JELLY.....335
BLACKBERRY WINE.....332
BLANC MANGE.....296
BLÄTTERTEIG.....269
BLINTZES.....241
BLINTZES, CHEESE.....240
BLINTZES, MEAT.....351
BLINTZES, SWEET.....240
BLITZKUCHEN.....250
BLUEBERRIES.....167
BOHEMIAN CREAM.....297
BOHEMIAN KOLATCHEN.....226
BOHEMIAN SALAD.....154
BOLA.....221
BORDELAISE SAUCE.....68
BORSHT.....28
BOSTON ROAST.....148
BOUILLON.....29
BRAIN
    APPETIZER.....16
    CALF'S (SOUR).....76
    CALF'S FRIED.....76
    DEVILED.....77
    SALAD.....165
    SWEET AND SOUR.....76
    WITH EGG SAUCE.....77
BRANDY SAUCE....311
BRAUNE MEHLSUPPE-BROWN FLOUR SOUP No.1.....38
BREAD
    BRAN....232
    CRUMBS....71
    PUDDING....304
    STICKS....217
    GLUTEN....213
    GRAHAM....213
    PANCAKES....239
    POTATO....213
    POTATO-RYE....214
    RAISIN....214
    ROLLED OATS....214
    RYE (AMERICAN) No. 1....215
    RYE No. 2.....215

BREAD continued
  VARIETY.....216
  WHITE.....211
  WHITE NUT.....232

BREMEN APPLE TORTE.....259
BRISKET OF BEEF (BRUSTDECKEL).....86
BRISKET OF BEEF WITH SAUERKRAUT.....86
BRODTORTE.....260
BROWN BETTY.....303
BROWN BREAD.....231
BROWN BREAD SANDWICHES.....22
BROWN FLOUR SOUP, No. 1.....38
BROWN FLOUR SOUP, No. 2.....38
BROWN SAUCE.....68
BROWN STOCK.....28
BRUNSWICK STEW.....89
BRUSSELS SPROUTS.....128
BUCKWHEAT CAKES.....238
BUNS.....217
BUNS, CINNAMON.....237
BUNS, RAISIN OR CURRANT.....217
BUNT KUCHEN, BAKING POWDER.....249
BUNT, PLAIN OR NAPF KUCHEN.....220
BURNT ALMOND TORTE.....261
BUTTER SAUCE, DRAWN..... 64
BUTTER, Maître d'hôtel.....65
BUTTER, RENDERED.....219
BUTTERBARCHES.....212

CABBAGE
  BELGIAN RED.....120
  BOILED.....117
  COLD SLAW.....117
  CREAMED NEW.....118
  HOT SLAW.....118
  FILLED.....119
  FRIED.....118
  RED.....120
  SALAD.....155
  STRUDEL.....190
  STEWED.....119
CAFÉ Á LA GLACÉ.....320
CAKE
  ANGEL FOOD.....258
  APPLE JELLY.....253
  APPLE SAUCE.....252
  BAKING POWDER CINNAMON.....250
  CARAMEL LAYER 254

CAKE continued
    CHOCOLATE LAYER 254
    COCONUT LAYER.....254
    CREAM LAYER.....254
    EGGLESS, BUTTERLESS, MILKLESS.....253
    GOLD.....248
    GRAFTON.....247
    GREEN TREE LAYER AND ICING.....252
    HUCKLEBERRY.....255
    LEMON.....249
    LITTLE FRENCH.....247
    LOAF COCONUT.....251
    MARBLE.....249
    NUT.....251
    NUT HONEY.....264
    ONE EGG.....247
    ORANGE 249
    POTATO.....249
    POTATO FLOUR SPONGE.....356
    POUND.....249
    SMALL SPONGE.....257
    SPICE.....252
    SPONGE.....256
    SUNSHINE   258
    VIENNA PRATER.....259
    WEDDING FRUIT CAKE.....251
    WHITE.....248
CALF'S FEET, PRUNES AND CHESTNUTS.....79
CALF'S FEET, SCHARF.....80
CALF'S FOOT JELLY, No. 1.....80
CALF'S LIVER SMOTHERED IN ONIONS.....82
CANDIED CHERRIES, PINEAPPLE & FRUITS.....322
CANDIED LEMON AND ORANGE PEEL.....360
CANNED FRUIT FROZEN.....318
CARAMEL CUSTARD.....295
CARAMEL SAUCE.....311
CARAWAY SEED COOKIES.....291
CARAWAY, OR KIMMEL SAUCE.....69
CARDAMOM COOKIES.....287
CARNATZLICH (ROMANIAN).....91
CARP, PAPRIKA.....55
CARROT
    BOILED WITH CABBAGE.....118
    CARROTS.....114
    CARROTS & PEAS.....122
    COMPOTE (RUSSIAN).....115
    FLEMISH.....115
    LEMON.....114
    PUDDING.....308
    PUDDING.....354

CARROT continued
    SCHALET.....187
    SIMMERED.....114
    WITH BRISKET OF BEEF 115
CAULIFLOWER
    CAULIFLOWER 112
    CAULIFLOWER OR ASPARAGUS.....113
    CREAM SOUP.....36
    CROQUETTES.....74
    ROMANIAN   113
    SALAD.....155
    SCALLOPED.....113
    SPANISH.....112
    WITH BROWN CRUMBS.....113
CAVIAR AND SALMON SANDWICHES.....25
CAVIAR CANAPÉS.....16
CELERIAC.....112
CELERIAC PURÉE.....112
CELERY RELISH.....19
CELERY ROOT BASKETS.....154
CELERY ROOT, BOILED SALAD.....154
CELERY SANDWICHES.....22
CELERY, CREAMED.....113
CELERY, CREAM OF SOUP.....35
CHEESE
    BALLS.....18
    BALLS, No. 1.....207
    BALLS, No. 2.....207
    BOILED.....206
    BREAD.....208
    CHEESE AND NUT SANDWICHES.....22
    CHEESE AND SWEET GREEN PEPPERS.....209
    CHEESE CAKE OR PIE.....229
    CHEESE CAKE, COVERED.....250
    CHEESE CAKES (HUNGARIAN).....224
    FONDUE.....209
    KREPLICH.....177
    SOUFFLÉ.....207
    STRAWS.....274
    TIMBALS FOR TWELVE PEOPLE.....207
    TOASTED SANDWICHES.....24
CHERRY
    BOUNCE.....333
    BRANDY.....332
    CAKE.....229
    CONSERVE.....339
    DIPLOMATE.....318
    MOCK PIE.....280
    PIE, No. 1.....276
    PIE, No. 2.....276

CHERRY continued
    PUDDING.....306
    PUDDING.....308
    ROLEY-POLEY.....183
    SOUP.....41
    STRUDEL......190
    SYRUP.....332

CHESTNUT
    & PRUNES.....148
    & RAISINS.....148
    BOILED.....147
    PAN-ROASTED.....147

CHESTNUTS continued
    PUDDING.....302
    PURÉE.....147
    SALAD.....155
    SANDWICHES.....24
    STUFFING.....108
    TORTE.....263
    WITH CELERY (TURKISH).....147

CHICKEN
    Á LA ITALIENNE.....102
    Á LA SWEETBREAD.....79
    BOILED & BAKED.....98
    BROILED SPRING.....98
    BROTH......29
    CASSEROLE.....98
    CROQUETTES, No. 1.....73
    CROQUETTES, No. 2.....74
    CURRY.....101
    FRICASSEE.....99
    FRICASSEE, WITH NOODLES.....78
    FRIED SPRING.....99
    GIBLETS.....99
    HOMEMADE TAMALES.....78
    JELLIED.....77
    LIVER PASTE, No. 1.....16
    LIVER PASTE, No. 2.....17
    LIVERS.....82
    PAPRIKA WITH RICE.....101
    PRESSED.....77
    ROAST.....98
    SALAD.....164
    SALAD FOR TWENTY PEOPLE.....164
    SANDWICHES.....25
    SANDWICHES WITH MAYONNAISE.....26
    SMOTHERED.....101
    SOUP, No. 1.....29
    SOUP, No. 2.....29
    STUFFED (TURKISH).....100

CHICKEN continued
    TURKISH.....100
    WITH RICE.....100
    WITH SPAGHETTI *EN CASSEROLE*.....100
CHIFFONADE SALAD.....153
CHILI CON CARNE.....101
CHILE CON CARNE, MOCK.....146
CHOCOLATE
    BRODTORTE.....261
    CAKE.....357
    COFFEE CAKE.....221
    COOKIES.....293
    CORNSTARCH PUDDING.....296
    CUSTARD.....295
    ÉCLAIRS.....255
CHOCOLATE continued
    ICE CREAM, No. 1.....315
    ICE CREAM, No. 2.....315
    ICED.....326
    NECTAR.....326
    SAUCE, No. 1.....311
    SAUCE, No. 2.....311
    SYRUP.....326
    TORTE.....262
CHOPPED ONION AND CHICKEN FAT.....16
CHRIMSEL FILLING.....361
CHRIMSEL, KENTUCKY.....347
CHRIMSEL, No. 1.....346
CHRIMSEL, No. 2.....347
CIDER EGG NOG.....333
CINNAMON ROLLS OR SCHNECKEN.....220
CINNAMON STICKS.....358
CITRON COOKIES.....291
CLARET CUP.....331
COCOA, BREAKFAST.....325
COCOA, RECEPTION.....325
COCONUT KISSES.....292
COCONUT LEMON PIE.....277
COCONUT PIE.....277
COCONUT PUDDING.....353
COD FISH BALLS.....62
COFFEE
    BOILED.....324
    COFFEE CAKE.....226
    COFFEE CAKE DOUGH.....219
    COFFEE CAKE, GERMAN.....250
    COFFEE CAKE, QUICK.....250
    COFFEE FILLING.....267
    FILTERED 324
    FRENCH.....325

COFFEE continued
    COFFEE FOR TWENTY PEOPLE.....325
    ICE CREAM.....315
    ICED.....326
    TURKISH.....324
COLD OATMEAL.....192
COLD SLAW.....117
COLD SLAW DRESSING.....155
COLD SLAW OR CABBAGE SALAD.....155
COLD SOUR SOUP.....42
CONSOMMÉ.....29
COOKIES.....284
COOKIES.....358
CORDIAL.....331
CORN BREAD.....231
CORN FRITTERS.....242
CORN OFF THE COB.....116
CORN ON THE COB   115
CORN PUDDING.....306
CORN, CREAM OF SOUP.....36
CORNED BEEF, BOILED.....92
CORNFLAKE COCONUT KISSES.....293
CORNMEAL MUSH.....193
CORNMEAL MUSH, SAUTÉED.....193
CORNMEAL PUDDING.....305
COTTAGE CHEESE (POT CHEESE).....206
COTTAGE CHEESE SALAD.....159
CRAB-APPLE, BAKED PRESERVES.....334
CRABAPPLE JELLY.....336
CRACKERS AND CHEESE.....210
CRANBERRIES
    BAKED OR CHERRY PRESERVES.....334
    STEWED.....68
    JELLY.....338
    SAUCE.....68
CREAM CHEESE.....207
CREAM CHEESE SALAD.....159
CREAM CHEESE SALAD WITH PINEAPPLES.....160
CREAM FILLING.....267
CREAM PIE.....277
CREAM PUFFS.....255
CROQUANTE CAKES.....288
CROQUETTES.....73
CROQUETTES OF CALF'S BRAINS.....74
CROUTONS.....44
CRULLERS.....236
CUCUMBER SALAD.....155
CUCUMBER SAUCE.....64
CUCUMBERS, FRIED.....116
CUCUMBERS, STUFFED.....116

CUP CAKE.....248
CURRANT JELLY.....335
CURRANTS, FROSTED.....323
CURRY SAUCE.....66
CUSTARD CUP FOR SIX.....295
CUSTARD PIE.....277
CUSTARD, BOILED.....295
CUSTARD, FROZEN.....315

D AMSON JAM.....338
DANDELIONS.....116
DATES
    CAKE.....357
    DATE AND FIG SANDWICHES.....2
    MACAROONS.....292
    PUDDING.....308
    TORTE.....262
    STUFFED WITH FONDANT.....323
    STUFFED WITH GINGER AND NUTS.....323
    STUFFED 322
DESSERT WITH WHIPPED CREAM.....298
DIMPES DAMPES (APPLE SLUMP).....305
DIVINITY.....321
DOBOS TORTE.....256
DOMINOES.....257
DOUGH FOR OPEN FACE PIES.....237
DOUGHNUTS.....236
DOUGHNUTS, FRENCH.....236
DRAWN BUTTER SAUCE.....64
DRESSING
    BOILED.....152
    BOILED WITH OLIVE OIL.....152
    BREAD FOR FOWL.....107
    CRUMB.....107
    MEAT FOR POULTRY.....108
DRIED PEA FRITTERS.....243
DUCK.....104
DUCK Á LA MODE IN JELLY.....105
DUCK, MOCK.....87
DUCK, ROAST.....105
DUMPLINGS
    FOR CREAM SOUPS.....46
    FOR STEW.....178
    DROP.....46
    SPONGE.....46
DUTCH STUFFED MONKEYS.....284

EGGS
  Á LA MEXICANA 202
  AND CHEESE RAMEKINS.....210
  AND OLIVE SANDWICHES.....25
  APPETIZER.....18
  BAKED.....198
  BAKED WITH CHEESE   198
  BAKED WITH TOMATOES.....198
  BARLEY.....176
  BOILED 197
  CURRIED.....203
  CUSTARD.....44
  DEVILED WITH HOT SAUCE.....18
  DUMPLINGS FOR SOUPS.....45
  EGGS BAKED IN RICE.....195
  EN MARINADE.....204
  FRICASSEED.....204
  FRIED.....198
  MARMALADE.....359
  PIQUANT.....201
  POACHED WITH FRIED TOMATOES.....201
  POACHED OR DROPPED.....197
  POACHED IN TOMATO SAUCE.....201
  POACHED SANDWICHES.....24
  RAREBIT.....203
  SANDWICHES.....23
  SPANISH.....203
  SCALLOPED.....202
  SCALLOPED (FLEISCHIG).....204
  SCRAMBLED.....198
  SCRAMBLED WITH BRAINS.....204
  SCRAMBLED WITH SAUSAGE.....204
  STUFFED 19
  WITH CREAM DRESSING.....202
EGGNOG.....331
EGGPLANT
  BAKED.....121
  BROILED.....121
  BROILED OR FRIED.....121
  CROQUETTES (ROMANIAN).....75
  FRIED.....122
  FRIED IN OIL (TURKISH).....121
  ROMANIAN.....122
  SALAD (ROMANIAN).....156
  SALAD (TURKISH).....156
EINLAUF (EGG DROP).....45
ENCHILADAS.....93
ERBSEN LIEVANZEN (DRIED PEA FRITTERS).....243

FARINA
- FARINA.....193
- DUMPLINGS.....45
- DUMPLINGS.....182
- PUDDING WITH PEACHES.....302
- PUDDING, No. 2.....303
- SOUP.....31

FARSOLE.....144
FARSOLE DULCE.....144
FIG DESSERT.....299
FIG FILLING.....267
FIG SANDWICHES.....23
FIG SAUCE.....172
FIGS, STUFFED.....323
FILLED BUTTER CAKES.....284
FINNAN HADDIE.....62
FINNAN HADDIE AND MACARONI.....62
FISH
- BAKED.....49
- BAKED - TURKISH.....58
- BOILED.....48
- BROILED.....49
- CAKES, RUSSIAN.....52
- CHOWDER.....36
- CROQUETTES.....75
- ENGLISH LEMON STEWED.....345
- FILLED - TURKISH STYLE No. 1.....53
- JEWISH FRIED.....49
- LEMON.....50
- MOCK CHOWDER.....36
- PIQUANT.....55
- ROE, SCALLOPED.....59
- SALAD.....161
- SALAD FOR TWENTY PEOPLE.....161
- SANDWICHES.....22
- SAUTÉED.....50
- SCALLOPED No. 1.....63
- SCALLOPED No. 2.....63
- STOCK.....51
- SWEET AND SOUR.....51
- SWEET SOUR.....50
- SWEET SOUR WITH WINE.....51
- SWISS CREAMED.....62
- WITH GARLIC.....59
- WITH HORSERADISH SAUCE.....56
- WITH SAUERKRAUT.....56

FLOATING ISLAND.....296
FLOUNDERS, BAKED.....58
FLOUR BALLS WITH ALMONDS, BOILED.....45
FOAM SAUCE.....311
FOAM TORTE.....355

FORCE-MEAT FOR KREPLECH.....43
FRENCH ARTICHOKES WITH TOMATO SAUCE.....110
FRENCH COFFEE CAKE (SAVARIN).....221
FRENCH DRESSING.....152
FRENCH FRIED POTATOES.....139
FRENCH FRIED SWEET POTATOES.....142
FRENCH PUFFS (WINDBEUTEL).....243
FRESH COD OR STRIPED BASS.....54
FRIED GREEN TOMATOES.....132
FRITADA No. 2......53
FRITTER BATTER.....241
FRITTER BEANS.....46
FROSTING, INSTANTANEOUS.....266
FROSTING, MOCHA.....267
FROSTING, PLAIN.....266
FROZEN CREAM CHEESE WITH PRESERVED FIGS.....317
FROZEN PUDDINGS.....316
FRUIT AND NUT SALAD.....160
FRUIT JUICES.....331
FRUIT LOAF.....322
FRUIT PUNCH FOR TWENTY PEOPLE.....328
FRUIT SALAD.....160
FRUIT SAUCES.....312
FRUIT SOUP.....42
FRUIT TARTLETS.....272
FRUIT WHEELS 237
FRUITS, DRIED 172
FUDGE.....321

GÄNSEKLEIN.....103
GANSLEBER IN SULZ (GOOSE LIVER ASPIC).....81
GANSLEBER PURÉE IN SULZ.....81
GARLIC SAUCE.....70
GEFILLTE FISCH.....52
GEFILLTTE FISCH WITH EGG SAUCE.....53
GERMAN HAZELNUT TORTE.....262
GERMAN PANCAKES, No. 1.....238
GERMAN PANCAKES, No. 2.....238
GERMAN PANCAKES, No. 3.....238
GERMAN PUFFS.....349
GERÖSTETE FERVELCHEN PFARVEL (EGG BARLEY).....176
GESCHUNDENE GANS.....103
GEWETSH (SERBIAN).....96
GIBLETS.....99
GINGER GEMS, EGGLESS.....235
GINGER WAFERS.....291
GINGERBREAD 232
GINGERBREAD WITH CHEESE.....232
GLACÉ FOR CANDIES.....322

GLOBE ARTICHOKE OR TURNIP SOUP.....36
GLÜHWEIN.....327
GLUTEN GEMS.....235
GOLDEN BUCK.....208
GOOSE
    BREASTS, ROAST.....104
    CRACKLINGS (GRIEBEN).....103
    GÄNSEKLEIN.....103
    GESCHUNDENE GANS.....103
    LIVER.....81
    LIVER ASPIC.....81
    LIVER WITH GLACÉED CHESTNUTS.....81
    LIVER WITH MUSHROOM SAUCE.....82
    MINCED (HUNGARIAN).....104
    MINCED SANDWICHES.....26
    ROAST.....102
    STEWED PIQUANTE.....104
GRAPE JELLY.....336
GRAPE JUICE, UNFERMENTED.....331
GRAPE PIE.....279
GRAPEFRUIT.....168
GRAPEFRUIT COCKTAIL.....20
GRAPEFRUIT SALAD.....160
GRAPES, SPICED.....339
GRATED EGG FOR SOUP.....44
GREEN CORN, TOMATOES AND CHEESE.....208
GREEN PEA PURÉE.....39
GREEN PEA SOUP.....32
GREEN PEAS AND EGG BARLEY (PFARVEL).....123
GREEN PEAS AND RICE.....123
GREEN SALADS.....153
GRIMSLICH.....239
GROUND MEAT WITH RAISINS (ROMANIAN)   91

HAMBURGER STEAK.....90
HARD SAUCE.....312
HARICOT BEANS AND BEEF.....143
HASHED BROWN POTATOES, LYONNAISE.....138
HASTY PUDDING.....356
HECHT (PICKEREL).....53
HERRING
    BAKED CHOPPED.....60
    CHOPPED.....17
    CREAM OF SOUP (RUSSIAN)   36
    MARINIRTE (PICKLED)   60
    SALAD, No. 1.....162
    SALAD, No. 2.....162
    SALT.....60
    SOUSED.....   61
    STUFFED.....59

HESTERLISTE.....244
HOLLANDAISE SAUCE.....65
HOMINY.....193
HONEY CAKES, No. 1.....293
HONEY CAKES, No. 2.....293
HONEY CORN CAKES.....288
HONEY PUDDING.....310
HORSERADISH SAUCE, No. 1.....69
HORSERADISH SAUCE, No. 2.....70
HOT CHOCOLATE.....326
HOT MILK PUNCH.....333
HOT SLAW.....118
HOT WINE (GLÜHWEIN).....327
HUCKLEBERRY
    COMPOTE.....172
    DUMPLINGS.....182
    KUCHEN.....230
    PIE.....230
    PIE.....279
    PUDDING.....306
HUNGARIAN ALMOND COOKIES.....286
HUNGARIAN FRUIT SALAD.....160
HUNGARIAN GOULASH.....90
HUNGARIAN VEGETABLE SALAD.....162
HURRY UPS (OATMEAL).....292

ICEBOX CAKE.....300
ICING see also FROSTING
    ALMOND.....266
    BOILED.....265
    CHOCOLATE GLAZING.....266
    CHOCOLATE UNBOILED.....266
    COCONUT.....265
    MAPLE SUGAR.....265
    NUT.....265
    ORANGE.....266
    UNBOILED.....265
    WHITE CARAMEL.....265
IMBERLACH.....358
IRISH POTATO, GRATED.....44
IRISH STEW.....95

JELLIED QUINCES.....338
JELLY ROLL.....258
JELLY SAUCE.....312
JERUSALEM ARTICHOKE.....110
JOHNNIE CAKE.....232
JULIENNE SOUP.....30

KAFFEEKUCHEN (CINNAMON).....219
KAL DOLMAR.....119
KALE.....130
KARTOFFELKLÖßE (POTATO DUMPLINGS).....180
KÄSEKNÖPFLI (CHEESE KREPLICH).....177
KEDGEREE.....62
KIDNEY BEANS WITH BROWN SAUCE.....147
KIMMEL SAUCE.....69
KINDEL.....288
KINDLECH.....225
KIRSCH SAUCE.....312
KISCHKES   83
KISCHKES - RUSSIAN STYLE.....82
KNOBLAUCH SAUCE (GARLIC SAUCE).....70
KNÖDEL, POTATO PLUM (HUNGARIAN).....350
KOCH KÄSE (BOILED CHEESE).....206
KOHL-RABI.....130
KOHL-RABI WITH BREAST OF LAMB.....130
KOLATCHEN.....226
KOLATCHEN, SOUR CREAM.....226
KÖNIGKUCHEN.....251
KRAUS GEBACKENES.....243
KRAUT KUGEL.....184
KREMSLEKH.....358
KREPLECH OR BUTTERFLIES.....43
KROSPHADA.....203
KRULLER OR CRULLERS.....236
KUCHEN APPLE CAKE.....228
KUCHEN BLITZKUCHEN.....250
KUCHEN KÖNIGKUCHEN.....251
KUGEL.....184
KUGEL (SCHARFE).....184

LADYFINGERS.....257
LAMB AND MACARONI.....95
LAMB STEW - TOCANE.....95
LAMPLICH.....274
LEAF PUFFS.....301
LEBERKLÖSE (LIVER DUMPLINGS).....46
LEBERKNÖDEL (CALF LIVER DUMPLINGS).....179
LEBKUCHEN.....294
LEBKUCHEN, OLD-FASHIONED.....294
LEEK SOUP.....39
LEFT-OVER CEREALS.....196
LEFTOVER MEAT.....92
LEKACH.....294
LEMON
        CREAM FILLING.....361
        FILLED.....21

LEMON continued
    GINGER SHERBET.....319
    ICE.....319
    JELLY FOR LAYER CAKE.....268
    PIE, No. 1.....278
    PIE, No. 2.....278
    PRESERVES.....360
    PUFFS.....301
    SAUCE.....69
    SAUCE.....301
    SAUCE, No.....312
    SAUCE, No. 2.....312
    TART (FLEISCHIG).....273
LEMONADE IN LARGE QUANTITIES.....328
LEMONADE, EGG.....329
LEMONADE, MARASCHINO.....329
LEMONADE, MILK.....329
LEMONADE, QUICK.....328
LENTIL SAUSAGES.....146
LENTIL SOUP (LINZEN), No. 1.....33
LENTIL SOUP, No. 2.....33
LENTIL, CREAM OF SOUP.....37
LENTILS, BAKED (LINZEN).....144
LETTUCE
    BOILED.....114
    CREAM OF SOUP.....37
    DRESSING.....152
    LETTUCE.....153
    SANDWICHES.....23
LIMA BEAN SALAD.....157
LIMA BEANS, DRIED BAKED.....144
LIMA BEANS, GREEN.....114
LINSER TART.....273
LINZERTORTE.....262
LIVER DUMPLINGS.....46
LIVER DUMPLINGS.....179
LIVER, SPANISH.....82

MACARONI
    AND CHEESE.....209
    AND CHEESE, BAKED.....178
    BOILED.....177
    SAVORY.....178
MACAROON ISLAND.....298
MACAROON TARTS.....273
MACKEREL
    BAKED.....59
    BOILED SALT.....60
    BROILED SALT.....60
    SALAD.....163

MACROTES.....244
Maître d'hôtel SAUCE.....70
MAMOURAS (TURKISH).....349
MANDEL (ALMOND) STRUDEL.....190
MANDELCHEN.....292
MAPLE BISQUE.....317
MAPLE MOUSSE.....317
MARINIRTE (PICKLED) HERRING.....60
MARINIRTE FISH.....61
MARMELITTA.....193
MARROW DUMPLINGS.....344
MARSHMALLOW FILLING.....267
MARSHMALLOW SALAD.....159
MATRIMONIES.....242
MATZOTH
    CHARLOTTE, No. 1.....351
    CHARLOTTE, No. 2.....352
    DIPPED IN EGGS, No. 1..... 348
    DIPPED IN EGGS, No. 2 348
    EIRKUCHEN.....348
    KLEIS, FILLED 345
    KLEIS, No. 1.....344
    KLEIS, No. 2.....345
    KUGEL.....352
    MEAL CAKE.....351
    MEAL KLEIS, No. 1.....343
    MEAL KLEIS, No. 2.....344
    MEAL MACAROONS.....348
    PLUM PUDDING.....353
    SHALET.....352
    SPICE CAKE.....351
    SCRAMBLED EGGS (ÜBERSCHLAGENE).....347
    SCRAMBLED.....347
MAYONNAISE
    COLORED.....151
    DRESSING.....151
    ESPECIALLY FOR SALMON.....163
    FLOUNDER.....161
    TOMATOES (WHOLE).....156
    WITH WHIPPED CREAM.....151
    WHITE.....151
MEAT AND BOILED HOMINY CROQUETTES.....74
MEAT BLINTZES.....351
MEAT CROQUETTES.....74
MEAT LOAF.....90
MEAT OLIVES.....89
MEAT PIE.....92
MERBERDECK.....186
MERBERKUCHEN.....285
MERBERTEIG.....271
MERINGUE.....271

MILK AND CHEESE SOUP.....40
MILK, CLABBERED.....329
MILK, OR CREAM SOUP.....36
MILK, SOUR SOUP.....39
MINA (TURKISH).....350
MINCE PIE.....279
MINCE PIE, MOCK.....278
MINT SAUCE.....69
MIRLITIOUS.....274
MOCHA MOUSSE.....317
MOCHA TORTE.....259
MOCK DUCK.....87
MOCK TURTLE SOUP.....30
MOHN
    CAKES, SMALL.....223
    MOHNTORTE.....223
    MOHNTORTE.....282
    PLÄTZCHEN.....290
    POPPY SEED) ROLEY POLEY.....222
    WACHTEL.....223
MOLASSES COOKIES, OLD-FASHIONED.....286
MONTEREY SALAD.....163
MOTHER'S DELICIOUS COOKIES.....285
MUFFINS
    BRAN.....233
    CORN No. 1.....233
    CORN No. 2.....234
    GRAHAM.....234
    RICE.....234
    RYE FLOUR.....234
    WHEAT.....234
MULLED WINE.....330
MULLIGATAWNY SOUP.....31
MUSHROOMS
    AND BARLEY SOUP.....31
    BROILED.....125
    CREAMED.....125
    FRESH WITH EGGS.....203
    SAUTÉED.....126
    SCALLOPED.....125
MUSK MELONS.....21
MUSTARD
    MUSTARD.....340
    DRESSING.....152
    PASTE FOR SANDWICHES.....25
    SAUCE.....65
    SAUCE, CREAM.....66
MUTTON
    BREAST & STEWED CARROTS.....96
    BROTH.....30

MUTTON continued
    OR LAMB CHOPS.....97
    CURRIED 95
    ROAST WITH POTATOES.....96
    SHOULDER STUFFED.....97

NAPKIN PUDDING.....308
NEAPOLITAN JELLY.....337
NEAPOLITAN SALAD.....166
NESSELRODE PUDDING.....318
NIAGARA SALAD.....164
NOODLES
    AND APPLES.....176
    AND MUSHROOMS.....176
    BROAD.....175
    KUGEL.....184
    MATZOTH MEAL.....344
    MILK OR POTATO.....179
    NOODLES.....43
    POTATO FLOUR.....343
    PUDDING.....309
    PUFFS.....244
    SCHALET.....186
    SOUP.....31
    WITH BUTTER.....175
    WITH CHEESE.....175
    SCALLOPED AND PRUNES.....176
    SNIP FRIED.....244
    THIN.....175
NUT AND CHEESE RELISH.....19
NUT AND RAISIN SANDWICHES.....22
NUT LOAF.....148
NUT ROAST.....149
NUT SALAD.....161
NUTMEG CAKES (PFEFFERNUESSE).....286

OATMEAL PORRIDGE.....192
OATMEAL WITH CHEESE.....192
OKRA GUMBO SOUP (SOUTHERN).....32
OKRA, BOILED.....126
OLIVE SANDWICHES.....23
OMELET also see EGGS
    CHEESE.....209
    CORN.....200
    HERB.....200
    PLAIN.....199
    RUM.....200

OMELETTE continued
    SOUFFLÉ.....202
    SPANISH.....199
    SWEET.....199
    SWEET ALMOND.....200
    SWEET FOR ONE.....199
    WHITE SAUCE.....202
ONION
    BOILED.....126
    SAUCE.....69
    SCALLOPED.....126
    SOUP.....38
    SPANISH RAREBIT.....126
    ZWIEBEL MATZOTH.....348
ORANGE CHIPS 322
ORANGE FRITTERS.....242
ORANGE ICE.....319
ORANGEADE.....329
ORANGES.....168
OXTAIL SOUP.....31
OXTAILS, BRAISED.....89
OYSTER PLANT - SALSIFY.....128

PALESTINE SOUP.....343
PANCAKE, FRENCH.....240
PANCAKES, SOUR MILK.....240
PARSNIPS.....127
PARVE COOKIES.....287
PARVE, COOKIE AND PIE DOUGH.....271
PATÉ DE FOIS GRAS, IMITATION.....17
PEA PURÉE.....146
PEA, DRIED SOUP.....33
PEACH
    COCKTAIL.....20
    COMPOTE.....171
    CREAM PIE.....280
    CREAM TARTS.....279
    DUMPLINGS.....183
    KUCHEN.....229
    PEACHES.....168
    PICKLED.....339
    PIE, No. 1.....280
    PIE, No. 2.....280
    PUDDING.....309
    SHORTCAKE.....259
    SWEET ENTRÉE OF RIPE.....173
PEANUT AND RICE CROQUETTES.....75
PEANUTS, SALTED.....21

PEAR DUMPLING (BIRNE KLÖßE).....182
PEAR KUGEL.....184
PEARS, COMPOTE OF.....171
PEAS AND EGG BARLEY (PFARVEL).....123
PEAS AND RICE.....123
PEAS, GREEN 122
PEAS, SUGAR.....122
PECAN, WALNUT, HICKORY NUT MACAROONS.....292
PEPPERS
     AND CHEESE SALAD.....157
     BROILED GREEN.....124
     GREEN.....123
     GREEN FOR SALAD.....157
     GREEN STUFFED WITH VEGETABLES.....124
     SALAD.....157
     STEWED.....124
     STUFFED WITH MEAT.....123
     STUFFED WITH NUTS.....124
     STUFFED 124
     STUFFED 123
PESACH CAKE WITH WALNUTS.....357
PETER PAN DESSERT.....318
PFANNKUCHEN 223
PFARVEL - FLEISCHIG.....177
PFARVEL OR GRATED EGG FOR SOUP.....44
PFEFFERNUESSE.....286
PICKEREL.....53
PICKLE SAUCE.....65
PICKLED RED CABBAGE (HUNGARIAN STYLE).....340
PIE CRUST.....348
PIE CRUST (MERBERTEIG).....271
PIE CRUST, FLEISCHIG.....270
PIE, WHIPPED CREAM.....275
PIGEON PIE.....106
PIGEON SOUP.....32
PIKE WITH EGG SAUCE.....51
PILAF.....196
PILAF (RUSSIAN).....102
PILAF (TURKISH).....102
PINEAPPLE
     COMPOTE 171
     PINEAPPLE.....168
     AND BANANA COCKTAIL.....20
     FRITTERS.....241
     ICE.....320
     LEMONADE.....328
     PIE, No. 1.....280
     PIE, No. 2.....281
     SOUFFLÉ.....169

PINOCHE....321
PIQUANTE SAUCE.....66
PISTACHIO CREAM.....299
PLAIN WAFERS....290
PLÄTCHEN....43
PLUMS
    KNÖDEL (HUNGARIAN)....182
    PIE.....281
    PUDDING (FOR THANKSGIVING DAY)....310
    PUDDING, No. 2....310
    SWEET POTATOES AND MEAT....129
POCKET BOOKS....221
POLENTA....194
POLISH SALAD, OR SALAD PIQUANT....166
POPOVERS....235
POPPY SEED COOKIES (MOHN PLÄTZCHEN)....290
POTATOES
    AND CORN....139
    AND PEARS....139
    AU GRATIN....138
    BAKED No. 1....136
    BAKED No. 2....136
    BALLS WITH PARSLEY....137
    BOHEMIAN PUFF....140
    BOILED....136
    BOILED IN THEIR JACKETS....136
    CAKES....139
    CAKES....240
    CARAWAY SEEDS....139
    CREAMED....138
    CROQUETTES....75
    CURRIED....138
    DUMPLINGS....80
    FLOUR PUDDING....357
    FOR TWENTY PEOPLE....136
    FRENCH FRIED....139
    GERMAN FRIED....138
    HASHED BROWN LYONNAISE....138
    HUNGARIAN....141
    MARBLES....350
    MASHED 137
    NEW....137
    PANCAKES....239
    PLUM KNÖDEL (HUNGARIAN)....350
    PUDDING....352
    PUDDING, BOILED....188
    PUFF....141
    RIBBON....140
    SALAD, No. 1....157
    SALAD, No. 2....157
    SALAD, No 3....158

POTATOES continued
    SARATOGA CHIPS....138
    SCALLOPED No. 1....137
    SCALLOPED No. 2....137
    SCHALET....188
    SOUP....39
    STEWED 140
    STEWED SOUR....140
    STEWED WITH ONIONS....140
    STUFFED....140
    STUFFING....108
    SURPRISE....141
POUND CAKE....249
PRINCE ALBERT PUDDING....309
PRUNES
    AND RAISIN PIE....281
    BLINTZES....351
    BAKED....173
    CAKE (KUCHEN)....230
    CAKE, FRESH (KUCHEN)....229
    CUSTARD....298
    PIE....281
    PRUNES....360
    PUDDING....303
    PUDDING....309
    SAUCE....313
    SOUFFLÉ....173
    STEAMED....173
    STEWED....172
    STUFFED....323
    WHIP....297
    WITHOUT SUGAR....173
PUDDING Á LA GRANDE BELLE....306
PUFF PASTE OR BLÄTTERTEIG....269
PUFFS (PURIM)....225
PUMPKIN PIE....279
PUNCH ICES....320
PURIM CAKES....287
PURIM KRAPFEN....223

Q

QUARK STRUDEL (DUTCH CHEESE)....191
QUEEN BREAD PUDDING....304
QUEEN FRITTERS....242
QUEEN OF TRIFLES....300
QUINCE JELLY....337
QUINCES, BAKED....334

RADISH PRESERVES (RUSSIAN STYLE)....359
RADISHES....125
RAHM STRUDEL....189
RAISINS
    AND RHUBARB PIE....283
    PIE....283
    SAUCE....69
    STUFFING....108
    WINE, No. 1....342
    WINE, No. 2....343
RASPBERRIES
    COMPOTE....171
    AND CURRANTS....167
    AND CURRANT JELLY....335
    COCKTAIL....20
    ICE....320
    JAM....338
    JELLY....335
    RASPBERRIES....167
    VINEGAR....332
RED CABBAGE....120
RED CABBAGE (HUNGARIAN STYLE)....340
RED CABBAGE WITH CHESTNUTS AND PRUNES....120
RED MULLET IN CASES....346
RED PEPPER CANAPÉS....21
RED RASPBERRY OR CURRANT FLOAT....296
RED SNAPPER WITH TOMATO SAUCE....56
RED WINE SOUP....40
RHUBARB
    BAKED....172
    PIE....282
    PUDDING....302
    SAUCE....172
RIBBON SANDWICHES....25
RICE
    AND CHEESE....208
    AND NUT LOAF....195
    BAKED....195
    BOILED....194
    BOILED WITH PINEAPPLE....195
    BROTH....30
    CROQUETTES, No. 1....76
    CROQUETTES, No. 2....76
    CUSTARD....297
    IN MILK....194
    KUGEL....185
    PANCAKES OR GRIDDLE CAKES....239
    PUDDING....303
    RICE WITH GRATED CHOCOLATE....194

RICE continued
    SPANISH....196
    STEAMED....195
    SWEET....195
ROAST BEEF
    BRAISED BEEF....85
    EASY POT ROAST....85
    RUSSIAN....88
    No. 1....87
    No. 2....87
ROLLS....216
ROLLS, CRESCENT....216
ROLLS, FRENCH....217
ROLLS, TEA....216
ROSEL, BEET VINEGAR....342
ROTE GRITZE....297
RUM PUDDING....317
RUM SAUCE....360
RUSSIAN DRESSING....151
RUSSIAN FRUIT SALAD....161
RUSSIAN GOULASH....90
RUSSIAN HAMBURGER STEAK....91
RUSSIAN PUNCH TORTE....263
RUSSIAN SALAD....163
RUSSIAN SANDWICHES....25
RUSSIAN TEA CAKES....226
RYE BREAD PUDDING....307
RYE BREAD TORTE....260

SAGO PUDDING WITH STRAWBERRY JUICE....301
SALAD PIQUANT....166
SALMON
    AND BROWN BREAD SANDWICHES....24
    CREAM....61
    CUTLETS....55
    LOAF....61
    PICKLE FOR....61
    SALAD....162
SALSIFY....128
SALSIFY, SCALLOPED....129
SAND TORTE....260
SARATOGA CHIPS....138
SARDELLEN....19
SARDELLEN, OR HERRING SAUCE....65
SARDINE CANAPÉS....15
SARDINE SANDWICHES....23
SAUCE BORDELAISE....68
SAUCE PIQUANTE....66
SAUCE TARTARE (TARTAR SAUCE)....66

SAUERBRATEN....86
SAUERKRAUT....341
SAUERKRAUT, BOILED....117
SAVOY CABBAGE....128
SAVOY CABBAGE WITH RICE....119
SCALLOPED PEACHES....302
SCHALET DOUGH (MERBERDECK)....186
SCHALET OR TSCHOLNT (SHABBAS SOUP)....28
SCHALET, SEVEN LAYER....187
SCHNECKEN....220
SCHWEM KLÖßE....45
SHABBAS KUGEL....183
SHAD ROE....58
SHAD, BAKED....59
SHAVINGS (KRAUS GEBACKENES)....243
SHERRY COBBLER....330
SHORT RIBS AND YELLOW TURNIPS....89
SICKEL PEARS, BAKED....334
SLAITTA (ROMANIAN)....144
SMELTS, BONED SAUTÉED....56
SNOWBALLS....276
SNOWBALLS (HESTERLISTE)....244
SNOWFLAKES....68
SODA CREAM....330
SOLE Á LA CREOLE, FILLET OF....57
SOLE Á LA MOUQUIN, FILLET OF....57
SOLE WITH WINE (FRENCH)....346
SOUP MEAT....91
SOUP STOCK....27
SOUR CREAM DRESSING....152
SOUR MILK COOKIES....286
SOUR SOUP FOR PURIM....33
SPAGHETTI....177
SPAGHETTI AND MEAT....92
SPANISH PIE....102
SPANISH RICE....196
SPANISH SAUCE....67
SPÄTZEN or SPÄTZLE....44
SPATZEN, SOUR....179
SPÄTZLEN OR SPATZEN....178
SPICE ROLL....227
SPINACH....127
SPINACH - FLEISCHIG....128
SPINACH SOUP....37
SPINACH WITH CREAM SAUCE....128
SPLIT PEA SOUP (MILCHIG)....40
SPONGE CAKE, No. 1....356
SPONGE CAKE, No. 2....356
SPRINGELE....287
SQUAB EN CASSEROLE....106
SQUABS, BROILED....105

SQUABS, OR NEST PIGEONS....105
SQUASH FRITTERS....243
SQUASH, STEWED 127
STEAK, FRIED WITH ONIONS....88
STEAMED BERRY PUDDING....308
STOLLEN....228
STRAWBERRIES
    STRAWBERRIES....167
    Á LA "BRIDGE"....300
    COCKTAIL....20
    DESSERT....361
    JELLY....335
    PIE....282
    SHERBET....330
    SHORTCAKE (BISCUIT DOUGH....237
    SHORTCAKE WITH MATZOTH-MEAL....356
STRING BEANS WITH LAMB....134
STRING BEANS WITH TOMATOES....134
STRING OR GREEN SNAP BEANS....134
STRING OR WAX-BEANS, SWEET AND SOUR....134
STRIPED BASS OR FRESH COD....54
STRUDEL AUS KALBSLUNGE....191
STUFFED PEPPERS (ARDAY-INFLUS)....124
STUFFING, CHESTNUT....108
STUFFING, POTATO 108
STUFFING, RAISIN....108
SUCCOTASH....116
SUET PUDDING WITH PEARS....306
SUGAR COOKIES....284
SUGAR PEAS....122
SUGAR SYRUP....361
SULZ....81
SULZE VON KALBSFUESSEN....80
SUMMER DRINK, DELICIOUS AND NOURISHING....330
SURPRISE SANDWICHES....25
SWEET POTATO
    AND APPLES....142
    BOILED....142
    CANDIED 142
    CROQUETTES....75
    PIE....282
    PUDDING....188
    FRENCH FRIED....142
    FRIED....142
    ROASTED....142
SWEETBREAD
    CROQUETTES....74
    GLACÉ SAUCE JARDINAIRE....78
    SALAD....165
    SAUTÉ WITH MUSHROOMS....79

SWEETBREAD continued
        SWEETBREADS....79
        STEWED....349
        VEAL (FRIED....79
SWISS CHARD....131

TAPIOCA CUSTARD....298
    TARTAR SAUCE....66
    TARTLETS....272
TCHORBA - TURKISH SOUP....32
TEA....326
TEA (RUSSIAN STYLE)....327
TEA, RUSSIAN ICED....327
TEIGLECH....288
TIPSY PUDDING....299
TOAST, BUTTERED....217
TOAST, CINNAMON FOR TEA....218
TOAST, MILK OR CREAM....218
TOCANE....95
TOM AND JERRY....333
TOMATO
        BAKED AND EGGPLANT....133
        CANNED STEWED....131
        CHEESE SALAD....156
        CREAM SOUP....37
        CREOLE....133
        CUSTARDS....133
        EGGS AND CHEESE (HUNGARIAN)....210
        FRIED....131
        FRIED GREEN....132
        PURÉE....132
        RIPE....169
        SALAD (FRENCH DRESSING)....156
        SAUCE....67
        SCALLOPED....132
        SOUP....34
        SOUP WITH RICE....40
        STEWED 131
        STUFFED....132
        STUFFED 156
        STUFFED YELLOW....18
        WITH EGG....198
        WITH RICE....132
TONGUE
        BOILED (SWEET AND SOUR)....83
        BOILED, SMOKED, PICKLED SANDWICHES....26
        DEVILED SANDWICHES....26

TONGUE continued
    FILLED....84
    PICKLED BEEF....84
    SMOKED 84
    SMOTHERED....84
TOPFA DALKELN - (HUNGARIAN)....224
TORTE
    ALMOND CAKE 260
    BREMEN APPLE....259
    BRODTORTE....260
    BURNT ALMOND....261
    CHOCOLATE BRODTORTE....261
    CHESTNUT....263
    CHOCOLATE 262
    DATE....262
    GERMAN HAZELNUT....262
    LINZERTORTE....262
    MOCHA....259
    RUSSIAN PUNCH....263
    RYE BREAD....260
    SAND....260
    ZWIEBACK....261
TRIPE Á LA CREOLE....83
TRIPE, FAMILY STYLE....83
TROUT, BOILED....54
TSIMESS....129
TURKEY
    NECK, STUFFED (TURKISH)....107
    SOUP....32
    ROAST....106
TURNIPS....129
TURNIPS, BOILED....129
TURNIPS, HASHED....130
TUTTI-FRUTTI....169
TUTTI-FRUTTI ICE CREAM....316

ÜBERSCHLAGENE....347

VANILLA COOKIES....286
VANILLA ICE CREAM, No. 1....314
VANILLA ICE CREAM, No. 2....314
VANILLA OR CREAM SAUCE....313
VEAL
    CROQUETTES....74
    FRICASSEED WITH CAULIFLOWER....94
    LOAF....94

VEAL continued
    SALAD....165
    SANDWICHES....26
    SOUP....34
    ROAST....93
    ROASTED BREAST....93
    SHOULDER OR NECK - HUNGARIAN....95
    STEWED 94
    STUFFED SHOULDER....94
VEGETABLE "MEAT" PIE....149
VEGETABLE FRITTERS....242
VEGETABLE HASH....120
VEGETABLE SOUP....34
VEGETABLE SOUP (MILCHIG)....38
VIENNA PASTRY FOR KIPFEL....274
VIENNA PRATER CAKE....259
VIENNA ROAST....88
VIENNA SAUSAGE....93
VINAIGRETTE SAUCE 65
VINEGAR PIE....282

WAFFLES, ONE-EGG 235
WAFFLES, THREE-EGG....236
WALDORF SALAD....158
WALNUT TORTE, No. 1....263
WALNUT TORTE, No. 2....263
WATER-LILY SALAD....159
WATERMELON SHERBET....320
WATERMELONS....168
WEDDING CAKE, FRUIT CAKE....251
WELSH RAREBIT....208
WHEAT CEREALS....193
WHIPPED CREAM....298
WHIPPED CREAM FILLING, MOCK....361
WHITE AND BROWN BREAD SANDWICHES....24
WHITE CAVIAR....15
WHITE FONDANT....321
WHITE SAUCE FOR VEGETABLES....66
WHITE STOCK....28
WIENER BRATEN - VIENNA ROAST....88
WIENER KARTOFFELKLÖßE....180
WIENER KIPFEL....227
WIENER STUDENTEN KIPFEL   227
WINDBEUTEL....243
WINE SAUCE....360
WINE SAUCE, No. 1....313

WINE SAUCE, No. 2....313
WINE, COLD EGG....329
WINE, CREAM SOUP....38
WINTER JELLY....337

YEAST KRANTZ....228
YOM-TOV SOUP....343

ZUCCHINI SQUASH SALAD (TURKISH)....158
ZUEMIMO SAUCE....58
ZWIEBACK....226
ZWIEBACK TORTE....261
ZWIEBEL MATZOTH....348
ZWIEBELPLATZ....215

More Cookbooks from New York History Review

German Cookery for the American Home
by Ella Oswald, 1910

Janowski Gardens Cookbook
by Diane Janowski

Our Own Book - A Victorian Guide to Life
Homespun Cuisine, Health, Romance, Etiquette,
Raising Children and Farm Animals

Notes

Notes

www.ingramcontent.com/pod-product-compliance
Lightning Source LLC
Chambersburg PA
CBHW022058150426
43195CB00008B/188